Fundamentals of Business, 4th edition

This book is dedicated to reducing the cost of education in business.

– S. Skripak

Fundamentals of Business, 4th edition

ADAPTED BY RON POFF

PREVIOUSLY ADAPTED BY STEPHEN J. SKRIPAK

PDF AND EPUB FREE ONLINE AT: HTTPS://DOI.ORG/10.21061/FUNDAMENTALSOFBUSINESS4E

VIRGINIA TECH PAMPLIN COLLEGE OF BUSINESS IN ASSOCIATION WITH VIRGINIA TECH PUBLISHING
BLACKSBURG, VA

© Ron Poff, 2023. *Fundamentals of Business, 4th Edition* by Ron Poff is licensed under a Creative Commons Attribution-NonCommercial-ShareAlike 4.0 International License, except where otherwise noted.

With contributions from Howard Haines and John Andy Travers.
Previously adapted by Stephen J. Skripak.

Attribution for third-party materials can be found within each chapter and on the acknowledgments page.

You are free to copy, share, adapt, remix, transform, and build on the material for any primarily noncommercial purpose as long as you follow the terms of the license: https://creativecommons.org/licenses/by-nc-sa/4.0.

> **You must:**
> - Attribute—You must give appropriate credit, provide a link to the license, and indicate if changes were made. You may do so in any reasonable manner, but not in any way that suggests the licensor endorses you or your use.
> - ShareAlike—If you remix, transform, or build on the material, you must distribute your contributions under the same license as the original.
>
> **You may not:**
> - NonCommercial—You may not use the work for primarily commercial use.
> - Additional restrictions—You may not add any legal terms or technological measures that legally restrict others from doing anything the license permits.

Suggested citation: Poff, Ron and Skripak, Stephen J. (2023). *Fundamentals of Business, 4th edition.* Blacksburg, VA: Pamplin College of Business. https://doi.org/10.21061/fundamentalsofbusiness4e Licensed with CC BY-NC-SA 4.0 https://creativecommons.org/licenses/by-nc-sa/4.0.

Publisher: This work is published by the Virginia Tech Pamplin College of Business in association with Virginia Tech Publishing, a division of the University Libraries at Virginia Tech. Supplemental funding and technical assistance was provided by the Open Education Initiative of the University Libraries at Virginia Tech.

Virginia Tech Pamplin College of Business, 1030 Pamplin Hall, Blacksburg, VA 24061 USA https://pamplin.vt.edu

Virginia Tech Publishing, University Libraries at Virginia Tech, 560 Drillfield Drive, Blacksburg, VA 24061 USA https://publishing.vt.edu publishing@vt.edu

Peer review: This work benefited from peer review by a recent Virginia Tech alumna.

Accessibility statement: Virginia Tech Publishing is committed to making its publications accessible in accordance with the Americans with Disabilities Act of 1990. The Pressbooks (HTML) and ePub versions of this text are tagged structurally and include alternative text, which allows for machine readability.

Publication cataloging information:
Poff, Ron and Skripak, Stephen J., adapted by
Fundamentals of Business, 4th edition / Ron Poff and Stephen J. Skripak
Pages cm
ISBN 978-1-957213-25-5 (Print, B&W)
ISBN 978-1-957213-24-8 (Print, color)
ISBN 978-1-957213-21-7 (PDF)
ISBN 978-1-957213-23-1 (Pressbooks) https://pressbooks.lib.vt.edu/fundamentalsofbusiness4e
ISBN 978-1-957213-22-4 (ePub)
URI (Universal Resource Identifier): http://hdl.handle.net/10919/111385
DOI: https://doi.org/10.21061/fundamentalsofbusiness4e
1. Business
2. Business -- Textbooks
    Title HF1008 .S57 2023
    658

Cover art: Lukas via Pexels (Pexels license), Fauxels via Pexels (Pexels license), Alena Darmel via Pexels (Pexels license), Cedric Fauntleroy via Pexels (Pexels license), mscamilaalmeida via Pixabay (Pixabay license), and Wladyslaw via https://commons.wikimedia.org/wiki/File:Eiffel_Tower_and_La_D%C3%A9fense_from_the_Tour_Montparnasse,_October_2010.jpg (CC BY 3.0).

Cover design: Kindred Grey

Disclaimers: All product names and registered trademarks are property of their respective owners. Company, product, and service names used in this book are for identification purposes only. Use of these names, trademarks, and brands does not imply endorsement.

This work may contain components (e.g., illustrations or quotations) not covered by the license. Every effort has been made to clearly identify these components but ultimately it is your responsibility to independently evaluate the copyright status of any work or component part of a work you use, in light of your intended use. Please check the references at the end of each chapter before redistributing.

Contents

An Open Letter to Students — vi

Introduction — vii

Instructor Resources — x

Acknowledgments — xii

1. Teamwork in Business — 1
2. The Foundations of Business — 20
3. Economics and Business — 31
4. Ethics and Social Responsibility — 50
5. Business in a Global Environment — 85
6. Forms of Business Ownership — 114
7. Entrepreneurship and Small Business Development — 129
8. Management and Leadership — 172
9. Structuring Organizations — 193
10. Operations Management — 206
11. Motivating Employees — 230
12. Managing Human Resources — 238
13. Union/Management Issues — 270
14. Marketing: Providing Value to Customers — 280
15. Pricing Strategy — 308
16. Hospitality and Tourism — 321
17. Accounting and Financial Information — 350
18. Personal Finances — 376
19. Technology in Business — 391

About the Author — 427

Version Notes — 431

An Open Letter to Students

Dear Student,

Welcome to the fourth edition of the *Fundamentals of Business* textbook!

We imagine that if you are reading this that you are beginning a new path to learn more about business. We are very excited to be a part of that learning development with you.

This textbook, an Open Education Resource (OER), was developed in response to the increased prices of textbooks for college students. We recognized that the financial burden for students and families continues to increase and we wanted to change that with a free textbook. However, just because the textbook has no price does not diminish the value of the content inside.

Fundamentals of Business provides a foundation of business terms, concepts, and an understanding of the global business environment so as to inspire you in your business journey. It covers the following topics in business: teamwork; economics; ethics; entrepreneurship; business ownership, management, and leadership; organizational structures and operations management; human resources and motivating employees; managing in labor union contexts; marketing and pricing strategy; hospitality and tourism, accounting and finance, technology in business and personal finances.

I hope that you find this resource worthwhile and that it provides insights to help you discover more about business.

Kindest regards,

Ron Poff

Introduction

If you are an instructor reviewing, adopting, or adapting this textbook, please inform us at http://bit.ly/business-interest.

Purpose of This Book

Fundamentals of Business, 4th edition is intended to serve as a no-cost, instructor-customizable primary text for one-semester undergraduate introductory business courses. It serves as the primary text for Virginia Tech's MGT 1104 Foundations of Business, a required, introductory level course which builds the foundational structure for all business majors at Virginia Tech. MGT 1104 is part of Virginia Tech's First-Year Experience program and serves as an elective for students exploring majors in business.

Target Audience

This book has also been adopted at over 100 colleges and universities! *Fundamentals of Business*, 4th edition is intended for a wide range of undergraduate business students including those majoring or considering majors in marketing, management, business administration, accounting, finance, real estate, business information technology, and hospitality and tourism.

Scope

This text enables undergraduate students' exploration of their chosen or prospective major in business, and introduces them to new ideas and concepts, career possibilities, and real-world examples. The text covers most if not all functions of business including: Teamwork; economics; ethics; business in a global environment; business ownership; entrepreneurship and small business development; management, and leadership; organizational structures and operations management; human resources and motivating employees; managing in labor union contexts; marketing and pricing strategy; hospitality and tourism, accounting and finance, personal finances, and technology in business.

Features

- Example-rich narrative
- Updated graphic elements which illustrate and reinforce concepts
- Interactive self-test quizzes with feedback
- Section-level videos and key takeaways
- Linked end of section references for additional reading
- Embedded navigation and image alt-text for screen readers
- Free online, PDF, ePub, and in print at vendor cost of production
- Open license, CC BY-NC-SA 4.0 https://creativecommons.org/licenses/by-nc-sa/4.0 permits customization and sharing

Instructor Resources

- Instructor community portal for sharing of ancillary resources
- Interest form allows instructors to opt in to receive book updates
- Errata and report-an-error/share-a-suggestion forms promote currency
- Test bank available to instructors upon request

See the Instructor Resource section for further information.

Attribution and Scope of Revision

This textbook is an update of the 3rd edition of Fundamentals of Business (2020) http://hdl.handle.net/10919/99283, an openly licensed text published by the Pamplin College of Business in association with Virginia Tech Publishing. The 4th edition uses the same structure as the 3rd (2020) edition. A detailed list of changes by chapter is available in the Version Notes at the back of the book. Attribution details are available in the Acknowledgments section.

Impact

Our hope for this textbook is that it will engage students who are learning about business. Also, it is hoped that instructors in other colleges and universities will appreciate this text, adopt it for their students, and adapt and share it, thus providing a student textbook solution at no cost. If you are an instructor reviewing, adopting, or adapting this textbook, please inform us at http://bit.ly/business-interest.

Instructor Resources

Open Access Availability

This book is available to anyone with internet access and at no charge in the following electronic formats:

HTML at: https://pressbooks.lib.vt.edu/fundamentalsofbusiness4e

PDF and ePub https://doi.org/10.21061/fundamentalsofbusiness4e

Get it in Print

This book is available at the manufacturer's lowest cost of print in color or black and white. Visit https://doi.org/10.21061/fundamentalsofbusiness4e for further information.

How to Adopt This Book

Instructors reviewing, adopting, or adapting this textbook are encouraged to register at http://bit.ly/business-interest. This assists Virginia Tech's Open Education Initiative in assessing the impact of the book and allows us to more easily alert instructors of new editions, supplements, and other additional resources.

This is an open textbook. Open textbooks are full, complete textbooks that have been funded, published, and licensed to be freely used, adapted, and distributed. As a particular type of Open Educational Resource (OER), this open textbook is intended to provide authoritative, accurate, and comprehensive subject content at no cost, to anyone including those who utilize technology to read and those who cannot afford or choose not to acquire traditional fee-based textbooks. Unless otherwise noted, this book is licensed with a Creative Commons Attribution NonCommercial-ShareAlike 4.0 license, which permits customization and sharing under the same license with attribution.

Instructors and other readers may be interested in localizing, rearranging, or adapting content, or in transforming the content into other formats with the goal of better addressing student learning needs, and/or making use of various teaching methods. Open textbooks in a variety of disciplines are available via the Open Textbook Library: https://open.umn.edu/opentextbooks.

Locating Additional Resources for Your Course

The following additional resources are available:

- Instructor-only test bank http://hdl.handle.net/10919/93404 (Ch 1-18)
- Instructor resource sharing portal https://www.oercommons.org/groups/fundamentals-of-business-user-group/1379
- 1st edition (2016) http://hdl.handle.net/10919/70961, 2nd edition (2018) http://hdl.handle.net/10919/84848, and 3rd edition (2020) http://hdl.handle.net/10919/99283
- Instructor listserv https://groups.google.com/a/vt.edu/forum/#!forum/fundamentalsofbusiness-g
- Links to additional resources will be added here http://hdl.handle.net/10919/111385

Sharing Resources You've Created

Have you created any supplementary materials for use with *Fundamentals of Business* such as presentation slides, activities, test items, or question banks? If so, please consider sharing your materials related to this open textbook. Please tell us about resources you wish to share by using this form: http://bit.ly/business-interest or by directly sharing non-assessment resources under an open license to the public-facing instructor sharing portal https://www.oercommons.org/groups/fundamentals-of-business-user-group/1379.

Request for Feedback

The editor and author of this book are actively soliciting feedback from individuals, classes, and faculty using this book. You may submit private or anonymous suggestions, errors to correct, or feedback to the editor and author of *Fundamentals of Business* by using this form: http://bit.ly/business-feedback.

Additional suggestions or feedback may be submitted via email at: publishing@vt.edu

Acknowledgments

This adapted edition is produced through the University Libraries at Virginia Tech's Open Education Initiative (https://guides.lib.vt.edu/oer/grantees) which funded Pamplin College faculty, and University Libraries' faculty and staff labor. This included grant and technical support from the University Libraries' Open Education Initiative https://guides.lib.vt.edu/oer/grants. Support for Ron Poff's contributions was provided by the Pamplin College of Business at Virginia Tech.

Attributions

This book updates the first, second, and third editions of *Fundamentals of Business*, adapted by Stephen Skripak, et al. Version notes located in the back of the book describe changes and updates implemented in the fourth edition.

Much of the content in Chapters 1-15 and 17-18 is based on an openly licensed text hosted by the Saylor Foundation. The Saylor Foundation has given permission to adapt and redistribute http://www.saylor.org/site/textbooks/Exploring%20Business.docx via a Creative Commons Attribution NonCommercial-ShareAlike 3.0 (CC BY NC-SA) license: https://creativecommons.org/licenses/by-nc-sa/3.0. The Saylor Foundation previously adapted this work under a Creative Commons Attribution-NonCommercial-ShareAlike 3.0 (CC BY NC-SA) license and without attribution as requested by the work's original creator or licensee.

Selected text and figures were used in Chapter 16 from *Introduction to Tourism and Hospitality in BC*: https://opentextbc.ca/introtourism. Morgan Westcott, Editor and © Capilano University. The copyright holder has given permission to adopt and redistribute via a Creative Commons Attribution 4.0 (CC BY) license: https://creativecommons.org/licenses/by/4.0.

OpenStax has given permission to adapt and redistribute *Introduction to Business* https://openstax.org/details/books/introduction-business via a Creative Commons Attribution 4.0 (CC BY) license: http://creativecommons.org/licenses/by/4.0.

- Content adapted for Chapter 4
    - Understanding Business Ethics, Section 2.1. Retrieved from: https://openstax.org/books/introduction-business/pages/2-1-understanding-business-ethics
    - Blowing the Whistle on Financial Fraud in Buying and Selling at Securities Exchanges, Section 16.7. Retrieved from: https://openstax.org/books/introduction-business/pages/16-7-buying-and-selling-at-securities-exchanges
- Content adapted for Chapter 7
    - Making Smarter Homes [Video]. Retrieved from: https://youtu.be/kMt4wqZfgmU

- Content adapted for Chapter 8
  - Summary of Learning Outcomes, Chapter 6. Retrieved from: https://openstax.org/books/introduction-business/pages/6-8-trends-in-management-and-leadership
- Content adapted for Chapter 14
  - Trends in Social Media, Section 12.10. Retrieved from: https://openstax.org/books/introduction-business/pages/12-10-trends-in-social-media
- Content adapted for Chapter 17
  - Exploring Business Careers, Chapter 16. Retrieved from: https://openstax.org/books/introduction-business/pages/16-introduction
  - Role of Finance and the Financial Manager, Section 16.1. Retrieved from: https://openstax.org/books/introduction-business/pages/16-1-the-role-of-finance-and-the-financial-manager
- Content adapted to create nearly the whole of Chapter 19
  - Using Technology to Manage Information, Chapter 13. Retrieved from: https://openstax.org/books/introduction-business/pages/13-introduction

The following copyright holder has generously given written permission to reproduce this image:

- (c) "The PowerSki Jetboard." Figure 10.1 Permission granted for this and future versions of this text by copyright owner Bob Montgomery.

Cover image attributions:

- Front cover: Photo by Lukas from Pexels (https://www.pexels.com/photo/close-up-photo-of-survey-spreadsheet-590022/)(Pexels license) and photo by fauxels from Pexels (https://www.pexels.com/photo/close-up-photo-of-survey-spreadsheet-590022/)(Pexels license).
- Back cover: Photo by Alena Darmel from Pexels (https://www.pexels.com/photo/businessman-and-women-in-the-meeting-room-8133867/)(Pexels license), photo by Cedric Fauntleroy from Pexels (https://www.pexels.com/photo/women-in-hijab-sitting-at-table-with-laptops-8154524/)(Pexels license), photo by mscamilaalmeida from Pixabay (https://pixabay.com/photos/empire-state-building-1350511/?download)(Pixabay license), and photo by Wladyslaw from WikimediaCommons (https://commons.wikimedia.org/wiki/File:Eiffel_Tower_and_La_D%C3%A9fense_from_the_Tour_Montparnasse,_October_2010.jpg)(CC BY 3.0).

Additional sources are referenced at the end of each chapter.

1. Teamwork in Business

Learning Objectives

- Define a team and describe its key characteristics.
- Explain why organizations use teams and describe different types of teams.
- Explain why teams may be effective or ineffective.
- Identify factors that contribute to team cohesiveness.
- Understand the importance of learning to participate in team-based activities.
- Identify the skills needed by team members and the roles that members of a team might play.
- Learn how to survive team projects in college (and actually enjoy yourself).
- Explain the skills and behaviors that foster effective team leadership.

The Team with the RAZR's Edge

The publicly traded company Motorola Mobility was created when Motorola spun off its Mobile Devices division, creating a new entity. The newly-formed company's executive team was under intense pressure to come out with a smartphone that could grab substantial market share from Apple's iPhone 4S and Samsung's Galaxy Nexus. To do this, the team oversaw the design of an Android version of the Motorola RAZR, which was once the best-selling phone in the world. The hope of the executive team was that past customers who loved the RAZR would love the new ultra-thin smartphone—the Droid RAZR. The Droid RAZR was designed by a team, as are other Motorola products. To understand the team approach at Motorola, let's review the process used to design the RAZR.

By winter 2003, the company that for years had run in circles around their competition had been bumped from the top spot in worldwide sales.[1] Motorola found itself stuck in the number-three slot. Their sales had declined because consumers were less than enthusiastic about the uninspired style of Motorola phones, and for many people, style is just as important in picking a cell phone as features. As a reviewer for one industry publication put it, "We just want to see the look on people's faces when we slide [our phones] out of our pockets to take a call."

Yet there was a glimmer of hope at Motorola. Despite its recent lapse in cell phone fashion sense, Motorola still maintained a concept-phone unit—a group responsible for designing futuristic new product features such as speech-recognition capability, flexible touchscreens, and touch-sensitive body covers. In every concept-phone unit, developers engage in an ongoing struggle to balance the two often-opposing demands of cell phone design: building the smallest possible phone with the largest possible screen. The previous year, Motorola had unveiled the rough model of an ultra-trim phone—at 10 millimeters, about half the width of the average flip-top or "clamshell" design. It was on this concept that Motorola decided to stake the revival of its reputation as a cell phone maker who knew how to package functionality with a wow factor.

The next step in developing a concept phone is actually building it. Teamwork becomes critical at this point. The process requires some diversity in expertise. An electronics engineer, for example, knows how to apply energy to transmit information through a system but not how to apply physics to the design and manufacture of the system; that's the specialty of a mechanical engineer. Engineers aren't designers—the specialists who know how to enhance the marketability of a product through its aesthetic value. Designers bring their own unique value to the team.

Figure 1.1: Woman on the phone.

In addition, when you set out to build any kind of innovative high-tech product, you need to become a master of trade-offs—in Motorola's case, compromises resulted from the demands of state-of-the-art functionality on one hand and fashionable design on the other. Negotiating trade-offs is a team process: it takes at least two people to resolve design disputes.

The responsibility for assembling and managing the Motorola "thin-clam" team fell to veteran electronic engineer Roger Jellicoe. His mission: create the world's thinnest phone, do it in one year, and try to keep it a secret. Before the project was completed, the team had grown to more than twenty members, and with increased creative input and enthusiasm came increased confidence and clout. Jellicoe had been warned by company specialists in such matters that no phone wider than 49 millimeters could be held comfortably in the human hand. When the team had finally arrived at a satisfactory design that couldn't work at less than 53 millimeters, they ignored the "49 millimeters warning," built a model, passed it around, and came to a consensus: as one team member put it, "People could hold it in their hands and say, 'Yeah, it doesn't feel like a brick.'" Four millimeters, they decided, was an acceptable trade-off, and the new phone went to market at 53 millimeters. While small by today's standards, at the time, 53 millimeters was a gamble.

Team members liked to call the design process the "dance." Sometimes it flowed smoothly and sometimes people stepped on one another's toes, but for the most part, the team moved in lockstep toward its goal. After a series of trade-offs about what to call the final product (suggestions ranged from Razor Clam to V3), Motorola's new RAZR was introduced in July 2004. Recall that the product was originally conceived as a high-tech toy—something to restore the luster to Motorola's tarnished image. It wasn't supposed to set sales records, and sales in the fourth quarter of 2004, though promising, were in fact fairly modest. Back in September, however, a new executive named Ron Garriques had taken over Motorola's cell phone division; one of his first decisions was to raise the bar for RAZR. Disregarding a 2005 budget that called for sales of two million units, Garriques pushed expected sales for the RAZR up to twenty million. The RAZR topped that target, shipped ten million in the first quarter of 2006, and hit the fifty-million mark at midyear. Talking on a RAZR, declared hip-hop star Sean "P. Diddy" Combs, "is like driving a Mercedes versus a regular ol' ride."[2]

Jellicoe and his team were invited to attend an event hosted by top executives, receiving a standing ovation, along with a load of stock options. One of the reasons for the RAZR's success, said Jellicoe, was that "it took the world by surprise. Very few Motorola products do that." For a while, the new RAZR was the best-selling phone in the world.

The Team and the Organization

What Is a Team? How Does Teamwork Work?

A **team** (or a work team) is a group of people with complementary skills who work together to achieve a specific goal.[3] In the case of Motorola's RAZR team, the specific **goal** was to develop (and ultimately bring to market) an ultra-thin cell phone that would help restore the company's reputation. The team achieved its goal by integrating specialized but complementary skills in engineering and design and by making the most of its authority to make its own decisions and manage its own operations.

Teams versus Groups

As Bonnie Edelstein, a consultant in organizational development suggests, "A group is a bunch of people in an elevator. A team is also a bunch of people in an elevator, but the elevator is broken."[4] This distinction may be a little oversimplified, but as our tale of teamwork at Motorola reminds us, a team is clearly something more than a mere group of individuals. In particular, members of a **group**—or, more accurately, a working group—go about their jobs independently and meet primarily to work towards a shared objective. A group of department-store managers, for example, might meet monthly to discuss their progress in cutting plant costs. However, each manager is focused on the goals of his or her department because each is held accountable for meeting those goals.

Some Key Characteristics of Teams

To put teams in perspective, let's identify five key characteristics. Teams:[5]

- share accountability for achieving specific common goals,
- function interdependently,
- require stability,
- hold authority and decision-making power, and
- operate in a social context.

Why Organizations Build Teams

Why do major organizations now rely so much on teams to improve operations? Executives at Xerox have reported that team-based operations are 30 percent more productive than conventional operations. General Mills says that factories organized around team activities are 40 percent more productive than traditionally organized factories. FedEx says that teams reduced service errors (lost packages, incorrect bills) by 13 percent in the first year.[6]

Today it seems obvious that teams can address a variety of challenges in the world of corporate activity. Before we go any further, however, we should remind ourselves that the data we've just cited aren't necessarily definitive. For one thing, they may not be objective—companies are more likely to report successes than failures. As a matter of fact, teams don't always work. According to one study, team-based projects fail 50–70 percent of the time.[7]

The Effect of Teams on Performance

Research shows that companies build and support teams because of their effect on overall workplace performance, both organizational and individual. If we examine the impact of team-based operations according to a wide range of relevant criteria, we find that overall organizational performance generally improves. Figure 1.2 lists several areas in which we can analyze workplace performance and indicates the percentage of companies that have reported improvements in each area.

Area of performance	Firms reporting improvement
Product and service quality	70%
Customer service	67%
Worker satisfaction	66%
Quality of work life	63%
Productivity	61%
Competitiveness	50%
Profitability	45%
Absenteeism/turnover	23%

Figure 1.2: Performance improvements due to team-based operations.

Types of Teams

Teams can improve company and individual performance in a number of areas. Not all teams, however, are formed to achieve the same goals or charged with the same responsibilities. Nor are they organized in the same way. Some, for instance, are more autonomous than others—less accountable to those higher up in the organization. Some depend on a team leader who's responsible for defining the team's goals and making sure that its activities are performed effectively. Others are more or less self-governing: though a leader lays out overall goals and strategies, the team itself chooses and manages the methods by which it pursues its goals and implements its strategies.[8] Teams also vary according to their membership. Let's look at several categories of teams.

Manager-Led Teams

As its name implies, in the **manager-led team** the manager is the team leader and is in charge of setting team goals, assigning tasks, and monitoring the team's performance. The individual team members have relatively little autonomy. For example, the key employees of a professional football team (a manager-led team) are highly trained (and highly paid) athletes, but their activities on the field are tightly controlled by a head coach. As team manager, the coach is responsible both for developing the strategies by which the team pursues its goal of winning games and for the outcome of each game and season. They're also solely responsible for interacting with managers above them in the organization. The players are responsible mainly for executing plays.[9]

Figure 1.3: Virginia Tech head football coach, Brent Pry.

Self-Managed Teams

Self-managed teams (also known as self-directed teams) have considerable autonomy. They are usually small and often absorb activities that were once performed by traditional supervisors. A manager or team leader may determine overall goals, but the members of the self-managed team control the activities needed to achieve those goals.

Self-managed teams are the organizational hallmark of Whole Foods Market, the largest natural-foods grocer in the United States. Each store is run by 10 departmental teams, and virtually every store employee is a member of a team. Each team has a designated leader and its own performance targets. (Team leaders also belong to a store team, and store-team leaders belong to a regional team.) To do its job, every team has access to the kind of information—including sales and even salary figures—that most companies reserve for traditional managers.[10]

Not every self-managed team enjoys the same degree of autonomy. Companies vary widely in choosing which tasks teams are allowed to manage and which ones are best left to upper-level management only. As you can see in figure 1.4 for example, self-managed teams are often allowed to schedule assignments, but they are rarely allowed to fire coworkers.

Figure 1.4: Duties of self-managed teams.

Cross-Functional Teams

Figure 1.5: Cross-functional teams.

Many companies use **cross-functional teams**—teams that, as the name suggests, cut across an organization's functional areas (operations, marketing, finance, and so on). A cross-functional team is designed to take advantage of the special expertise of members drawn from different functional areas of the company. For example, when the Internal Revenue Service wanted to study the effects of a major change in information systems on employees, it created a cross-functional team composed of people from a wide range of departments. The final study reflected expertise in such areas as job analysis, training, change management, industrial psychology, and ergonomics.[11]

Cross-functional teams figure prominently in the product-development process at Nike, where they take advantage of expertise from both inside and outside the company. Typically, team members include not only product designers, marketing specialists, and accountants but also sports-research experts, coaches, athletes, and even consumers. Likewise, Motorola's RAZR team was a cross-functional team; the responsibility for developing the new product wasn't passed along from the design team to the engineering team, but rather was entrusted to a special team composed of both designers and engineers.

Committees and task forces, both of which are dedicated to specific issues or tasks, are often cross-functional teams. Problem-solving teams, which are created to study such issues as improving quality or reducing waste, may be either intradepartmental or cross-functional.[12]

Virtual Teams

Technology now makes it possible for teams to function not only across organizational boundaries like functional areas, but also across time and space. Technologies such as videoconferencing allow people to interact simultaneously and in real time, offering a number of advantages in conducting the business of a **virtual team**.[13] Members can participate from any location or at any time of day, and teams can "meet" for as long as it takes to achieve a goal or solve a problem—a few days, weeks, or months. Early in the Covid-19 pandemic, many companies, organizations, governments and learning institutions were forced to move to virtual settings in order to curve the spread of the virus. This transition allowed for continuity of operations as best as possible.

Team size does not seem to be an obstacle when it comes to virtual-team meetings; in building the F-35 Strike Fighter, US defense contractor Lockheed Martin staked the $225 billion project on a virtual product-team of unprecedented global dimension, drawing on designers and engineers from the ranks of eight international partners from Canada, the United Kingdom, Norway, and Turkey.[14]

 An interactive H5P element has been excluded from this version of the text. You can view it online here: https://pressbooks.lib.vt.edu/fundamentalsofbusiness4e/?p=40#h5p-1

Why Teamwork Works

Now that we know a little bit about how teams work, we need to ask ourselves why they work. Not surprisingly, this is a fairly complex issue. In this section, we'll explore why teams are often effective and when they ineffective.

Factors in Effective Teamwork

First, let's begin by identifying several factors that contribute to **effective teamwork**. Teams are most effective when the following factors are met:

- Members depend on each other. When team members rely on each other to get the job done, team productivity and efficiency tend to be high.
- Members trust one another.
- Members work better together rather than individually. When team members perform better as a group than alone, collective performance exceeds individual performance.
- Members become boosters. When each member is encouraged by other team members to do his or her best, collective results improve.
- Team members enjoy being on the team.
- Leadership rotates.

Some of these factors may seem intuitive. Because such issues are rarely clear-cut, we need to examine the issue of group effectiveness from another perspective—one that considers the effects of factors that aren't quite so straightforward.

Group Cohesiveness

The idea of **group cohesiveness** refers to the attractiveness of a team to its members. If a group is high in cohesiveness, membership is quite satisfying to its members. If it's low in cohesiveness, members are unhappy with it and may try to leave it.[15]

What Makes a Team Cohesive?

Numerous factors may contribute to team cohesiveness, but in this section, we'll focus on five of the most important:

- **Size**. The bigger the team, the less satisfied members tend to be. When teams get too large, members find it harder to interact closely with other members; a few members tend to dominate team activities, and conflict becomes more likely.
- **Similarity**. People usually get along better with people like themselves, and teams are generally more cohesive when members perceive fellow members as people who share their own attitudes and experience.
- **Success**. When teams are successful, members are satisfied, and other people are more likely to be attracted to their teams.
- **Exclusiveness**. The harder it is to get into a group, the happier the people who are already in it. Team status also increases members' satisfaction.
- **Competition**. Membership is valued more highly when there is motivation to achieve common goals and outperform other teams.

Maintaining team focus on broad organizational goals is crucial. If members get too wrapped up in immediate team goals, the whole team may lose sight of the larger organizational goals toward which it's supposed to be working. Let's look at some factors that can erode team performance.

Groupthink

It's easy for leaders to direct members toward team goals when members are all on the same page—when there's a basic willingness to conform to the team's rules. When there's too much conformity, however, the group can become ineffective: the group may resist fresh ideas and, even worse, end up adopting its own dysfunctional tendencies as its way of doing things. Such tendencies may also encourage a phenomenon known as **groupthink**—the tendency to conform to group pressure in making decisions, while failing to think critically or to consider outside influences.

Figure 1.6: The space shuttle Challenger's first launch in 1983.

Groupthink is often cited as a factor in the explosion of the space shuttle Challenger in January 1986: engineers from a supplier of components for the rocket booster warned that the launch might be risky because of the weather but were persuaded to set aside their warning by NASA officials who wanted the launch to proceed as scheduled.[16]

Motivation and Frustration

Remember that teams are composed of people, and whatever the roles they happen to be playing at a given time, people are subject to psychological ups and downs. As members of workplace teams, they need motivation, and when motivation is low, so are effectiveness and productivity. The difficulty of maintaining a high level of motivation is the chief cause of frustration among members of teams. As such, it's also a chief cause of ineffective teamwork, and that's one reason why more employers now look for the ability to develop and sustain motivation when they're hiring new managers.[17]

Other Factors that Erode Performance

Let's take a quick look at three other obstacles to success in introducing teams into an organization:[18]

- **Unwillingness to cooperate**. Failure to cooperate can occur when members don't or won't commit to a common goal or set of activities. What if, for example, half the members of a product-development team want to create a brand-new product and half want to improve an existing product? The entire team may get stuck on this point of contention for weeks or even months. Lack of cooperation between teams can also be problematic to an organization.
- **Lack of managerial support**. Every team requires organizational resources to achieve its goals, and if management isn't willing to commit the needed resources— say, funding or key personnel—a team will probably fall short of those goals.
- **Failure of managers to delegate authority**. Team leaders are often chosen from the ranks of successful supervisors—first-line managers give instructions on a day-to-day basis and expect to have them carried out. This approach to workplace activities may not work very well in leading a team—a position in which success depends on building a consensus and letting people make their own decisions.

 An interactive H5P element has been excluded from this version of the text. You can view it online here: https://pressbooks.lib.vt.edu/fundamentalsofbusiness4e/?p=40#h5p-2

The Team and Its Members

"Life Is All About Group Work"

"I'll work extra hard and do it myself, but please don't make me have to work in a group."

Like it or not, you've probably already noticed that you'll have team-based assignments in college. More than two-thirds of all students report having participated in the work of an organized team, and if you're in business school, you will almost certainly find yourself engaged in team-based activities.[19]

Why do we put so much emphasis on something that, reportedly, makes many students feel anxious and academically drained? Here's one college student's practical-minded answer to this question:

> "In the real world, you have to work with people. You don't always know the people you work with, and you don't always get along with them. Your boss won't particularly care, and if you can't get the job done, your job may end up on the line. Life is all about group work, whether we like it or not. And school, in many ways, prepares us for life, including working with others."[20]

She's right. In placing so much emphasis on teamwork skills and experience, business colleges are doing the responsible thing—preparing students for the business world. A survey of Fortune 1000 companies reveals that 79 percent use self-managing teams and 91 percent use other forms of employee work groups. Another survey found that the skill that most employers value in new employees is the ability to work in teams.[21] Consider the advice of former Chrysler Chairman Lee Iacocca: "A major reason that capable people fail to advance is that they don't work well with their colleagues."[22] The importance of the ability to work in teams was confirmed in a survey of leadership practices of more than sixty of the world's top organizations.[23]

Figure 1.7: Teamwork makes the dream work!

When top executives in these organizations were asked what causes the careers of high-potential leadership candidates to derail, 60 percent of the organizations cited "inability to work in teams." Interestingly, only 9 percent attributed the failure of these executives to advance to "lack of technical ability."

To put it in plain terms, the question is not whether you'll find yourself working as part of a team. You will. The question is whether you'll know how to participate successfully in team-based activities.

Will You Make a Good Team Member?

What if your instructor decides to divide the class into teams and assigns each team to develop a new product plus a business plan to get it on the market? What teamwork skills could you bring to the table, and what teamwork skills do you need to improve? Do you possess qualities that might make you a good team leader?

What Skills Does the Team Need?

Sometimes we hear about a sports team made up of mostly average players who win a championship because of coaching genius, flawless teamwork, and superhuman determination.[24] But not terribly often. In fact, we usually hear about such teams simply because they're newsworthy—exceptions to the rule. Typically a team performs well because its members possess some level of talent. Members' talents must also be managed in a collective effort to achieve a common goal.

In the final analysis, a team can succeed only if its members provide the skills that need managing. In particular, every team requires some mixture of three sets of skills:

- **Technical skills**. Because teams must perform certain tasks, they need people with the skills to perform them. For example, if your project calls for a lot of math work, it's good to have someone with the necessary quantitative skills.
- **Decision-making and problem-solving skills**. Because every task is subject to problems, and because handling every problem means deciding on the best solution, it's good to have members who are skilled in identifying problems, evaluating alternative solutions, and deciding on the best options.
- **Interpersonal skills**. Because teams need direction and motivation and depend on communication, every group benefits from members who know how to listen, provide feedback, and resolve conflict. Some members must also be good at communicating the team's goals and needs to outsiders.

The key is ultimately to have the right mix of these skills. Remember, too, that no team needs to possess all these skills—never mind the right balance of them—from day one. In many cases, a team gains certain skills only when members volunteer for certain tasks and perfect their skills in the process of performing them. For the same reason, effective teamwork develops over time as team members learn how to handle various team-based tasks. In a sense, teamwork is always work in progress.

What Roles Do Team Members Play?

As a student and later in the workplace, you'll be a member of a team more often than a leader. Team members can have as much impact on a team's success as its leaders. A key is the quality of the contributions they make in performing non-leadership **roles**.[25]

What, exactly, are those roles? At this point, you've probably concluded that every team faces two basic challenges:

- Accomplishing its assigned task, and
- Maintaining or improving group cohesiveness.

Whether you affect the team's work positively or negatively depends on the extent to which you help it or hinder it in meeting these two challenges.[26] We can thus divide teamwork roles into two categories, depending on which of these two challenges each role addresses. These two categories (task-facilitating roles and relationship-building roles) are summarized here:

Task-facilitating roles	Example	Relationship-building roles	Example
Direction giving	"Jot down a few ideas and we'll see what everyone has come up with."	Supporting	"Now, that's what I mean by a practical application."
Information seeking	"Does anyone know if this is the latest data we have?"	Harmonizing	"Actually, I think you're both saying pretty much the same thing."
Information giving	"Here are the latest numbers from …"	Tension relieving	"Before we go on, would anyone like a drink?"
Elaborating	"I think a good example of what you're talking about is …"	Confronting	"How does that suggestion relate to the topic that we're discussing?"
Urging	"Let's try to finish this proposal before we adjourn."	Energizing	"It's been a long time since I've had this many laughs at a meeting in this department."
Monitoring	"If you'll take care of the first section, I'll make sure that we have the second by next week."	Developing	"If you need some help pulling the data together, let me know."
Process analyzing	"What happened to the energy level in this room?"	Consensus building	"Do we agree on the first four points even if number five needs a little more work?"
Reality testing	"Can we make this work and stay within budget?"	Empathizing	"It's not you. The numbers are confusing."
Enforcing	"We're getting off track. Let's try to stay on topic."	Summarizing	"Before we jump ahead, here's what we've decided so far."

Figure 1.8: Team member roles.

Task-facilitating roles

Task-facilitating roles address challenge number one—accomplishing the team goals. As you can see from Table P.6, such roles include not only providing information when someone else needs it but also asking for it when you need it. In addition, it includes monitoring (checking on progress) and enforcing (making sure that team decisions are carried out). Task facilitators are especially valuable when assignments aren't clear or when progress is too slow.

Relationship-building roles

When you challenge unmotivated behavior or help other team members understand their roles, you're performing a **relationship-building role** and addressing challenge number two—maintaining or improving group cohesiveness. This type of role includes activities that improve team "chemistry," from empathizing to confronting.

Bear in mind three points about this model: (1) Teams are most effective when there's a good balance between task facilitation and relationship-building; (2) it's hard for any given member to perform both types of roles, as some people are better at focusing on tasks and others on relationships; and (3) overplaying any facet of any role can easily become counterproductive. For example, elaborating on something may not be the best strategy when the team needs to make a quick decision; and consensus building may cause the team to overlook an important difference of opinion.

Blocking roles

Finally, review figure 1.9, which summarizes a few characteristics of another kind of team-membership role. So-called **blocking roles** consist of behavior that inhibits either team performance or that of individual members. Every member of the team should know how to recognize blocking behavior. If teams don't confront dysfunctional members, they can destroy morale, hamper consensus building, create conflict, and hinder progress.

Blocking behavior	Tactics
Dominate	Talk as much as possible; interrupt and interject
Overanalyze	Split hairs and belabor every detail
Stall	Frustrate efforts to come to conclusions: decline to agree, sidetrack the discussion, rehash old ideas
Remain passive	Stay on the fringe; keep interaction to a minimum; wait for others to take on work
Overgeneralize	Blow things out of proportion; float unfounded conclusions
Find fault	Criticize and withhold credit whenever possible
Make premature decisions	Rush to conclusions before goals are set, information is shared, or problems are clarified
Present opinions as facts	Refuse to seek factual support for ideas that you personally favor
Reject	Object to ideas by people who tend to disagree with you
Pull rank	Use status or title to push through ideas, rather than seek consensus on their value
Resist	Throw up roadblocks to progress; look on the negative side
Deflect	Refuse to stay on topic; focus on minor points rather than main points

Figure 1.9: Types and examples of blocking behaviors.

Class Team Projects

In your academic career you'll participate in a number of team projects. To get insider advice on how to succeed on team projects in college, let's look at some suggestions offered by students who have gone through this experience.[27]

- **Draw up a team charter**. At the beginning of the project, draw up a team charter that includes: the goals of the group; ways to ensure that each team member's ideas are considered; timing and frequency of meeting. A more informal way to arrive at a team charter is to simply set some ground rules to which everyone agrees.
- **Contribute your ideas**. Share your ideas with your group. The worst that could happen is that they won't be used (which is what would happen if you kept quiet).
- **Never miss a meeting or deadline**. Pick a weekly meeting time and write it into your schedule as if it were a class. Never skip it.
- **Be considerate of each other**. Be patient, listen to everyone, involve everyone in decision making, avoid infighting, build trust.
- **Create a process for resolving conflict**. Do so before conflict arises. Set up rules to help the group decide how conflict will be handled.
- **Use the strengths of each team member**. All students bring different strengths. Utilize the unique value of each person.
- **Don't do all the work yourself**. Work with your team to get the work done. The project output is often less important than the experience.

What Does It Take to Lead a Team?

To borrow from Shakespeare, "Some people are born leaders, some achieve leadership, and some have leadership thrust upon them." At some point in a successful career, you will likely be asked to lead a team. What will you have to do to succeed as a leader?

Like so many of the questions that we ask in this book, this question doesn't have any simple answers. We can provide one broad answer: A *leader must help members develop the attitudes and behavior that contribute to team success: interdependence, collective responsibility, shared commitment, and so forth.*

Team leaders must be able to *influence* their team members. Notice that we say influence: except in unusual circumstances, giving commands and controlling everything directly doesn't work very well.[28] As one team of researchers puts it, team leaders are more effective when they work *with* members rather than *on* them.[29] Hand-in-hand with the ability to influence is the ability to gain and keep the trust of team members. People aren't likely to be influenced by a leader whom they perceive as dishonest or selfishly motivated.

Assuming you were asked to lead a team, there are certain leadership skills and behaviors that would help you influence your team members and build trust. Let's look briefly at some of them:

- **Demonstrate integrity**. Do what you say you'll do and act in accordance with your stated values. Be honest in communicating and follow through on promises.
- **Be clear and consistent**. Let members know that you're certain about what you want and remember that being clear and consistent reinforces your credibility.
- **Generate positive energy**. Be optimistic and compliment team members. Recognize their progress and success.
- **Acknowledge common points of view**. Even if you're about to propose some kind of change, recognize the value of the views that members already hold in common.
- **Manage agreement and disagreement**. When members agree with you, confirm your shared point of view. When they disagree, acknowledge both sides of the issue and support your own with strong, clearly-presented evidence.
- **Encourage and coach**. Buoy up members when they run into new and uncertain situations and when success depends on their performing at a high level.
- **Share information**. Give members the information they need and let them know that you're knowledgeable about team tasks and individual talents. Check with team members regularly to find out what they're doing and how the job is progressing.

An interactive H5P element has been excluded from this version of the text. You can view it online here:
https://pressbooks.lib.vt.edu/fundamentalsofbusiness4e/?p=40#h5p-3

Key Takeaways

- A **team** (or a work team) is a group of people with complementary skills and diverse areas of expertise who **work together** to achieve a specific **goal**.
- Work teams have five key characteristics. They are **accountable for achieving specific common goals**. They function **interdependently**. They are **stable**. They have **authority**. And they operate in a **social context**.
- Work teams may be of several types:

    - In the traditional **manager-led team**, the leader defines the team's goals and activities and is responsible for its achieving its assigned goals.
    - The leader of a **self-managed team** may determine overall goals, but employees control the activities needed to meet them.
    - A **cross-functional team** is designed to take advantage of the special expertise of members drawn from different functional areas of the company.
    - On **virtual teams**, geographically dispersed members interact electronically in the process of pursuing a common goal.

- Group **cohesiveness** refers to the attractiveness of a team to its members. If a group is high in cohesiveness, membership is quite satisfying to its members; if it's low in cohesiveness, members are unhappy with it and may even try to leave it.
- As the business world depends more and more on teamwork, it's increasingly important for incoming members of the workforce to develop skills and experience in team-based activities.
- Every team requires some mixture of three skill sets:

    - **Technical skills**: skills needed to perform specific tasks
    - **Decision-making and problem-solving skills**: skills needed to identify problems, evaluate alternative solutions, and decide on the best options
    - **Interpersonal skills**: skills in listening, providing feedback, and resolving conflict

Figure References

Figure 1.1: Woman on the phone. Good Faces. 2021. Unsplash license. https://unsplash.com/photos/lY8ZoxeGUhU.

Figure 1.2: Performance improvements due to team-based operations. Adapted from Edward E. Lawler, S. A. Mohman, and G. E. Ledford (1992). Creating High Performance Organizations: Practices and Results of Employee Involvement and Total Quality in Fortune 1000 Companies. San Francisco: Wiley. Reprinted with permission of John Wiley & Sons Inc.

Figure 1.3: Virginia Tech head football coach, Brent Pry. SneakinDeacon. 2021. CC BY-SA 2.0. https://flic.kr/p/2mP1fd6.

Figure 1.4: Duties of self-managed teams. Kindred Grey. 2022. CC BY 4.0. https://archive.org/details/1.5_20220621.

Figure 1.5: Cross-functional teams. Kindred Grey. 2022. CC BY 4.0. Added person by Richa from Noun Project (Noun Project license). https://archive.org/details/1.6_20220621.

Figure 1.6: The space shuttle Challenger's first launch in 1983. U.S. federal government. 1983. Public domain. https://commons.wikimedia.org/wiki/File:Space_Shuttle_Challenger_(04-04-1983).JPEG.

Figure 1.7: Teamwork makes the dream work! Ivan Samkov. 2021. Pexels license. https://www.pexels.com/photo/coworkers-looking-at-a-laptop-in-an-office-8127690/.

Figure 1.8: Team member roles. Adapted from David A. Whetten and Kim S. Cameron (2007). Developing Management Skills, 7th ed. Upper Saddle River, NJ: Pearson Education. Pp. 517, 519.

Figure 1.9: Types and examples of blocking behaviors. Adapted from David A. Whetten and Kim S. Cameron (2007). Developing Management Skills, 7th ed. Upper Saddle River, NJ: Pearson Education. Pp. 519-20.

Notes

1. The Motorola vignette is based on the following sources: Adam Lashinsky (2006). "RAZR's Edge." Fortune. Retrieved from: http://archive.fortune.com/magazines/fortune/fortune_archive/2006/06/12/8379239/index.htm; Scott D. Anthony (2005). "Motorola's Bet on the RAZR's Edge." HBS Working Knowledge. Retrieved from: http://hbswk.hbs.edu/archive/4992.html; Roger O. Crockett (2005). "The Leading Edge is RAZR-Thin." Bloomberg. Retrieved from: http://www.bloomberg.com/news/articles/2005-12-04/the-leading-edge-is-razr-thin; Arik Hessedahl (2004). "Motorola vs. Nokia." Forbes.com. Retrieved from: http://www.forbes.com/2004/01/19/cx_ah_0119mondaymatchup.html; Vlad Balan (2007). "10 Coolest Concept Phones Out There." Cameraphones Plaza. Retrieved from: http://www.cameraphonesplaza.com/10-coolest-concept-phones-out-there/.
2. Roger O. Crockett (2005). "The Leading Edge is RAZR-Thin." Bloomberg. Retrieved from: http://www.bloomberg.com/news/articles/2005-12-04/the-leading-edge-is-razr-thin
3. This section is based in part on Leigh L. Thompson (2008). *Making the Team: A Guide for Managers*. Upper Saddle River, NJ: Pearson Education. p. 4.
4. Wilderdom.com (2006). "Team Building Quotes." Retrieved from: http://www.wilderdom.com/teambuilding/Quotes.html
5. Adapted from Leigh L. Thompson (2008). *Making the Team: A Guide for Managers*. Upper Saddle River, NJ: Pearson

Education. p. 4-5; C. P. Alderfer (1977). "Group and Intergroup Relations," in *Improving Life at Work*. J. R. Hackman and J. L. Suttle ed. (1977). Palisades, CA: Goodyear. pp. 277-96.

6. Kimball Fisher (1999). *Leading Self-Directed Work Teams: A Guide to Developing New Team Leadership Skills*, rev. ed. New York: McGraw-Hill Professional; Jerald Greenberg and Robert A. Baron (2008). *Behavior in Organizations*, 9th ed. Upper Saddle River, NJ: Pearson Education. pp. 315-16.
7. Jerald Greenberg and Robert A. Baron (2008). *Behavior in Organizations*, 9th ed. Upper Saddle River, NJ: Pearson Education. p. 316; Leigh L. Thompson (2008). *Making the Team: A Guide for Managers*. Upper Saddle River, NJ: Pearson Education. p. 5.
8. Leigh L. Thompson (2008). *Making the Team: A Guide for Managers*. Upper Saddle River, NJ: Pearson Education. pp. 8-13.
9. Ibid. p. 9
10. Charles Fishman (1996). "Whole Foods Is All Teams." Fast Company. Retrieved from: http://www.fastcompany.com/26671/whole-foods-all-teams
11. Human Resources Development Council (n.d.). "Organizational Learning Strategies: Cross-Functional Teams." Getting Results through Learning. Retrieved from: http://www.humtech.com/ForestService/sites/GRTL/ols/ols3.htm
12. Stephen P. Robbins and Timothy A. Judge (2009). *Organizational Behavior*, 13th ed. Upper Saddle River, NJ: Pearson Education. pp. 340-42.
13. Jennifer M. George and Gareth R. Jones (2008). *Understanding and Managing Organizational Behavior*, 5th ed. Upper Saddle River, NJ: Pearson Education. pp. 381-82.
14. Adept Scientific (n.d.). "Lockheed Martin Chooses Mathcad as a Standard Design Package for F-35 Joint Strike Fighter Project." Retrieved from: http://www.adeptscience.co.uk/media-room/press_room/lockheed-martin-chooses-mathcad-as-a-standard-design-package-for-f-35-joint-strike-fighter-project.html
15. This section based on: David A. Whetten and Kim S. Cameron (2007). *Developing Management Skills*, 7th ed. Upper Saddle River, NJ: Pearson Education. p. 497.
16. John Schwartz and Matthew L. Wald (2003). "The Nation: NASA's Curse? 'Groupthink' Is 30 Years Old, And Still Going Strong." New York Times. Retrieved from: http://www.nytimes.com/2003/03/09/weekinreview/the-nation-nasa-s-curse-groupthink-is-30-years-old-and-still-going-strong.html
17. This section is based on Jerald Greenberg and Robert A. Baron (2008). *Behavior in Organizations*, 9th ed. Upper Saddle River, NJ: Pearson Education. pp. 317-18.
18. Leigh L. Thompson (2008). *Making the Team: A Guide for Managers*. Upper Saddle River, NJ: Pearson Education. pp. 323-324.
19. David A. Whetten and Kim S. Cameron (1991). *Developing Management Skills*, 7th ed. Upper Saddle River, NJ: Pearson Education. pp. 498-99; Richard S. Wellins, William C. Byham, and Jeanne M. Wilson (1991). *Empowered Teams*. San Francisco: Jossey-Bass.
20. Lauren Elrick (2015). "The Importance of Teamwork Skills in Work and School." Rasmussen College, College Life Blog. Retrieved from: http://www.rasmussen.edu/student-life/blogs/college-life/importance-of-teamwork-skills-in-work-and-school/
21. David A. Whetten and Kim S. Cameron (1991). *Developing Management Skills*, 7th ed. Upper Saddle River, NJ: Pearson Education. pp. 498-499; Edward E. Lawler (2003). *Treat People Right*. San Francisco: Jossey-Bass.
22. Lee Iacocca and William Novak (2007). *Iacocca*. New York: Bantam. p. 61.
23. The Hay Group (1999). "What Makes Great Leaders: Rethinking the Route to Effective Leadership: Findings from the Fortune Magazine/Hay Group 1999 Executive Survey of Leadership Effectiveness." Retrieved from: http://www.lrhartley.com/seminars//great-leaders.pdf
24. Stephen P. Robbins and Timothy A. Judge (2009). *Organizational Behavior*, 13th ed. Upper Saddle River, NJ: Pearson Education. pp. 346-7.
25. David A. Whetten and Kim S. Cameron (1991). *Developing Management Skills*, 7th ed. Upper Saddle River, NJ: Pearson Education. pp. 516-520.
26. Ibid.
27. Kristen Feenstra (n.d.). "Study Skills: Teamwork Skills for Group Projects." Powertochange.com. Retrieved from: http://powertochange.com/students/academics/groupproject/
28. David A. Whetten and Kim S. Cameron (1991). *Developing Management Skills*, 7th ed. Upper Saddle River, NJ: Pearson Education. p. 520.
29. Kristen Feenstra (n.d.). "Study Skills: Teamwork Skills for Group Projects." Powertochange.com. Retrieved from: http://powertochange.com/students/academics/groupproject/

2. The Foundations of Business

Learning Objectives

- Describe the concept of stakeholders and identify the stakeholder groups relevant to an organization.
- Discuss and be able to apply the PESTEL macro-business-environment model to an industry or emerging technology.
- Explain other key terms related to this chapter including entrepreneur, profit, and revenue.

Why Is Apple Successful?

In 1976 Steve Jobs and Steve Wozniak created their first computer, the Apple I.[1] They invested a mere $1,300 and set up business in Jobs' garage. Three decades later, their business—Apple Inc.—has become one of the world's most influential and successful companies. Jobs and Wozniak were successful **entrepreneurs**: those who take the risks and reap the rewards associated with starting a new business enterprise. Did you ever wonder why Apple flourished while so many other young companies failed? How did it grow from a garage start-up to a company generating over $365 billion in sales in 2021? How was it able to transform itself from a nearly bankrupt firm to a multinational corporation with locations all around the world? You might conclude that it was the company's products, such as the Apple I and II, the Macintosh, or more recently its wildly popular Apple watch, iPhone, and iPad. Or, you could decide that it was its dedicated employees, management's wiliness to take calculated risks, or just plain luck—that Apple simply was in the right place at the right time.

Figure 2.1: Steve Jobs.

Before we draw any conclusions about what made Apple what it is today and what will propel it into a successful future, you might like to learn more about Steve Jobs, the company's cofounder and former CEO. Jobs was instrumental in the original design of the Apple I and, after being ousted from his position with the company, returned to save the firm from destruction and lead it onto its current path. Growing up, Jobs had an interest in computers. He attended lectures at Hewlett-Packard after school and worked for the company during the summer months. He took a job at Atari after graduating from high school and saved his money to make a pilgrimage to India in search of spiritual enlightenment. Following his India trip, he attended Steve Wozniak's "Homebrew Computer Club" meetings, where the idea for building a personal computer surfaced.[2] "Many colleagues describe Jobs as a brilliant man who could be a great motivator and positively charming. At the same time his drive for perfection was so strong that employees who did not meet his demands [were] faced with blistering verbal attacks."[3] Not everyone at Apple appreciated Jobs' brilliance and ability to motivate. Nor did they all go along with his willingness to do whatever it took to produce an innovative, attractive, high-quality product. So at age thirty, Jobs found himself ousted from Apple by John Sculley, whom Jobs himself had hired as president of the company several years earlier. It seems that Sculley wanted to cut costs and thought it would be easier to do so without Jobs around. Jobs sold $20 million of his stock and went on a two-month vacation to figure out what he would do for the rest of his life. His solution: start a new personal computer company called NextStep. In 1993, he was invited back to Apple (a good thing, because neither his new company nor Apple was doing well).

Steve Jobs was definitely not known for humility, but he was a visionary and had a right to be proud of his accomplishments. Some have commented that "Apple's most successful days occurred with Steve Jobs at the helm."[4]

Jobs did what many successful CEOs and managers do: he learned, adjusted, and improvised.[5] Perhaps the most important statement that can be made about him is this: He never gave up on the company that once turned its back on him. With Jobs being one of the most admired CEOs of all time, Tim Cook, Apple's current CEO, had big shoes to fill when he took over from Jobs in 2011. Despite doubt from many, Apple has released popular products under Cook's leadership, such as the Apple Watch and AirPods, with Apple's worth approaching $3 trillion in 2022.

Introduction

As the story of Apple suggests, today is an interesting time to study business. Advances in technology are bringing rapid changes in the ways we produce and deliver goods and services. The internet and other improvements in communication, such as smartphones, video conferencing, and social networking, now affect the way we do business. Companies are expanding international operations, and the workforce is more diverse than ever. Corporations are being held responsible for the behavior of their executives, and more people share the opinion that companies should be good corporate citizens. Because of the role they played in the worst financial crisis since the Great Depression, businesses today face increasing scrutiny and negative public sentiment.[6]

Economic turmoil that began in the housing and mortgage industries as a result of troubled subprime mortgages quickly spread to the rest of the economy. In 2008, credit markets froze up and banks stopped making loans. Lawmakers tried to get money flowing again by passing a $700 billion Wall Street bailout, however now-cautious banks became reluctant to extend credit. Without money or credit, consumer confidence in the economy dropped and consumers cut back on spending. Unemployment rose as troubled companies shed the most jobs in five years, and 760,000 Americans marched to the unemployment lines.[7] The stock market reacted to the financial crisis and its stock prices dropped by 44 percent while millions of Americans watched in shock as their savings and retirement accounts took a nosedive. In fall 2008, even Apple, a company that had enjoyed strong sales growth over the past five years, began to cut production of its popular iPhone. Without jobs or cash, consumers would no longer flock to Apple's fancy retail stores or buy a prized iPhone.[8] Apple eventually recovered and continued to grow, reaching an all time high stock price of $325 in February 2020. However, Apple then faced economic turmoil yet again with the COVID-19 pandemic causing its stock prices to plummet almost 30% to $224. By June 2020, Apple had rebounded from this, reaching a new record stock price of $362.[9]

As you go through the course with the aid of this text, you'll explore the exciting world of business. We'll introduce you to the various activities in which business people engage—accounting, finance, information technology, management, marketing, and operations. We'll help you understand the roles that these activities play in an organization, and we'll show you how they work together. We hope that by exposing you to the things that businesspeople do, we'll help you decide whether business is right for you and, if so, what areas of business you'd like to study further.

Getting Down to Business

A business is any activity that provides goods or services to consumers for the purpose of making a profit. Be careful not to confuse the terms *revenue* and *profit*. **Revenue** represents the funds an enterprise receives in exchange for its goods or services. **Profit** is what's left (hopefully) after all the bills are paid. When Steve Jobs and Steve Wozniak launched the Apple I, they created the Apple Computer in Jobs' family garage in the hope of making a profit. Before we go on, let's make a couple of important distinctions concerning the terms in our definitions. First, whereas Apple produces and sells *goods* (Mac, iPhone, iPod, iPad, Apple Watch), many businesses provide *services*. Your bank is a service company, as is your Internet provider. Hotels, airlines, law firms, movie theaters, and hospitals are also service companies. Many companies provide both goods and services. For example, your local car dealership sells goods (cars) and also provides services (automobile repairs). Second, some organizations are not set up to make profits. Many are established to provide social or educational services. Such not-for-profit (or nonprofit) organizations include the United Way of America, Habitat for Humanity, the Boys and Girls Clubs, the Sierra Club, the American Red Cross, and many colleges and universities. Most of these organizations, however, function in much the same way as a business. They establish goals and work to meet them in an effective, efficient manner. Thus, most of the business principles introduced in this text also apply to nonprofits.

An interactive H5P element has been excluded from this version of the text. You can view it online here: https://pressbooks.lib.vt.edu/fundamentalsofbusiness4e/?p=46#h5p-4

Business Participants and Activities

Let's begin our discussion of business by identifying the main participants of business and the functions that most businesses perform. Then we'll finish this section by discussing the external factors that influence a business' activities.

Participants

Every business must have one or more **owners** whose primary role is to invest money in the business. When a business is being started, it's generally the owners who polish the business idea and bring together the resources (money and people) needed to turn the idea into a business. The owners also hire **employees** to work for the company and help it reach its goals. Owners and employees depend on a third group of participants—**customers**. Ultimately, the goal of any business is to satisfy the needs of its customers in order to generate a profit for the owners.

Stakeholders

Consider your favorite restaurant. It may be an outlet or franchise of a national chain (more on franchises in a later chapter) or a local "mom and pop" without affiliation to a larger entity. Whether national or local, every business has **stakeholders**—those with a legitimate interest in the success or failure of the business and the policies it adopts. Stakeholders include customers, vendors, employees, landlords, bankers, and others (see figure 2.2). All have a keen interest in how the business operates, in most cases for obvious reasons. If the business fails, employees will need new jobs, vendors will need new customers, and banks may have to write off loans they made to the business. Stakeholders do not always see things the same way—their interests sometimes conflict with each other. For example, lenders are more likely to appreciate high profit margins that ensure the loans they made will be repaid, while customers would probably appreciate the lowest possible prices. Pleasing stakeholders can be a real balancing act for any company.

Figure 2.2: Business stakeholders.

The Foundations of Business | 23

An interactive H5P element has been excluded from this version of the text. You can view it online here: https://pressbooks.lib.vt.edu/fundamentalsofbusiness4e/?p=46#h5p-5

Functional Areas of Business

The activities needed to operate a business can be divided into a number of **functional areas**. Examples include: management, operations, marketing, accounting, and finance. Let's briefly explore each of these areas.

Management

Managers are responsible for the work performance of other people. **Management** involves planning for, organizing, leading, and controlling a company's resources so that it can achieve its goals. Managers *plan* by setting goals and developing strategies for achieving them. They *organize* activities and resources to ensure that company goals are met and staff the organization with qualified employees and managers *lead* them to accomplish organizational goals. Finally, managers design *controls* for assessing the success of plans and decisions and take corrective action when needed.

Operations

All companies must convert resources (labor, materials, money, information, and so forth) into goods or services. Some companies, such as Apple, convert resources into *tangible* products—Macs, iPhones, Apple Watch, etc. Others, such as hospitals, convert resources into *intangible* products—e.g., health care. The person who designs and oversees the transformation of resources into goods or services is called an **operations manager**. This individual is also responsible for ensuring that products are of high quality.

Marketing

Marketing consists of everything that a company does to identify customers' needs (i.e., market research) and design products to meet those needs. Marketers develop the benefits and features of products, including price and quality. They also decide on the best method of delivering products and the best means of promoting them to attract and keep customers. They manage relationships with customers and make them aware of the organization's desire and ability to satisfy their needs.

Accounting

Managers need accurate, relevant and timely financial information, which is provided by accountants. **Accountants** measure, summarize, and communicate financial and managerial information and advise other managers on financial matters. There are two fields of accounting. *Financial accountants* prepare financial statements to help users, both inside and outside the organization, assess the financial strength of the company. *Managerial accountants* prepare information, such as reports on the cost of materials used in the production process, for internal use only.

Finance

Finance involves planning for, obtaining, and managing a company's funds. Financial managers address questions such as the following: How much money does the company need? How and where will it get the necessary money? How and when will it pay the money back? What investments should be made in plant and equipment? How much should be spent on research and development? Good financial management is particularly important when a company is first formed, because new business owners usually need to borrow money to get started.

External Forces That Influence Business Activities

Apple and other businesses don't operate in a vacuum; they're influenced by a number of external factors. These include the economy, government, consumer trends, technological developments, public pressure to act as good corporate citizens, and other factors. Collectively, these forces constitute what is known as the "**macro-environment**"—essentially the big picture world external to a company over which the business exerts very little if any control. Figure 2.3 sums up the relationship between a business and the outside forces that influence its activities. One industry that's clearly affected by all these factors is the fast-food industry. Companies such as Taco Bell, McDonald's, Cook-Out and others all compete in this industry. A strong **economy** means people have more money to eat out. Food standards are monitored by a **government** agency, the Food and Drug Administration. Preferences for certain types of foods are influenced by **consumer trends**, for example, fast food companies are being pressured to make their menus healthier. Finally, a number of decisions made by the industry result from its desire to be a good corporate citizen. For example, several fast-food chains have responded to **environmental** concerns by eliminating Styrofoam containers.[10]

Figure 2.3: Business and its environment—PESTEL.

Of course, all industries are impacted by external factors, not just the food industry. As people have become more conscious of the environment, they have begun to choose new **technologies**, like all-electric cars to replace those that burn fossil fuels. Both established companies, like Nissan with its Nissan Leaf, and brand new companies like Tesla have entered the market for all-electric vehicles. While the market is still small, it is expected to grow at a compound annual growth rate of 21.1 percent between 2019 and 2030.[11]

PESTEL Analysis

One useful tool for analyzing the external environment in which an industry or company operates is the PESTEL model. PESTEL is an acronym, with each of the letters representing an aspect of the macro-environment that a business needs to consider in its planning. Let's briefly run through the meaning of each letter.

P stands for the political environment. Governments influence the environment in which businesses operate in many ways, including taxation, tariffs, trade agreements, labor regulations, and environmental regulations.

E represents the economic environment. As we will see in detail in a later chapter, whether the economy is growing or not is a major concern to business. Numerous economic indicators have been created for the specific purpose of measuring the health of the economy.

S indicates the sociocultural environment, which is a category that captures societal attitudes, trends in national demographics, and even fashion trends. The term *demographics* applies to any attribute that can be used to describe people, such as age, income level, gender, race, and so on. As a society's attitudes or its demographics change, the market for goods and services can shift right along with it.

T is for technological factors. In the last several decades, perhaps no force has impacted business more than the emergence of the internet. Nearly instantaneous access to information, e-commerce, social media, and even the ability to control physical devices from remote locations have all come about due to technological forces.

The second E stands for environmental forces, which in this case means natural resources, pollution levels, recycling, etc. While the attitudes of a society towards the natural environment would be considered a sociocultural force, the level of pollution, the supply of oil, etc. would be grouped under this second E for environment.

Finally, the L represents legal factors. These forces often coincide with the political factors already discussed, because it is politicians (i.e., government) that enacts laws. However, there are other legal factors that can impact businesses as well, such as decisions made by courts that may have broad implications beyond the case being decided.

When conducting PESTEL analysis, it is important to remember that there can be considerable overlap from category to category. It's more important that businesses use the model to thoroughly assess its external environment, and much less important that they get all the forces covered under the "right" category. It is also important to remember that an individual force, in itself, is not inherently positive or negative but rather presents either an opportunity or a threat to different businesses. For example, societal attitudes moving in favor of green energy are an opportunity for those with capabilities in wind, solar, and other renewables, while presenting a threat, or at least a need to change, to companies whose business models depend exclusively on fossil fuels.

As you read through the description of the PESTEL model, it may have occurred to you to ask, "Where would COVID-19 fit in using this model?" since this pandemic had a major impact on all sorts of businesses and on every economy in the world. In other models that analyze the macro-environment, there is a force called "Natural" that essentially equates to the environmental force in the PESTEL model. So, the natural environment is usually equated to the forces described above, like natural resources and pollution, but a broader view of this force would logically include something like a pandemic. And consistent with other types of forces, COVID-19 has been hugely unfavorable to some industries and yet a boost to business for others. Any business in the realm of tourism has probably suffered large revenue losses and employee layoffs and furloughs, while makers of personal protective equipment (PPE)[12] have been challenged just to meet the increase in demand.[13]

 An interactive H5P element has been excluded from this version of the text. You can view it online here: https://pressbooks.lib.vt.edu/fundamentalsofbusiness4e/?p=46#h5p-6

Chapter Video

This video covers the six macro-environmental forces that make up the PESTEL model.

To view this video, visit https://vtechworks.lib.vt.edu/handle/10919/88014

> *Key Takeaways*
>
> - The main participants in a **business** are its **owners**, **employees**, and **customers**.
> - Every business must consider its **stakeholders**, and their sometimes conflicting interests, when making decisions.
> - The activities needed to run a business can be divided into **functional areas**. The business functions correspond fairly closely with many majors found within a typical college of business.
> - Businesses are influenced by such **external factors** as the **economy**, **government**, and other forces external to the business. The PESTEL model is a useful tool for analyzing these forces.

References

Figures

Figure 2.1: Steve Jobs. segagman. 2011. CC BY 2.0. https://flic.kr/p/atjY6C.

Figure 2.2: Business stakeholders. Kindred Grey. 2022. CC BY 4.0. https://archive.org/details/2.2_20220621.

Figure 2.3: Business and its environment—PESTEL. Kindred Grey. 2022. CC BY 4.0. https://archive.org/details/2.3_20220621.

Video

Video 1: The PESTEL Model. Alyssa Duong. 2019. CC BY 3.0. https://vtechworks.lib.vt.edu/handle/10919/88014.

Notes

1. This vignette is based on an honors thesis written by Danielle M. Testa (2007). "Apple, Inc.: An Analysis of the Firm's Tumultuous History, in Conjunction with the Abounding Future." Lehigh University.
2. Lee Angelelli (1994). "Steve Paul Jobs." Retrieved from: http://ei.cs.vt.edu/~history/Jobs.html
3. Ibid.
4. Cyrus Farivar (2006). "Apple's first 30 years; three decades of contributions to the computerIndustry." Macworld. p. 2.
5. Dan Barkin (2006). "He made the iPod: How Steve Jobs of Apple created the new millennium's signature invention." Knight Ridder Tribune Business News. p. 1.
6. Jon Hilsenrath, Serena Ng, and Damian Paletta (2008). "Worst Crisis Since '30s, With No End Yet in Sight." Wall Street Journal, Markets. Retrieved from: http://www.wsj.com/articles/SB122169431617549947
7. Steve Hargreaves (2008). "How the Economy Stole the Election." CNN.com. Retrieved from: http://money.cnn.com/galleries/2008/news/0810/gallery.economy_election/index.html
8. Dan Gallagher (2008). "Analyst Says Apple Is Cutting Back Production as Economy Weakens." MarketWatch. Retrieved from: http://www.marketwatch.com/story/apple-cutting-back-iphone-production-analyst-says?amp;dist=msr_1

9. Shawn Tully (2020). "After Apple's Stratospheric Rise, Investors are Facing a New Threat: Simple Math." Fortune. Retrieved from https://fortune.com/2020/06/30/apple-stock-aapl-shares-whats-next-coronavirus-pandemic-covid-19-nasdaq
10. David Baron (2003). "Facing-Off in Public." Stanford Business. pp. 20-24. Retrieved from: https://www.gsb.stanford.edu/sites/gsb/files/2003August.pdf
11. Markets and Markets (2018). "Electric Vehicle Market by Vehicle, Vehicle Class, Propulsion, EV Sales, Charging Station & Region - Global Forecast to 2030." Retrieved from: https://www.marketsandmarkets.com/Market-Reports/electric-vehicle-market-209371461.html
12. Kate Rogers and Betsy Spring (2020). "Personal Protective Equipment Is in High Demand as Coronavirus Spreads." CNBC. Retrieved from: https://www.cnbc.com/2020/03/06/personal-protective-equipment-is-in-high-demand-as-coronavirus-spreads.html13 Taylor Borden and Allana Akhtar (2020). "The Coronavirus Outbreak Has Triggered Unprecedented Mass Layoffs and Furloughs. Here Are the Major companies That Have Announced They Are Downsizing Their Workforces." Business Insider. Retrieved from: https://www.businessinsider.com/coronavirus-layoffs-furloughs-hospitality-service-travel-unemployment-2020#airbnb-announced-it-is-laying-off-about-25-of-its-workforce-or-1900-employees-on-may-5-its-severance-package-includes-several-months-pay-a-year-of-healthcare-and-support-finding-a-new-job-2
13. Taylor Borden and Allana Akhtar (2020). "The coronavirus outbreak has triggered unprecedented mass layoffs and furloughs. Here are the major companies that have announced they are downsizing their workforces." Business Insider, May 18, 2020. Retrieved from: https://www.businessinsider.com/coronavirus-layoffs-furloughs-hospitality-service-travel-unemployment-2020#airbnb-announced-it-is-laying-off-about-25-of-its-workforce-or-1900-employees-on-may-5-its-severance-package-includes-several-months-pay-a-year-of-healthcare-and-support-finding-a-new-job-2

3. Economics and Business

> *Learning Objectives*
>
> - Describe the foundational philosophies of capitalism and socialism.
> - Discuss private property rights and why they are key to economic development.
> - Discuss the concept of gross domestic product (GDP).
> - Explain the difference between fiscal and monetary policy.
> - Discuss the concept of the unemployment rate measurement.
> - Discuss the concepts of inflation and deflation.
> - Explain other key terms related to this chapter including supply, demand, equilibrium price, monopoly, recession, and depression.

What Is Economics?

To appreciate how a business functions, we need to know something about the economic environment in which it operates. We begin with a definition of economics and a discussion of the resources used to produce goods and services.

Resources: Inputs and Outputs

Economics is the study of the production, distribution, and consumption of goods and services. **Resources** are the inputs used to produce outputs. Resources may include any or all of the following:

- Land and other natural resources
- Labor (physical and mental)
- Capital, including buildings and equipment
- Entrepreneurship
- Knowledge

Resources are combined to produce goods and services. Land and natural resources provide the needed raw materials. Labor transforms raw materials into goods and services. Capital (equipment, buildings, vehicles, cash, and so forth) are needed for the production process. Entrepreneurship provides the skill, drive and creativity needed to bring the other resources together to produce a good or service to be sold to the marketplace.

Because a business uses resources to produce things, we also call these resources **factors of production**. The factors of production used to produce a shirt would include the following:

- The land that the shirt factory sits on, the electricity used to run the plant, and the raw cotton from which the shirts are made
- The laborers who make the shirts
- The factory and equipment used in the manufacturing process, as well as the money needed to operate the factory
- The entrepreneurship skills and production knowledge used to coordinate the other resources to make the shirts and distribute them to the marketplace

Input and Output Markets

Many of the factors of production are provided to businesses by households. For example, households provide businesses with labor (as workers), land and buildings (as landlords), and capital (as investors). In turn, businesses pay households for these resources by providing them with income, such as wages, rent, and interest. The resources obtained from households are then used by businesses to produce **goods** and **services**, which are sold to provide businesses with revenue. The revenue obtained by businesses is then used to buy additional resources, and the cycle continues. This is described in figure 3.1, which illustrates the dual roles of households and businesses:

- Households not only provide factors of production (or resources) but also consume goods and services.
- Businesses not only buy resources but also produce and sell both goods and services.

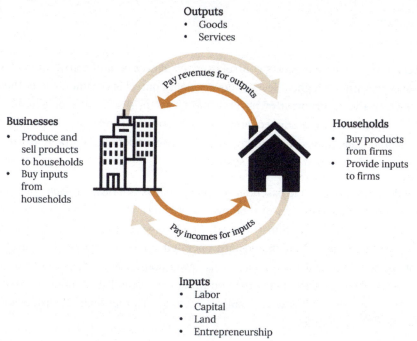

Figure 3.1: Circular flow of inputs and outputs.

Economic Systems

Economists study the interactions between households and businesses and look at the ways in which the factors of production are combined to produce the goods and services that people need. Basically, economists try to answer three sets of questions:

- What goods and services should be produced to meet consumers' needs? In what quantity? When?
- How should goods and services be produced? Who should produce them, and what resources, including technology, should be combined to produce them?
- Who should receive the goods and services produced? How should they be allocated among consumers?

The answers to these questions depend on a country's **economic system**—the means by which a society (households, businesses, and government) makes decisions about allocating resources to produce products and about distributing those products. The degree to which individuals and business owners, as opposed to the government, enjoy freedom in making these decisions varies according to the type of economic system.

Generally speaking, economic systems can be divided into two systems: planned systems and free market systems.

Planned Systems

In a **planned system**, the government exerts control over the allocation and distribution of all or some goods and services. The system with the highest level of government control is communism. In theory, a communist economy is one in which the government owns all or most enterprises. Central planning by the government dictates which goods or services are produced, how they are produced, and who will receive them. In practice, pure communism is practically nonexistent today, and only a few countries (notably North Korea and Cuba) operate under rigid, centrally planned economic systems.

Under **socialism**, industries that provide essential services, such as utilities, banking, and health care, may be government owned. Some businesses may also be owned privately. Central planning allocates the goods and services produced by government-run industries and tries to ensure that the resulting wealth is distributed equally. In contrast, privately owned companies are operated for the purpose of making a profit for their owners. In general, workers in socialist economies work fewer hours, have longer vacations, and receive more health care, education, and child-care benefits than do workers in capitalist economies. To offset the high cost of public services, taxes are generally steep. Examples of countries that lean towards a socialistic approach include Venezuela, Sweden, and France.

Free Market System

The economic system in which most businesses are owned and operated by individuals is the **free market system**, also known as **capitalism**. In a free market economy, **competition** dictates how goods and services will be allocated. Business is conducted with more limited government involvement concentrated on regulations that dictate how businesses are permitted to operate. A key aspect of a free market system is the concept of **private property rights**, which means that business owners can expect to own their land, buildings, machines, etc., and keep the majority of their profits, except for taxes. The profit incentive is a key driver of any free market system. The economies of the United States and other countries, such as Japan, are based on capitalism. However, a purely capitalistic economy is as rare as one that is purely communist. Imagine if a service such as police protection, one provided by government in the United States, were instead allocated based on market forces. The ability to pay would then become a key determinant in who received these services, an outcome that few in American society would consider to be acceptable.

How Economic Systems Compare

In comparing economic systems, it can be helpful to think of a continuum with communism at one end and pure capitalism at the other, as in figure 3.2. As you move from left to right, the amount of government control over business diminishes. So, too, does the level of social services, such as health care, child-care services, social security, and unemployment benefits. Moving from left to right, taxes are correspondingly lower as well.

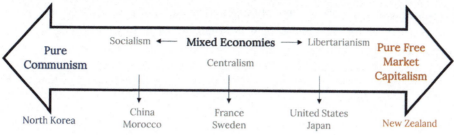

Figure 3.2: The economic spectrum.

Mixed Market Economies

Though it's possible to have a pure communist system, or a pure capitalist (free market) system, in reality many economic systems are mixed. A **mixed market economy** relies on both markets and the government to allocate resources. In practice, most economies are mixed, with a leaning towards either free market or socialistic principles, rather than being purely one or the other. Some previously communist economies, such as those of Eastern Europe and China, are becoming more mixed as they adopt more capitalistic characteristics and convert businesses previously owned by the government to private ownership through a process called **privatization**. By contrast, Venezuela is a country that has moved increasingly towards socialism, taking control of industries such as oil and media through a process called **nationalization**.

The U.S. Economic System

Like most countries, the United States features a mixed market system: though the U.S. economic system is primarily a free market system, the federal government controls some basic services, such as the postal service and air traffic control. The U.S. economy also has some characteristics of a socialist system, such as providing social security retirement benefits to retired workers.

The free market system was espoused by Adam Smith in his book *The Wealth of Nations*, published in 1776. According to Smith, competition alone would ensure that consumers received the best products at the best prices. In the kind of competition he assumed, a seller who tries to charge more for his product than other sellers would not be able to find any buyers. A job-seeker who asks more than the going wage won't be hired. Because the "invisible hand" of competition will make the market work effectively, there won't be a need to regulate prices or wages. Almost immediately, however, a tension developed among free market theorists between the principle of *laissez-faire*—leaving things alone—and government intervention. Today, it's common for the U.S. government to intervene in the operation of the economic system. For example, government exerts influence on the food and pharmaceutical industries through the Food and Drug Administration, which protects consumers by preventing unsafe or mislabeled products from reaching the market.

To appreciate how businesses operate, we must first get an idea of how prices are set in competitive markets. The next section, "Perfect Competition and Supply and Demand," begins by describing how markets establish prices in an environment of perfect competition.

 An interactive H5P element has been excluded from this version of the text. You can view it online here: https://pressbooks.lib.vt.edu/fundamentalsofbusiness4e/?p=57#h5p-7

Perfect Competition and Supply and Demand

Under a mixed economy, such as we have in the United States, businesses make decisions about which goods to produce or services to offer and how they are priced. Because there are many businesses making goods or providing services, customers can choose among a wide array of products. The competition for sales among businesses is a vital part of our economic system. Economists have identified four types of competition—perfect competition, monopolistic competition, oligopoly, and monopoly. We'll introduce the first of these—perfect competition—in this section and cover the remaining three in the following section.

Perfect Competition

Perfect competition exists when there are many consumers buying a standardized product from numerous small businesses. Because no seller is big enough or influential enough to affect price, sellers and buyers accept the going price. For example, when a commercial fisher brings his fish to the local market, he has little control over the price he gets and must accept the going market price.

The Basics of Supply and Demand

To appreciate how perfect competition works, we need to understand how buyers and sellers interact in a market to set prices. In a market characterized by perfect competition, price is determined through the mechanisms of supply and demand. Prices are influenced both by the supply of products from sellers and by the demand for products by buyers.

To illustrate this concept, let's create a *supply and demand schedule* for one particular good sold at one point in time. Then we'll define demand and create a demand curve and define *supply* and create a *supply curve*. Finally, we'll see how supply and demand interact to create an *equilibrium price*—the price at which buyers are willing to purchase the amount that sellers are willing to sell.

36 | Economics and Business

Demand and the Demand Curve

Demand is the quantity of a product that buyers are willing to purchase at various prices. The quantity of a product that people are willing to buy depends on its price. You're typically willing to buy *less* of a product when prices *rise* and *more* of a product when prices *fall*. Generally speaking, we find products more attractive at lower prices, and we buy more at lower prices because our income goes further.

Using this logic, we can construct a demand curve that shows the quantity of a product that will be demanded at different prices. Let's assume that the diagram in figure 3.3 represents the daily price and quantity of apples sold by farmers at a local market. Note that as the price of apples goes down, buyers' demand goes up. Thus, if a pound of apples sells for $0.80, buyers will be willing to purchase only 1,500 pounds per day. But if apples cost only $0.60 a pound, buyers will be willing to purchase two thousand pounds. At $0.40 a pound, buyers will be willing to purchase 2,500 pounds.

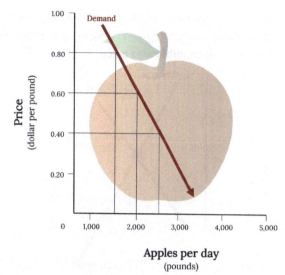

Figure 3.3: Demand curve.

Supply and the Supply Curve

Supply is the quantity of a product that sellers are willing to sell at various prices. The quantity of a product that a business is willing to sell depends on its price. Businesses are *more* willing to sell a product when the price *rises* and *less* willing to sell it when prices *fall*. Again, this fact makes sense: businesses are set up to make profits, and there are larger profits to be made when prices are high.

Now we can construct a supply curve that shows the quantity of apples that farmers would be willing to sell at different prices, regardless of demand. As you can see in figure 3.4, the supply curve goes in the opposite direction from the demand curve: as prices rise, the quantity of apples that farmers are willing to sell also goes up. The supply curve shows that farmers are willing to sell only a thousand pounds of apples when the price is $0.40 a pound, two thousand pounds when the price is $0.60, and three thousand pounds when the price is $0.80.

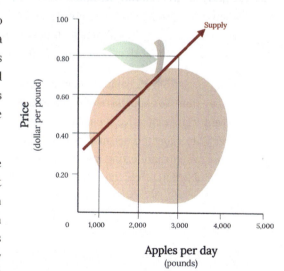

Figure 3.4: Supply curve.

Equilibrium Price

We can now see how the market mechanism works under perfect competition. We do this by plotting both the supply curve and the demand curve on one graph, as we've done in figure 3.5. The point at which the two curves intersect is the **equilibrium price**.

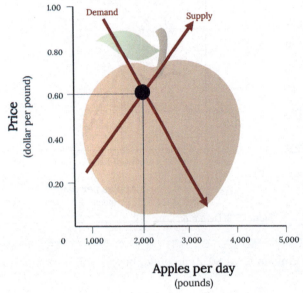

Figure 3.5: Equilibrium price.

You can see in figure 3.5 that the supply and demand curves intersect at the price of $0.60 and quantity of two thousand pounds. Thus, $0.60 is the equilibrium price: at this price, the quantity of apples demanded by buyers equals the quantity of apples that farmers are willing to supply. If a single farmer tries to charge more than $0.60 for a pound of apples, he won't sell very many because other suppliers are making them available for less. As a result, his profits will go down. If, on the other hand, a farmer tries to charge less than the equilibrium price of $0.60 a pound, he will sell more apples but his profit per pound will be less than at the equilibrium price. With profit being the motive, there is no incentive to drop the price.

What have we learned in this discussion? Without outside influences, markets in an environment of perfect competition will arrive at an equilibrium point at which both buyers and sellers are satisfied. But we must be aware that this is a very simplistic example. Things are more complex in the real world. For one thing, markets don't always operate without outside influences. For example, if a government set an artificially low price ceiling on a product to keep consumers happy, we would not expect producers to produce enough to satisfy demand, resulting in a **shortage**. If government set prices high to assist an industry, sellers would likely supply more of a product than buyers need; in that case, there would be a **surplus**.

Circumstances also have a habit of changing. What would happen, for example, if incomes rose and buyers were willing to pay more for apples? The demand curve would change, resulting in an increase in equilibrium price. This outcome makes intuitive sense: as demand increases, prices will go up. What would happen if apple crops were larger than expected because of favorable weather conditions? Farmers might be willing to sell apples at lower prices rather than letting part of the crop spoil. If so, the supply curve would shift, resulting in another change in equilibrium price: the increase in supply would bring down prices.

Monopolistic Competition, Oligopoly, and Monopoly

As mentioned previously, economists have identified four types of competition—perfect competition, monopolistic competition, oligopoly, and monopoly. Perfect competition was discussed in the last section; we'll cover the remaining three types of competition here.

Monopolistic Competition

In **monopolistic competition**, we still have many sellers, but not nearly as many as we had under perfect competition. And in addition to having fewer sellers, they don't sell identical products. Instead, they sell **differentiated** products—products that differ somewhat, or are perceived to differ, even though they serve a similar purpose. Products can be differentiated in a number of ways, including quality, style, convenience, location, and brand name. An example in this case might be toothpaste. Although many people are fiercely loyal to their favorites, most products in this category are quite similar and address the same consumer need. But what if there was a substantial price difference among products? In that case, many buyers would likely be persuaded to switch brands, at least on a trial basis.

How is product differentiation accomplished? Sometimes, it's simply geographical; you probably buy gasoline at the station closest to your home regardless of the brand. At other times, perceived differences between products are promoted by advertising designed to convince consumers that one product is different from the other—and better than it. Regardless of customer loyalty to a product, if its price goes too high the seller will lose business to a competitor. Therefore, under monopolistic competition, companies have only limited control over price.

Oligopoly

Oligopoly means few sellers. In an oligopolistic market, each seller supplies a large portion of all the products sold in the marketplace. In addition, because the cost of starting a business in an oligopolistic industry is usually high, the number of firms entering it is low. Companies in oligopolistic industries include such large-scale enterprises as automobile companies and airlines. As large firms supplying a sizable portion of a market, these companies have some control over the prices they charge. But there's a catch: because products are fairly similar, when one company lowers prices, others are often forced to follow suit to remain competitive. You see this practice all the time in the airline industry: When American Airlines announces a fare decrease, Delta, United Airlines, and others do likewise. When one automaker offers a special deal, its competitors usually come up with similar promotions.

Monopoly

In terms of the number of sellers and degree of competition, a **monopoly** lies at the opposite end of the spectrum from perfect competition. In perfect competition, there are many small companies, none of which can control prices; they simply accept the market price determined by supply and demand. In a monopoly, however, there's only one seller in the market. The market could be a geographical area, such as a city or a regional area, and doesn't necessarily have to be an entire country.

There are few monopolies in the United States because the government limits them. Most fall into one of two categories: natural and legal. **Natural monopolies** include public utilities, such as electricity and gas suppliers. Such enterprises require huge investments, and it would be inefficient to duplicate the products that they provide. They inhibit competition, but they're legal because they're important to society. In exchange for the right to conduct business without competition, they're regulated. For instance, they can't charge whatever prices they want, but they must adhere to government-controlled prices. As a rule, they're required to serve all customers, even if doing so isn't cost efficient.

A **legal monopoly** arises when a company receives a patent giving it exclusive use of an invented product or process. Patents are issued for a limited time, generally 20 years.[1] During this period, other companies can't use the invented product or process without permission from the patent holder. Patents allow companies a certain period to recover the heavy costs of researching and developing products and technologies. A classic example of a company that enjoyed a patent-based legal monopoly is Polaroid, which for years held exclusive ownership of instant-film technology.[2] Polaroid priced the product high enough to recoup, over time, the high cost of bringing it to market. Without competition, in other words, it enjoyed a monopolistic position in regard to pricing.

 An interactive H5P element has been excluded from this version of the text. You can view it online here: https://pressbooks.lib.vt.edu/fundamentalsofbusiness4e/?p=57#h5p-8

Measuring the Health of the Economy

Every day, we are bombarded with economic news (at least if you watch the business news stations). We're told about things like unemployment, home prices, and consumer confidence trends. As a student learning about business, and later as a business manager, you need to understand the nature of the U.S. economy and the terminology that we use to describe it. You need to have some idea of where the economy is heading, and you need to know something about the government's role in influencing its direction.

Economic Goals

The world's economies share three main goals:

- Growth
- High employment
- Price stability

Let's take a closer look at each of these goals, both to find out what they mean and to show how we determine whether they're being met.

Economic Growth

One purpose of an economy is to provide people with goods and services—cars, computers, video games, houses, rock concerts, fast food, amusement parks. One way in which economists measure the performance of an economy is by looking at a widely used measure of total output called the **gross domestic product** (GDP). The GDP is defined as the market value of all goods and services produced by the economy in a given year. The GDP includes only those goods and services produced domestically; goods produced outside the country are excluded. The GDP also includes only those goods and services that are produced for the final user; intermediate products are excluded. For example, the silicon chip that goes into a computer (an intermediate product) would not count directly because it is included when the finished computer is counted. By itself, the GDP doesn't necessarily tell us much about the direction of the economy. But change in the GDP does. If the GDP (after adjusting for inflation, which will be discussed later) goes up, the economy is growing. If it goes down, the economy is contracting.

The Business Cycle

The economic ups and downs resulting from expansion and contraction constitute the **business cycle**. A typical cycle runs from three to five years but could last much longer. Though typically irregular, a cycle can be divided into four general phases of prosperity, recession, depression (which the cycle generally skips), and recovery:

- During **prosperity**, the economy expands, unemployment is low, incomes rise, and consumers buy more products. Businesses respond by increasing production and offering new and better products.
- Eventually, however, things slow down. GDP decreases, unemployment rises, and because people have less money to spend, business revenues decline. This slowdown in economic activity is called a **recession**.
- Economists often say that we're entering a recession when GDP goes down for two consecutive quarters.
- Generally, a recession is followed by a **recovery** in which the economy starts growing again.
- If, however, a recession lasts a long time (perhaps a decade or so), while unemployment remains very high and production is severely curtailed, the economy could sink into a **depression**. Unlike for the term

recession, economists have not agreed on a uniform standard for what constitutes a depression, though they are generally characterized by their duration. Though not impossible, it's unlikely that the United States will experience another severe depression like that of the 1930s. The federal government has a number of economic tools (some of which we'll discuss shortly) with which to fight any threat of a depression.

Full Employment

To keep the economy going strong, people must spend money on goods and services. A reduction in personal expenditures for things like food, clothing, appliances, automobiles, housing, and medical care could severely reduce GDP and weaken the economy. Because most people earn their spending money by working, an important goal of all economies is making jobs available to everyone who wants one. In principle, **full employment** occurs when everyone who wants to work has a job. In practice, we say that we have full employment when about 95 percent of those wanting to work are employed.

The Unemployment Rate

The U.S. Department of Labor tracks unemployment and reports the **unemployment rate**: the percentage of the labor force that's unemployed and actively seeking work. The unemployment rate is an important measure of economic health. It goes up during recessionary periods because companies are reluctant to hire workers when demand for goods and services is low. Conversely, it goes down when the economy is expanding and there is high demand for products and workers to supply them.

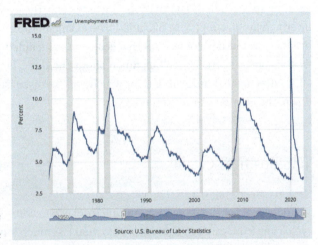

Figure 3.6: The U.S. unemployment rate (1970-present). Each of the last three peaks in unemployment (1982, 1992, and 2010) coincided with recessions (periods of declining GDP).

Figure 3.6 traces the U.S. unemployment rate between 1970 and 2020. Please be aware that there are multiple measures of unemployment and that this graph is based on what is known as U3, the most commonly used measurement. Another measurement, U6, is considered to provide a broader picture of unemployment in the United States. It includes two groups of people that U3 doesn't: those who are not actively looking for work but would like a job and have looked for one in the last 12 months; and those who would like to work full-time jobs but have settled for part-time positions because full-time work was not available to them. Since by definition, U6 is always higher than U3, it is likely that U3 is discussed more often because it paints a more favorable, if not completely accurate, picture.

Price Stability

A third major goal of all economies is maintaining price stability. Price stability occurs when the average of the prices for goods and services either doesn't change or changes very little. Rapidly rising prices are troublesome for both individuals and businesses. For individuals, rising prices mean people have to pay more for the things they need. For businesses, rising prices mean higher costs, and, at least in the short run, businesses might have trouble passing on higher costs to consumers. When the overall price level goes up, we have **inflation**. Figure 3.7 shows inflationary trends in the U.S. economy since 1960. When the price level goes down (which rarely happens), we have **deflation**. A deflationary situation can also be damaging to an economy. When purchasers believe they can expect lower prices in the future, they may defer making purchases, which has the effect of slowing economic growth (GDP) accompanied by a rise in unemployment. Japan experienced a long period of deflation which contributed to economic stagnation in that country from which it is only now beginning to recover.

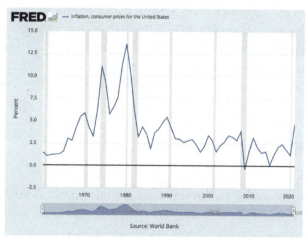

Figure 3.7: The U.S. inflation rate (1960-present). During both peak periods (1974 and 1979-1980) the price of oil doubled.

The Consumer Price Index

The most widely publicized measure of inflation is the **consumer price index** (CPI), which is reported monthly by the Bureau of Labor Statistics. The CPI measures the rate of inflation by determining price changes of a hypothetical basket of goods, such as food, housing, clothing, medical care, appliances, automobiles, and so forth, bought by a typical household.

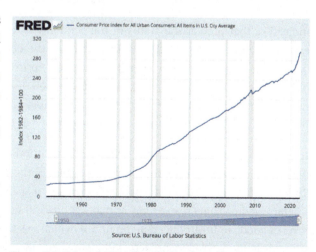

Figure 3.8: Selected CPI values (1950-present).

The CPI base period is 1982 to 1984, which has been given an average value of 100. Figure 3.8 gives CPI values computed for selected years. The CPI value for 1950, for instance, is 24. This means that $1 of typical purchases in 1982 through 1984 would have cost $0.24 in 1950. Conversely, you would have needed $2.18 to purchase the same $1 worth of typical goods in 2010. The difference registers the effect of inflation. In fact, that's what an inflation rate is—the percentage change in a price index.

Economics and Business | 43

Economic Forecasting

In the previous section, we introduced several measures that economists use to assess the performance of the economy at a given time. By looking at changes in the GDP, for instance, we can see whether the economy is growing. The CPI allows us to gauge inflation. These measures help us understand where the economy stands today. But what if we want to get a sense of where it's headed in the future? To a certain extent, we can forecast future economic trends by analyzing several leading economic indicators.

Economic Indicators

An **economic indicator** is a statistic that provides valuable information about the economy. There's no shortage of economic indicators, and trying to follow them all would be an overwhelming task. So in this chapter, we'll only discuss the general concept and a few of the key indicators.

Lagging and Leading Indicators

Economists use a variety of statistics to discuss the health of an economy. Statistics that report the status of the economy looking at past data are called **lagging economic indicators**. This type of indicator looks at trends to determine how strong an economy is and its direction. One such indicator is average length of unemployment. If unemployed workers have remained out of work for a long time, we may infer that the economy has been slow. Another lagging indicator is GDP growth. Even if the last several quarters have followed the same trend, though, there is no way to say with confidence that such a trend will necessarily continue.

Indicators that predict the status of the economy three to twelve months into the future are called **leading economic indicators**. If such an indicator rises, the economy is more likely to expand in the coming year. If it falls, the economy is more likely to contract. An example of a leading indicator is the number of permits obtained to build homes in a particular time period. If people intend to build more homes, they will be buying materials like lumber and appliances, and also employ construction workers. This type of indicator has a direct predictive value since it tells us something about what level of activity is likely in a future period.

In addition to housing, it is also helpful to look at indicators from sectors like labor and manufacturing. One useful indicator of the outlook for future jobs is the number of new claims for unemployment insurance. This measure tells us how many people recently lost their jobs. If it's rising, it signals trouble ahead because unemployed consumers can't buy as many goods and services as they could if they had paychecks. To gauge the level of goods to be produced in the future (which will translate into future sales), economists look at a statistic called average weekly manufacturing hours. This measure tells us the average number of hours worked per week by production workers in manufacturing industries. If it's on the rise, the economy will probably improve.

Since employment is such a key goal in any economy, the Bureau of Labor Statistics tracks total non-farm payroll employment from which the number of net new jobs created can be determined.

The Conference Board also publishes a consumer confidence index based on results of a monthly survey of five thousand U.S. households. The survey gathers consumers' opinions on the health of the economy and their plans for future purchases. It's often a good indicator of consumers' future buying intent.

 An interactive H5P element has been excluded from this version of the text. You can view it online here: https://pressbooks.lib.vt.edu/fundamentalsofbusiness4e/?p=57#h5p-9

Government's Role in Managing the Economy

Monetary Policy

Monetary policy is exercised by the Federal Reserve System ("the Fed"), which is empowered to take various actions that decrease or increase the money supply and raise or lower short-term interest rates, making it harder or easier to borrow money. When the Fed believes that inflation is a problem, it will use contractionary policy to decrease the money supply and raise interest rates. When rates are higher, borrowers have to pay more for the money they borrow, and banks are more selective in making loans. Because money is "tighter"—more expensive to borrow—demand for goods and services will go down, and so will prices. In any case, that's the theory.

The Fed will typically tighten or decrease the money supply during inflationary periods, making it harder to borrow money.

To counter a recession, the Fed uses expansionary policy to increase the money supply and reduce interest rates. With lower interest rates, it's cheaper to borrow money, and banks are more willing to lend it. We then say that money is "easy." Attractive interest rates encourage businesses to borrow money to expand production and encourage consumers to buy more goods and services. In theory, both sets of actions will help the economy escape or come out of a recession.

Fiscal Policy

Fiscal policy relies on the government's powers of spending and taxation. Both taxation and government spending can be used to reduce or increase the total supply of money in the economy—the total amount, in other words, that businesses and consumers have to spend. When the country is in a recession, government policy is typically to increase spending, reduce taxes, or both. Such expansionary actions will put more money in the hands of businesses and consumers, encouraging businesses to expand and consumers to buy more goods and services. When the economy is experiencing inflation, the opposite policy is adopted: the government will decrease spending or increase taxes, or both. Because such contractionary measures reduce spending by businesses and consumers, prices come down and inflation eases.

The National Debt

If, in any given year, the government takes in more money (through taxes) than it spends on goods and services (for things such as defense, transportation, and social services), the result is a **budget surplus**. If, on the other hand, the government spends more than it takes in, we have a **budget deficit** (which the government pays off by borrowing through the issuance of Treasury bonds). Historically, deficits have occurred much more often than surpluses; typically, the government spends more than it takes in. Consequently, the U.S. government now has a total **national debt** of more than $19 trillion (Note: This number is moving too quickly for the authors to keep the graph current—you can see the current debt at http://www.usdebtclock.org/).

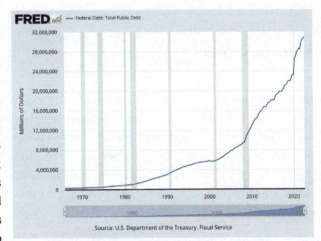

Figure 3.9: The National Debt (1966-present).

 An interactive H5P element has been excluded from this version of the text. You can view it online here: https://pressbooks.lib.vt.edu/fundamentalsofbusiness4e/?p=57#h5p-10

Chapter Video

This video presents a balanced view of capitalism and socialism and reinforces key points within the chapter. Since it is rather dry, it would be fine to watch only the first seven minutes or so.

 One or more interactive elements has been excluded from this version of the text. You can view them online here: https://www.youtube.com/watch?v=PBIXmXJwIuk

Key Takeaways

- **Economics** is the study of the production, distribution, and consumption of goods and services.
- Economists address these three questions: (1) What goods and services should be produced to meet consumer needs? (2) How should they be produced, and who should produce them? (3) Who should receive goods and services?
- The answers to these questions depend on a country's **economic system**. The primary economic systems that exist today are planned and free-market systems.
- In a **planned system**, such as communism and socialism, the government exerts control over the production and distribution of all or some goods and services.
- In a **free-market system**, also known as capitalism, business is conducted with limited government involvement. **Competition** determines what goods and services are produced, how they are produced, and for whom.
- When the market is characterized by **perfect competition**, many small companies sell identical products. The price is determined by supply and demand. Commodities like corn are an excellent example.
- **Supply** is the quantity of a product that sellers are willing to sell at various prices. Producers will supply more of a product when prices are high and less when they're low.
- **Demand** is the quantity of a product that buyers are willing to purchase at various prices; they'll buy more when the price is low and less when it's high.
- In a competitive market, the decisions of buyers and sellers interact until the market reaches an **equilibrium price**—the price at which buyers are willing to buy the same amount that sellers are willing to sell.
- There are three other types of competition in a free market system: monopolistic competition, oligopoly, and monopoly.
- In **monopolistic competition,** there are still many sellers, but products are **differentiated**, ie., differ slightly but serve similar purposes. By making consumers aware these differences, sellers

- exert some control over price.
- In an **oligopoly**, a few sellers supply a sizable portion of products in the market. They exert some control over price, but because their products are similar, when one company lowers prices, the others follow.
- In a **monopoly**, there is only one seller in the market. The "market" could be a specific geographical area, such as a city. The single seller is able to control prices.
- All economies share three goals: growth, high employment, and price stability.
- To get a sense of where the economy is headed in the future, we use statistics called **economic indicators**. Indicators that report the status of the economy a few months in the past are *lagging*. Those that predict the status of the economy three to twelve months in the future are called *leading* indicators.

References

Figures

Figure 3.1: Circular flow of inputs and outputs. Kindred Grey. 2022. CC BY 4.0. Added Home Sign from Clipart Library and building-clipart from Clipart Library (Clipart Library license). https://archive.org/details/3.1_20220621.

Figure 3.2: The economic spectrum. Kindred Grey. 2022. CC BY 4.0. https://archive.org/details/3.2_20220622.

Figure 3.3: Demand curve. Kindred Grey. 2022. CC BY 4.0. Added Simple Red Apple by sanja from Openclipart (Openclipart license). https://archive.org/details/3.3_20220622.

Figure 3.4: Supply curve. Kindred Grey. 2022. CC BY 4.0. Added Simple Red Apple by sanja from Openclipart (Openclipart license). https://archive.org/details/3.4_20220622.

Figure 3.5: Equilibrium price. Kindred Grey. 2022. CC BY 4.0. Added Simple Red Apple by sanja from Openclipart (Openclipart license). https://archive.org/details/3.5_20220622.

Figure 3.6: The U.S. unemployment rate (1970-present). U.S. Bureau of Labor Statistics, Unemployment Rate [UNRATE], retrieved from FRED, Federal Reserve Bank of St. Louis; https://fred.stlouisfed.org/series/UNRATE.

Figure 3.7: The U.S. inflation rate (1960-present). World Bank, Inflation, consumer prices for the United States [FPCPITOTLZGUSA], retrieved from FRED, Federal Reserve Bank of St. Louis; https://fred.stlouisfed.org/series/FPCPITOTLZGUSA.

Figure 3.8: Selected CPI values (1950-present). U.S. Bureau of Labor Statistics, Consumer Price Index for All Urban Consumers: All Items in U.S. City Average [CPIAUCSL], retrieved from FRED, Federal Reserve Bank of St. Louis; https://fred.stlouisfed.org/series/CPIAUCSL.

Figure 3.9: The National Debt (1966-present). U.S. Department of the Treasury. Fiscal Service, Federal Debt:

Total Public Debt [GFDEBTN], retrieved from FRED, Federal Reserve Bank of St. Louis; https://fred.stlouisfed.org/series/GFDEBTN.

Video

Video 1: Capitalism vs Socialism-A Balanced Approach. Guyus Seralius. 2013. Copyrighted. https://www.youtube.com/watch?v=PBIXmXJwIuk.

Notes

1. United States Patent and Trademark Office (2015). "General Information Concerning Patents." Retrieved from: http://www.uspto.gov/web/offices/pac/doc/general/index.html#laws
2. Mary Bellis (2015). "Learn About Edwin Land, Inventor of the Polaroid Camera." ThoughtCo. Retrieved from: http://inventors.about.com/library/inventors/blpolaroid.htm

4. Ethics and Social Responsibility

Learning Objectives

- Define business ethics and explain what it means to act ethically in business.
- Explain why we study business ethics.
- Identify ethical issues that you might face in business, such as insider trading, conflicts of interest, and bribery, and explain rationalizations for unethical behavior.
- Identify steps you can take to maintain your honesty and integrity in a business environment.
- Define corporate social responsibility and explain how organizations are responsible to their stakeholders, including owners, employees, customers, and the community.
- Discuss how you can identify an ethical organization, and how organizations can prevent behavior like sexual harassment.
- Learn how to avoid an ethical lapse, and why you should not rationalize when making decisions.

Introduction

"Mommy, Why Do You Have to Go to Jail?"

The one question Betty Vinson would have preferred to avoid is "Mommy, why do you have to go to jail?"[1] Vinson graduated with an accounting degree from Mississippi State and married her college sweetheart. After a series of jobs at small banks, she landed a mid-level accounting job at WorldCom, at the time still a small long-distance provider. Sparked by the telecom boom, however, WorldCom soon became a darling of Wall Street, and its stock price soared. Now working for a wildly successful company, Vinson rounded out her life by reading legal thrillers and watching her daughter play soccer.

Her moment of truth came in mid-2000, when company executives learned that profits had plummeted. They asked Vinson to make some accounting adjustments to boost income by $828 million. Vinson knew that the scheme was unethical (at the very least) but she gave in and made the adjustments. Almost immediately, she felt guilty and told her boss that she was quitting. When news of her decision came to the attention of CEO Bernard Ebbers and CFO Scott Sullivan, they hastened to assure Vinson that she'd never be asked to cook any more books. Sullivan explained it this way: "We have planes in the air. Let's get the planes landed. Once they've landed, if you still want to leave, then leave. But not while the planes are in the air."[2] Besides, she'd done nothing illegal, and if anyone asked, he'd take full responsibility. So Vinson decided to stay. After all, Sullivan was one of the top CFOs in the country; at age 37, he was already making $19 million a year.[3] Who was she to question his judgment?[4]

Six months later, Ebbers and Sullivan needed another adjustment—this time for $771 million. This scheme was even more unethical than the first: it entailed forging dates to hide the adjustment. Pretty soon, Vinson was making adjustments on a quarterly basis—first for $560 million, then for $743 million, and yet again for $941 million. Eventually, Vinson had juggled almost $4 billion, and before long, the stress started to get to her: she had trouble sleeping, lost weight, and withdrew from people at work. She decided to hang on when she got a promotion and a $30,000 raise.

By spring 2002, however, it was obvious that adjusting the books was business as usual at WorldCom. Vinson finally decided that it was time to move on, but, unfortunately, an internal auditor had already put two and two together and blown the whistle. The Securities and Exchange Commission charged WorldCom with fraud amounting to $11 billion—the largest in US history. Seeing herself as a valuable witness, Vinson was eager to tell what she knew. The government, however, regarded her as more than a mere witness. When she was named a co-conspirator, she agreed to cooperate fully and pleaded guilty to criminal conspiracy and securities fraud. But she won't be the only one doing time: Scott Sullivan will be in jail for five years, and Bernie Ebbers will be locked up for 25 years. Both maintain that they are innocent.[5]

So where did Betty Vinson, mild-mannered mid level executive and mother, go wrong? How did she manage to get involved in a scheme that not only bilked investors out of billions but also cost 17,000 people their jobs?[6] Ultimately, of course, we can only guess. Maybe she couldn't say no to her bosses; perhaps she believed that they'd take full responsibility for her accounting "adjustments." Possibly she was afraid of losing her job or didn't fully understand the ramifications of what she was doing. What we do know is that she disgraced herself and went to jail.[7]

Figure 4.1: Bernie Madoff's mug shot.

The WorldCom situation is not an isolated incident. Perhaps you have heard of Bernie Madoff, founder of Bernard L. Madoff Investment Securities and former chairman of the NASDAQ stock exchange.[8] Madoff is alleged to have run a giant Ponzi scheme[9] that cheated investors of up to $65 billion. His wrongdoings won him a spot at the top of Time Magazine's Top 10 Crooked CEOs. According to the SEC charges, Madoff convinced investors to give him large sums of money. In return, he gave them an impressive 8–12 percent return a year. But Madoff never really invested their money. Instead, he kept it for himself. He got funds to pay the first investors their return (or their money back if they asked for it) by bringing in new investors. Everything was going smoothly until the fall of 2008, when the stock market plummeted and many of his investors asked for their money. As he no longer had it, the game was over and he had to admit that the whole thing was just one big lie. Thousands of investors, including many of his wealthy friends, not-so-rich retirees who trusted him with their life savings, and charitable foundations, were financially ruined. Those harmed by Madoff either directly or indirectly were likely pleased when he was sentenced to jail for 150 years.

Unfortunately, ethical issues are not isolated to Wall Street and corporate CEOs. In 2016, Wells-Fargo was found guilty for creating 1.5 million fake deposit accounts and more than 500,000 fake credit cards.[10] Even though then CEO John Stumpf was fired as a result of the scandal he did not act alone. The Wells-Fargo scandal involved hundreds of managers, supervisors, and tellers at every level of the organization. You or your family members may even have been directly impacted by the fake account activity. This case reminds us that all employees play a role or are affected by the ethical culture of companies, clubs and organizations we belong to.

What can government, business and/or society do to reduce these types of ethical scandals?

Business Ethics

The Idea of Business Ethics

The nature of ethics in business continues to evolve. It is understood that the more ethical the organization is, the better it is positioned for long-term success. It's in the best interest of a company to operate ethically as trustworthy companies are better at attracting and keeping customers, talented employees, and capital. This long-term more "sustainable" and balanced model for business, allows business to grow in multiple ways. Today's definitions of "ethical business" suggest that these organizations are more in tune with their key stakeholders, including customers, suppliers, local community, and even their physical environment. Multiple studies suggest that more ethical companies are also more profitable, benefiting their shareholders.[11]

The cases above remind us that organizations tainted by questionable ethics suffer from dwindling customer bases, employee turnover, and investor mistrust. Ethical troubles and shortfalls can also be expensive, and these kinds of expenses do not lead to innovation or growth. Expenses related to legal problems and marketing efforts to rebuild brand equity also take time and present a significant distraction to the organization.

Let's begin this section by addressing this question: What can individuals, organizations, and government agencies do to foster an environment of ethical behavior in business? First, of course, we need to define the term.

What Is Ethics?

You probably already know what it means to be **ethical**: to know right from wrong and to know when you're practicing one instead of the other. We can say that **business ethics** is the application of ethical behavior in a business context. Acting ethically in business means more than simply obeying applicable laws and regulations: It also means being honest, doing no harm to others, competing fairly, and declining to put your own interests above those of your company, its owners, and its workers. If you're in business you obviously need a strong sense of what's right and wrong. You need the personal conviction to do what's right, even if it means doing something that's difficult or personally disadvantageous.

Why Study Ethics?

Ideally, prison terms, heavy fines, and civil suits would discourage corporate misconduct, but, unfortunately, many experts suspect that this assumption is a bit optimistic. There are always people who think they can outsmart the system or believe that rules don't apply to them. Again, we are reminded that ethical organizations are better positioned for long-term success. Whatever the condition of the ethical environment in the near future, one thing seems clear: the next generation entering business—which includes most of you—will find a world much different than the one that waited for the previous generation.

For example, cyberethics, user behavior and programmed computers may negatively impact people and society. In artificial intelligence (AI) programming decisions are built on assumptions in the code, so a programmer with a solid ethical foundation and awareness of how biases creep into code[12] will be more likely to develop more ethical decision-making tools through the technology being deployed. Recent history tells us in no uncertain terms that today's business students, many of whom are tomorrow's business leaders, need a much sharper understanding of the difference between what is and isn't ethically acceptable.

As a business student, one of your key tasks is learning how to recognize and deal with the ethical challenges that will confront you. Yes, you will be confronted with an ethical situation that could potentially snowball if your ethical radar is not in tune. Ethical dilemmas often start small like stealing of office supplies and cheating on expense reports. Openness to ethical lapses over time can result in more egregious activities like financial coverups, sexual harassment, and other illegal offenses. Employers are increasingly seeking ethical role models to help create a more ideal business environment.

> Asked what he looked for in a new hire, Warren Buffett, CEO of Berkshire Hathaway and one of the world's most successful investors, replied: "I look for three things. The first is personal integrity, the second is intelligence, and the third is a high energy level." He paused and then added, "But if you don't have the first, the second two don't matter."[13]

Identifying Ethical Issues and Dilemmas

Ethical issues are the difficult social questions that involve some level of controversy over what is the right thing to do. Environmental protection is an example of a commonly discussed ethical issue, because there can be trade offs between environmental and economic factors.

Ethical dilemmas are situations in which it is difficult for an individual to make decisions either because the right course of action is unclear or carries some potential negative consequences for the person or people involved.

Make no mistake about it: when you enter the business world, you'll find yourself in situations in which you'll have to choose the appropriate behavior. How, for example, would you answer questions like the following?

1. Is it OK to accept a pair of sports tickets from a supplier?
2. Can I buy office supplies from my brother-in-law?
3. Is it appropriate to donate company funds to a local charity?
4. If I find out that a friend is about to be fired, can I warn her?

Obviously, the types of situations are numerous and varied. Fortunately, we can break them down into a few basic categories: issues of honesty and integrity, conflicts of interest and loyalty, bribes versus gifts, theft, lying and deception, and whistleblowing. Let's look a little more closely at each of these categories.

Addressing Ethical Dilemmas

An **ethical dilemma** is a morally problematic situation: you must choose between two or more acceptable but often opposing alternatives that are important to different groups. Experts often frame this type of situation as a "right-versus-right" decision. As indicated at the beginning of the chapter the additional challenges of time and pressure can make ethical dilemmas and even basic ethical issues more stressful and dangerous. It's the sort of decision that Johnson & Johnson (known as J&J) CEO James Burke had to make in 1982. On September 30, twelve-year-old Mary Kellerman of Chicago died after her parents gave her Extra-Strength Tylenol. That same morning, 27-year-old Adam Janus, also of Chicago, died after taking Tylenol for minor chest pain. That night, when family members came to console his parents, Adam's brother and his wife took Tylenol from the same bottle and died within 48 hours. Over the next two weeks, four more people in Chicago died after taking Tylenol. The actual connection between Tylenol and the series of deaths wasn't made until an off-duty fireman realized from news reports that every victim had taken Tylenol. As consumers panicked, J&J pulled Tylenol off Chicago-area retail shelves. Researchers discovered Tylenol capsules containing large amounts of deadly cyanide. Because the poisoned bottles came from batches originating at different J&J plants, investigators determined that the tampering had occurred after the product had been shipped.[14]

So J&J wasn't at fault. But CEO Burke was still faced with an extremely serious dilemma: Was it possible to respond to the tampering cases without destroying the reputation of a highly profitable brand?

Burke had two options:

1. He could recall only the lots of Extra-Strength Tylenol that were found to be tainted with cyanide. In 1991, Perrier executives recalled only tainted product when they discovered that cases of their bottled water had been poisoned with benzine. This option favored J&J financially but possibly put more people at risk.
2. Burke could order a nationwide recall—of all bottles of Extra-Strength Tylenol. This option would reverse the priority of the stakeholders, putting the safety of the public above stakeholders' financial interests.

Burke opted to recall all 31 million bottles of Extra-Strength Tylenol on the market. The cost to J&J was $100 million, but public reaction was quite positive. Less than six weeks after the crisis began, Tylenol capsules were reintroduced in new tamper-resistant bottles, and by responding quickly and appropriately, J&J was eventually able to restore the Tylenol brand to its previous market position. When Burke was applauded for moral courage, he replied that he'd simply adhered to the long-standing J&J credo that put the interests of customers above those of other stakeholders. His only regret was that the perpetrator was never caught.[15]

If you're wondering what your thought process should be if you're confronted with an ethical dilemma, you might wish to remember the mental steps listed here—which happen to be the steps that James Burke took in addressing the Tylenol crisis:

1. **Define the problem.** How to respond to the tampering case without destroying the reputation of the Tylenol brand.
2. **Identify feasible options.** (1) Recall only the lots of Tylenol that were found to be tainted or (2) order a nationwide recall of all bottles of Extra-Strength Tylenol.
3. **Assess the effect of each option on stakeholders.** Option 1 (recalling only the tainted lots of Tylenol) is cheaper but puts more people at risk. Option 2 (recalling all bottles of Extra-Strength Tylenol) puts the safety of the public above stakeholders' financial interests.
4. **Establish criteria for determining the most appropriate action.** Adhere to the J&J credo, which puts the interests of customers above those of other stakeholders.
5. **Select the best option based on the established criteria.** In 1982, Option 2 was selected, and a nationwide recall of all bottles of Extra-Strength Tylenol was conducted.

Making Ethical Decisions

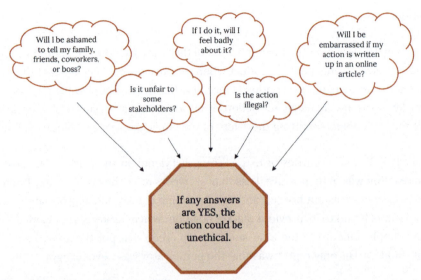

Figure 4.2: How to avoid an ethical lapse.

In contrast to the "right-versus-right" problem posed by an ethical dilemma, an **ethical decision** entails a "right-versus-wrong" decision—one in which there is clearly a right (ethical) choice and a wrong (unethical or illegal) choice. When you make a decision that's unmistakably unethical or illegal, you've committed an ethical lapse. If you're presented with this type of choice, asking yourself the questions in figure 4.2 will increase your odds of making an ethical decision.

To test the validity of this approach, let's take a point-by-point look at Betty Vinson's decisions:

1. Her actions were clearly illegal.
2. They were unfair to the workers who lost their jobs and to the investors who suffered financial losses (and also to her family, who shared her public embarrassment).
3. She definitely felt badly about what she'd done.
4. She was embarrassed to tell other people what she had done.
5. Reports of her actions appeared in her local newspaper (and just about every other newspaper in the country).

So Vinson could have answered "yes" to all five of our test questions. To simplify matters, remember the following rule of thumb: If you answer yes to any one of these five questions, odds are that you're about to do something you shouldn't.

Revisiting Johnson & Johnson

As discussed earlier, Johnson & Johnson received tremendous praise for the actions taken by its CEO, James Burke, in response to the 1982 Tylenol catastrophe. However, things change. To learn how a company can destroy its good **reputation**, let's fast forward to 2008 and revisit J&J and its credo, which states, "We believe our first responsibility is to the doctors, nurses and patients, to mothers and fathers and all others who use our products and services. In meeting their needs everything we do must be of high quality."[16] How could a company whose employees believed so strongly in its credo find itself under criminal and congressional investigation for a series of recalls due to defective products?[17] In a three-year period, the company recalled 24 products, including Children's, Infants' and Adults' Tylenol, Motrin, and Benadryl;[18] 1-Day Acuvue TruEye contact lenses sold outside the US;[19] and hip replacements.[20]

Unlike the Tylenol recall, no one had died from the defective products, but customers were certainly upset to find they had purchased over-the-counter medicines for themselves and their children that were potentially contaminated with dark particles or tiny specks of metal;[21] contact lenses that contained a type of acid that caused stinging or pain when inserted in the eye;[22] and defective hip implants that required patients to undergo a second hip replacement.[23]

Who bears the responsibility for these image-damaging blunders? Two individuals who were at least partially responsible were William Weldon, CEO, and Colleen Goggins, Worldwide Chairman of J&J's Consumer Group. Weldon has been criticized for being largely invisible and publicly absent during the recalls. Additionally, he admitted that he did not understand the consumer division where many of the quality control problems originated. Goggins was in charge of the factories that produced many of the recalled products. She was heavily criticized by fellow employees for her excessive cost-cutting measures and her propensity to replace experienced scientists with new hires.[24] In addition, she was implicated in scheme to avoid publicly disclosing another J&J recall of a defective product.

After learning that J&J had released packets of Motrin that did not dissolve correctly, the company hired contractors to go into convenience stores and secretly buy up every pack of Motrin on the shelves. The instructions given to the contractors were the following: "You should simply 'act' like a regular customer while making these purchases. THERE MUST BE NO MENTION OF THIS BEING A RECALL OF THE PRODUCT!"[25] In May 2010, when Goggins appeared before a congressional committee investigating the "phantom recall," she testified that she was not aware of the behavior of the contractors[26] and that she had "no knowledge of instructions to contractors involved in the phantom recall to not tell store employees what they were doing." In her September 2010 testimony to the House Committee on Oversight and Government Reform, she acknowledged that the company in fact wrote those very instructions. In 2020, Johnson & Johnson is discontinuing their baby powder, one of their flagship products, because of the cancer-related issues found from the talc, an ingredient in the powder. This time, they are being proactive.[27]

Refusing to Rationalize

Despite all the good arguments in favor of doing the right thing, why do many reasonable people act unethically (at least at times)? Why do good people make bad choices? According to one study, there are four common **rationalizations** (excuses) for justifying misconduct:[28]

1. **My behavior isn't really illegal or immoral.** Rationalizers try to convince themselves that an action is OK if it isn't downright illegal or blatantly immoral. They tend to operate in a gray area where there's no clear evidence that the action is wrong.
2. **My action is in everyone's best interests.** Some rationalizers tell themselves: "I know I lied to make the deal, but it'll bring in a lot of business and pay a lot of bills." They convince themselves that they're expected to act in a certain way.[29]
3. **No one will find out what I've done.** Here, the self-questioning comes down to "If I didn't get caught, did I really do it?" The answer is yes. There's a simple way to avoid succumbing to this rationalization: Always act as if you're being watched.
4. **The company will condone my action and protect me.** This justification rests on a fallacy. Betty Vinson may honestly have believed that her actions were for the good of the company and that her boss would, therefore, accept full responsibility (as he promised). When she goes to jail, however, she'll go on her own.

Here's another rule of thumb: If you find yourself having to rationalize a decision, it's probably a bad one.

Easy to Remember Ethical Tests to Help With Decision Making—What to do When the Light Turns Yellow

Ethical decision making can be difficult when balancing multiple stakeholder interests. It is compounded when there is added pressure and a lack of time for good analysis and review. There are a couple simple Ethical Strategies that can help with personal decision making or at least remind you to pump the brakes if needed.

- The Golden Rule – Treat others the way you expect to be treated.[30]
- The Grandma Rule – This is also called the Loved-one Rule. When balancing options, think about what an elder you respect may think of the options if you had to review it with them later.[31]
- The Sunshine Rule – This concept has been articulated in a number of ways. Think about how your plan may look in the light of day or on the front page of the newspaper. In this context it may be easier to consider if certain action is justified.[32]

- The Rule of the Big 4. When faced with a challenging situation or an option if you ask yourself these 4 questions it may help reveal if there is a linked ethical problem.[33]
    - Is the decision HAZY? Are there elements to the issue that appear to be hidden or unclear? Do those items need to be revealed?
    - Is the decision LAZY? Is the path forward or decision made with any effort? Is more work expected of you to make a good decision?
    - Is the decision based on GREED? Who stands to gain by the decision? Is the decision being made for the good of the company and the stakeholders involved or is it based on personal greed?
    - Is the decision made out of SPEED? Was there a rush to judgment without all of the facts?

What to Do When the Light Turns Yellow

Like our five questions, some ethical problems are fairly straightforward. Others, unfortunately, are more complicated, but it will help to think of our five-question test as a set of signals that will warn you that you're facing a particularly tough decision—that you should think carefully about it and perhaps consult someone else. The situation is like approaching a traffic light. Red and green lights are easy; you know what they mean and exactly what to do. Yellow lights are trickier. Before you decide which pedal to hit, try posing our five questions. If you get a single yes, you will almost surely be better off hitting the brake.[34]

Figure 4.3: Caution light.

 An interactive H5P element has been excluded from this version of the text. You can view it online here: https://pressbooks.lib.vt.edu/fundamentalsofbusiness4e/?p=927#h5p-12

Issues of Honesty and Integrity

Master investor Warren Buffet once told a group of business students the following: "I cannot tell you that honesty is the best policy. I can't tell you that if you behave with perfect **honesty** and **integrity** somebody somewhere won't behave the other way and make more money. But honesty is a good policy. You'll do fine, you'll sleep well at night and you'll feel good about the example you are setting for your coworkers and the other people who care about you."[35]

Ethics and Social Responsibility | 59

If you work for a company that settles for its employees' merely obeying the law and following a few internal regulations, you might think about moving on. If you're being asked to deceive customers about the quality or value of your product, you're in an ethically unhealthy environment.

Think About This Story:

"A chef put two frogs in a pot of warm soup water. The first frog smelled the onions, recognized the danger, and immediately jumped out. The second frog hesitated: The water felt good and he decided to stay and relax for a minute. After all, he could always jump out when things got too hot. As the water got hotter, however, the frog adapted to it, hardly noticing the change. Before long he was the main ingredient in frog-leg soup."[36]

Figure 4.4: Two frogs and two different responses.

So, what's the moral of the story? Don't sit around in an ethically compromised environment and lose your integrity a little at a time; get out before the water gets too hot and your options have evaporated. Fortunately, a few rules of thumb can guide you. We've summed them up in figure 4.5.

1. While at work, focus on your job, not on non-work-related activities, such as e-mails and personal phone calls.

2. Follow your own code of personal conduct; act according to your own convictions rather than doing what's convenient (or profitable) at the time.

3. Don't appropriate office supplies, products, or other company resources for your own use.

4. Be honest with customers, management, coworkers, competitors, and the public.

5. Remember that it's the small, seemingly trivial, day-to-day activities and gestures that build your character.

Figure 4.5: How to maintain honesty and integrity.

Time and Pressure

The frog example reminds us that decision making while under pressure can be pretty important. Unfortunately, we will often be short on time when we are facing some decisions. This is why it is so important to arm ourselves with good ethical models and to know the value of good ethical decision making. If we can practice this decision making in the classroom or in situations when we are not under pressure or out of time, we can be more equipped for those times when time is not available. A common example is practicing a play in sports. In practice a team may walk through the ideal steps in slow motion and do it over and over, so they will be more prepared for the same play or sequence of events during the game when time is not a luxury.

The realities of time and pressure are so important and are another reason why we practice making deadlines in our coursework. We need to manage time well and be aware of when we procrastinate. In many ways procrastination can be thought of as a lid on that heated pot, creating more pressure, and potential disaster. Unfortunately, procrastination is not the only way we can contribute to a potentially unethical environment. We will review some additional challenges in the sections to follow.

Conflicts of Interest

Conflicts of interest occur when individuals must choose between taking actions that promote their personal interests over the interests of others or taking actions that don't. A conflict can exist, for example, when an employee's own interests interfere with, or have the potential to interfere with, the best interests of the company's stakeholders (management, customers, and owners). Let's say that you work for a company with a contract to cater events at your college and that your uncle owns a local bakery. Obviously, this situation could create a conflict of interest (or at least give the appearance of one—which is a problem in itself). When you're called on to furnish desserts for a luncheon, you might be tempted to send some business your uncle's way even if it's not in the best interest of your employer. What should you do? You should disclose the connection to your boss, who can then arrange things so that your personal interests don't conflict with the company's.

The same principle holds that an employee shouldn't use private information about an employer for personal financial benefit. Say that you learn from a coworker at your pharmaceutical company that one of its most profitable drugs will be pulled off the market because of dangerous side effects. The recall will severely hurt the company's financial performance and cause its stock price to plummet. Before the news becomes public, you sell all the stock you own in the company. What you've done is called **insider trading**—acting on information that is not available to the general public, either by trading on it or providing it to others who trade on it. Insider trading is illegal, and you could go to jail for it.

Conflicts of Loyalty

You may one day find yourself in a bind between being **loyal** either to your employer or to a friend or family member. Perhaps you just learned that a coworker, a friend of yours, is about to be downsized out of his job. You also happen to know that he and his wife are getting ready to make a deposit on a house near the company headquarters. From a work standpoint, you know that you shouldn't divulge the information. From a friendship standpoint, though, you feel it's your duty to tell your friend. Wouldn't he tell you if the situation were reversed? So what do you do? As tempting as it is to be loyal to your friend, you shouldn't tell. As an employee, your primary responsibility is to your employer. You might be able to soften your dilemma by convincing a manager with the appropriate authority to tell your friend the bad news before he puts down his deposit.

Bribes vs. Gifts

It's not uncommon in business to give and receive small gifts of appreciation, but when is a gift unacceptable? When is it really a **bribe**?

There's often a fine line between a gift and a bribe. The following information may help in drawing it, because it raises key issues in determining how a gesture should be interpreted: the cost of the item, the timing of the gift, the type of gift, and the connection between the giver and the receiver. If you're on the receiving end, it's a good idea to refuse any item that's overly generous or given for the purpose of influencing a decision. Because accepting even small gifts may violate company rules, always check on company policy.

Google's "Code of Conduct," for instance, has an entire section on avoiding conflicts of interest. They outline where these conflicts might occur, such as accepting gifts, personal investments, and outside employment, and provide guidelines: "In each of these situations, the rule is the same—if you are considering entering into a business situation that creates a conflict of interest, don't. If you are in a business situation that may create a conflict of interest, or the appearance of a conflict of interest, review the situation with your manager and Ethics & Compliance."[37]

Theft

The work environment is full of resources, materials, tools and assets. None of them are yours until, as a consumer, you purchase a resulting product. If you are able to keep this basic rule in mind you can check yourself and others when tempted by **theft**.

From a labor management perspective, we are focused on the loss of employee time. We can think of the **"theft of time"** as an issue in a few different ways. First, the traditional concern is how an employee may just post in accurate time on a time card or in a timekeeping system. In this case the employee posts a time beyond the hours worked in an effort to be paid for time not worked, resulting in stealing wages from the company for work not performed.

Another example of time theft to be considered is when employees are simply not following the tasks, duties or the job's expectations but rather they are focused on doing other personal activities. Internet access and use of smartphones during working hours opens the door to this potential problem. In response, employers have employed a variety of types of monitoring technology to help with time management and supervision which allows the employer to have data for discussion during performance management meetings. While these monitoring practices may seem that there is a lack of trust, these types of practices can help to build trust as well. Employers have also had to re-evaluate job expectations, as a whole, and update job descriptions accordingly.

As a result of more employees working from home, a trend accelerated during the COVID pandemic, the ability to monitor employee time and activity became more complex. Many organizations were already facing a monitoring challenge, due to new technology in the workplace, but COVID then forced many organizations to make changes for which they were not fully prepared.

Historically, we would think of theft as the stealing of money, assets, or time from the company, but theft of information is a growing problem in our corporate climate. Data about customers, suppliers and the marketplace, has become more than just another tool for decision making. In many industries that same data has become a commodity, a commodity that is bought, sold, and in some cases stolen.

Lying and Deception

Unethical behavior in everyday life easily translates to the business environment. Lying is no exception. While similar to lying, deception is not the same thing. **Deception** can be thought of as the creation of something that does not exist. Deception may involve lying or some other form of misrepresentation. Deception could also simply be an act of providing less information than expected in an effort to mislead another party. **Lying** is saying things that are not true. Falsely assigning blame or inaccurately reporting conversations are examples of lying.[38]

If we make a practice of lying or deceiving others as a part of our job, we are misrepresenting the intentions of the company we represent. Not only is the relationship one's employment at risk, in many cases, there are legal implications for organizations and individuals.

- An organization that misrepresents the safety of the work environment may soon find itself facing OSHA (Occupational Safety and Health Administration) penalties.
- An organization that misrepresents the quality of its products could face enforcement actions with the FDA (Food and Drug Administration).
- An organization that misrepresents financial reporting may find itself dealing with the SEC (Security and Exchange Commission).

Your Actions Matter—See Something, Say Something

Unethical activity in an organization can be unhealthy. It can easily spread and be deadly to the life of a company. It is important to know that unethical actions often start small and they grow when they are unchecked or not corrected. The goal of this chapter is to help you identify issues early so that you can work with your peers and management to correct the behavior and act as a better model for others. While often small issues can be managed, sometimes there are systemic organizational issues that demand more significant action.

Whistleblowing

As we've seen, the misdeeds of Betty Vinson and her accomplices at WorldCom didn't go undetected. They caught the eye of Cynthia Cooper, the company's director of internal auditing. Cooper, of course, could have looked the other way, but instead she summoned up the courage to be a **whistleblower**—an individual who exposes illegal or unethical behavior in an organization. Like Vinson, Cooper had majored in accounting at Mississippi State and was a hard-working, dedicated employee. Unlike Vinson, however, she refused to be bullied by her boss, CFO Scott Sullivan. In fact, she had tried to tell not only Sullivan but also auditors from the Arthur Andersen accounting firm that there was a problem with WorldCom's books. The auditors dismissed her warnings, and when Sullivan angrily told her to drop the matter, she started cleaning out her office. But she didn't relent. She and her team worked late each night, conducting an extensive, secret investigation. Two months later, Cooper had evidence to take to Sullivan, who told her once again to back off. Again, however, she stood up to him, and though she regretted the consequences for her WorldCom coworkers, she reported the scheme to the company's board of directors. Within days, Sullivan was fired and the largest accounting fraud in history became public.[39]

As a result of Cooper's actions, executives came clean about the company's financial situation. The conspiracy of fraud was brought to an end, and though public disclosure of WorldCom's problems resulted in massive stock-price declines and employee layoffs, investor and employee losses would have been greater without Cooper's intervention. Even though Cooper did the right thing, and landed on the cover of Time magazine for it, the experience wasn't exactly gratifying.

A lot of people applauded her action, but many coworkers shunned her; some even blamed her for the company's troubles.[40]

Whistleblowing is sometimes career suicide. A survey of 200 whistleblowers conducted by the National Whistleblower Center found that half were fired for blowing the whistle.[41] Even those who keep their jobs can experience repercussions. As long as they stay, some will treat them (as one whistleblower put it) "like skunks at a picnic"; if they leave, they may be blackballed in the industry.[42] On a positive note, new Federal laws have been passed which are intended to protect whistleblowers.

For her own part, Cynthia Cooper doesn't regret what she did. As she told a group of students at Mississippi State: "Strive to be persons of honor and integrity. Do not allow yourself to be pressured. Do what you know is right even if there may be a price to be paid."[43] If your company tells employees to do whatever it takes, push the envelope, look the other way, and "be sure that we make our numbers," you have three choices: go along with the policy, try to change things, or leave. If your personal integrity is part of the equation, you're probably down to the last two choices.[44]

Legislative Action for Organizational Change

As part of the 2010 Dodd-Frank legislation passed by Congress in response to the 2008 financial crisis, the Securities and Exchange Commission (SEC) established a whistleblower-rewards program to provide employees and other individuals with the opportunity to report financial securities misconduct. According to a recent SEC report Fiscal year 2021 also was a record year for whistleblower awards, with the SEC awarding a total of $564 million to 108 whistleblowers. The whistleblower program also surpassed $1 billion in awards over the life of the program in financial penalties from companies that have done things to damage their own reputation as well as those of employees and other stakeholders.[45]

The whistleblower program is based on three key components: monetary awards, prohibition of employer retaliation, and protection of the whistleblower's identity. The program requires the SEC to pay out monetary awards to eligible individuals who voluntarily provide original information about a violation of federal securities laws that has occurred, is ongoing, or is about to take place. The information supplied must lead to a successful enforcement action or monetary sanctions exceeding $1 million. No awards are paid out until the sanctions are collected from the offending firm.

A whistleblower must be an individual (not a company), and that individual does not need to be employed by a company to submit information about that specific organization. A typical award to a whistleblower is between 10 and 30 percent of the monetary sanctions the SEC and others (for example, the U.S. attorney general) are able to collect from the company in question.

Despite criticisms from some financial institutions, the whistleblower-rewards program continues to be a success—reinforcing the point that financial fraud will not go unnoticed by the SEC, employees, and others individuals.[46]

Adapted from: OpenStax *Introduction to Business* (CC BY). Access for free at https://openstax.org/books/introduction-business/pages/16-7-buying-and-selling-at-securities-exchanges

The SEC publishes statements and press releases on their website about decisions on their cases including the company charged and the settlement amounts.[47]

An interactive H5P element has been excluded from this version of the text. You can view it online here: https://pressbooks.lib.vt.edu/fundamentalsofbusiness4e/?p=927#h5p-11

Government Changes Helped Introduce New Business Stakeholders

So far in this chapter we have discussed factors that have influenced ethical decision making within organizations. Over the past 100 years or so activities outside the organization have been a catalyst for change within the organization. As we walk through a very basic timeline of key events, we will see how national events and perceptions about business have changed, and led to a more ethical model for business which we have today.

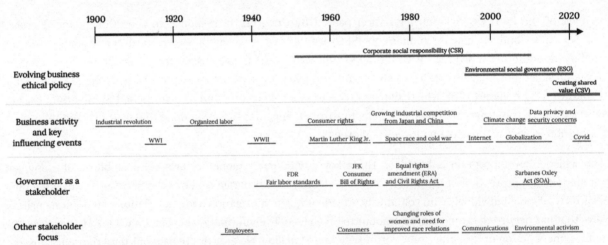

Figure 4.6: Overlap between government and stakeholders.

The Rise of Government Intervention in Business

Ryan Engleman's post, The Second Industrial Revolution, 1870-1914[48], describes societal changes, "The Second Revolution fueled the Gilded Age, a period of great extremes, great wealth and widespread poverty, great expansion and deep depression."[49] By the end of the Great Depression in 1938, it was evident that something needed to be done to better compensate American workers.[50] President Franklin Delano Roosevelt's administration passed the Fair Labor Standards Act in an attempt to give workers better working conditions and hours. Government stepped in to play a greater role in the relationship between worker and employer, and in doing so, a huge evolutionary step was taken. **Government** had become the first key stakeholder in American business, besides owners. **Employees**, then had become the second.

The Rise of the Consumer

In the 1960s a third key business stakeholder began to influence business in a more concerted way, the **consumer**. While it could be argued that consumers were the first stakeholder, prior to this time big business made goods they thought the consumer would want. Business did not seek out consumer preferences or feedback and consumers failed to leverage their collective influence. Henry Ford was famous for reflecting about consumer preferences of the Model T, "You can have it in any color, as long as it's black."[51]

Again like 1938, the government intervened and opened the door for action. Under President Kennedy the Consumer Bill of Rights was passed in 1960.[52] In 1965, Ralph Nader published his book *Unsafe at Any Speed*[53], further bolstering the need for greater consumer awareness and action towards business.[54] Consumer power has continued to grow and be more diversified with the advent of the internet.

Intervention in Business by Academia and Mass Media

The Civil Rights Act of 1964 ushered in the 1970s and a time of radical social change in the United States.[55] During this time large organizations of all kinds were questioned, including big government and big business. Academics also began to be more vocal. Nadar, Friedman, and others inserted **academia** and the **media** into the business stakeholder arena.[56,57]

Over the next few decades business attempted to regulate itself until a series of scandals created the need for more government action. Enron, Worldcom, Wells-Fargo, VW, Ford and others faced huge scandals and Congress was forced to act again. In 2002 the Sarbanes Oxley Act (SOX) was passed to help develop more audit controls and transparency for business operations.[58]

Frameworks for Business Ethics

We will look at several ethics frameworks used by businesses, including: **corporate social responsibility (CSR)**, **environmental, social, and governance (ESG)**, and **creating shared value (CSV)**.

Corporate Social Responsibility (CSR)

By the late 1900's we can see how business was now positioning itself in the marketplace to interact with more outside stakeholders. **Corporate social responsibility** refers to the approach that an organization takes in balancing its responsibilities toward different stakeholders when making legal, economic, ethical, and social decisions. Remember that we previously defined **stakeholders** as those with a legitimate interest in the success or failure of the business and the policies it adopts. The term social responsibility refers to the approach that an organization takes in balancing its responsibilities toward their various stakeholders.

What motivates companies to be "socially responsible"? We hope it's because they want to do the right thing, and for many companies, "doing the right thing" is a key motivator. The fact is, it's often hard to figure out what the "right thing" is: what's "right" for one group of stakeholders isn't necessarily just as "right" for another. One thing, however, is certain: companies today are held to higher standards than ever before. Consumers and other groups consider not only the quality and price of a company's products but also its character. If too many groups see a company as a poor corporate citizen, it will have a harder time attracting qualified employees, finding investors, and selling its products. Good corporate citizens, by contrast, are more successful in all these areas.

Environmental, Social, and Governance (ESG)

Environmental, social and governance is the second ethical business framework we will review. In this framework business acknowledges the additional influences of government and climate change. Business is no longer working in just a social context, there are also new rules to follow at all levels of the organization.

In the early 21st century there has also been a greater overall awareness about climate change. It is important to note that if we set aside the debate about climate change it is still clear that we are living in a world where there is greater competition for finite resources. Business needs a variety of resources, as raw material inputs. Business also often creates a variety of unwanted outputs in the production process, in the form of pollution. This management of resources has forced businesses to engage a variety of new stakeholders.

The internet and the electronic age of business has changed the business environment in more ways than one. Traditional and new kinds of business are able to reach a wider variety of people, as suppliers, customers and workers. This new diverse work environment has changed the way business looks at itself and it has challenged many traditional norms. Many businesses have had great success in developing a more diverse work environment and know that such change is key to attracting good talent.

Governance in this context is not limited to government oversight, even though government rules and regulations do play a role. A company's board of directors (BOD) also play a key role in this organizational structure. The company's board is often made up of key shareholders and stakeholders that are working to influence the organization and guide management. Organizations with a high level of governance will also have robust audit processes in place covering a myriad of activities from workplace safety and environmental impact to financial reporting integrity. Audit results are then passed on to the board for formal review and strategic decision making.

Many companies have grown to understand that the ideal balancing of environmental and social and governance influences can be a competitive advantage. Investors also see this as a possible benefit and therefore many seek companies with a strong ESG strategy.[59]

Rank	Company	Actions towards reducing CO_2 emissions
1	Alphabet	- Became carbon neutral in 2007 - By 2030 they pledge to become the first major company to operate full-time on carbon-free energy
2	Beyond Meat	- The Beyond Burger requires over 90% less land, 46% less energy, and produced 90% fewer greenhouse gas emissions compared to its cow counterpart
3	HP	- In 2019, HP eliminated power cord plastic ties and plastic document bags in its packaging - Launched the HP sustainable forest collaborative - By 2025 they plan to eliminate 75% of single-use plastic packaging
4	Unilever	By 2030, they plan to half their environmental footprint and become carbon negative
5	Johnson & Johnson	- In 2019, they received the Energy Star Partner of the Year Award - By 2025 all packaging will be 100% recyclable, reusable, or compostable - By 2050, facilities will be powered by 100% renewable energy
6	Tesla	- Has produced over 1 million electric cars, preventing close to 4 million tons of CO2 from entering the atmosphere - In 2018 and 2019, they provided disaster relief financial assistance for regions experiencing hurricanes and forest fires
7	Microsoft	- By 2025, company will shift to 100% renewable energy - By 2030, carbon negative - By 2050, remove all carbon that the company has been responsible for since its founding in 1975
8	Apple	- All facilities are entirely carbon neutral - Company has invested $300 million in China CLean Energy Fund
9	Nike	- All North American operations are powered on 100% renewable energy, with goals of extending this across the globe by 2025 - Nike Grind program has recycled 30 million pairs of sports shoes into new apparel
10	Hasbro	- In 2019, they began using a plant-based plastic material made from agricultural byproducts - By 2022, they plan to remove almost all plastic from new plastic packaging - Launched TerraCycle, which allows used toys to be transformed into materials for constructing outdoor play spaces

Figure 4.7: Top 10 publicly traded companies fighting climate change in 2022.

Although large companies are taking steps to reduce their carbon footprint, they are usually the biggest contributors to CO_2 in the atmosphere. A hundred of the largest companies are responsible for around 71% of all global emissions. It is important that companies (like these in figure 4.7) continue to produce less waste, use renewable energy, source sustainable materials and labor, and reuse materials when possible. It is important to hold big companies accountable to their pledges for the future. While big companies can make the biggest impact by going carbon neutral, it is also important for smaller companies to find ways to lead as well. Both large and small companies are responsible for reducing their carbon footprint.[60]

Creating Shared Value (CSV)

Creating shared value is an aspirational viewpoint developed by Michael Porter and Mark Kramer.[61] This framework views business in an ideal position to solve big problems. Porter and Kramer summarize their work as follows:

"Shared value focuses companies on the right kind of profits—profits that create societal benefits rather than diminish them."

In this model the great challenges or our time are viewed as opportunities and business is in an ideal position to meet those challenges. By having business focused on these issues it achieves a profit for its shareholders and it also solves problems, creating shared value.[62]

Figure 4.8 presents a model of corporate responsibility based on a company's relationships with its stakeholders. In this model, the focus is on managers—not owners—as the principals involved in these relationships. **Managers** act as representatives of the business organization and those that must balance stakeholder influences as they manage the organization. **Owners** or shareholders are the stakeholders who invest risk capital in the firm in expectation of a financial return. Other stakeholders include **employees**, **suppliers**, and the **communities** in which the firm does business. Proponents of this model hold that customers, who provide the firm with revenue, have a special claim on managers' attention. The arrows indicate the two-way nature of corporation-stakeholder relationships: All stakeholders have some claim on the firm's resources and returns, and management's job is to make decisions that balance these claims.[63]

Stakeholders of Business Ethics and Social Responsibility

Let's look at some of the ways in which companies can be "ethically and socially responsible" in considering the claims of various stakeholders.

Owners

Owners or shareholders invest money in companies. In return, the people who run a company have a responsibility to increase the value of owners' investments through profitable operations. In historical businesses of the early 1900's ownership was more concentrated. Now, through the stock market, company ownership is more diverse, with some

Figure 4.8: Management's relationship with stakeholders.

companies having thousands of "owners" through the company stock they own. Managers also have a responsibility to provide owners (as well as other stakeholders having financial interests, such as creditors and suppliers) with accurate, reliable information about the performance of the business. Clearly, this is one of the areas in which WorldCom managers fell down on the job. Upper-level management purposely deceived shareholders by presenting them with fraudulent financial statements

Managers

Managers have what is known as a fiduciary responsibility to owners: they're responsible for safeguarding the company's assets and handling its funds in a trustworthy manner. Yet managers experience what is called the agency problem; a situation in which their best interests do not align with those of the owners who employ them. To enforce managers' fiduciary responsibilities for a firm's financial statements and accounting records, the Sarbanes-Oxley Act of 2002 requires CEOs and CFOs to attest to their accuracy. The law also imposes penalties on corporate officers, auditors, board members, and any others who commit fraud. You'll learn more about this law in your accounting and business law courses.

Employees

Companies are responsible for providing **employees** with safe, healthy places to work—as well as environments that are free from sexual harassment and all types of discrimination. They should also offer appropriate wages and benefits. In the following sections, we'll take a closer look at these areas of corporate responsibility. The framework of corporate social responsibility (CSR) gives more weight to the interests of the employee, beyond basic safety and equality. In order to compete for good employees organizations need to consider personal fulfillment, individual creativity and flexibility as they think about the employee stakeholder. It is interesting to note that during the COVID pandemic of 2020-2022, even more resistant organizations were reminded that the concerted power of employees was compelling, often creating changes never imagined previously.

Wages and Benefits

At the very least, employers must obey laws governing minimum wage and overtime pay. A **minimum wage** is set by the federal government, though states can set their own rates as long as they are higher. As of 2022 the current federal rate, for example, is $7.25, while the rate in many states is far higher, with California at the extreme resting at $15.[64] By law, employers must also provide certain **benefits**—social security (retirement funds), unemployment insurance (protects against loss of income in case of job loss), and workers' compensation (covers lost wages and medical costs in case of on-the-job injury). Most large companies pay most of their workers more than minimum wage and offer broader benefits, including medical, dental, and vision care, as well as savings programs, in order to compete for talent. Companies may also pay a living wage, which is a sufficient wage that covers the basic cost of living for a specific location.[65,66]

Safety and Health

Though it seems obvious that companies should guard workers' **safety and health**, some simply don't. For over four decades, for example, executives at Johns Manville suppressed evidence that one of its products, asbestos, was responsible for the deadly lung disease developed by many of its workers.[67] The company concealed chest X-rays from stricken workers, and executives decided that it was simply cheaper to pay workers' compensation claims than to create a safer work environment. A New Jersey court was quite blunt in its judgment: Johns Manville, it held, had made a deliberate, cold-blooded decision to do nothing to protect at-risk workers, in blatant disregard of their rights.[68]

About four in 100,000 US workers die in workplace "incidents" each year. The Department of Labor categorizes deaths caused by conditions like those at Johns Manville as "exposure to harmful substances or environments." How prevalent is this condition as a cause of workplace deaths? See figure 4.9, which breaks down workplace fatalities by cause. Some jobs are more dangerous than others. For a comparative overview based on workplace deaths by occupation, see figure 4.10.

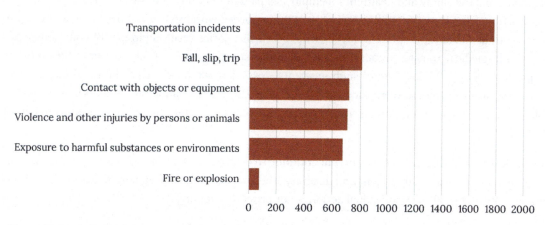

Figure 4.9: Workplace deaths by event or exposure (2020).

Occupation	% of total workplace deaths*
Transportation and material moving	26.91%
Construction and extraction	20.49%
Installation, maintenance, and repair	8.25%
Management	7.58%
Building and grounds cleaning and maintenance	6.44%
Farming, fishing, and forestry	5.54%
Protective service	4.81%
Production	4.70%
Sales and related	4.20%
Food preparation and serving related	1.72%

Figure 4.10: Workplace deaths by occupation, 2020.
*Data is selective. The categories listed represent the ones with the highest percentage of total workplace deaths.

Fortunately for most people, things are far better than they were at Johns Manville. Procter & Gamble (P&G), for example, considers the safety and health of its employees paramount and promotes the attitude that "Nothing we do is worth getting hurt for." With nearly 100,000 employees worldwide, P&G uses a measure of worker safety called "total incident rate per employee," which records injuries resulting in loss of consciousness, time lost from work, medical transfer to another job, motion restriction, or medical treatment beyond first aid. The company attributes the low rate of such incidents—less than one incident per hundred employees—to a variety of programs to promote workplace safety.[69] During the COVID pandemic of 2020 new issues related to employee health created a greater sense of social awareness forcing change within and outside of the organization.

While our culture and the business environment continue to evolve and be more welcoming, problems continue to exist in the areas of sexual harassment and diversity. These issues can plague an organization at an individual level or at a more cultural level if individual action is not properly supported.

Prevention of Sexual Harassment

Sexual harassment occurs when an employee makes "unwelcome sexual advances, requests for sexual favors, and other verbal or physical conduct of a sexual nature" to another employee. It's also considered sexual harassment when "submission to or rejection of this conduct explicitly or implicitly affects an individual's employment, unreasonably interferes with an individual's work performance or creates an intimidating, hostile or offensive work environment."[70]

To prevent sexual harassment—or at least minimize its likelihood—a company should adopt a formal anti-harassment **policy** describing prohibited conduct, asserting its objections to the behavior, and detailing penalties for violating the policy.[71] Employers also have an obligation to investigate harassment complaints. Failure to enforce anti-harassment policies can be very costly. In 1998, for example, Mitsubishi paid $34 million to more than 350 female employees of its Normal, Illinois, plant to settle a sexual harassment case supported by the **Equal Employment Opportunity Commission**. The EEOC reprimanded the company for permitting an atmosphere of verbal and physical abuse against women, charging that female workers had been subjected to various forms of harassment, ranging from exposure to obscene graffiti and vulgar jokes to fondling and groping.[72] Since the "#MeToo" movement gained traction in late 2017, there has been widespread discussion regarding the best ways to prevent sexual harassment.[73]

Workforce Diversity

In addition to complying with equal employment opportunity laws, many companies make special efforts to recruit employees who are underrepresented in the workforce according to sex, race, gender, or some other characteristic. In helping to build more **diverse** workforces, such initiatives contribute to competitive advantage for two reasons:

1. People from diverse backgrounds bring new talents and fresh perspectives to an organization, typically enhancing creativity in the development of new products.
2. By more accurately reflecting the demographics of the marketplace, a diverse workforce improves a company's ability to serve an ethnically diverse population.
3. Again, the best companies see good ethics, including diversity, not as a final checklist of things they should do, but as part of an integrated strategy to create a competitive advantage.

Customers

The purpose of any business is to satisfy **customers**, who reward businesses by buying their products. Sellers are also responsible—both ethically and legally—for treating customers fairly. As indicated above, the voice and interests of customers as key stakeholders became more significant when the rights of consumers were first articulated by President John F. Kennedy in 1962.[74] He submitted to Congress a presidential message devoted to consumer issues.[75] Kennedy identified four consumer rights:

1. **The right to safe products.** A company should sell no product that it suspects of being unsafe for buyers. Thus, producers have an obligation to safety-test products before releasing them for public consumption. The automobile industry, for example, conducts extensive safety testing before introducing new models (though recalls remain common).
2. **The right to be informed about a product.** Sellers should furnish consumers with the product information that they need to make an in- formed purchase decision. That's why pillows have labels identifying the materials used to make them, for instance.
3. **The right to choose what to buy.** Consumers have a right to decide which products to purchase, and sellers should let them know what their options are. Pharmacists, for example, should tell patients when a prescription can be filled with a cheaper brand-name or generic drug. Telephone companies should explain alternative calling plans.
4. **The right to be heard.** Companies must tell customers how to contact them with complaints or concerns. They should also listen and respond.

Companies share the responsibility for the legal and ethical treatment of consumers with several government agencies: the **Federal Trade Commission (FTC)**, which enforces consumer-protection laws; the **Food and Drug Administration (FDA)**, which oversees the labeling of food products; and the **Consumer Product Safety Commission**, which enforces laws protecting consumers from the risk of product-related injury.

Local Communities

For obvious reasons, most **communities** see getting a new business as an asset and view losing one—especially a large employer—as a detriment. After all, the economic impact of business activities on local communities is substantial: They provide jobs, pay taxes, and support local education, health, and recreation programs. Both big and small businesses donate funds to community projects, encourage employees to volunteer their time, and donate equipment and products for a variety of activities. The Amazon process to select a new second headquarters is an interesting example of how communities may actually compete for some additional business investment.[76] Larger companies can make greater financial contributions. Let's start by taking a quick look at the philanthropic activities of a few US corporations.

Philanthropy

Many large corporations support various charities, an activity called **philanthropy**. Some donate a percentage of sales or profits to worthwhile causes. Other companies have more sophisticated strategies where philanthropy is actually integrated more with the overall corporate strategy and mission. Retailer Target, for example, donates 5 percent of its profits—about $2 million per week—to schools, neighborhoods, and local projects across the country; its store-based grants underwrite programs in early childhood education, the arts, and family-violence prevention.[77] The late actor Paul Newman donated 100 percent of the profits from "Newman's Own" foods (salad dressing, pasta sauce, popcorn, and other products sold in eight countries). His company continues his legacy of donating all profits and distributing them to thousands of organizations, including the Hole in the Wall Gang camps for seriously ill children.[78]

For example, the LEGO Group consistently ranks as a top organization globally because of their commitment to Corporate Social Responsibility. According to their website in 2020, the LEGO Group has their commitment to sustainability broken into three categories: Children, Environment and People. Here are some examples of their specific CSR initiatives:

Children	Environment	People
LEGO is partnered with Unicef to provide safeguards for children and support their wellbeing.	Pledged to implement sustainable packaging by 2025	Through their local community engagement partnerships, LEGO provides opportunities for their employees to volunteer
Support children affected by crisis (e.g. natural disasters, armed conflict)	Pledged to make all core products from sustainable materials by 2030	Pledged to build a diverse and inclusive organization

Figure 4.11: LEGO Group commitment to corporate social responsibility (CSR).

Ethical Organizations

How Can You Recognize an Ethical Organization?

One goal of anyone engaged in business should be to foster **ethical behavior** in the organizational environment. How do we know when an organization is behaving ethically? Most lists of ethical organizational activities include the following criteria:

- Treat employees, customers, investors, and the public fairly.
- Hold every member personally accountable for his or her action.
- Communicate core values and principles to all members.
- Demand and reward integrity from all members in all situations.[79]

Employees at companies that consistently make 3BL Media's annual list of the "100 Best Corporate Citizens" regard the items on the previous list as business as usual in the workplace. Companies at the top of the 2022 list include Owens Corning, PepsiCo, Inc, Apple Inc, HP Inc, and Cisco Systems, Inc..[80]

By contrast, employees with the following attitudes tend to suspect that their employers aren't as ethical as they should be:

- They consistently feel uneasy about the work they do.
- They object to the way they're treated.
- They're uncomfortable about the way coworkers are treated.
- They question the appropriateness of management directives and policies.[81]

The Individual Approach to Ethics

Betty Vinson didn't start out at WorldCom with the intention of going to jail. She undoubtedly knew what the right behavior was, but the bottom line is that she didn't do it. How can you make sure that you do the right thing in the business world? How should you respond to the kinds of challenges that you'll be facing? Because your actions in the business world will be strongly influenced by your moral character, let's begin by assessing your current moral condition. Which of the following best applies to you (select one)?

1. I'm always ethical.
2. I'm mostly ethical.
3. I'm somewhat ethical.
4. I'm seldom ethical.
5. I'm never ethical.

Now that you've placed yourself in one of these categories, here are some general observations. Few people put themselves below the second category. Most of us are ethical most of the time, and most people assign themselves to category number two—"I'm mostly ethical." Why don't more people claim that they're always ethical?

Apparently, most people realize that being ethical all the time takes a great deal of moral energy. If you placed yourself in category number two, ask yourself this question: How can I change my behavior so that I can move up a notch? The answer to this question may be simple. Just ask yourself an easier question: How would I like to be treated in a given situation?[82]

Unfortunately, practicing this philosophy might be easier in your personal life than in the business world. Ethical challenges arise in business because companies, especially large ones, have multiple stakeholders who sometimes make competing demands. Making decisions that affect multiple stakeholders isn't easy even for seasoned managers; and for new entrants to the business world, the task can be extremely daunting. You can, however, get a head start in learning how to make ethical decisions by looking at two types of challenges that you'll encounter in the business world: ethical dilemmas and ethical decisions.

Chapter Video

Foxconn is a major supplier to Apple. All of its factories are in China and Taiwan, although it recently announced building a new one in the United States. Working conditions are much different than in a typical US factory. As you watch the video, think about what responsibilities Apple has in this situation. They don't own Foxconn or its factories, yet their reputation can be nevertheless impacted.

To view this video, visit: https://youtu.be/Jk-xqPKOxl4?t=39

Key Takeaways

- Business ethics is the application of ethical behavior in a business context. Ethical (trustworthy) companies are better able to attract and keep customers, talented employees, and capital.
- Acting ethically in business means more than just obeying laws and regulations. It also means being honest, doing no harm to others, competing fairly, and declining to put your own interests above those of your employer and coworkers.
- In the business world, you'll encounter conflicts of interest: situations in which you'll have to choose between taking action that promotes your personal interest and action that favors the interest of others.
- Corporate social responsibility refers to the approach that an organization takes in balancing its responsibilities toward different stakeholders (owners, employees, customers, and the communities in which they conduct business) when making legal, economic, ethical, and social decisions.
- Managers have several responsibilities: to increase the value of owners' investments through profitable operations, to provide owners and other stakeholders with accurate, reliable financial information, and to safeguard the company's assets and handle its funds in a trustworthy manner.
- Companies have a responsibility to pay appropriate wages and benefits, treat all workers fairly, and provide equal opportunities for all employees. In addition, the must guard workers' safety and health and to provide them with a work environment that's free from sexual harassment.
- Consumers have certain legal rights: to use safe products, to be informed about products, to choose what to buy, and to be heard. Sellers must comply with these requirements.
- Businesspeople face two types of ethical challenges: ethical dilemmas and ethical decisions.
- An ethical dilemma is a morally problematic situation in which you must choose competing and often conflicting options which do not satisfy all stakeholders.
- An ethical decision is one in which there's a right (ethical) choice and a wrong (unethical or downright illegal) choice.

References

Figures

Figure 4.1: Bernie Madoff's mug shot. U.S. Department of Justice. 2009. Public domain. https://commons.wikimedia.org/wiki/File:BernardMadoff.jpg.

Figure 4.2: How to avoid an ethical lapse. Kindred Grey. 2022. CC BY 4.0. https://archive.org/details/4.6_20220714.

Figure 4.3: Caution light. Tom Barrett. 2021. Unsplash license. https://unsplash.com/photos/m8H0Ppm2IVk.

Figure 4.4: Two frogs and two different responses. Kindred Grey. 2022. CC BY 4.0. Added frog by GREY Perspective from Noun Project and from by
Ealancheliyan from Noun Project (Noun Project license). https://archive.org/details/frogs_20220714.

Figure 4.5: How to maintain honesty and integrity. Kindred Grey. 2022. CC BY 4.0. https://archive.org/details/4.2_20220714.

Figure 4.6: Overlap between government and stakeholders. Kindred Grey. 2022. CC BY 4.0. https://archive.org/details/timeline_202207.

Figure 4.7: Top 10 publicly traded companies fighting climate change in 2022. Adapted from https://www.leafscore.com/blog/top-10-publicly-traded-companies-fighting-climate-change-in-2021.

Figure 4.8: Management's relationship with stakeholders. Kindred Grey. 2022. CC BY 4.0. Added house by Alex Muravev from Noun Project, city building by Graphiqu from Noun Project, people by kitzsingmaniiz from Noun Project, and businesswoman by Timothy Miller from Noun Project (Noun Project license). https://archive.org/details/4.3_20220714.

Figure 4.9: Workplace deaths by event or exposure (2020). Kindred Grey. 2022. CC BY 4.0. Data from https://www.bls.gov/news.release/pdf/cfoi.pdf (page 7). https://archive.org/details/4.4_20220714.

Figure 4.10: Workplace deaths by occupation, 2020. Data from https://www.bls.gov/news.release/pdf/cfoi.pdf (page 8).

Figure 4.11: LEGO Group commitment to corporate social responsibility (CSR). Information from https://www.lego.com/en-us/sustainability#:~:text=We%20are%20committed%20to%20protecting,all%20our%20boxes%20by%202025..

Video

Video 1: Foxconn: An Exclusive Inside Look. ABC News. 2012. Copyrighted. https://www.youtube.com/watch?v=Jk-xqPKOxl4&amp=&t=39s

Notes

1. This case is based on Susan Pullman (2003). "How Following Orders Can Harm Your Career." Wall Street Journal. Retrieved from: http://ww2.cfo.com/human-capital-careers/2003/10/how-following-orders-can-harm-your-career/
2. Ibid.
3. Amanda Ripley (2002). "The Night Detective." Time. Retrieved from: http://content.time.com/time/magazine/article/0,9171,1003990,00.html
4. Jeff Clabaugh (2005). "WorldCom's Betty Vinson Gets 5 Months in Jail." Washington Business Journal. Retrieved from: http://www.bizjournals.com/washington/stories/2005/08/01/daily51.html
5. Scott Reeves (2005). "Lies, Damned Lies and Scott Sullivan." Forbes. Retrieved from: http://www.forbes.com/2005/02/17/cx_sr_0217ebbers.html; David A. Andelman (2005). "Scott Sullivan Gets Slap on the Wrist—WorldCom Rate Race." Forbes. Retrieved from: http://www.mindfully.org/Industry/2005/Sullivan-WorldCom-Rat12aug05.htm
6. Susan Pullman (2003). "How Following Orders Can Harm Your Career." Wall Street Journal. Retrieved from: http://ww2.cfo.com/human-capital-careers/2003/10/how-following-orders-can-harm-your-career/
7. David Hancock (2002). "World-Class Scandal at WorldCom." CBS News. Retrieved from: http://www.cbsnews.com/news/world-class-scandal-at-worldcom
8. Time (2009). "Top 10 Crooked CEO's." Retrieved from: http://content.time.com/time/specials/packages/article/0,28804,1903155_1903156_1903160,00.html
9. Fred Langan (2008). "The -billion BMIS Debacle: How a Ponzi Scheme Works." CBC News. Retrieved from: http://www.cbc.ca/news/business/the-50-billion-bmis-debacle-how-a-ponzi-scheme-works-1.709409
10. Ethan Wolff-Mann (2019). "Wells Fargo scandals: The complete list." Yahoo! Finance. Retrieved from: https://finance.yahoo.com/news/wells-fargo-scandals-the-complete-timeline-141213414.html
11. Karpe, Alankar (2015) Being ethical is profitable. Project Management Institute: Newtown Square. and Karim, Khondkar; Suh, SangHyun, and Tang, Jiali (2016) Do ethical firms create value? Social Responsibility Journal v12 n1: 54-68
12. Noble, Safiya Umoja (2018). Algorithms of Oppression: How Search Engines Reinforce Racism. NYU Press: New York.
13. Adrian Gostick and Dana Telford (2003). The Integrity Advantage. Salt Lake City: Gibbs Smith. pp. 3–4.
14. Tamara Kaplan (1998). "The Tylenol Crisis: How Effective Public Relations Saved Johnson & Johnson." Aerobiological Engineering, Inc. Retrieved from: http://www.aerobiologicalengineering.com/wxk116/TylenolMurders/crisis.html
15. Ibid.
16. Yaakov Weber (1999). "CEO Saves Company's Reputation, Products." New Sunday Times. Retrieved from: https://web.archive.org/web/20030712124829/http:/adtimes.nstp.com.my/jobstory/jun13.htm
17. Ibid.
18. McNeil Consumer Healthcare (2011). "Product Recall Information." Retrieved from: http://web.archive.org/web/20110808021741/http://www.mcneilproductrecall.com
19. Bill Berkrot (2010). "J&J Confirms Widely Expanded Contact Lens Recall." Reuters. Retrieved from: http://www.reuters.com/article/us-jandj-recall-idUSTRE6B05G620101201
20. Natasha Singer (2010). "Johnson & Johnson Recalls Hip Implants." New York Times. Retrieved from: http://www.nytimes.com/2010/08/27/business/27hip.html
21. Mina Kimes (2010). "Why J&J's Headache Won't Go Away." Fortune. Retrieved from: http://archive.fortune.com/2010/08/18/news/companies/jnj_drug_recalls.fortune/index.htm
22. Jonathan D. Rockoff and Jon Kamp (2010). "J&J Contact Lenses Recalled." Wall Street Journal. Retrieved from: http://online.wsj.com/article/SB10001424052748703846604575447430303567108.html
23. Natasha Singer (2010). "Johnson & Johnson Recalls Hip Implants." New York Times. Retrieved from: http://www.nytimes.com/2010/08/27/business/27hip.html
24. Mina Kimes (2010). "Why J&J's Headache Won't Go Away." Fortune. Retrieved from: http://archive.fortune.com/2010/08/18/news/companies/jnj_drug_recalls.fortune/index.htm
25. ibid
26. Johnson and Johnson (2010). "Testimony of Ms. Colleen A. Goggins, Worldwide Chairman, Consumer Group, Johnson & Johnson, before the Committee on Oversight and Government Reform, U.S. House of Representatives." Retrieved from: http://www.blogjnj.com/wp-content/uploads/2010/05/Testimony-of-Colleen-A-Goggins2.pdf

27. Jen Christensen (2020). "Johnson & Johnson will stop selling talc-based baby powder." CNN Health. Retrieved from: https://www.cnn.com/2020/05/20/health/johnson-and-johnson-stops-selling-talc-based-baby-powder-trnd/index.html
28. Saul W. Gellerman (2003). "Why 'Good' Managers Make Bad Ethical Choices" in *Harvard Business Review on Corporate Ethics*. Boston: Harvard Business School Press. p. 59.
29. Adrian Gostick and Dana Telford (2003). *The Integrity Advantage*. Salt Lake City: Gibbs Smith. p. 12.
30. Wikipedia (n.d.). Golden Rule. Retrieved from: https://en.wikipedia.org/wiki/Golden_Rule
31. Triple Crown Leadership (2013). Ethical Decision-Making: Simple Tests. Retrieved from: https://triplecrownleadership.com/ethical-decision-making-simple-tests
32. Kym Middleton (2016). "Ethics Explainer: The Sunlight Test." The Ethics Centre. Retrieved from: https://ethics.org.au/ethics-explainer-the-sunlight-test
33. V. Vivekanandan (2013). "Approach to Ethics Paper. Vetrii IAS Academy. Retrieved from: https://issuu.com/vetriias/docs/approach_to_ethics_paper/133
34. Online Ethics Center for Engineering and Science (2004). "Advice from the Texas Instruments Ethics Office: Article Number 280: What do you do when the light turns yellow?" Onlineethics.org. Retrieved from: https://web.archive.org/web/20060517161459/http://onlineethics.org/corp/help.html
35. Ibid. p. 103.
36. Ibid. Adapted from p. 16.
37. Travis H. Brown (2015). "Living Wage vs. Minimum Wage: What's the Difference?" How Money Walks. Retrieved from: https://www.howmoneywalks.com/living-wage-vs-minimum-wage-whats-the-difference/
38. Lawrence Gitman, et al. (2018). "2.1 Understanding Business Ethics," Introduction to Business. OpenStax (CC BY 4.0). Retrieved from: https://openstax.org/books/introduction-business/pages/2-1-understanding-business-ethics. OpenStax *Introduction to Business* may be accessed for free at: https://openstax.org/books/introduction-business/pages/1-introduction.
39. Susan Pulliam and Deborah Solomon (2002). "How Three Unlikely Sleuths Exposed Fraud at WorldCom." Wall Street Journal. Retrieved from: http://www.wsj.com/articles/SB1035929943494003751
40. Gostick and Telford (2003). The Integrity Advantage. Salt Lake City: Gibbs Smith. p. 13.
41. National Whistleblower Center (2002). "Labor Day Report: The National Status of Whistleblower Protection on Labor Day 2002." Retrieved from: https://web.archive.org/web/20060130104004/http://www.whistleblowers.org/labordayreport.htm
42. Paula Dwyer, Dan Carney et al. (2002). "Year of the Whistleblower." BusinessWeek. Retrieved from: http://www.bloomberg.com/news/articles/2002-12-15/year-of-the-whistleblower
43. Scott Waller (2003). "Whistleblower Tells Students to Have Personal Integrity." The (Jackson, MS) Clarion-Ledger. Retrieved from: http://www.yourlawyer.com/articles/title/whistleblower-tells-students-to-have-personal-integrity
44. Gostick and Telford (2003). The Integrity Advantage. Salt Lake City: Gibbs Smith. pp. 98-99.
45. U.S. Securities and Exchange Commission (2021). "SEC Announces Enforcement Results for FY 2021" Retrieved from: https://www.sec.gov/news/press-release/2021-238
46. Lawrence Gitman, et al. (2018)."Ethics in Practice" in Chapter 16 Understanding Financial Management and Securities Markets, Introduction to Business (CC BY 4.0). OpenStax. Retrieved from: https://openstax.org/books/introduction-business/pages/16-7-buying-and-selling-at-securities-exchanges. OpenStax *Introduction to Business* may be accessed for free at: https://openstax.org/books/introduction-business/pages/1-introduction.
47. Office of the Whistleblower (n.d.). Retrieved from: https://www.sec.gov/whistleblower/pressreleases
48. Engleman, Ryan (no date). The Second Industrial Revolution, 1870-1914. U.S. History Scene. Retrieved from https://ushistoryscene.com/article/second-industrial-revolution
49. Engelman, R., Stern, A. E., & Silva, J. O. (2020, October 25). The Second Industrial Revolution, 1870-1914. US History Scene. Retrieved from: https://ushistoryscene.com/article/second-industrial-revolution/
50. U.S. Department of Labor Wage and Hour Division. (2011, May). The Fair Labor Standards Act Of 1938, As Amended. dol.gov. Retrieved from: https://www.dol.gov/sites/dolgov/files/WHD/legacy/files/FairLaborStandAct.pdf
51. Abhinand. (2018, July 7). The Ford Model T Came in Only Black for Several Years - Here's Why! Retrieved from: https://www.drivespark.com/four-wheelers/2018/why-ford-model-t-came-in-black-colour-only-025093.html
52. Encyclopædia Britannica, inc. (n.d.). Civil Rights Act. Encyclopædia Britannica. Retrieved from: https://www.britannica.com/event/Civil-Rights-Act-United-States-1964
53. Nader, Ralph (1972) Unsafe at Any Speed: The Designed-in Dangers of the American Automobile. Grossman: New York.

54. History.com Editors (Ed.). (2010, January 27). Ralph Nader's "Unsafe at Any Speed" Hits Bookstores. History.com. Retrieved from: https://www.history.com/this-day-in-history/unsafe-at-any-speed-hits-bookstores
55. Ibid.
56. 1912-2006. (2021, October 8). Milton Friedman. Econlib. Retrieved from: https://www.econlib.org/library/Enc/bios/Friedman.html
57. Denning, S. (2022, April 14). The Origin of 'the World's Dumbest Idea': Milton Friedman. Forbes. Retrieved from: https://www.forbes.com/sites/stevedenning/2013/06/26/the-origin-of-the-worlds-dumbest-idea-milton-friedman/?sh=c77a732870e8
58. Blokhin, A. (2022, July 13). The Impact of the Sarbanes-Oxley Act of 2002. Investopedia. Retrieved from: https://www.investopedia.com/ask/answers/052815/what-impact-did-sarbanesoxley-act-have-corporate-governance-united-states.asp
59. What is ESG? Definition and Meaning. Market Business News. (2021, August 30). Retrieved from: https://marketbusinessnews.com/financial-glossary/esg-definition-meaning/
60. Green Business Bureau (2022, April 7). Comparing the Carbon Footprint of Small Businesses to Large Corporations. Green Business Bureau. Retrieved from: https://greenbusinessbureau.com/topics/carbon-accounting/comparing-the-carbon-footprint-of-small-businesses-to-large-corporations
61. Porter ME and Kramer MR (2011) The Big Idea: Creating Shared Value. Harvard Business Review v89 n1-2
62. Porter, M. and Kramer, M. (n.d.). Creating Shared Value. FSG Reimagining Social Change. Retrieved from: https://www.fsg.org/resource/creating-shared-value
63. David P. Baron (2003). Business and Its Environment, 4th ed. Upper Saddle River. NJ: Prentice Hall. pp. 650– 52.
64. Labor Law Center, (2022). Law Law Center. Retrieved from: https://www.laborlawcenter.com/state-minimum-wage-rates
65. U.S. Department of Labor (2016). "Minimum Wage Laws in the States." Retrieved from: https://www.dol.gov/whd/minwage/america.htm
66. Ibid.
67. Saul W. Gellerman (2003). "Why 'Good' Managers Make Bad Ethical Choices" in Harvard Business Review on Corporate Ethics. Boston: Harvard Business School Press. pp. 49–66.
68. Ibid. p. 53.
69. Procter & Gamble (2003). *Sustainability Report* 2003. Retrieved from: http://us.pg.com/sustainability/at_a_glance/sustainability_reports
70. Alan Axelrod (2004). *My First Book of Business Ethics*. Philadelphia: Quirk Books. p. 7.
71. U.S. Equal Employment Opportunity Commission (2002). "Facts about Sexual Harassment." Retrieved from: https://www.eeoc.gov/facts/fs-sex.html
72. Joanna Grossman (2002). "Sexual Harassment in the Workplace: Do Employers' Efforts Truly Prevent Harassment, or Just Prevent Liability." FindLaw. Retrieved from: http://writ.news.findlaw.com/grossman/20020507.html
73. Stefanie K. Johnson, Ksenia Keplinger, Jessica F. Kirk and Liza Barnes (2019). "Has Sexual Harassment at Work Decreased Since #MeToo?" Harvard Business Review. Retrieved from: https://hbr.org/2019/07/has-sexual-harassment-at-work-decreased-since-metoo
74. Encyclopædia Britannica, inc. (n.d.). Civil Rights Act. Encyclopædia Britannica. Retrieved from: https://www.britannica.com/event/Civil-Rights-Act-United-States-1964
75. John F. Kennedy (1962). "Special Message to the Congress on Protecting the Consumer Interest." The American Presidency Project. Retrieved from: http://www.presidency.ucsb.edu/ws/?pid=9108
76. Weise, E. (2019, February 14). Amazon HQ2 Timeline: The Winners are New York City and Arlington, Virginia. USA Today. Retrieved from: https://www.usatoday.com/story/tech/science/2018/09/12/timeline-amazons-search-hq-2-its-second-headquarters/1273275002/
77. Target Brands Inc. (2012). " Million Every Week: A Brief History of Target's Community Giving." Target. Retrieved from: https://corporate.target.com/article/2012/10/4-million-every-week-a-brief-history-of-target-s-c
78. Jennifer Barrett (2003). "A Secret Recipe for Success: Paul Newman and A. E. Hotchner Dish Up Management Tips from Newman's Own." Newsweek. Retrieved from: http://www.newsweek.com/secret-recipe-success-133673
79. Alan Axelrod (2004). *My First Book of Business Ethics*. Philadelphia: Quirk Books. p. 7.
80. CR Magazine (2019). "100 Best Corporate Citizens." CR Magazine. Retrieved from https://www.3blassociation.com/files/yMblCg/100BestCorporateCitizens_2019.pdf

81. Alan Axelrod (2004). *My First Book of Business Ethics*. Philadelphia: Quirk Books. p. 7.
82. John C. Maxwell (2003). *There's No Such Thing as "Business Ethics": There's Only One Rule for Making Decisions*. New York: Warner Books. pp. 19–21.

5. Business in a Global Environment

Learning Objectives

- Explain why nations and companies participate in international trade.
- Describe the concepts of absolute and comparative advantage.
- Explain how trade between nations is measured.
- Define importing and exporting.
- Explain how companies enter the international market through licensing agreements or franchises.
- Describe how companies reduce costs through contract manufacturing and outsourcing.
- Explain the purpose of international strategic alliances and joint ventures.
- Understand how US companies expand their businesses through foreign direct investments and international subsidiaries.
- Appreciate how cultural, economic, legal, and political differences between countries create challenges to successful business dealings.
- Describe the ways in which governments and international bodies promote and regulate global trade.
- Discuss the various initiatives designed to reduce international trade barriers and promote free trade.

Do you wear Nike shoes or Timberland boots? Buy groceries at Giant Stores or Stop & Shop? Listen to Halsey, Billie Eilish, or Drake on Spotify? If you answered yes to any of these questions, you're a global business customer. Both Nike and Timberland manufacture most of their products overseas. The Dutch firm Royal Ahold owns all three supermarket chains. And Spotify is a Swedish enterprise.

Figure 5.1: Orchard Road in Singapore.

Take an imaginary walk down Orchard Road, the most fashionable shopping area in Singapore. You'll pass department stores such as Tokyo-based Takashimaya and London's very British Marks & Spencer, both filled with such well-known international labels as Ralph Lauren Polo, Burberry, and Chanel. If you need a break, you can also stop for a latte at Seattle-based Starbucks.

When you're in the Chinese capital of Beijing, don't miss Tiananmen Square. Parked in front of the Great Hall of the People, the seat of Chinese government, are fleets of black Buicks, cars made by General Motors in Flint, Michigan. If you're adventurous enough to find yourself in Faisalabad, a medium-size city in Pakistan, you'll see Hamdard University, located in a refurbished hotel. Step inside its computer labs, and the sensation of being in a faraway place will likely disappear: on the computer screens, you'll recognize the familiar Microsoft flag—the same one emblazoned on screens in Microsoft's hometown of Seattle and just about everywhere else on the planet.

The Globalization of Business

The **globalization of business** is bound to affect you. Not only will you buy products manufactured overseas, but it's highly likely that you'll meet and work with individuals from various countries and cultures as customers, suppliers, colleagues, employees, or employers. The bottom line is that the globalization of world commerce has an impact on all of us. Therefore, it makes sense to learn more about how globalization works. Although globalization has been the trend towards increased connections and interdependence in the world's economies, there has been talk about nationalism from the impact of COVID-19 and trade agreements. However, this has yet to be determined, therefore, this chapter will focus on globalization as defined above.

Never before has business spanned the globe the way it does today. But why is international business important? Why do companies and nations engage in international trade? What strategies do they employ in the global marketplace? How do governments and international agencies promote and regulate international trade? These questions and others will be addressed in this chapter. Let's start by looking at the more specific reasons why companies and nations engage in international trade.

Why Do Nations Trade?

Why does the United States import automobiles, steel, digital phones, and apparel from other countries? Why don't we just make them ourselves? Why do other countries buy wheat, chemicals, machinery, and consulting services from us? Because no national economy produces all the goods and services that its people need. In fact, countries have been trading for thousands of years. Marco Polo established trade between Europe and China in the late thirteenth century, introducing gun powder to China and citrus and spices to Europe.[1] Countries are **importers** when they buy goods and services from other countries; when they sell products to other nations, they're **exporters**. (We'll discuss importing and exporting in greater detail later in the chapter.) The monetary value of international trade is enormous. In 2020, the total value of worldwide trade in merchandise and commercial services was $17.5 trillion. In comparison, this figure stood at around 6.45 trillion US dollars in 2000. The rise in the value of goods exported around the world reflects developments in international trade, globalization, and advances in technology.[2]

Absolute and Comparative Advantage

To understand why certain countries import or export certain products, you need to realize that every country (or region) can't produce the same products. The cost of labor, the availability of natural resources, and the level of know-how vary greatly around the world. Most economists use the concepts of absolute advantage and comparative advantage to explain why countries import some products and export others.

Absolute Advantage

A nation has an **absolute advantage** if (1) it's the only source of a particular product or (2) it can make more of a product using fewer resources than other countries. Because of climate and soil conditions, for example, France had an absolute advantage in wine making until its dominance of worldwide wine production was challenged by the growing wine industries in Italy, Spain, and the United States. Unless an absolute advantage is based on some limited natural resource, it seldom lasts. That's why there are few, if any, examples of absolute advantage in the world today.

Comparative Advantage

How can we predict, for any given country, which products will be made and sold at home, which will be imported, and which will be exported? This question can be answered by looking at the concept of **comparative advantage**, which exists when a country can produce a product at a lower opportunity cost compared to another nation. But what's an opportunity cost? **Opportunity costs** are the products that a country must forego making in order to produce something else. When a country decides to specialize in a particular product, it must sacrifice the production of another product. Countries benefit from specialization—focusing on what they do best, and trading the output to other countries for what those countries do best. The United States, for instance, is increasingly an exporter of knowledge-based products, such as software, movies, music, and professional services (management consulting, financial services, and so forth). America's colleges and universities, therefore, are a source of comparative advantage, and students from all over the world come to the United States for the world's best higher-education system.

France and Italy are centers for fashion and luxury goods and are leading exporters of wine, perfume, and designer clothing. Japan's engineering expertise has given it an edge in such fields as automobiles and consumer electronics. And with large numbers of highly skilled graduates in technology, India has become the world's leader in low-cost, computer-software engineering.

How Do We Measure Trade Between Nations?

To evaluate the nature and consequences of its international trade, a nation looks at two key indicators. We determine a country's **balance of trade** by subtracting the value of its **imports** from the value of its **exports**. If a country sells more products than it buys, it has a favorable balance, called a trade surplus. If it buys more than it sells, it has an unfavorable balance, or a trade deficit.

For many years, the United States has had a **trade deficit**: we buy far more goods from the rest of the world than we sell overseas. This fact shouldn't be surprising. With high income levels, we not only consume a sizable portion of our own domestically produced goods but enthusiastically buy imported goods. Other countries, such as China and Taiwan, which manufacture high volumes for export, have large trade surpluses because they sell far more goods overseas than they buy.

Managing the National Credit Card

Are trade deficits a bad thing? Not necessarily. They can be positive if a country's economy is strong enough both to keep growing and to generate the jobs and incomes that permit its citizens to buy the best the world has to offer. That was certainly the case in the United States in the 1990s. Some experts, however, are alarmed at our trade deficit. Investment guru Warren Buffet, for example, cautions that no country can continuously sustain large and burgeoning trade deficits. Why not? Because creditor nations will eventually stop taking IOUs from debtor nations, and when that happens, the national spending spree will have to cease. "Our national credit card," he warns, "allows us to charge truly breathtaking amounts. But that card's credit line is not limitless."[3]

By the same token, **trade surpluses** aren't necessarily good for a nation's consumers. Japan's export-fueled economy produced high economic growth in the 1970s and 1980s. But most domestically made consumer goods were priced at artificially high levels inside Japan itself—so high, in fact, that many Japanese traveled overseas to buy the electronics and other high-quality goods on which Japanese trade was dependent.

CD players and televisions were significantly cheaper in Honolulu or Los Angeles than in Tokyo. How did this situation come about? Though Japan manufactures a variety of goods, many of them are made for export. To secure shares in international markets, Japan prices its exported goods competitively. Inside Japan, because competition is limited, producers can put artificially high prices on Japanese-made goods. Due to a number of factors (high demand for a limited supply of imported goods, high shipping and distribution costs, and other costs incurred by importers in a nation that tends to protect its own industries), imported goods are also expensive.[4]

Balance of Payments

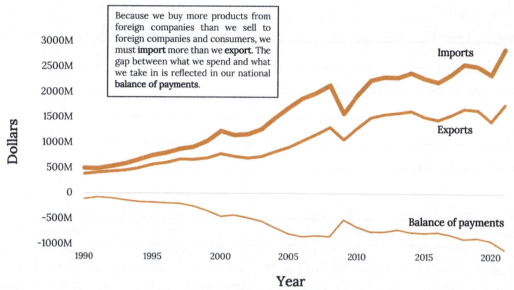

Figure 5.2: Imports, exports, and balance of payments (1990-2021).

The second key measure of the effectiveness of international trade is **balance of payments**: the difference, over a period of time, between the total flow of money coming into a country and the total flow of money going out. As in its balance of trade, the biggest factor in a country's balance of payments is the money that flows as a result of imports and exports. But balance of payments includes other cash inflows and outflows, such as cash received from or paid for foreign investment, loans, tourism, military expenditures, and foreign aid. For example, if a US company buys some real estate in a foreign country, that investment counts in the US balance of payments, but not in its balance of trade, which measures only import and export transactions. In the long run, having an unfavorable balance of payments can negatively affect the stability of a country's currency. The United States has experienced unfavorable balances of payments since the 1970s which has forced the government to cover its debt by borrowing from other countries.[5] Figure 5.2 provides a brief historical overview to illustrate the relationship between the United States' balance of trade and its balance of payments.

Opportunities in International Business

The fact that nations exchange billions of dollars in goods and services each year demonstrates that international trade makes good economic sense. For a company wishing to expand beyond national borders, there are a variety of ways it can get involved in international business. Let's take a closer look at the more popular ones.

Figure 5.3: Key strategies for reaching global markets.

Importing and Exporting

Importing (buying products overseas and reselling them in one's own country) and **exporting** (selling domestic products to foreign customers) are the oldest and most prevalent forms of international trade. For many companies, importing is the primary link to the global market. American food and beverage wholesalers, for instance, import for resale in US supermarkets the bottled waters Evian and Fiji from their sources in the French Alps and the Fiji Islands respectively.[6] Other companies get into the global arena by identifying an international market for their products and becoming exporters. The Chinese, for instance, are fond of fast foods cooked in soybean oil. Because they also have an increasing appetite for meat, they need high-protein soybeans to raise livestock.[7] In 2020, the value of U.S. soybean exports to the world reached a record $25.7 billion, up nearly 40 percent ($7 billion) by value and up 23 percent (11.9 million tons) by volume from the prior year. Exports to China jumped $6.2 billion (up 77 percent) from last year, significantly contributing to the rise in total exports. The total value of U.S. soybean exports was more than $4 billion (18 percent) above the 5-year average of 2013-2017.[8]

Licensing and Franchising

A company that wants to get into an international market quickly while taking only limited financial and legal risks might consider **licensing agreements** with foreign companies. An international licensing agreement allows a foreign company (the licensee) to sell the products of a producer (the licensor) or to use its intellectual property (such as patents, trademarks, copyrights) in exchange for what is known as royalty fees. Here's how it works: You own a company in the United States that sells coffee-flavored popcorn. You're sure that your product would be a big hit in Japan, but you don't have the resources to set up a factory or sales office in that country. You can't make the popcorn here and ship it to Japan because it would get stale. So you enter into a licensing agreement with a Japanese company that allows your licensee to manufacture coffee-flavored popcorn using your special process and to sell it in Japan under your brand name. In exchange, the Japanese licensee would pay you a royalty fee—perhaps a percentage of each sale or a fixed amount per unit.

Another popular way to expand overseas is to sell **franchises**. Under an international franchise agreement, a company (the franchiser) grants a foreign company (the franchisee) the right to use its brand name and to sell its products or services. The franchisee is responsible for all operations but agrees to operate according to a business model established by the franchiser. In turn, the franchiser usually provides advertising, training, and new-product assistance. Franchising is a natural form of global expansion for companies that operate domestically according to a franchise model, including restaurant chains, such as McDonald's and Kentucky Fried Chicken, and hotel chains, such as Holiday Inn and Best Western.

Figure 5.4: The franchise Marriott in Budapest.

Contract Manufacturing and Outsourcing

Because of high domestic labor costs, many US companies manufacture their products in countries where labor costs are lower. This arrangement is called international **contract manufacturing**, a form of **outsourcing**. A US company might contract with a local company in a foreign country to manufacture one of its products. It will, however, retain control of product design and development and put its own label on the finished product. Contract manufacturing is quite common in the US apparel business, with most American brands being made in a number of Asian countries, including China, Vietnam, Indonesia, and India.[9]

Thanks to twenty-first-century information technology, non-manufacturing functions can also be outsourced to nations with lower labor costs. US companies increasingly draw on a vast supply of relatively inexpensive skilled labor to perform various business services, such as software development, accounting, and claims processing. For years, American insurance companies have processed much of their claims-related paperwork in Ireland. With a large, well-educated population with English language skills, India has become a center for software development and customer-call centers for American companies. In the case of India, as you can see in figure 5.5, the attraction is not only a large pool of knowledge workers but also significantly lower wages.

Occupation	Hourly wage in the US (per year)	Hourly wage in India (per year)
Accountant	$23.92 ($53,498)	$1.60 ($3,495)
Information technology analyst	$31.23 ($75,711)	$2.74 ($6,448)
Cleaner	$15.42 ($36,009)	$1.12 ($2,552)

Figure 5.5: Hourly wage comparisons for U.S. and India.

Strategic Alliances and Joint Ventures

What if a company wants to do business in a foreign country but lacks the expertise or resources? Or what if the target nation's government doesn't allow foreign companies to operate within its borders unless it has a local partner? In these cases, a firm might enter into a strategic alliance with a local company or even with the government itself.

A **strategic alliance** is an agreement between two companies (or a company and a nation) to pool resources in order to achieve business goals that benefit both partners. For example, Korean automaker Hyundai Motor Co agreed to jointly develop electric vehicles with California startup Canoo in addition to investing $110 million in UK startup Arrival to jointly develop electric commercial vehicles.[10]

An alliance can serve a number of purposes:

- Enhancing marketing efforts
- Building sales and market share
- Improving products
- Reducing production and distribution costs
- Sharing technology

Alliances range in scope from informal cooperative agreements to **joint ventures**—alliances in which the partners fund a separate entity (perhaps a partnership or a corporation) to manage their joint operation. Magazine publisher Hearst, for example, has joint ventures with companies in several countries. So, young women in Israel can read Cosmo Israel in Hebrew, and Russian women can pick up a Russian-language version of Cosmo that meets their needs. The US edition serves as a starting point to which nationally appropriate material is added in each different nation. This approach allows Hearst to sell the magazine in more than 50 countries.[11]

Foreign Direct Investment and Subsidiaries

Many of the approaches to global expansion that we've discussed so far allow companies to participate in international markets without investing in foreign plants and facilities. As markets expand, however, a firm might decide to enhance its competitive advantage by making a direct investment in operations conducted in another country. **Foreign direct investment** (FDI) refers to the formal establishment of business operations on foreign soil—the building of factories, sales offices, and distribution networks to serve local markets in a nation other than the company's home country. On the other hand, offshoring occurs when the facilities set up in the foreign country replace US manufacturing facilities and are used to produce goods that will be sent back to the United States for sale. Shifting production to low-wage countries is often criticized as it results in the loss of jobs for US workers.[12]

FDI is generally the most expensive commitment that a firm can make to an overseas market, and it's typically driven by the size and attractiveness of the target market. For example, German and Japanese automakers, such as BMW, Mercedes, Toyota, and Honda, have made serious commitments to the US market: most of the cars and trucks that they build in plants in the South and Midwest are destined for sale in the United States.

A common form of FDI is the **foreign subsidiary**: an independent company owned by a foreign firm (called the parent). This approach to going international not only gives the parent company full access to local markets but also exempts it from any laws or regulations that may hamper the activities of foreign firms. The parent company has tight control over the operations of a subsidiary, but while senior managers from the parent company often oversee operations, many managers and employees are citizens of the host country. Not surprisingly, most very large firms have foreign subsidiaries. IBM and Coca-Cola, for example, have both had success in the Japanese market through their foreign subsidiaries (IBM-Japan and Coca-Cola-Japan). FDI goes in the other direction, too, and many companies operating in the United States are in fact subsidiaries of foreign firms. Gerber Products, for example, is a subsidiary of the Swiss company Novartis, while Stop & Shop and Giant Food Stores belong to the Dutch company Royal Ahold. Where does most FDI capital end up? Figure 5.6 provides an overview of amounts, destinations (high to low income countries), and trends.

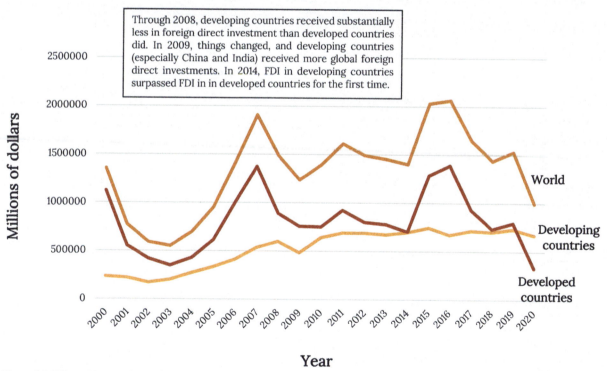

Figure 5.6: *Where FDI goes (2000–2020).*

Business in a Global Environment | 93

An interactive H5P element has been excluded from this version of the text. You can view it online here: https://pressbooks.lib.vt.edu/fundamentalsofbusiness4e/?p=75#h5p-13

All these strategies have been employed successfully in global business. But success in international business involves more than finding the best way to reach international markets. Global business is a complex, risky endeavor. Over time, many large companies reach the point of becoming truly multi-national.

Company	Industry	Headquarters	Revenue in 2015 (in billions)	Revenue in 2021 (in billions)
1. Walmart	General merchandise	USA	485.7	559.2
2. State Grid	Utilities	China	339.4	386.6
3. Amazon	Internet services and retailing	USA	89.0	386.1
4. China National Petroleum	Petroleum	China	428.6	284.0
5. Sinopec Group	Petroleum	China	446.8	283.8
6. Apple	Computers	USA	182.8	274.5
7. CVS Health	Health services	USA	139.4	268.7
8. UnitedHealth Group	Healthcare	USA	130.5	257.1
9. Toyota Motor	Automobile	Japan	247.7	256.7
10. Volkswagen	Automobile	Germany	268.6	254.0
11. Berkshire Hathaway	Insurance	USA	194.7	245.5
12. McKesson	Healthcare	USA	181.2	238.2
13. China State Construction Engineering	Construction	China	129.9	234.4
14. Saudi Aramco	Petroleum	Petroleum	N/A*	229.8
15. Samsung Electronics	Electronics	South Korea	195.8	200.7

Figure 5.7: Fortune top 15 multinational firms by revenue (2021).
*Saudi Aramco released their first financial statement in 2018.

Multinational Corporations

A company that operates in many countries is called a **multinational corporation** (MNC). Fortune magazine's roster of the top 500 MNCs speaks for the growth of non-US businesses. Five of the top 10 MNCs are headquartered in the US (see figure 5.7 above): Wal-Mart (number 1), Amazon, Apple, CVS Health and UnitedHealth Group. Two others are in the top 15: Berkshire Hathaway and McKesson. The others are non-US firms. Interestingly, of the 15 top companies, three are energy suppliers (in 2018, there were seven listed in the Top 15), two are motor vehicle companies, and two are consumer electronics or computer companies. Also interesting is the difference between company revenues and profits: the list would look quite different arranged by profits instead of revenues!

MNCs often adopt the approach encapsulated in the motto "Think globally, act locally." They often adjust their operations, products, marketing, and distribution to mesh with the environments of the countries in which they operate. Because they understand that a "one-size-fits-all" mentality doesn't make good business sense when they're trying to sell products in different markets, they're willing to accommodate cultural and economic differences. Increasingly, MNCs supplement their mainstream product line with products designed for local markets. Coca-Cola, for example, produces coffee and citrus-juice drinks developed specifically for the Japanese market.[13] When Nokia and Motorola design cell phones, they're often geared to local tastes in color, size, and other features. For example, Nokia introduced a cell phone for the rural Indian consumer that has a dust-resistant keypad, anti-slip grip, and a built-in flashlight.[14] McDonald's provides a vegetarian menu in India, where religious convictions affect the demand for beef and pork.[15] In Germany, McDonald's caters to local tastes by offering beer in some restaurants and a Shrimp Burger in Hong Kong and Japan.[16]

Likewise, many MNCs have made themselves more sensitive to local market conditions by decentralizing their decision making. While corporate headquarters still maintain a fair amount of control, home-country managers keep a suitable distance by relying on modern telecommunications. Today, fewer managers are dispatched from headquarters; MNCs depend instead on local talent. Not only does decentralized organization speed up and improve decision making, but it also allows an MNC to project the image of a local company. IBM, for instance, has been quite successful in the Japanese market because local customers and suppliers perceive it as a Japanese company. Crucial to this perception is the fact that the vast majority of IBM's Tokyo employees, including top leadership, are Japanese nationals.[17]

Criticism of MNCs

The global reach of MNCs is a source of criticism as well as praise. Critics argue that they often destroy the livelihoods of home-country workers by moving jobs to developing countries where workers are willing to labor under poor conditions and for less pay. They also contend that traditional lifestyles and values are being weakened, and even destroyed, as global brands foster a global culture of American movies; fast food; and cheap, mass-produced consumer products. Still others claim that the demand of MNCs for constant economic growth and cheaper access to natural resources do irreversible damage to the physical environment. All these negative consequences, critics maintain, stem from the abuses of international trade—from the policy of placing profits above people, on a global scale. These views surfaced in violent street demonstrations in Seattle in 1999 and Genoa, Italy, in 2000, and since then, meetings of the International Monetary Fund (IMF) and World Bank have regularly been assailed by protestors.

In Defense of MNCs

Supporters of MNCs respond that huge corporations deliver better, cheaper products for customers everywhere; create jobs; and raise the standard of living in developing countries. They also argue that globalization increases cross-cultural understanding. Anne O. Kruger, first deputy managing director of the IMF, says the following:

> "The impact of the faster growth on living standards has been phenomenal. We have observed the increased well-being of a larger percentage of the world's population by a greater increment than ever before in history. Growing incomes give people the ability to spend on things other than basic food and shelter, in particular on things such as education and health. This ability, combined with the sharing among nations of medical and scientific advances, has transformed life in many parts of the developing world.
>
> Infant mortality has declined from 180 per 1,000 births in 1950 to 60 per 1,000 births. Literacy rates have risen from an average of 40 percent in the 1950s to over 70 percent today. World poverty has declined, despite still-high population growth in the developing world."[18]

The Global Business Environment

In the classic movie *The Wizard of Oz*, a magically misplaced Midwest farm girl takes a moment to survey the bizarre landscape of Oz and then comments to her little dog, "I don't think we're in Kansas anymore, Toto." That sentiment probably echoes the reaction of many businesspeople who find themselves in the midst of international ventures for the first time. The differences between the foreign landscape and the one with which they're familiar are often huge and multifaceted. Some are quite obvious, such as differences in language, currency, and everyday habits (say, using chopsticks instead of silverware). But others are subtle, complex, and sometimes even hidden.

Success in international business means understanding a wide range of cultural, economic, legal, and political differences between countries. Let's look at some of the more important of these differences.

The Cultural Environment

Even when two people from the same country communicate, there's always a possibility of misunderstanding. When people from different countries get together, that possibility increases substantially. Differences in communication styles reflect differences in culture: the system of shared beliefs, values, customs, and behaviors that govern the interactions of members of a society. Cultural differences create challenges to successful international business dealings. Let's look at a few of these challenges.

Language

English is the international language of business. The natives of such European countries as France and Spain certainly take pride in their own languages and cultures, but nevertheless English is the business language of the European community.

Whereas only a few educated Europeans have studied Italian or Norwegian, most have studied English. Similarly, on the South Asian subcontinent, where hundreds of local languages and dialects are spoken, English is the official language. In most corners of the world, English-only speakers—such as most Americans—have no problem finding competent translators and interpreters. So why is language an issue for English speakers doing business in the global marketplace? In many countries, only members of the educated classes speak English. The larger population—which is usually the market you want to tap—speaks the local tongue. Advertising messages and sales appeals must take this fact into account. More than one English translation of an advertising slogan has resulted in a humorous (and perhaps serious) blunder. Some classics are listed in figure 5.8.

- In Belgium, the translation of the slogan of an American auto-body company, "Body by Fisher," came out as "Corpse by Fisher."
- Translated into German, the slogan "Come Alive with Pepsi" became "Come out of the grave with Pepsi."
- A U.S. computer company in Indonesia translated "software" as "underwear."
- A German chocolate product called "Zit" didn't sell well in the United States.
- An English-speaking car-wash company in Francophone, Quebec advertised itself as a "lavement d'auto" ("car enema") instead of the correct "lavage d'auto."
- One false word in a Mexican commercial for an American shirt maker changed "When I used this shirt, I felt good" to "Until I used this shirt, I felt good."
- In the 1970s, GM's Chevy Nova didn't get on the road in Puerto Rico, in part because Nova in Spanish means "It doesn't go."
- A U.S. appliance ad fizzled in the Middle East because it showed a well-stocked refrigerator featuring a large ham, thus offending the sensibilities of Muslim consumers, who don't eat pork.

Figure 5.8: Lost in translation.

Furthermore, relying on translators and interpreters puts you as an international businessperson at a disadvantage. You're privy only to interpretations of the messages that you're getting, and this handicap can result in a real competitive problem. Maybe you'll misread the subtler intentions of the person with whom you're trying to conduct business. The best way to combat this problem is to study foreign languages. Most people appreciate some effort to communicate in their local language, even on the most basic level. They even appreciate mistakes you make resulting from a desire to demonstrate your genuine interest in the language of your counterparts in foreign countries. The same principle goes doubly when you're introducing yourself to non-English speakers in the United States. Few things work faster to encourage a friendly atmosphere than a native speaker's willingness to greet a foreign guest in the guest's native language.

Time and Sociability

Americans take for granted many of the cultural aspects of our business practices. Most of our meetings, for instance, focus on business issues, and we tend to start and end our meetings on schedule. These habits stem from a broader cultural preference: we don't like to waste time. (It was an American, Benjamin Franklin, who coined the phrase "Time is money.") This preference, however, is by no means universal. The expectation that meetings will start on time and adhere to precise agendas is common in parts of Europe (especially the Germanic countries), as well as in the United States, but elsewhere—say, in Latin America and the Middle East—people are often late to meetings and it is an acceptable custom.

High- and Low-Context Cultures

Likewise, don't expect businesspeople from these regions—or businesspeople from most of Mediterranean Europe, for that matter—to "get down to business" as soon as a meeting has started. They'll probably ask about your health and that of your family, inquire whether you're enjoying your visit to their country, suggest local foods, and generally appear to be avoiding serious discussion at all costs. For Americans, such topics are conducive to nothing but idle chitchat, but in certain cultures, getting started this way is a matter of simple politeness and hospitality and expected.

Intercultural Communication

Different cultures have different communication styles—a fact that can take some getting used to. For example, degrees of animation in expression can vary from culture to culture. Southern Europeans and Middle Easterners are quite animated, favoring expressive body language along with hand gestures and raised voices. Northern Europeans are far more reserved. The English, for example, are famous for their understated style and the Germans for their formality in most business settings. In addition, the distance at which one feels comfortable when talking with someone varies by culture. People from the Middle East like to converse from a distance of a foot or less, while Americans prefer more personal space.

Finally, while people in some cultures prefer to deliver direct, clear messages, others use language that's subtler or more indirect. North Americans and most Northern Europeans fall into the former category and many Asians into the latter. But even within these categories, there are differences. Though typically polite, Chinese and Koreans are extremely direct in expression, while Japanese are indirect: They use vague language and avoid saying "no" even if they do not intend to do what you ask. They worry that turning someone down will result in their "losing face," i.e., an embarrassment or loss of credibility, and so they avoid doing this in public.

In summary, learn about a country's culture and use your knowledge to help improve the quality of your business dealings. Learn to value the subtle differences among cultures, but don't allow cultural stereotypes to dictate how you interact with people from any culture. Treat each person as an individual and spend time getting to know what he or she is about.

The Economic Environment

If you plan to do business in a foreign country, you need to know its level of economic development. You also should be aware of factors influencing the value of its currency and the impact that changes in that value will have on your profits.

Economic Development

If you don't understand a nation's level of economic development, you'll have trouble answering some basic questions, such as: Will consumers in this country be able to afford the product I want to sell? Will it be possible to make a reasonable profit? A country's level of economic development can be evaluated by estimating the annual income earned per citizen. The World Bank, which lends money for improvements in underdeveloped nations, divides countries into four income categories:

World Bank Country and Lending Groups (by Gross National Income per Capita 2021)[19]

- High income—$12,536 or higher (United States, Germany, Japan)
- Upper-middle income—$4,046 to $12,535 (China, South Africa, Mexico)
- Lower-middle income—$1,036 to $4,045 (Kenya, Philippines, India)
- Low income—$1,035 or less (Afghanistan, South Sudan, Haiti)

Note that even though a country has a low annual income per citizen, it can still be an attractive place for doing business. India, for example, is a lower-middle-income country, yet it has a population of a billion, and a segment of that population is well educated—an appealing feature for many business initiatives.

The long-term goal of many countries is to move up the economic development ladder. Some factors conducive to economic growth include a reliable banking system, a strong stock market, and government policies to encourage investment and competition while discouraging corruption. It's also important that a country have a strong infrastructure—its systems of communications (telephone, Internet, television, newspapers), transportation (roads, railways, airports), energy (gas and electricity, power plants), and social facilities (schools, hospitals). These basic systems will help countries attract foreign investors, which can be crucial to economic development.

Currency Valuations and Exchange Rates

If every nation used the same currency, international trade and travel would be a lot easier. Of course, this is not the case. There are around 175 currencies in the world: Some you've heard of, such as the British pound; others are likely unknown to you, such as the manat, the official currency of Azerbaijan. If you were in Azerbaijan you would exchange your US dollars for Azerbaijan manats. The day's foreign exchange rate will tell you how much one currency is worth relative to another currency and so determine how many manats you will receive. If you have traveled abroad, you already have personal experience with the impact of exchange rate movements.

The Legal and Regulatory Environment

One of the more difficult aspects of doing business globally is dealing with vast differences in legal and regulatory environments. The United States, for example, has an established set of laws and regulations that provide direction to businesses operating within its borders. But because there is no global legal system, key areas of business law—for example, contract provisions and copyright protection—can be treated in different ways in different countries. Companies doing international business often face many inconsistent laws and regulations. To navigate this sea of confusion, American business people must know and follow both US laws and regulations and those of nations in which they operate.

Business history is filled with stories about American companies that have stumbled in trying to comply with foreign laws and regulations. Coca-Cola, for example, ran afoul of Italian law when it printed its ingredients list on the bottle cap rather than on the bottle itself. Italian courts ruled that the labeling was inadequate because most people throw the cap away.[20]

One approach to dealing with local laws and regulations is hiring lawyers from the host country who can provide advice on legal issues. Another is working with local businesspeople who have experience in complying with regulations and overcoming bureaucratic obstacles.

Foreign Corrupt Practices Act

One U.S. law that creates unique challenges for American firms operating overseas is the Foreign Corrupt Practices Act, which prohibits the distribution of bribes and other favors in the conduct of business. Unfortunately, though they're illegal in this country, such tactics as kickbacks and bribes are business-as-usual in many nations. According to some experts, American businesspeople are at a competitive disadvantage if they're prohibited from giving bribes or undercover payments to foreign officials or business people who expect them. In theory, because the Foreign Corrupt Practices Act warns foreigners that Americans can't give bribes, they'll eventually stop expecting them.

Where are American businesspeople most likely and least likely to encounter bribe requests and related forms of corruption? Transparency International, an independent German-based organization, annually rates nations according to "perceived corruption," (see figure 5.9) which it defines as "the abuse of entrusted power for private gain."[21]

Rank	Country	CPI score
1	Denmark	88
1	Finland	88
1	New Zealand	88
7	Switzerland	84
11	United Kingdom	78
13	Canada	74
27	United States	67
124	Mexico	31
174	North Korea	16
178	Syria	13
180	South Sudan	11

Figure 5.9: Corruption perceptions around the world (2021). A score of 100 is perfect, and anything below 30 means that corruption is considered rampant. Note that since 2015, the United States has dropped 9 points on the CPI scale.

Trade Controls

The debate about the extent to which countries should control the flow of foreign goods and investments across their borders is as old as international trade itself. Governments continue to control trade. To better understand how and why, let's examine a hypothetical case. Suppose you're in charge of a small country in which people do two things—grow food and make clothes. Because the quality of both products is high and the prices are reasonable, your consumers are happy to buy locally made food and clothes. But one day, a farmer from a nearby country crosses your border with several wagonloads of wheat to sell. On the same day, a foreign clothes maker arrives with a large shipment of clothes. These two entrepreneurs want to sell food and clothes in your country at prices below those that local consumers now pay for domestically made food and clothes. At first, this seems like a good deal for your consumers: they won't have to pay as much for food and clothes. But then you remember all the people in your country who grow food and make clothes. If no one buys their goods (because the imported goods are cheaper), what will happen to their livelihoods? And if many people become unemployed, what will happen to your national economy? That's when you decide to protect your farmers and clothes makers by setting up trade rules. Maybe you'll increase the prices of imported goods by adding a tax to them; you might even make the tax so high that they're more expensive than your homemade goods. Or perhaps you'll help your farmers grow food more cheaply by giving them financial help to defray their costs. The government payments that you give to the farmers to help offset some of their costs of production are called **subsidies**. These subsidies will allow the farmers to lower the price of their goods to a point below that of imported competitors' goods. What's even better is that the lower costs will allow the farmers to export their own goods at attractive, competitive prices.

The United States has a long history of subsidizing farmers. Subsidy programs guarantee farmers (including large corporate farms) a certain price for their crops, regardless of the market price. This guarantee ensures stable income in the farming community but can have a negative impact on the world economy. How? Critics argue that in allowing American farmers to export crops at artificially low prices, US agricultural subsidies permit them to compete unfairly with farmers in developing countries. A reverse situation occurs in the steel industry, in which a number of countries—China, Japan, Russia, Germany, and Brazil—subsidize domestic producers.

U.S. trade unions charge that this practice gives an unfair advantage to foreign producers and hurts the American steel industry, which can't compete on price with subsidized imports.

Whether they push up the price of imports or push down the price of local goods, such initiatives will help locally produced goods compete more favorably with foreign goods. Both strategies are forms of trade controls—policies that restrict free trade. Because they protect domestic industries by reducing foreign competition, the use of such controls is often called **protectionism**. Though there's considerable debate over the pros and cons of this practice, all countries engage in it to some extent. Before debating the issue, however, let's learn about the more common types of trade restrictions: tariffs, quotas, and, embargoes.

Tariffs

Tariffs are taxes on imports. Because they raise the price of the foreign-made goods, they make them less competitive. The United States, for example, protects domestic makers of synthetic knitted shirts by imposing a stiff tariff of 32.5 percent on imports.[22] Tariffs are also used to raise revenue for a government. Shoe imports alone are worth $2.7 billion annually to the federal government.[23]

In 2018 and 2019, the United States government implemented a round of four different tariffs meant to reduce the trade deficit along with punishing China for alleged unfair trading practices and intellectual property theft. The US imposed tariffs on more than $360 billion worth of Chinese goods which then triggered a similar response from the Chinese government with tariffs on more than $110 billon of US made products. This US–China trade war led to uncertainties not only in both markets but globally as well. Finally, in 2020, the United States and China reached an historic and enforceable agreement on a Phase One trade deal that requires structural reforms and other changes to China's economic and trade regime in the areas of intellectual property, technology transfer, agriculture, financial services, and currency and foreign exchange.[24]

Quotas

A **quota** imposes limits on the quantity of a good that can be imported over a period of time. Quotas are used to protect specific industries, usually new industries or those facing strong competitive pressure from foreign firms. US import quotas take two forms. An absolute quota fixes an upper limit on the amount of a good that can be imported during the given period. A tariff-rate quota permits the import of a specified quantity and then adds a high import tax once the limit is reached.

Sometimes quotas protect one group at the expense of another. To protect sugar beet and sugar cane growers, for instance, the United States imposes a tariff-rate quota on the importation of sugar—a policy that has driven up the cost of sugar to two to three times world prices.[25] These artificially high prices push up costs for American candy makers, some of whom have moved their operations elsewhere, taking high-paying manufacturing jobs with them. Life Savers, for example, were made in the United States for 90 years but are now produced in Canada, where the company saves $9 million annually on the cost of sugar.[26]

An extreme form of quota is the **embargo**, which, for economic or political reasons, bans the import or export of certain goods to or from a specific country. The United States, for example, bans nearly every commodity originating in Cuba, although this may soon change.

Dumping

A common political rationale for establishing tariffs and quotas is the need to combat **dumping**: the practice of selling exported goods below the price that producers would normally charge in their home markets (and often below the cost of producing the goods). Usually, nations resort to this practice to gain entry and market share in foreign markets, but it can also be used to sell off surplus or obsolete goods. Dumping creates unfair competition for domestic industries, and governments are justifiably concerned when they suspect foreign countries of dumping products on their markets. They often retaliate by imposing punitive tariffs that drive up the price of the imported goods.

The Pros and Cons of Trade Controls

Opinions vary on government involvement in international trade. Proponents of controls contend that there are a number of legitimate reasons why countries engage in protectionism. Sometimes they restrict trade to protect specific industries and their workers from foreign competition—agriculture, for example, or steel making. At other times, they restrict imports to give new or struggling industries a chance to get established. Finally, some countries use protectionism to shield industries that are vital to their national defense, such as shipbuilding and military hardware.

Despite valid arguments made by supporters of trade controls, most experts believe that such restrictions as tariffs and quotas—as well as practices that don't promote level playing fields, such as subsidies and dumping—are detrimental to the world economy. Without impediments to trade, countries can compete freely. Each nation can focus on what it does best and bring its goods to a fair and open world market. When this happens, the world will prosper, or so the argument goes. International trade is certainly heading in the direction of unrestricted markets.

 An interactive H5P element has been excluded from this version of the text. You can view it online here: https://pressbooks.lib.vt.edu/fundamentalsofbusiness4e/?p=75#h5p-14

Reducing International Trade Barriers

A number of organizations work to ease barriers to trade, and more countries are joining together to promote trade and mutual economic benefits. Let's look at some of these important initiatives.

Trade Agreements and Organizations

Free trade is encouraged by a number of agreements and organizations set up to monitor trade policies. The two most important are the General Agreement on Tariffs and Trade and the World Trade Organization.

General Agreement on Tariffs and Trade

After the Great Depression and World War II, most countries focused on protecting home industries, so international trade was hindered by rigid trade restrictions. To rectify this situation, 23 nations joined together in 1947 and signed the **General Agreement on Tariffs and Trade** (GATT), which encouraged free trade by regulating and reducing tariffs and by providing a forum for resolving trade disputes.

The highly successful initiative achieved substantial reductions in tariffs and quotas, and in 1995 its members founded the World Trade Organization to continue the work of GATT in overseeing global trade.

World Trade Organization

Based in Geneva, Switzerland, with nearly 150 members, the **World Trade Organization** (WTO) encourages global commerce and lower trade barriers, enforces international rules of trade, and provides a forum for resolving disputes. It is empowered, for instance, to determine whether a member nation's trade policies have violated the organization's rules, and it can direct "guilty" countries to remove disputed barriers (though it has no legal power to force any country to do anything it doesn't want to do). If the guilty party refuses to comply, the WTO may authorize the plaintiff nation to erect trade barriers of its own, generally in the form of tariffs.

Affected members aren't always happy with WTO actions. For example, the European Commission is having to wait on a WTO action regarding whether it can impose tariffs against the United States over subsidies for Boeing (BA.N). They claim it is unjustified and harms the bloc's right to retaliate.[27]

Financial Support for Emerging Economies: The IMF and the World Bank

A key to helping developing countries become active participants in the global marketplace is providing financial assistance. Offering monetary assistance to some of the poorest nations in the world is the shared goal of two organizations: the International Monetary Fund and the World Bank. These organizations, to which most countries belong, were established in 1944 to accomplish different but complementary purposes.

The International Monetary Fund

The International Monetary Fund (IMF) loans money to countries with troubled economies, such as Mexico in the 1980s and mid-1990s and Russia and Argentina in the late 1990s. There are, however, strings attached to IMF loans: in exchange for relief in times of financial crisis, borrower countries must institute sometimes painful financial and economic reforms. In the 1980s, for example, Mexico received financial relief from the IMF on the condition that it privatize and deregulate certain industries and liberalize trade policies. The government was also required to cut back expenditures for such services as education, health care, and workers' benefits.[28]

The World Bank

The World Bank is an important source of economic assistance for poor and developing countries. With backing from wealthy donor countries (such as the United States, Japan, Germany, and United Kingdom), the World Bank has committed $42.5 billion in loans, grants, and guarantees to some of the world's poorest nations.[29] Loans are made to help countries improve the lives of the poor through community-support programs designed to provide health, nutrition, education, infrastructure, and other social services.

Trading Blocs: NAFTA and the European Union

So far, our discussion has suggested that global trade would be strengthened if there were no restrictions on it—if countries didn't put up barriers to trade or perform special favors for domestic industries. The complete absence of barriers is an ideal state of affairs that we haven't yet attained. In the meantime, economists and policymakers tend to focus on a more practical question: Can we achieve the goal of free trade on the regional level? To an extent, the answer is yes. In certain parts of the world, groups of countries have joined together to allow goods and services to flow without restrictions across their mutual borders. Such groups are called **trading blocs**. Let's examine two of the most powerful trading blocs—NAFTA and the European Union.

North American Free Trade Association

Figure 5.10: A business lobby in Ottawa, Canada.

The North American Free Trade Association (NAFTA) is an agreement among the governments of the United States, Canada, and Mexico to open their borders to unrestricted trade. The effect of this agreement is that three very different economies are combined into one economic zone with almost no trade barriers. From the northern tip of Canada to the southern tip of Mexico, each country benefits from the comparative advantages of its partners: each nation is free to produce what it does best and to trade its goods and services without restrictions.

When the agreement was ratified in 1994, it had no shortage of skeptics. Many people feared, for example, that without tariffs on Mexican goods, more US manufacturing jobs would be lost to Mexico, where labor is cheaper. Almost two decades later, most such fears have not been realized, and, by and large, NAFTA has been a success.

Since it went into effect, the value of trade between the United States and Mexico has grown substantially, and Canada and Mexico are now the United States' top trading partners.

Shortly after taking office in 2017, concerned with deficiencies and mistakes from the original NAFTA, President Trump and representatives from the Office of the United States Trade Representative, began negotiating a new trade agreement between the United States, Mexico and Canada. Signed in 2018 and later ratified by all three nations, the new United States–Mexico–Canada Agreement (USMCA) replaces the 25-year-old trade agreement known as NAFTA. Implemented in July 2020, the USMCA works to mutually beneficial trade between all three nations with the goal of leading to freer markets, fairer trade, and robust economic growth in North America.[30]

The European Union

The forty-plus countries of Europe have long shown an interest in integrating their economies. The first organized effort to integrate a segment of Europe's economic entities began in the late 1950s, when six countries joined together to form the European Economic Community (EEC). Over the next four decades, membership grew, and in the late 1990s, the EEC became the European Union. Today, the **European Union** (EU) is a group of 27 countries that have eliminated trade barriers among themselves (see the map in figure 5.11).

The forty-plus countries of Europe have long shown an interest in integrating their economies. The first organized effort to integrate a segment of Europe's economic entities began in the late 1950s, when six countries joined together to form the European Economic Community (EEC). Over the next four decades, membership grew, and in the late 1990s, the EEC became the European Union. Today, the **European Union** (EU) is a group of 27 countries that have eliminated trade barriers among themselves (see the map in figure 5.11).

At first glance, the EU looks similar to NAFTA. Both, for instance, allow unrestricted trade among member nations. But the provisions of the EU go beyond those of NAFTA in several important ways. Most importantly, the EU is more than a trading organization: it also enhances political and social cooperation and binds its members into a single entity with authority to require them to follow common rules and regulations. It is much like a federation of states with a weak central government, with the effect not only of eliminating internal barriers but also of enforcing common tariffs on trade from outside the EU. In addition, while NAFTA allows goods and services as well as capital to pass between borders, the EU also allows people to come and go freely: if you possess an EU passport, you can work in any EU nation.

Figure 5.11: Members of the European Union.

The Euro

A key step toward unification occurred in 1999, when most (but not all) EU members agreed to abandon their own currencies and adopt a joint currency. The actual conversion occurred in 2002, when a common currency called the **euro** replaced the separate currencies of participating EU countries. The common currency facilitates trade and finance because exchange-rate differences no longer complicate transactions.[31]

Its proponents argued that the EU would not only unite economically and politically distinct countries but also create an economic power that could compete against the dominant players in the global marketplace. Individually, each European country has limited economic power, but as a group, they could be an economic superpower.[32] Over time, the value of the euro has been questioned. Many of the "euro" countries (Spain, Italy, Greece, Portugal, and Ireland in particular) have been financially irresponsible, piling up huge debts and experiencing high unemployment and problems in the housing market. But because these troubled countries share a common currency with the other "euro countries," they are less able to correct their economic woes.[33] Many economists fear that the financial crisis precipitated by these financially irresponsible countries threaten the very survival of the euro.[34] Keep a close eye on Greece because if an exit from the Euro occurs, it will likely start there.

Only time will tell whether the trend toward regional trade agreements is good for the world economy. Clearly, they're beneficial to their respective participants; for one thing, they get preferential treatment from other members. But certain questions still need to be answered more fully. Are regional agreements, for example, moving the world closer to free trade on a global scale—toward a marketplace in which goods and services can be traded anywhere without barriers?

An interactive H5P element has been excluded from this version of the text. You can view it online here: https://pressbooks.lib.vt.edu/fundamentalsofbusiness4e/?p=75#h5p-15

Key Takeaways

- Nations **trade** because they don't produce all the products that their inhabitants need.
- The cost of labor, the availability of natural resources, and the level of know-how vary greatly around the world, so not every country has the same resources or is good at producing the same products.
- To explain how countries decide what products to **import** and **export**, economists use the concepts of absolute and comparative advantage: A nation has an **absolute advantage** if it's the only source of a particular product or can make more of a product with the same amount of or fewer resources than other countries. A **comparative advantage** exists when a country can produce a product at a lower opportunity cost than other nations.
- We determine a country's **balance of trade** by subtracting the value of its imports from the value of its exports. If a country sells more products than it buys, it has a favorable balance, called a **trade surplus**. If it buys more than it sells, it has an unfavorable balance, or a **trade deficit**.
- The **balance of payments** is the difference, over a period of time, between the total flow coming

- into a country and the total flow going out. The biggest factor in a country's balance of payments is the money that comes in and goes out as a result of exports and imports.
- A company that operates in many countries is called a **multinational corporation** (MNC).
- For a company in the United States wishing to expand beyond national borders, there are a variety of ways to get involved in international business:
    - **Importing** involves purchasing products from other countries and reselling them in one's own.
    - **Exporting** entails selling products to foreign customers.
    - Under a **franchise agreement**, a company grants a foreign company the right to use its brand name and sell its products.
    - A **licensing agreement** allows a foreign company to sell a company's products or use its intellectual property in exchange for royalty fees.
    - Through **international contract manufacturing**, or **outsourcing**, a company has its products manufactured or services provided in other countries.
    - A **joint venture** is a type of **strategic alliance** in which a separate entity funded by the participating companies is formed.
    - **Foreign direct investment** (FDI) refers to the formal establishment of business operations on foreign soil.
    - A common form of FDI is the **foreign subsidiary**, an independent company owned by a foreign firm.
- Success in international business requires an understanding an assortment of cultural, economic, and legal/regulatory differences between countries. **Cultural challenges** stem from differences in **language**, **concepts of time** and **sociability**, and **communication styles**.
- Because they protect domestic industries by reducing foreign competition, the use of controls to restrict free trade is often called **protectionism**.
    - **Tariffs** are taxes on imports. Because they raise the price of the foreign-made goods, they make them less competitive.
    - **Quotas** are restrictions on imports that impose a limit on the quantity of a good that can be imported over a period of time. They're used to protect specific industries, usually new industries or those facing strong competitive pressure from foreign firms.
    - An **embargo** is a quota that, for economic or political reasons, bans the import or export of certain goods to or from a specific country.
- A common rationale for tariffs and quotas is the need to combat **dumping**—the practice of selling exported goods below the price that producers would normally charge in their home markets (and often below the costs of producing the goods).
- **Free trade** is encouraged by a number of agreements and organizations set up to monitor trade policies.

- The **General Agreement on Tariffs and Trade** (GATT) regulates free trade, reduces tariffs and provides a forum for resolving trade disputes.
- The **World Trade Organization** (WTO) encourages global commerce and lower trade barriers, enforces international rules of trade, and provides a forum for resolving disputes.

- The **International Monetary Fund** (IMF) and the **World Bank** both provide monetary assistance to the world's poorest countries.
- In certain parts of the world, groups of countries have formed **trading blocs** to allow goods and services to flow without restrictions across their mutual borders.

  - Examples include the **North American Free Trade Association** (NAFTA) (United States, Canada, and Mexico) and the **European Union** (EU), a group of 27 countries that have eliminated trade barriers among themselves.

- Globalization is essentially the trend towards increased connections and interdependence in the world's economies.

References

Figures

Figure 5.1: Orchard Road in Singapore. Hannah Sibayan. 2020. Unsplash license. https://unsplash.com/photos/KZhMBYzKtNg.

Figure 5.2: Imports, exports, and balance of payments (1990-2021). Kindred Grey. 2022. CC BY 4.0. Data from https://www.census.gov/foreign-trade/statistics/historical/goods.pdf. https://archive.org/details/5.2_20220622.

Figure 5.3: Key strategies for reaching global markets. Kindred Grey. 2022. CC BY 4.0. https://archive.org/details/5.3_20220622.

Figure 5.4: The franchise Marriott in Budapest. Eugene Chystiakov. 2020. Unsplash license. https://unsplash.com/photos/qpkKR3N6AJ0.

Figure 5.5: Hourly wage comparisons for U.S. and India. Data from indeed.com.

Figure 5.6: Where FDI goes (2000–2020). Kindred Grey. 2022. CC BY 4.0. Data from http://unctadstat.unctad.org/wds/TableViewer/tableView.aspx?ReportId=96740. https://archive.org/details/5.6_20220622.

Figure 5.7: Fortune top 15 multinational firms by revenue (2021). Data from https://fortune.com/global500/2021/search/.

Figure 5.8: Lost in translation. Kindred Grey. 2022. CC BY 4.0. Added Shallow Focus Photo of Man Reading Newspaper by Andrea Piacquadio from Pexels (Pexels license). https://archive.org/details/5.8_20220622.

Figure 5.9: Corruption perceptions around the world (2021). Data from https://www.transparency.org/en/cpi/2021.

Figure 5.10: A business lobby in Ottawa, Canada. Trang Doan. 2018. Pexels license. https://www.pexels.com/photo/people-in-couch-1024248/.

Figure 5.11: Members of the European Union. Kindred Grey. 2022. CC BY 4.0. Added Special member state territories in Europe and the European Union by Glentamara from Wikimedia commons (public domain). https://archive.org/details/5.12_20220622.

Notes

1. Silk Road Foundation (n.d.). "Marco Polo and His Travels." Silk Road Foundation. Retrieved from: http://www.silkroadfoundation.org/artl/marcopolo.shtml#:~:text=Marco Polo (1254-1324),predecessors, beyond Mongolia to China.
2. Sabanoglu, T. (2021, May 7). Worldwide Export Trade Value 1950-2020. Statista. Retrieved from: https://www.statista.com/statistics/264682/worldwide-export-volume-in-the-trade-since-1950
3. Warren E. Buffet and Carol Loomis (2003). "America's Growing Trade Deficit Is Selling The Nation Out From Under Us. Here's A Way To Fix The Problem—And We Need To Do It Now." Fortune. Retrieved from: http://archive.fortune.com/magazines/fortune/fortune_archive/2003/11/10/352872/index.htm
4. Anonymous (2003). "Why Are Prices in Japan So Damn High?" The Japan FAQ.com. Retrieved from: http://www.thejapanfaq.com/FAQ-Prices.html
5. U.S. Census Bureau (2015). "U.S. Trade in Goods and Services—Balance of Payments (BOP) Basis, 1960 thru 2014." Retrieved from: http://www.census.gov/foreign-trade/statistics/historical/gands.txt
6. Fine Waters Media (2016). "Bottled Waters of France." Retrieved from: http://www.finewaters.com/bottled-waters-of-the-world/france/evian; Fiji Water (2016). "Fiji water history." Retrieved from: https://store.fijiwater.com/about-fiji-water-bottle-delivery
7. H. Frederick Gale (2003). "China's Growing Affluence: How Food Markets Are Responding." U.S. Department of Agriculture. Retrieved from: http://www.ers.usda.gov/amber-waves/2003-june/chinas-growing-affluence.aspx#.Vz-JUfkrIqM
8. USDA Foreign Agricultural Service. (2021). U.S. Soybeans Exports in 2021 . Foreign Agricultural Service. Retrieved from: https://www.fas.usda.gov/commodities/soybeans#:~:text=U.S.%20Soybeans%20Exports%20in%202021&text=In%202020%2C%20the%20value%20of,volume%20from%20the%20prior%20year
9. Gary Gereffi and Stacey Frederick (2010). "The Global Apparel Value Chain, Trade and the Crisis: Challenges and Opportunities for Developing Countries." World Bank. Retrieved from: http://www19.iadb.org/intal/intalcdi/PE/2010/05413.pdf
10. Paul Lienert and Joyce Lee (2020). "Hyundai Signs Development Deal With Another Electric Vehicle Startup." Reuters. Retrieved from: https://www.reuters.com/article/us-autos-hyundai-motor-electric-idUSKBN2052MI
11. Clothing, Makeup and Beauty Tips (2012). Lihi Griner Cosmopolitan Israel. Retrieved from: http://www.magxone.com/cosmopolitan/lihi-griner-cosmopolitan-israel-may-2012/attachment/lihi-griner-cosmopolitan-israel/; CountryMagazines.Blogspot.com (2015). Retrieved from: http://country-magazines.blogspot.com/2015/09/tennis-maria-sharapova-cosmopolitan.html
12. Michael Mandel (2007). "The Real Cost of Offshoring." Bloomberg Businessweek. Retrieved from: http://www.bloomberg.com/news/articles/2007-06-17/the-real-cost-of-offshoring
13. James C. Morgan and Jeffrey Morgan (1991). *Cracking the Japanese Market*. New York: Free Press. p. 102.
14. Case Study Inc. (2010). "Glocalization Examples—Think Globally and Act Locally." CaseStudyInc.com. Retrieved from:

15. http://www.casestudyinc.com/glocalization-examples-think-globally-and-act-locally
16. McDonald's India (n.d.). "McDonald's India." Retrieved from: http://www.mcdonaldsindia.com/McDonaldsinIndia.pdf
17. Susan L. Nasr (2009). "10 Unusual Items from McDonald's International Menu." HowStuffWorks. Retrieved from: http://money.howstuffworks.com/10-items-from-mcdonalds-international-menu5.htm
18. James C. Morgan and J. Jeffrey Morgan (1991). *Cracking the Japanese Market*. New York: Free Press. p. 117.
19. Anne O. Krueger (2002). "Supporting Globalization." Eisenhower National Security Conference: "National Security for the 21st Century: Anticipating Challenges, Seizing Opportunities, Building Capabilities." Retrieved from: http://www.imf.org/external/np/speeches/2002/092602a.htm
20. World Bank Group (2016). "Country and Lending Groups." Retrieved from: http://data.worldbank.org/about/country-and-lending-groups
21. David Ricks (1999). *Blunders in International Business*. Malden, MA: Blackwell. p. 137.
22. Transparency.org (2016). "What is Corruption?" Retrieved from: http://www.transparency.org/
23. Daniel Griswold (2009). "The Protectionist Swindle: How Trade Barriers Cheat the Poor and Middle Class." Insider Online. Retrieved from: http://www.insideronline.org/2009/12/the-protectionist-swindle-how-trade-barriers-cheat-the-poor-and-middle-class/
24. Footwear Distributors and Retailers of America (2015). "Tariff Reduction Initiatives." Retrieved from: http://fdra.org/key-issues-and-advocacy/legislative-initiatives/
25. China phase one agreement. USDA Foreign Agricultural Service. (n.d.). Retrieved from: https://www.fas.usda.gov/topics/china-phase-one-agreement
26. Chris Edwards (2007). "The Sugar Racket." CATO Institute Tax and Budget Bulletin. Retrieved from: http://www.cato.org/pubs/tbb/tbb_0607_46.pdf
27. James Pritchard (2002). "Sole U.S. Life Savers plant closing, moving to Canada." Southeast Missourian. Retrieved from: http://www.semissourian.com/story/70976.html
28. Philip Blenkinsop (2020). "EU is 'very concerned' by delayed WTO decision on tariffs vs US." Reuters. Retrieved from: https://www.reuters.com/article/us-usa-trade-eu/eu-is-very-concerned-by-delayed-wto-decision-on-tariffs-vs-u-s-idUSKBN23W2L7
29. 1 Bernard Sanders (1998). "The International Monetary Fund Is Hurting You." Z Magazine. Retrieved from: http://www.thirdworldtraveler.com/IMF_WB/IMF_Sanders.html
30. World Bank (2016). "Fiscal Year Data 2011-15." Retrieved from: http://www.worldbank.org/en/about/annual-report/fiscalyeardata#1
31. USMCA (2019). "Agreement between the United States of America, the United Mexican States, and Canada." Office of the United States Trade Representative. Retrieved from: https://ustr.gov/trade-agreements/free-trade-agreements/united-states-mexico-canada-agreement/agreement-between
32. European Commission on Economic, and Financial Affairs (2015). "Why the Euro?" Retrieved from: http://ec.europa.eu/economy_finance/euro/why/index_en.htm
33. Ibid.
34. "Paul Krugman (2011). "The Economic Failure of the Euro." National Public Radio. Retrieved from: http://www.npr.org/2011/01/25/133112932/paul-krugman-the-economic-failure-of-the-euro
35. Willem Buiter (2010). "Three Steps to Survival for Euro Zone." Wall Street Journal. Retrieved from: http://online.wsj.com/article/SB10001424052748703766704576009423447485768.html

6. Forms of Business Ownership

Learning Objectives

- Identify the questions to ask in choosing the appropriate form of ownership for a business.
- Describe the sole proprietorship and partnership forms of organization, and specify the advantages and disadvantages.
- Identify the different types of partnerships, and explain the importance of a partnership agreement.
- Explain how corporations are formed and how they operate.
- Discuss the advantages and disadvantages of the corporate form of ownership.
- Examine special types of business ownership, including limited-liability companies and not-for-profit corporations.
- Define mergers and acquisitions, and explain why companies are motivated to merge or acquire other companies.

The Ice Cream Men

Who would have thought it? Two ex-hippies with strong interests in social activism would end up starting one of the best-known ice cream companies in the country—Ben & Jerry's. Perhaps it was meant to be. Ben Cohen (the "Ben" of Ben & Jerry's) always had a fascination with ice cream. As a child, he made his own mixtures by smashing his favorite cookies and candies into his ice cream. But it wasn't until his senior year in high school that he became an official "ice cream man," happily driving his truck through neighborhoods filled with kids eager to buy his ice cream pops. After high school, Ben tried college but it wasn't for him. He attended Colgate University for a year and a half before he dropped out to return to his real love: being an ice cream man. He tried college again—this time at Skidmore, where he studied pottery and jewelry making—but, in spite of his selection of courses, still didn't like it.

In the meantime, Jerry Greenfield (the "Jerry" of Ben & Jerry's) was following a similar path. He majored in pre-med at Oberlin College in the hopes of one day becoming a doctor. But he had to give up on this goal when he was not accepted into medical school. On a positive note, though, his college education steered him into a more lucrative field: the world of ice cream making. He got his first peek at the ice cream industry when he worked as a scooper in the student cafeteria at Oberlin. So, 14 years after they first met on the junior high school track team, Ben and Jerry reunited and decided to go into ice cream making big time. They moved to Burlington, Vermont—a college town in need of an ice cream parlor—and completed a $5

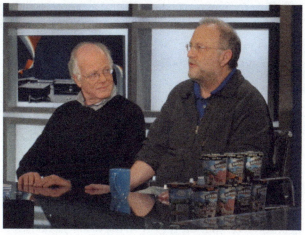

Figure 6.1: Ben Cohen and Jerry Greenfield.

correspondence course from Penn State on making ice cream. After getting an A in the course—not surprising, given that the tests were open book—they took the plunge: with their life savings of $8,000 and $4,000 of borrowed funds they set up an ice cream shop in a made-over gas station on a busy street corner in Burlington.[1] The next big decision was which form of business ownership was best for them. This chapter introduces you to their options.

Factors to Consider

If you're starting a new business, you have to decide which legal form of ownership is best for you and the strategy you plan on pursuing. Do you want to own the business yourself and operate as a sole proprietorship? Or, do you want to share ownership, operating as a partnership or a corporation? Before we discuss the pros and cons of these three types of ownership, let's address some of the questions that you'd probably ask yourself in choosing the appropriate legal form for your business.

1. In setting up your business, do you want to minimize the costs of getting started? Do you hope to avoid complex government regulations and reporting requirements?
2. How much control would you like? How much responsibility for running the business are you willing to share? What about sharing the profits?
3. Do you want to avoid special taxes?
4. Do you have all the skills needed to run the business?
5. Are you likely to get along with your co-owners over an extended period of time?
6. Is it important to you that the business survive you?
7. What are your financing needs and how do you plan to finance your company?
8. How much personal exposure to liability are you willing to accept? Do you feel uneasy about accepting personal liability for the actions of fellow owners?

No single form of ownership will give you everything you desire. You'll have to make some trade-offs. Because each option has both advantages and disadvantages, your job is to decide which one offers the features that are most important to you. In the following sections we'll compare three ownership options (sole proprietorship, partnership, corporation) on these eight dimensions.

Sole Proprietorship and Its Advantages

In a **sole proprietorship**, as the owner, you have complete control over your business. You make all important decisions and are generally responsible for all day-to-day activities. In exchange for assuming all this responsibility, you get all the income earned by the business. Profits earned are taxed as personal income and delineated on your tax return, so the business doesn't pay any special federal and state income taxes.

Disadvantages of Sole Proprietorships

For many people, however, the sole proprietorship is not suitable. The flip side of enjoying complete control is having to supply all the different talents that may be necessary to make the business a success. And when you're gone, the business dissolves. You also have to rely on your own resources for financing: in effect, you are the business and any money borrowed by the business is loaned to you personally. Even more important, the sole proprietor bears **unlimited liability** for any losses incurred by the business. The principle of unlimited personal liability means that if the business incurs a debt or suffers a catastrophe (say, getting sued for causing an injury to someone), the owner is personally liable. As a sole proprietor, you put your personal assets (your bank account, your car, maybe even your home) at risk for the sake of your business. You can lessen your risk with insurance, yet your liability exposure can still be substantial. Given that Ben and Jerry decided to start their ice cream business together (and therefore the business was not owned by only one person), they could not set their company up as a sole proprietorship.

Partnership

A **partnership** (or general partnership) is a business owned jointly by two or more people. About 10 percent of US businesses are partnerships[2] and though the vast majority are small, some are quite large. For example, the big four public accounting firms are partnerships. Setting up a partnership is more complex than setting up a sole proprietorship, but it's still relatively easy and inexpensive. The cost varies according to size and complexity. It's possible to form a simple partnership without the help of a lawyer or an accountant, though it's usually a good idea to get professional advice.

Professionals can help you identify and resolve issues that may later create disputes among partners.

The Partnership Agreement

The impact of disputes can be lessened if the partners have executed a well-planned **partnership agreement** that specifies everyone's rights and responsibilities. The agreement might provide such details as the following:

- Amount of cash and other contributions to be made by each partner
- Division of partnership income (or loss)
- Partner responsibilities—who does what
- Conditions under which a partner can sell an interest in the company
- Conditions for dissolving the partnership
- Conditions for settling disputes

Unlimited Liability and the Partnership

A major problem with partnerships, as with sole proprietorships, is **unlimited liability**: in this case, each partner is personally liable not only for his or her own actions but also for the actions of all the partners. If your partner in an architectural firm makes a mistake that causes a structure to collapse, the loss your business incurs impacts you just as much as it would him or her. And here's the really bad news: if the business doesn't have the cash or other assets to cover losses, you can be personally sued for the amount owed. In other words, the party who suffered a loss because of the error can sue you for your personal assets. Many people are understandably reluctant to enter into partnerships because of unlimited liability. Certain forms of businesses allow owners to limit their liability. These include limited partnerships and corporations.

Limited Partnerships

The law permits business owners to form a **limited partnership** which has two types of partners: a single general partner who runs the business and is responsible for its liabilities, and any number of limited partners who have limited involvement in the business and whose losses are limited to the amount of their investment.

Advantages and Disadvantages of Partnerships

The partnership has several advantages over the sole proprietorship. First, it brings together a diverse group of talented individuals who share responsibility for running the business. Second, it makes financing easier: the business can draw on the financial resources of a number of individuals. The partners not only contribute funds to the business but can also use personal resources to secure bank loans. Finally, continuity needn't be an issue because partners can agree legally to allow the partnership to survive if one or more partners die.

Still, there are some negatives. First, as discussed earlier, partners are subject to unlimited liability. Second, being a partner means that you have to share decision making, and many people aren't comfortable with that situation. Not surprisingly, partners often have differences of opinion on how to run a business, and disagreements can escalate to the point of jeopardizing the continuance of the business. Third, in addition to sharing ideas, partners also share profits. This arrangement can work as long as all partners feel that they're being rewarded according to their efforts and accomplishments, but that isn't always the case. While the partnership form of ownership is viewed negatively by some, it was particularly appealing to Ben Cohen and Jerry Greenfield. Starting their ice cream business as a partnership was inexpensive and let them combine their limited financial resources and use their diverse skills and talents. As friends they trusted each other and welcomed shared decision making and profit sharing. They were also not reluctant to be held personally liable for each other's actions. However, friendship should not be the basis of going into business together. Unfortunately, being in business together can sometimes drive a wedge into the friendship.

Corporation

A **corporation** (sometimes called a regular or C-corporation) differs from a sole proprietorship and a partnership because it's a legal entity that is entirely separate from the parties who own it. It can enter into binding contracts, buy and sell property, sue and be sued, be held responsible for its actions, and be taxed. Once businesses reach any substantial size, it is advantageous to organize as a corporation so that its owners can limit their liability. Corporations, then, tend to be far larger, on average, than businesses using other forms of ownership. As figure 6.2 shows, corporations account for roughly 18 percent of all US businesses but generate over 82 percent of the revenues.

Most large well-known businesses are corporations, but so are many of the smaller firms with which likely you do business.

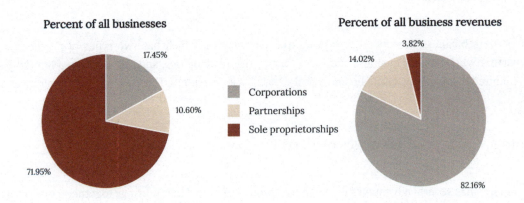

Figure 6.2: Types of U.S. businesses.

Ownership and Stock

Corporations are owned by **shareholders** who invest money in the business by buying shares of **stock**. The portion of the corporation they own depends on the percentage of stock they hold. For example, if a corporation has issued 100 shares of stock, and you own 30 shares, you own 30 percent of the company. The shareholders elect a **board of directors**, a group of people (primarily from outside the corporation) who are legally responsible for governing the corporation, but not for the daily operations. . The board oversees the major policies and decisions made by the corporation, sets goals and holds management accountable for achieving them, and hires and evaluates the top executive, generally called the CEO (**chief executive officer**). The board also approves the distribution of income to shareholders in the form of cash payments called dividends.

Benefits of Incorporation

The corporate form of organization offers several advantages, including limited liability for shareholders, greater access to financial resources, specialized management, and continuity.

Limited Liability

The most important benefit of incorporation is the **limited liability** to which shareholders are exposed: they are not responsible for the obligations of the corporation, and they can lose no more than the amount that they have personally invested in the company. Limited liability would have been a big plus for the unfortunate individual whose business partner burned down their dry cleaning establishment. Had they been incorporated, the corporation would have been liable for the debts incurred by the fire. If the corporation didn't have enough money to pay the debt, the individual shareholders would not have been obligated to pay anything. They would have lost all the money that they'd invested in the business, but no more.

Financial Resources

Incorporation also makes it possible for businesses to raise funds by selling stock. This is a big advantage as a company grows and needs more funds to operate and compete. Depending on its size and financial strength, the corporation also has an advantage over other forms of business in getting bank loans. An established corporation can borrow its own funds, but when a small business needs a loan, the bank usually requires that it be guaranteed by its owners.

Specialized Management

Because of their size and ability to pay high sales commissions and benefits, corporations are generally able to attract more skilled and talented employees than are proprietorships and partnerships.

Continuity and Transferability

Another advantage of incorporation is **continuity**. Because the corporation has a legal life separate from the lives of its owners, it can (at least in theory) exist forever.

Transferring ownership of a corporation is easy: shareholders simply sell their stock to others. Some founders, however, want to restrict the transferability of their stock and so choose to operate as a privately-held corporation. The stock in these corporations is held by only a few individuals, who are not allowed to sell it to the general public.

Companies with no such restrictions on stock sales are called public corporations; stock is available for sale to the general public.

Drawbacks to Incorporation

Like sole proprietorships and partnerships, corporations have both positive and negative aspects. In sole proprietorships and partnerships, for instance, the individuals who own and manage a business are the same people. Corporate managers, however, don't necessarily own stock, and shareholders don't necessarily work for the company. This situation can be troublesome if the goals of the two groups differ significantly.

Managers, for example, are often more interested in career advancement than the overall profitability of the company. Stockholders might care more about profits without regard for the well-being of employees. This situation is known as the **agency problem**, a conflict of interest inherent in a relationship in which one party is supposed to act in the best interest of the other. It is often quite difficult to prevent self-interest from entering into these situations.

Another drawback to incorporation—one that often discourages small businesses from incorporating—is the fact that corporations are more costly to set up. When you combine filing and licensing fees with accounting and attorney fees, incorporating a business could set you back by $1,000 to $6,000 or more depending on the size and scope of your business.[3] Additionally, corporations are subject to levels of regulation and governmental oversight that can place a burden on small businesses. Finally, corporations are subject to what's generally called "**double taxation**." Corporations are taxed by the federal and state governments on their earnings. When these earnings are distributed as dividends, the shareholders pay taxes on these dividends. Corporate profits are thus taxed twice—the corporation pays the taxes the first time and the shareholders pay the taxes the second time.

Five years after starting their ice cream business, Ben Cohen and Jerry Greenfield evaluated the pros and cons of the corporate form of ownership, and the "pros" won. The primary motivator was the need to raise funds to build a $2 million manufacturing facility. Not only did Ben and Jerry decide to switch from a partnership to a corporation, but they also decided to sell shares of stock to the public (and thus become a public corporation). Their sale of stock to the public was a bit unusual: Ben and Jerry wanted the community to own the company, so instead of offering the stock to anyone interested in buying a share, they offered stock to residents of Vermont only. Ben believed that "business has a responsibility to give back to the community from which it draws its support."[4] He wanted the company to be owned by those who lined up in the gas station to buy cones. The stock was so popular that one in every hundred Vermont families bought stock in the company.[5] Eventually, as the company continued to expand, the stock was sold on a national level, and the company acquired by Unilever in 2000. Although there were initial fears of it being a hostile takeover, Unilever claims "to achieve our collective vision of a global economy where all business works to create a more shared and durable prosperity for all."[6]

An interactive H5P element has been excluded from this version of the text. You can view it online here: https://pressbooks.lib.vt.edu/fundamentalsofbusiness4e/?p=79#h5p-16

Other Types of Business Ownership

In addition to the three commonly adopted forms of business organization—sole proprietorship, partnership, and regular corporations—some business owners select other forms of organization to meet their particular needs. We'll look at two of these options:

- Limited-liability companies
- Not-for-profit corporations

Limited-Liability Companies

How would you like a legal form of organization that provides the attractive features of the three common forms of organization (corporation, sole proprietorship and partnership) and avoids the unattractive features of these three organization forms? The **limited-liability company (LLC)** accomplishes exactly that. This form provides business owners with limited liability (a key advantage of corporations) and no "double taxation" (a key advantage of sole proprietorships and partnerships). Let's look at the LLC in more detail.

In 1977, Wyoming became the first state to allow businesses to operate as limited-liability companies. Twenty years later, in 1997, Hawaii became the last state to give its approval to the new organization form. Since then, the limited-liability company has increased in popularity. Its rapid growth was fueled in part by changes in state statutes that permit a limited-liability company to have just one member. The trend to LLCs can be witnessed by reading company names on the side of trucks or on storefronts in your city. It is common to see names such as Jim Evans Tree Care, LLC, and For-Cats-Only Veterinary Clinic, LLC. But LLCs are not limited to small businesses. Companies such as Crayola, Domino's Pizza, Ritz-Carlton Hotel Company, and iSold It (which helps people sell their unwanted belongings on eBay) are operating under the limited-liability form of organization.

In a limited-liability company, owners (called members rather than shareholders) are not personally liable for debts of the company, and its earnings are taxed only once, at the personal level (thereby eliminating double taxation).

We have touted the benefits of limited liability protection for an LLC. We now need to point out some circumstances under which an LLC member (or a shareholder in a corporation) might be held personally liable for the debts of his or her company. A business owner can be held personally liable if he or she:

- Personally guarantees a business debt or bank loan which the company fails to pay.
- Fails to pay employment taxes to the government.
- Engages in fraudulent or illegal behavior that harms the company or someone else.
- Does not treat the company as a separate legal entity, for example, uses company assets for personal uses.

Not-for-Profit Corporations

A **not-for-profit corporation** (sometimes called a nonprofit) is an organization formed to serve some public purpose rather than for financial gain. As long as the organization's activity is for charitable, religious, educational, scientific, or literary purposes, it can be exempt from paying income taxes. Additionally, individuals and other organizations that contribute to the not-for-profit corporation can take a tax deduction for those contributions. The types of groups that normally apply for nonprofit status vary widely and include churches, synagogues, mosques, and other places of worship; museums; universities; and conservation groups.

There are more than 1.5 million not-for-profit organizations in the United States.[7] Some are extremely well funded, such as the Bill and Melinda Gates Foundation, which has an endowment of approximately $40 billion and has given away $36.7 billion since its inception.[8] Others are nationally recognized, such as United Way, Goodwill Industries, Habitat for Humanity, and the Red Cross. Yet the vast majority is neither rich nor famous, but nevertheless makes significant contributions to society.

An interactive H5P element has been excluded from this version of the text. You can view it online here:
https://pressbooks.lib.vt.edu/fundamentalsofbusiness4e/?p=79#h5p-17

Mergers and Acquisitions

The headline read, "Wanted: More than 2,000 in Google Hiring Spree."[9] The largest Web search engine in the world was disclosing its plans to grow internally and increase its workforce by more than 2,000 people, with half of the hires coming from the United States and the other half coming from other countries. The added employees will help the company expand into new markets and battle for global talent in the competitive Internet information providers industry. When properly executed, internal growth benefits the firm.

An alternative approach to growth is to merge with or acquire another company. The rationale behind growth through merger or acquisition is that 1 1 = 3: the combined company is more valuable than the sum of the two separate companies. This rationale is attractive to companies facing competitive pressures. To grab a bigger share of the market and improve profitability, companies will want to become more cost efficient by combining with other companies.

Mergers and Acquisitions

Though they are often used as if they're synonymous, the terms merger and acquisition mean slightly different things. A **merger** occurs when two companies combine to form a new company. An **acquisition** is the purchase of one company by another. An example of an acquisition is the creation of the "New T-Mobile" in 2020 resulting from T-Mobile acquiring Sprint.[10]

Another example of an acquisition is the purchase of Reebok by Adidas for $3.8 billion.[11] The deal was expected to give Adidas a stronger presence in North America and help the company compete with rival Nike. Once this acquisition was completed, Reebok as a company ceased to exist, though Adidas still sells shoes under the Reebok brand.

Motives Behind Mergers and Acquisitions

Companies are motivated to merge or acquire other companies for a number of reasons, including the following.

Forms of Business Ownership | 123

Gain complementary products

Acquiring **complementary products** was the motivation behind Adidas's acquisition of Reebok. As then Adidas CEO Herbert Hainer stated in a conference call, "This is a once-in-a-lifetime opportunity. This is a perfect fit for both companies, because the companies are so complementary … Adidas is grounded in sports performance with such products as a motorized running shoe and endorsement deals with such superstars as British soccer player David Beckham. Meanwhile, Reebok plays heavily to the melding of sports and entertainment with endorsement deals and products by Nelly, Jay-Z, and 50 Cent. The combination could be deadly to Nike." Of course, Nike has continued to thrive, but one can't blame Hainer for his optimism.[12]

Attain new markets or distribution channels

Gaining new markets was a significant factor in the 2005 merger of US Airways and America West. US Airways was a major player on the East Coast, the Caribbean, and Europe, while America West was strong in the West. The expectations were that combining the two carriers would create an airline that could reach more markets than either carrier could do on its own.[13]

Realize synergies

The purchase of Pharmacia Corporation (a Swedish pharmaceutical company) by Pfizer (a research-based pharmaceutical company based in the United States) in 2003 created one of the world's largest drug makers and pharmaceutical companies, by revenue, in every major market around the globe.[14] The acquisition created an industry giant with more than $48 billion in revenue and a research-and-development budget of more than $7 billion. Each day, almost forty million people around the globe are treated with Pfizer medicines.[15] Its subsequent $68 billion purchase of rival drug maker Wyeth further increased its presence in the pharmaceutical market.[16]

In pursuing these acquisitions, Pfizer likely identified many **synergies**: quite simply, a whole that is greater than the sum of its parts. There are many examples of synergies. A merger typically results in a number of redundant positions; the combined company does not likely need two vice presidents of marketing, two chief financial officers, and so on. Eliminating the redundant positions leads to significant cost savings that would not be realized if the two companies did not merge. Let's say each of the companies was operating factories at 50 percent of capacity, and by merging, one factory could be closed and sold. That would also be an example of a synergy. Companies bring different strengths and weaknesses into the merged entity. If the newly-combined company can take advantage of the marketing capabilities of the stronger entity and the distribution capabilities of the other (assuming they are stronger), the new company can realize synergies in both of these functions.

Hostile takeover

What happens, though, if one company wants to acquire another company, but that company doesn't want to be acquired? The outcome could be a **hostile takeover**—an act of assuming control that's resisted by the targeted company's management and its board of directors. Ben Cohen and Jerry Greenfield found themselves in one of these situations: Unilever—a very large Dutch/British company that owns three ice cream brands—wanted to buy Ben & Jerry's, against the founders' wishes. Most of the Ben & Jerry's stockholders sided with Unilever. They had little confidence in the ability of Ben Cohen and Jerry Greenfield to continue managing the company and were frustrated with the firm's social-mission focus. The stockholders liked Unilever's offer to buy their Ben & Jerry's stock at almost twice its current market price and wanted to take their profits. In the end, Unilever won; Ben & Jerry's was acquired by Unilever in a hostile takeover.[17] Despite fears that the company's social mission would end, it didn't happen. Though neither Ben Cohen nor Jerry Greenfield are involved in the current management of the company, they have returned to their social activism roots and are heavily involved in numerous social initiatives sponsored by the company.

An interactive H5P element has been excluded from this version of the text. You can view it online here: https://pressbooks.lib.vt.edu/fundamentalsofbusiness4e/?p=79#h5p-18

Chapter Video

Here is a short video providing a simple and straightforward recap of the key points of each form of business ownership.

One or more interactive elements has been excluded from this version of the text. You can view them online here: https://www.youtube.com/watch?v=4-yE5JduTIo

Key Takeaways

- A **sole proprietorship,** a business owned by only one person, accounts for 72 percent of all US businesses.
- Advantages include: complete control for the owner, easy and inexpensive to form, and owner gets to keep all of the profits.
- Disadvantages include: unlimited liability for the owner, complete responsibility for talent and financing, and business dissolves if the owner dies.
- A **general partnership** is a business owned jointly by two or more people, and accounts for about 10 percent of all US businesses.
- Advantages include: more resources and talents come with an increase in partners, and the business can continue even after the death of a partner.
- Disadvantages include: partnership disputes, unlimited liability, and shared profits.
- A **limited partnership** has a single general partner who runs the business and is responsible for its liabilities, plus any number of limited partners who have limited involvement in the business and whose losses are limited to the amount of their investment.
- A **corporation** is a legal entity that's separate from the parties who own it, the shareholders who invest by buying shares of stock. Corporations are governed by a Board of Directors, elected by the shareholders.
- Advantages include: limited liability, easier access to financing, and unlimited life for the corporation.
- Disadvantages include: the agency problem, double taxation, and incorporation expenses and regulations.
- A **limited-liability company** (LLC) is a business structure that combines the tax treatment of a partnership with the liability protection of a corporation.
- A **not-for-profit corporation** is an organization formed to serve some public purpose rather than for financial gain. It enjoys favorable tax treatment.
- A **merger** occurs when two companies combine to form a new company.
- An **acquisition** is the purchase of one company by another with no new company being formed. A **hostile takeover** occurs when a company is purchased even though the company's management and Board of Directors do not want to be acquired.

References

Figures

Figure 6.1: Ben Cohen and Jerry Greenfield. Megan Robertson. 2012. CC BY 2.0. https://commons.wikimedia.org/wiki/File:Ben_Cohen_and_Jerry_Greenfield_on_the_Dylan_Ratigan_Show_(2012).jpg.

Figure 6.2: Types of U.S. businesses. Kindred Grey. 2022. CC BY 4.0. Data from https://www.irs.gov/statistics/soi-tax-stats-integrated-business-data [Note: figure includes "number of returns" as percent of all business and "total receipts" as percent of all business revenues from Table 1. Also note: 2015 is the most recently reported data as of July 2022.] https://archive.org/details/6.2_20220710.

Video

Video 1: Business Structure – Choosing the right Structure for your Business. TRUiC. 2020. Copyrighted. https://www.youtube.com/watch?v=4-yE5JduTIo.

Notes

1. Fred Chico Lager (1994). *Ben & Jerry's: The Inside Scoop*. New York: Crown Publishers.
2. IRS (2015). "Table 1. Number of Returns, Total Receipts, Business Receipts, Net Income (less deficit), Net Income, and Deficit, by Form of Business, Tax Years 1980-2015." Retrieved from: https://www.irs.gov/statistics/soi-tax-stats-integrated-business-data.
3. AllBusiness Editors (2016). "How Much Does it Cost to Incorporate?" AllBusiness.com. Retrieved from: http://allbusiness.sfgate.com/legal/contracts-agreements-incorporation/2531-1.htm
4. Fred Chico Lager (1994). *Ben & Jerry's: The Inside Scoop*. New York: Crown Publishers. p. 91.
5. Fred Chico Lager (1994). *Ben & Jerry's: The Inside Scoop*. New York: Crown Publishers. p. 103.
6. Elizabeth Freeburg (n.d.). "Unilever, Multinationals, and the B Corp Movement." Certified B Corporation. Retrieved from: https://bcorporation.net/news/unilever-multinationals-and-b-corp-movement
7. Urban Institute National Center for Charitable Statistics (2010). "Number of Nonprofit Organizations in the United States, 1999 – 2009." Urban Institute National Center for Charitable Statistics. Retrieved from: http://nccsdataweb.urban.org/PubApps/profile1.php?state=US
8. The Bill and Melinda Gates Foundation (2016). "Who We Are: Foundation Fact Sheet." Retrieved from: http://www.gatesfoundation.org/Who-We-Are/General-Information/Foundation-Factsheet
9. Alexei Oreskovic (2010). "Wanted: More Than 2,000 in Google Hiring Spree." Reuters. Retrieved from: http://www.reuters.com/article/us-google-idUSTRE6AI05820101119
10. Uncarrier (2020). "T-Mobile Completes Merger with Sprint to Create the New T-Mobile." T-Mobile.com. Retrieved from: https://www.t-mobile.com/news/un-carrier/t-mobile-sprint-one-company
11. Theresa Howard (2005). "Adidas, Reebok Lace up for a Run Against Nike." USA Today. Retrieved from: http://usatoday30.usatoday.com/money/industries/manufacturing/2005-08-02-adidas-usat_x.htm
12. Ibid.
13. CNN (2005). "America West, US Air in Merger Deal." CNN Money. Retrieved from: http://money.cnn.com/2005/05/19/news/midcaps/airlines/index.htm
14. Robert Frank and Scott Hensley (2002). "Pfizer to Buy Pharmacia for Billion in Stock." The Wall Street Journal. Retrieved from: http://www.wsj.com/articles/SB1026684057282753560
15. Pfizer (2003). "2003: Pfizer and Pharmacia Merger." Pfizer.com. Retrieved from: http://www.pfizer.com/about/history/

pfizer_pharmacia

16. Andrew Ross Sorkin and Duff Wilson (2009). "Pfizer Agrees to Pay Billion for Rival Drug Maker Wyeth." New York Times. Retrieved from: http://www.nytimes.com/2009/01/26/business/26drug.html?pagewanted=2&_r=0
17. CNN (2000). "Ben and Jerry's Scooped Up." CNN Money. Retrieved from: http://money.cnn.com/2000/04/12/deals/benandjerrys/

7. Entrepreneurship and Small Business Development

> *Learning Objectives*
>
> - Define entrepreneur and describe what it means to be entrepreneurial.
> - Identify common roles or activities needed to start your own business.
> - Explain the conditions of when entrepreneurship takes place.
> - Describe the different kinds of funding approaches to starting a company.
> - Identify different parts of an entrepreneurial ecosystem that entrepreneurs can leverage when starting up.
> - Explain the assumptions that can cause some startups to fail.

What is Entrepreneurship? What does Entrepreneurial Mean?

Entrepreneurship as a social science is the study of how people turn an idea into reality to create a new social agreement or institution (most often a new business). Social agreements are taken for granted ways of organizing so that the social world works and usually for the benefit or safety of a greater societal whole.

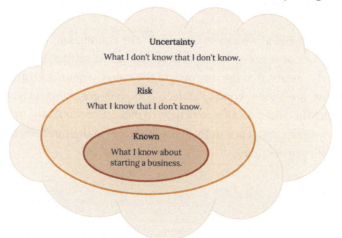

Figure 7.1: *Entrepreneurial boundaries.*

Entrepreneurs try to change the status quo or existing social agreements to new ways of doing things that are beneficial for a particular group of people. This proactive process of overcoming constraints to create value in new ways is what is meant by the adjective "**entrepreneurial**". An entrepreneurial spirit refers to someone that challenges the status quo and tries new ways to solve a problem. It can also refer to someone who is able to take limited resources—a constraint—and create something valuable. Historically speaking, the term entrepreneur was used to describe individuals who take on the financial risk that something might not work out believing they can take action that will generate a profit. Economists have further specified that entrepreneurs act under conditions of **uncertainty** rather than **risk**. Risk is something you can guess the results of, a kind of probability. Uncertainty is a kind of knowledge problem that doesn't have probabilities and can't really be guessed.

To illustrate the concept of uncertainty versus risk imagine that this cloud encompasses everything that you need to know to successfully run the business you want to start. Now imagine within the cloud there is a smaller circle that represents everything you are aware of in relation to starting the business, and finally inside of that circle is an even smaller circle about what you already know how to do to start the business. All that stuff that is outside your **circle of knowledge** that you are aware of is **risk** and all the other stuff that is outside your circle of awareness is **uncertainty**. It is the things that you don't even know you should worry about. It also represents stuff you can't know because it is dependent upon the future action of yourself and others like potential customers or competitors. As entrepreneurs take action and interact with others under these kinds of conditions they are able to reduce the uncertainty associated with a new venture.

The Nature of Entrepreneurship

If we look a little more closely at the definition of **entrepreneurship**, we can identify three characteristics of entrepreneurial activity:[1]

1. **Innovation**. Entrepreneurship generally means offering a new product, applying a new technique or technology, opening a new market, or developing a new form of organization for the purpose of producing or enhancing a product.
2. **Running a business**. A business, as we saw in Chapter 1 "The Foundations of Business," combines resources to produce goods or services. Entrepreneurship means setting up a business to make a profit.
3. **Risk taking**. The term risk means that the outcome of the entrepreneurial venture can't be known. Entrepreneurs, therefore, are always working under a certain degree of uncertainty, and they can't know the outcomes of many of the decisions that they have to make. Consequently, many of the steps they take are motivated mainly by their confidence in the innovation and in their understanding of the business environment in which they're operating.

A Few Things to Know about Going into Business for Yourself

Mark Zuckerberg founded Facebook while a student at Harvard. By age 27 he built up a personal wealth of $13.5 billion. By age 31, his net worth was $37.5 billion.

So what about you? Do you ever wonder what it would be like to start your own business? You might even turn into a "serial entrepreneur" like Marcia Kilgore.[2] After high school, she moved from Canada to New York City to attend Columbia University. But when her financial aid was delayed, Marcia abandoned her plans to attend college and took a job as a personal trainer (a natural occupation for a former bodybuilder and middleweight title holder). But things got boring in the summer when her

Figure 7.2: Facebook founder Mark Zuckerberg.

wealthy clients left the city for the Hamptons. To keep busy, she took a skin care course at a Manhattan cosmetology institute. As a teenager, she was self-conscious about her complexion and wanted to know how to treat it herself. She learned how to give facials and work with natural remedies. She started giving facials to her fitness clients who were thrilled with the results. As demand for her services exploded, she started her first business—Bliss Spa—and picked up celebrity clients, including Madonna, Oprah Winfrey, and Jennifer Lopez. The business went international, and she sold it for more than $30 million.[3]

But the story doesn't end here; she launched two more companies: Soap and Glory, a supplier of affordable beauty products sold at Target, and FitFlops, which sells sandals that tone and tighten your leg muscles as you walk. Oprah loves Kilgore's sandals and plugged them on her show.[4] You can't get a better endorsement than that. Kilgore never did finish college, but when asked if she would follow the same path again, she said, "If I had to decide what to do all over again, I would make the same choices…I found by accident what I'm good at, and I'm glad I did."

So, a few questions to consider if you want to go into business for yourself:

- How do I find a problem to solve and know it is an opportunity worth pursuing?
- How do I come up with a business idea?
- Should I build a business from scratch, buy an existing business, or invest in a franchise?
- What steps are involved in developing a business plan?
- Where could I find help in getting my business started?
- How can I increase the likelihood that I'll succeed?

In this chapter, we'll provide some answers to questions like these.

Why Start Your Own Business?

What sort of characteristics distinguishes those who start businesses from those who don't? Or, more to the point, why do some people actually follow through on the desire to start up their own businesses? The most common reasons for starting a business are the following:

- To be your own boss
- To accommodate a desired lifestyle
- To achieve financial independence
- To enjoy creative freedom
- To use your skills and knowledge

The **Small Business Administration** (SBA) points out, though, that these are likely to be advantages only "for the right person." How do you know if you're one of the "right people"? The SBA suggests that you assess your strengths and weaknesses by asking yourself a few relevant questions:[5]

- Am I a self-starter? You'll need to develop and follow through on your ideas.
- How well do I get along with different personalities? Strong working relationships with a variety of people are crucial.
- How good am I at making decisions? Especially under pressure.....
- Do I have the physical and emotional stamina? Expect six or seven work days of about twelve hours every week.
- How well do I plan and organize? Poor planning is the culprit in most business failures.
- How will my business affect my family? Family members need to know what to expect: long hours and, at least initially, a more modest standard of living.

Before we discuss why businesses fail we should consider why a huge number of business ideas never even make it to the grand opening. One business analyst cites four reservations (or fears) that prevent people from starting businesses:[6]

- **Money**. Without cash, you can't get very far. What to do: line up initial financing early or at least have done enough research to have a plan to raise money.
- **Security**. A lot of people don't want to sacrifice the steady income that comes with the nine-to-five job. What to do: don't give up your day job. Run the business part-time or connect with someone to help run your business—a "co-founder."
- **Competition**. A lot of people don't know how to distinguish their business ideas from similar ideas. What to do: figure out how to do something cheaper, faster, or better.
- **Lack of ideas**. Some people simply don't know what sort of business they want to get into. What to do: find out what trends are successful. Turn a hobby into a business. Think about a franchise. Find a solution to something that annoys you—entrepreneurs call this a "pain point"—and try to turn it into a business.

If you're interested in going into business for yourself, try to regard such drawbacks as mere obstacles to be overcome by a combination of planning, talking to potential customers, and creative thinking.

Who is an Entrepreneur?

You might be thinking, "All that sounds great, but I'm not an entrepreneur." While some research has found some correlation between personality traits, like openness to new experiences, to be common among entrepreneurs; entrepreneurs are not that different from you. You can learn to act entrepreneurially and decide if starting your own business is right for you now or in the future. While many people choose to be single founders of their own company (sometimes referred to as solopreneurs) most of entrepreneurship requires working with others in some way.

Founding Teams

One of the most effective ways to get more done is to collaborate with others. Founding Teams increases your capacity and provides additional knowledge and experience from which to draw during any problem-solving process. Working with others can also provide emotional support and motivation to persist when obstacles or failures are encountered. However, there is also a cost to collaboration requiring time and effort to ensure everyone's actions are aligned to support one another, and that everyone agrees on what those actions are and how they should be accomplished. It can get tricky when you started something together but then start to see different opportunities.

Figure 7.3: Collaborative teams yield the best results!

A **founding team** can be comprised of two (most common) or more co-founders that own the company together, take the chance to capitalize on an opportunity and are usually working for free as you get things off the ground.

When organizing a team it is good to start with yourself and an understanding of what you can do. Among entrepreneurship scholars, there is a bit of a debate and mixed results regarding the best kind of founding team. A diverse founding team can give you additional expertise, expand your network and access to additional knowledge and resources, as well as providing unique ways of seeing the world when it comes to problem-solving. Whereas, a founding team where members are more similar can reduce those benefits but it can also reduce the collaboration costs if you and you co-founders have the same kinds of backgrounds, experience, and goals which make communication and coordination more efficient for shared leadership.

If you are considering working with a co-founder start first by identifying what *you* can do, then consider what other skills or roles would allow you to achieve your goals of launching a new venture. Some common roles within a startup generally include someone who:

- Had the idea/pathfinder;
- Manages the project/company;
- Raises money or makes connections;
- Brings in the revenues;
- Built the product (or performs the services)

Now you may be able to do all of them pretty well yourself but you still only have 24 hours in a day and may need to spend your time doing something that no one else on your team can do, or using the time to work on your business rather than in it.

Identifying Co-Founders

How do you find co-founders once you know what you are looking for? You can start with your personal networks. Share your vision or what you are looking for and ask them to refer you to anyone they think would be interested and a good fit for what you are looking for. You can also try to put yourself in places where you are more likely to meet potential co-founders whether that is online or offline. You can search according to expertise. For example, if you're experienced on the making side but not as experienced on the business side you might go to a business networking event. If the situation were reversed and you had some business acumen but didn't know how to actually build say a software product you might go to a hackathon to find people that know how to code and develop software. In either case be sure you are bringing something to the relationship besides just an idea. Again, when recruiting, share your passion for the vision and why you need help. It is helpful to be very clear about the role they would fill as you work together. Because you are starting a new relationship try working together on a small project that would move things forward that can be completed in a week or two. Remember, you do not have to decide on how to divide the work and the ownership right away and in fact should probably make the amount of ownership contingent upon certain milestones completed.

When Does Entrepreneurship Occur? When Does it End?

Organization Lifecycle

An organizational lifecycle refers to the different stages that organizations pass through. Similarly, industries and products also experience this same kind of lifecycle, as you'll see in Chapter 15.

As the entrepreneur or founding team begins their journey of turning their idea into a new organization they are in the **startup phase**. This phase is usually characterized by large amounts of uncertainty associated with customer demand, operational capabilities, and the financial feasibility of the business model. After the startup phase the business continues on to the **growth phase** when founders have figured out how to provide the product profitably and are implementing systems to find and reach more customers. After that stage the **mature phase** occurs when growth slows and the focus is more on optimization and resource allocation rather than exploring how to create additional value. The final stage is the **decline or rebirth stage**. A decline occurs when there is negative growth or profits. Instead of shutting down the company many will try a rebirth stage where they attempt to change what they do and find new customers. This stage doesn't have to be after or during a decline but can occur whenever the company chooses to explore new products or services that create new value. This is when corporate entrepreneurship happens. However, the absence of uncertainty about what to create or how to create value signals the end of entrepreneurship and entrepreneurial thinking, but can resurface as the organization decides to launch a new product or faces uncertain market conditions.

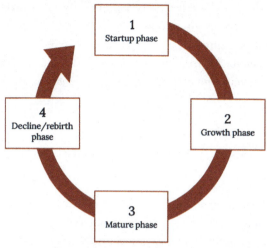

Figure 7.4: The organization life cycle.

 An interactive H5P element has been excluded from this version of the text. You can view it online here: https://pressbooks.lib.vt.edu/fundamentalsofbusiness4e/?p=564#h5p-19

Uncertainty

When we talk about uncertainty experienced by entrepreneurs we are often referring to various **knowledge problems** they encounter during the startup or rebirth stages. Uncertainty is one kind of knowledge problem that happens when you cannot know what action is likely to lead to a desired outcome. Other common knowledge problems entrepreneurs deal with are complexity, ambiguity, and equivocality. **Complexity** occurs because of the number of variables that make up a problem and the number of interactions between those variables that could influence outcomes. **Ambiguity** occurs when there isn't clarity around what is important or even what might happen. **Equivocality** occurs when there are multiple meanings or interpretations of what is important and what is possible. Each of these knowledge problems are navigated differently. For example, suppose you find yourself confronted with a complexity or equivocality knowledge problem and decide you just need more information before you make a decision. You have just added to your problems by creating more complexity to sift through or more possible options to consider. However, for knowledge problems like uncertainty and ambiguity additional information might help you to understand what will or will not work.[7]

These knowledge problems are why many people do not attempt entrepreneurship and why startups fail despite resources and effort. The judgement and action under these conditions are what define the domain of entrepreneurship. Once there has been a reduction in uncertainty and the other knowledge problems have been overcome to at least a level of probabilistic risk then as the emphasis shifts from exploration to optimization to minimize or to estimate the known risks.

Where Does Entrepreneurship Occur?

Entrepreneurship occurs in all sorts of different settings and industries. Each industry has its own set of norms, resources, and constraints. While new ideas can happen by bringing what has worked in one industry to another; it can also be challenging because of these differences of context. The common element in all the contexts is the creation of value under conditions of uncertainty.

Value is a subjective term that represents the perceived importance or preference of a good or service. Companies are able to capture some of that value because of the price they charge for delivering that value. Customers also receive enough value that they are willing and able to pay that price and receive enough of a benefit for doing so. An entrepreneur works with potential customers to understand and create a system that can continue to produce enough value for the customer to make providing a good or service worth doing. Let's look at different types of entrepreneurship to see how context and other factors matter in value creation.

Figure 7.5: Value creation.

 An interactive H5P element has been excluded from this version of the text. You can view it online here:
https://pressbooks.lib.vt.edu/fundamentalsofbusiness4e/?p=564#h5p-53

136 | Entrepreneurship and Small Business Development

Types of Entrepreneurship

Lifestyle versus High-Growth

One way to classify startups are by the goals or aspirations of the founders and the market size they choose to serve. On one end of the continuum, we have startups that grow up to be commonly called **lifestyle businesses** (also referred to as small businesses). These tend to create value for a niche group of customers that benefit from their service, product, or platform. These "small" businesses can still be very profitable and employ upwards of 500 people. This kind of business makes up the largest quantity of businesses, however, despite the sheer number of them, in total, they produce less than the type of business at the other end of the continuum,, which are usually referred to as **high-growth ventures**. High-growth venture startups tend to create value for much larger sized markets and become or are acquired by large and often publicly-traded corporations. They tend to employ thousands or tens of thousands of employees within one country though often have a larger global market that they serve.

Social Entrepreneurship

Traditionally all entrepreneurship seeks to systematize value creation in a way that generates enough profits to continue to create value through providing beneficial experiences or solving problems. **Social entrepreneurship** seeks to use a startup or company to not only generate enough profit but also enough social and/or environmental impact. This might mean addressing a social need experienced by those unable to pay for a solution on their own due to conditions of poverty. This might mean the company donates part of its revenue or profit to a charitable cause. It might also mean that the company is set up and supported to be able to provide a service at a price that normally wouldn't be sustainable. It also might look like a charity or non-profit that uses donations and grants instead of service or product revenue to address a social issue. It could also be a for-profit entity selling a service, product, or platform through a business model that provides employment to underemployed groups or areas. In most social entrepreneurship, the startup measures their success according to not only profits, but social and environmental impact referred to as a **triple bottom line**. Though both entrepreneurship and social entrepreneurship add value and do good, what differentiates them are the kind of constraints a founder must address.

Corporate Entrepreneurship/Intrapreneurship

When we think of entrepreneurship most of the time we think of new startup companies, but entrepreneurship can happen within an existing organization as well. As was mentioned in the organization lifecycle section, as a company grows it may sell its service or product to everyone within a particular market such that the demand for what they produce eventually declines. Intrapreneurship is entrepreneurship within an established organization. Instead of closing the organization because of a lack of demand, they can redeploy resources to make additional products or improve upon old ones to extend the lifecycle of the organization. Established companies might not wait until their current product is no longer in demand. Instead they build a better product that competes against their own product before someone else can. Existing businesses may also need to change different parts of their existing business model due to changes outside the company like competitors or environmental constraints. Some companies have separate divisions dedicated to exploring ways they can create new products, such as research and development (R&D) or a corporate venture capital division, while other companies encourage and rely on employees to suggest new ideas and improvements without any changes to dedicated roles or structures. In the figure below the dotted line represents the point at which intrapreneurship tends to take place during the lifecycle of the organization.

Figure 7.6: *When intrepreneurship happens with the organization's lifecycle.*

Intrapreneurship or entrepreneurship in this corporate setting tends not to have the same constraints found in new startups, like a lack of resources or legitimacy. Entrepreneurs within corporations must instead deal with constraints like institutional inertia and internal politics. Institutional inertia comes from the fact that the company is largely known for and focused on optimizing what they do well. The company does not want to risk a reputation in the market and is reluctant to compete against itself at times.

There is also the matter of not using the company's resources efficiently. Most choices about what project to invest in are made using assumptions about risk. Unfortunately, these same approaches do not account for conditions of uncertainty, and innovation projects are often rejected through the normal project evaluation process because they will be seen as too risky. New ideas are often met with resistance because it means someone has to do something different or because there are differences about what or how the different things should be. New ideas might not receive support because of the internal competition for resources or power. Intrapreneurship requires a slightly different skill set that is able to navigate rejection and internal politics to generate enough momentum and internal support to be able to move an idea forward.

Health Entrepreneurship

While every industry has its own set of challenges, rules, and norms, the health industry is one that is very regulated. Health entrepreneurship requires extra time to bring a new product to market. Within the United States, the Food and Drug Administration is responsible for ensuring the safety and efficacy of food, drugs, biologics, medical devices, cosmetics, and other health-related categories. This requires getting approval or a (510k) exemption from the agency before being able to sell your product. Drugs in particular need to go through a series of experiments to make sure they work as they should without side effects first on animals and then on people. Even on an accelerated track, these tests can take a lot of time and money.

Another unique aspect of the U.S. health industry for entrepreneurs to navigate is the role of the insurance companies. Insurance companies have a series of medical codes that classify different kinds of treatments or devices that some insurance plans will pay on behalf of the consumer while others will not. In addition, each insurance company has different agreements regarding how much will be paid to the medical providers. Introducing new products or services requires understanding how the insurance coding and claims process works so that the insurance payor system will be able to finance what you are doing. Just because consumers like your health product doesn't mean they will be able to afford it without it being covered by their insurance. These kinds of systemic constraints are experienced in the health industry in addition to the uncertainty associated with entrepreneurship.

Digital Entrepreneurship

Digital entrepreneurship is a term that has surfaced as a result of the increase in the use of technological advances that can be used to start a new venture. Often these kinds of new ventures create value by leveraging existing technological platforms or services to create and automate traditional business or organizational processes. Digital entrepreneurship also encompasses the use of digital products that only exist and can be used online. Often this kind of entrepreneurship lowers the cost to start but also introduces more complexities that make it difficult to understand which process and activities will create value that can be captured and delivered in a sustainable way. The internet context also introduces additional security concerns of protecting data that is used, collected, and stored.

Type	Definition
Lifestyle	Creates value for a niche group of customers that benefit from their service, product, or platform and grow-up to be small businesses (less than 500 employees)
High growth	Creates value for much larger sized markets and grow-up to be large corporations
Social	Use a startup or company to not only generate enough profit but also enough social and/or environmental impact.
Corporate/intrapreneurship	Creates a new product or service within an existing company
Digital	Creates value by leveraging existing technological platforms or services to automate traditional organizational processes or other digital products that only exist and can be used online.
Health/life science	Creates value with products that improve health outcomes while overcoming the constraints of regulation and insurance systems

Figure 7.7: Types of startups.

 An interactive H5P element has been excluded from this version of the text. You can view it online here:
https://pressbooks.lib.vt.edu/fundamentalsofbusiness4e/?p=564#h5p-59

Entrepreneurial Ecosystem

Each of these types and contexts is also part of a larger ecosystem that can make it easier or more difficult to go through the entrepreneurial process. When you hear the word ecosystem your mind might flash back to the first time you were introduced to biology and saw how things were connected. An **entrepreneurial ecosystem** refers to a community or network of people, spaces, and available resources that interact around the creation of new ventures. Traditionally, entrepreneurial ecosystems have been geographically oriented allowing for more frequent interactions between different groups of people who exchange information, connections, and resources. However, more and more entrepreneurs are turning to online ecosystems that can provide some of the same access.

Some common spaces where you are likely to find entrepreneurs within an ecosystem include coworking spaces, incubators, and accelerators. **Coworking spaces** are open areas where entrepreneurs and business professionals can work out of. The spaces can be free or accessible by paying for a membership to get access. Usually, those just getting started or solopreneurs tend to leverage these spaces. **Incubators** are basically a bunch of offices in the same area that are rented out to particular startup companies. The rent is usually below what you would find out in the current market to provide low-cost options for those getting started. There are also usually shared spaces or services to facilitate community amongst the tenants. **Accelerators** are programs that provide money, space, services, and some sort of training or mentoring to startups selected to participate in their program usually in exchange for equity. Accelerators often are for a limited time frame (e.g. 3 months) and end in a demo day when startups show off or demonstrate what they have done in front of other external investors.

There are also different variations on these kinds of spaces and programs in different ecosystems. For example, on a university campus you might find something similar to the Apex Center for Entrepreneurs, located at Virginia Tech in Blacksburg, Virginia, that is dedicated to helping students, faculty, and/or alumni turn their passion and purpose into action through various programs and entrepreneurial experiences. You might also find other organizations that support and provide services to entrepreneurs sponsoring these spaces. So don't be surprised to find lawyers, accountants, consultants, bankers, and investors at these places or other entrepreneurial events and activities.

See Virginia Tech Apex Center for Entrepreneurs' annual report here: https://www.apex.vt.edu/about/annual-report

Figure 7.8: Glenn Feit, of grand prize winner QuickTech, pitches the team's product.

How to do entrepreneurship?

Process/Approaches

The process of starting a new venture is a dynamic series of experiences that can be approached in a variety of ways. Some ventures may begin with an idea, others may come across a new technology, while some founders experience a problem they want to solve for themselves and discover others want a similar solution. Getting access to new resources or a desire to work with a particular group can be the start of finding ways to create value utilizing those talents, connections, or resources. This means that you can start from just about anywhere though you'll quickly discover the need to engage in other experiences to help reduce uncertainty as you figure out how it all fits together.

While the entrepreneurial journey can be started from different places most of the time in the early stage it begins with one of the following 5 scenarios:

Figure 7.9: *Different entrepreneurial journeys.*

Each of these is an on-ramp to a similar path with slight deviations depending on the industry and contextual factors. The entrepreneurs' path is about creating a vision, reducing the unknowns by validating assumptions associated with that vision, gathering resources needed to execute, and generating enough collective agreement to execute on the vision. It is usually best to start with the riskiest or most impactful assumption. The following assumptions are frequently found to be the challenge:

- Assumption #1: Your envisioned customer has the problem you are trying to solve
- Assumption #2: Your solution solves the problem in a unique and desirable way
- Assumption #3: You know how to find and attract enough of your customers
- Assumption #4: Your customers are willing to pay you for the solution
- Assumption #5: You can build or provide the solution
- Assumption #6: You can recruit the talent needed to create, capture, and deliver value
- Assumption #7: You can establish partnerships that allow you to scale

Assumption #1 Your envisioned customer has the problem you are trying to solve

Many people tend to come up with and get excited about product ideas or solutions without fully understanding the customers' problems. This can be problematic because they are at risk of only paying attention to information that can be used to justify that they are right instead of figuring out what the real problem is that customers actually care about. Another version of this underlying assumption is keeping the idea a secret, for fear of someone stealing the idea, until it is ready to buy instead of getting feedback along the way. This prevents entrepreneurs from taking advantage of the perspectives and ideas of others to refine and improve the idea. In both cases, the potential downside is that the entrepreneur puts in the time, effort, and resources to build something that no one really wants. Sure it might be annoying to the customer but so what? It isn't that big of a deal, at least enough that it would motivate them to buy something to solve it. Before falling in love with your solution make sure you understand the problem so you can create the right solution. Reducing the uncertainty associated with this assumption can be done by identifying the emotional evidence of the problem. In addition, understanding what the core problem is and not just the symptoms can reduce uncertainty around what would be valued.

Assumption #2 Your solution solves the problem in a unique and desirable way

This assumption is closely related to the first one but has more to do with gauging market timing or demand rather than understanding the motivations of your buyer. One way to figure that out is to talk with potential customers about their current experience when they encounter the problem you are interested in solving. You are listening to hear if they have the problem and are actively trying to solve it with workarounds, trying new products, or doing a bunch of research but just are not happy with the outcomes. These are the people most ready to buy and are your Early Adopters. Early adopters also tend to tell other people about new solutions through word of mouth. In order to gauge market timing, you are trying to find problem spaces in which the majority of the people you talk to are the early adopters. However, many times people will simply acknowledge the problem but just deal with it instead of trying to solve it. They'll be annoyed or discount the problem someway. Others won't have a problem with the current outcomes due to their own preferences or priorities. If you talk to 10 people that you believe have the problem but only 2 or 3 are actively trying to address the issue with time, money, or effort then it probably isn't the right time. This means you will end up spending a lot of time educating your customers about the problem and convincing them it is worth solving. You can choose to do that it just usually takes a lot more time, money, and motivation to generate enough momentum.

Once you have talked to early adopters about their experiences you can decide which problems you can or want to address. Now that the problem has been identified it is time to come up with a novel, useful, and valued solution. Ideation techniques and tools help entrepreneurs come up with those solutions. This process usually involves divergent thinking that generates as many kinds of solutions as possible before engaging in convergent thinking that narrows down choices to help us make a decision and move forward. Associative thinking that encourages unlikely recombinations of concepts or contexts has also been used to inspire novel ideas. Ultimately the idea needs to address the unmet needs of your early adopters.

Assumption #3: You know how to find and attract enough of your customers

Many entrepreneurs have the thought that as soon as they launch their website or app or if they just build it then people will immediately start buying. However, in most cases, people are so inundated with information or only use particular channels to get their information thereby making it difficult to even make them aware that your startup exists. As you talk to your early adopters figure out where they heard about the last new product, service, or platform that they considered buying. That can help you identify the marketing channels to start with but don't stop there. The cost to acquire a new customer, referred to as customer acquisition cost (CAC), is one of the most uncertain costs associated with your business that can make or break how profitable you can be. Some entrepreneurs assume those costs can be low because "social media is free". It still costs time to create, post, and interact with content even if it is your own time. Be sure to track how much it takes to get a new follower, put an hourly wage to that time, and include that in your CAC. You are trying to create a system that can continuously find and attract those early adopters who in turn will help you get more customers. You want to try to find what is most effective but also what brings in the largest quantity of potential customers. Because not everyone that sees your social media post will click on it, and not everyone that clicks on will, go to your website. Not everyone that comes to your website will be ready to buy and in fact, you'll have a much smaller percentage of potential customers that will result in a conversion or sale than what you started out with. Keeping track of how many potential customers move from one stage to the next can help you do a better job at finding and attracting more customers.

Assumption #4: Your customers are willing to pay you for the solution

If potential customers do make it to the point of purchase they may still be unwilling to pay the price you are asking them to pay. Determining the right price for a new product or service can be tricky. Many factors outside of your control can influence this like what the competition or alternatives for the buyer are and how much value is perceived by the customer. You can use a market comparables approach where you look at potential alternatives to what you're selling and either offer at a premium price or a discounted price. You can also try a cost-plus approach where you figure out how much it costs you to deliver the service, product, or platform and then add a particular markup percentage that represents your profits. Or you can attempt to quantify the subjective value that your early adopters place upon what you are creating. [8]

Sometimes the value created by a startup is not in a new service, product, or platform but rather, in the way they make it available to potential customers. A startup may sell its product at a loss or at a lower profit margin if they also have additional products or services that will be purchased by that customer over a lifetime. The lifetime value of a customer (LTV) is an assumed amount that each new customer will spend in the future. In most startup cycles lifetime means the next twelve to eighteen months.

Assumption #5: You can build or provide the solution

Many a potential entrepreneur has come up with an idea but have no idea how to actually make or build their idea. Some of that may be because of a lack of personal knowledge or skill in which case you will have to recruit the talent needed but it also may be because of the limitations of current technologies. Or it can be built but not at a cost anyone is ready to pay for. Remember as an entrepreneur you are wanting to create a system that can continuously create value. But you have to do it the first time before you can grow or scale it. This usually involves creating a prototype or a simple version of the product or service to learn what it would take to produce it and if it can work as envisioned. A prototype doesn't need to be completely functional in order to learn. You could even use competitors' products as your prototype and find out what needs to change or stay the same. Regardless in most cases, you'll make multiple versions of a product or service after having received feedback from potential customers before arriving at the finished outcome, which includes a repeatable process.

Assumption #6: You can recruit talent needed to create, capture, & deliver value

This builds off of the prior assumption that you don't have the necessary skills or knowledge to create, capture, and deliver value to your customers in a profitable way. This is often where passion for an idea can bring similarly passionate people together to work towards achieving a better future. However, while people might be interested in an idea, they are also interested in being well paid on a consistent basis. A lack of ability to pay people's salaries puts startups at a considerable disadvantage when recruiting. However, you may be able to offer longer-term benefits such as equity or the chance to gain experience by working on things they're not qualified to attempt in the general labor market. Or you can find experienced individuals who are willing to be a part of your advisory board and give you a few hours every month or so to help you know things that you are not aware of.

Assumption #7: You can establish partnerships that allow you to scale

Most of the time startups can't do everything and need to partner with others. This might be suppliers or raw material providers that provide parts or resources, Or it could be manufacturers, distributors, wholesalers, or retailers. It might also look like bankers, accountants, consultants, or independent contractors who provide expertise on particular parts of your business. However, like the prior recruiting assumption they tend to want to be paid or guaranteed they won't lose money for helping you. Finding partners who are willing to work with you as you figure out the best way can be challenging. Often personal networks and referrals are utilized to find partners willing to take a chance on a new startup. Contracts also become a common tool to spell out expectations and recourse if things do not go well.

Figure 7.10: Establish partnerships that allow you to scale.

Each assumption or area has experiences, milestones, or artifacts, a few of which we've mentioned above. The image below is an attempted visual roadmap of various stages/artifacts.

Startup Financing

While a lot of the process can be done without any money there are eventual costs that need to be covered to be able to create, capture, and deliver value. Often founders struggle to get started because of a lack of resources, this section talks about different ways the startup can be funded along a continuum that goes from straightforward to more complex.

Level	Name	Team	Problem and vision	Value prop	Product	Market	Business model	Scale	Exit	Type of funding typically closed at this level
9	Exit in sight	Team positioned to navigate M&A, IPO	Global leader in stated vision	Cited as the top solution in the industry solving this problem	Product recognized as top in industry	Clear line-of-sight to industry dominance	Minimum 2x revenue growth for multiple years	Strong unit economics for multiple customer segments	Growth with exit	Acquirers
8	Scaling up	Team is recognized as market leaders in the industry	Systems-level change validated	Multiple renewals with low sales effort. Customers in multiple markets love the product	Strong customer product feedback in multiple markets	Brand established. Hard-to-beat partnerships for distribution, marketing, and growth	MOM revenue meets industry standard	Growth of customer base accelerates month-to-month	Team has turned down acquisition offer	Close institutional VC for recurring revenue + growth
7	Hitting product-market fit	C-suite as good or better than founding CEO and can stay with company through its growth and exit phases	Impact is successfully validated	Majority of first sales in target market are inbound	Product is built for scale and additional offerings in progress	Sales cycles meet or exceed industry standard	Business model validated—validation of strong unit economics	Evidence of strong unit economics across multiple markets	Team has strong relationships with multiple acquirers	Close institutional VC for recurring revenue + growth
6	Moving beyond early adopters	Team has proven sales, product dev skills, and management ability to support a growing team for scale	Sales validate impact tied to solution and grow as solution scales	Sales beyond initial target customers. Customers love it and are referring the product to others	Complete product with strong user experience feedback	Supply/distribution partners see their success aligned with the company's success	Sales begin to map to projections. Evidence of decreasing CAC with growing customer base buying at target price	Company has cleared regulatory challenges and (if applicable) is implementing a strong IP strategy	Team has identified specific acquirer(s) or other exit environment	Close institutional VC for 1st sales, market expansion
5	Providing a profitable business model	Team has cleat sales/ops understanding and strategy	Evidence of impact tied to solution—the company has evidence that by growing the business, company solves the problem	Target customers love the product and want to keep using it	Fully functional prototype with completion of product for wide commercial distribution in sight	Team is having conversations with strategic partners to capture their market faster/cheaper than the competition	Financial model with evidence of valid projections to reach positive unit economics	Vision and initial evidence of positive unit economics in two markets	Inbound interest from large strategics	Close round with angel and early VC
4	Validating an investable market	Team has clear understanding of how their target market operates and has string industry contacts in this market	The company can articulate system-level change—how this solution would transform the industry	Evidence of differentiation through initial target customer feedback that the solution solves their problem significantly better than others in the market	Team has cleat understanding of product development costs and how to build the initial product cos-effectively	Evidence of $1B+ total addressable market	Team has financial model with cost and revenue projections articulated and a strategy for hitting these projections	Initial evidence that multiple types of customers find value in the solution or in an extension of the product that the company is well-positioned to develop	Evidence of growth trajectory that cound lead to IPO, acquisition, or self-liquidating exit	- Angel/seed funding starts - Friends, family, bootstrap
3	Solidifying the value proposition	Team has technical ability to build fully functional product and has a clear understanding of the value chain and cost structures in their industry	The company can articulate why they're the best ones to solve this problem	Evidence that customers will pay the target price. For B2C-100 customers, for B2B-5 customers and conversations with multiple stakeholders in each	Team has built a working prototype and a product roadmap	Initial evidence through sales that team can capture initial target market	Team can articulate projected costs along the value chain and target cost points to reach positive unit economics	Clear strategy to move to multiple markets	Initial evidence that the solution already solves the problem better than any incumbents	- Grants for R&D (hardware) - Friends, family, bootstrap
2	Setting the vision	Team has senior members with lived experience of the problem and/or deep understanding of their target customer's problem	The team can solve the problem and can articulate its vision at scale—what does the world look like if they succeed?	The team has potential customers who provide evidence that solution solves key pain point—product is a painkiller, not vitamin	Team has a basic low-fidelity prototype that solves the problem	Team understands any regulatory hurdles to entering the market and has a strategy to overcome them	Company can point to pricing and business models of similar products in the industry as further evidence that their revenue assumptions hold	Initial evidence that multiple markets experience this problem	Vision for growth has company solving a large piece of the global problem in 10 years	- Grants for R&D (hardware) - Friends, family, bootstrap
1	Establishing the founding team	Strong founding team—at least 2 people with differentiated skillsets	Team has identified a specific, important, and large problem	Team has identified their hypothesis of their target customer—the specific type of person whose problem they are solving	Team has ability to develop low-fidelity prototype and has freedom to operate—not blocked by other patents	Team can clearly articulate total addressable market, the percentage they will capture, and initial target market	Team has identified an outline of revenue model	Team has identified multiple possible markets or customer segments and has aspiration to scale	Team understands what an exit is and has a vision for how they will ultimately provide a return for their investors	Friends, family, bootstrap

Figure 7.11: Different types of funding for viral pathways.

Bootstrapping is when the founders use their own funds to start a company. This might be income from their full-time job, it might savings, or the use of their personal credit cards. They can also get favorable invoice or line of credit terms from suppliers so that they can have the product made and sell it before they have to pay for the cost of production. However, this often requires a personal guarantee from the founder exposing their personal assets to risk. As you progress along this continuum, founders might be funded with a gift or loan by friends or family members who want to help them start the business. Sometimes government institutions like universities or other ecosystem stakeholders might provide grants or competition prizes that allow the founder to get started. Some founders can pre-sell their ideas getting the money prior to building a product like on **crowdfunding** platforms. For those that need a lot of money to start their venture due to the kinds of equipment or property needed to create value, they may need to pursue debt financing like a bank loan. Others might be able to convince suppliers or manufacturers to extend a line of credit so that they have time to sell the service or products before the invoice comes due.

All these are ways to get to the primary funding mechanism of any business, revenue from paying customers. However, even if a startup has initial revenue, it may not be able to afford the changes needed to support rapid growth to reach large amounts of customers. This is when external investors may become involved. Investors will give the founders money in exchange for some equity or ownership of the company. Investors, in general, want a return on their investment which means the value of the company they invest in must increase considerably and have a way for them to get their money back. This becomes important for founders to understand as not all companies are investable due to the market size or growth potential. It doesn't mean that they won't be profitable just not enough for investors to get what they want or need. Below is an example of a Venture Investment-Readiness and Awareness Levels framework used by venture capital firms to help startups understand when they would be ready to be considered for investment.

The two primary types of investors in investable startups are angels and venture capitalists. **Angel investors** invest their own money either on their own or with a group of others. They might invest for a variety of reasons (a product they'd use, want to be involved in something exciting, desire to help a passionate founder, etc.) besides just the chance to make money but are often hoping to get a return on their money in a three to a five-year window through an acquisition or during the next round (Seed, Series A, B, C, etc.) of funding with venture capitalists. **Venture capitalists** invest primarily other people's money promising high returns in seven to ten years to those individuals who contribute to their fund. The venture capitalists then search for a portfolio of high-growth ventures that serve large amounts of customers. They hope that some of the ventures will be acquired and that at least one of them will get really big, really fast to become a publicly-traded stock so they can cash out and return the promised money to their clients. Angel investors invest smaller amounts than venture capitalists but also don't need the company to grow as much as the venture capitalist to get the desired return. Whereas venture capitalists have a fiduciary responsibility or to act in good faith on behalf of their clients. The tricky part is being able to tell which startups will be the ones to be that high-growth success with all the uncertainty that exists.

 An interactive H5P element has been excluded from this version of the text. You can view it online here:
https://pressbooks.lib.vt.edu/fundamentalsofbusiness4e/?p=564#h5p-20

 An interactive H5P element has been excluded from this version of the text. You can view it online here:
https://pressbooks.lib.vt.edu/fundamentalsofbusiness4e/?p=564#h5p-52

Beyond Founding

A key aspect of the entrepreneurial journey is the creation of a service, product, or platform. In order to build a system that creates value through one of these creations requires some experimentation and rapid learning to develop an offering that is enough to merit revenue transactions. Besides launching your own company the skills developed during the commercialization process tend to be those used by product managers within existing corporations and are often a career path for those that study entrepreneurship in higher education.

Distinguishing Entrepreneurs from Small Business Owners

Though most entrepreneurial ventures begin as small businesses, not all small business owners are entrepreneurs. **Entrepreneurs** are innovators who start companies to create new or improved products. They strive to meet a need that's not being met, and their goal is to grow the business and eventually expand into other markets.

In contrast, many people either start or buy small businesses for the sole purpose of providing an income for themselves and their families. They do not intend to be particularly innovative, nor do they plan to expand significantly. This desire to operate is what's sometimes called a "lifestyle business."[9] The neighborhood pizza parlor or beauty shop, the self-employed consultant who works out of the home, and even a local printing company—many of these are typically lifestyle businesses.

The Importance of Small Business to the US Economy

What Is a "Small Business"?

To assess the value of small businesses to the US economy, we first need to know what constitutes a small business. Let's start by looking at the criteria used by the Small Business Administration. According to the SBA, a **small business** is one that is independently owned and operated, exerts little influence in its industry, and (with a few exceptions) has fewer than 500 employees.[10]

Why Are Small Businesses Important?

There are more than 30.7 million small businesses in this country, and they generate about 47.3 percent of jobs in the US.[11] The millions of individuals who have started businesses in the United States have shaped the business world as we know it today. Some small business founders like Henry Ford and Thomas Edison have even gained places in history. Others, including Bill Gates (Microsoft), Sam Walton (Wal-Mart), Steve Jobs (Apple Computer), and Larry Page and Sergey Brin (Google), have changed the way business is done today.

Aside from contributions to our general economic well-being, founders of small businesses also contribute to growth and vitality in specific areas of economic and socioeconomic development. In particular, small businesses do the following:

- **Create jobs**
- **Spark innovation**
- **Provide opportunities** for many people, including women and minorities, to achieve financial success and independence

In addition, they complement the economic activity of large organizations by providing them with components, services, and distribution of their products. Let's take a closer look at each of these contributions.

Job Creation

The majority of US workers first entered the business world working for small businesses. Although the split between those working in small companies and those working in big companies is about even, small firms hire more frequently and fire more frequently than do big companies.[12] Why is this true? At any given point in time, lots of small companies are started and some expand. These small companies need workers and so hiring takes place. But the survival and expansion rates for small firms is poor, and so, again at any given point in time, many small businesses close or contract and workers lose their jobs. Fortunately, over time more jobs are added by small firms than are taken away, which results in a net increase in the number of workers, as seen in figure 7.12.

Job gains	Job losses	Net change
Openings: 85.5	Closings: 82.1	
Expansions: 326.5	Contractions: 320.7	
412	402.8	9.2

Figure 7.12: Small business job gains and losses, 2000-2021 (in millions of jobs).

The size of the net increase in the number of workers for any given year depends on a number of factors, with the economy being at the top of the list. A strong economy encourages individuals to start small businesses and expand existing small companies, which adds to the workforce. A weak economy does just the opposite: discourages start-ups and expansions, which decreases the workforce through layoffs. Figure 7.12 reports the job gains from start-ups and expansions and job losses from business closings and contractions.

Innovation

Given the financial resources available to large businesses, you'd expect them to introduce virtually all the new products that hit the market. Yet according to the SBA, small companies develop more patents per employee than do larger companies. During a recent four-year period, large firms generated 1.7 patents per hundred employees, while small firms generated an impressive 26.5 patents per employee.[13] Over the years, the list of important innovations by small firms has included the airplane, air-conditioning, DNA "fingerprinting," and overnight national delivery.[14]

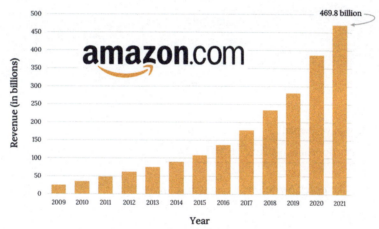

Figure 7.13: Amazon annual revenue growth (2009-2021).

Small business owners are also particularly adept at finding new ways of doing old things. In 1994, for example, a young computer-science graduate working on Wall Street came up with the novel idea of selling books over the Internet. During the first year of operations, sales at Jeff Bezos' new company—Amazon.com—reached half a million dollars. In less than 20 years, annual sales had topped $107 billion.[15] Not only did his innovative approach to online retailing make Bezos enormously rich, but it also established a viable model for the e-commerce industry.

Why are small businesses so innovative? For one thing, they tend to offer environments that appeal to individuals with the talent to invent new products or improve the way things are done. Fast decision making is encouraged, their research programs tend to be focused, and their compensation structures typically reward top performers.

According to one SBA study, the supportive environments of small firms are roughly 13 times more innovative per employee than the less innovation-friendly environments in which large firms traditionally operate.[16]

The success of small businesses in fostering creativity has not gone unnoticed by big businesses. In fact, many large companies have responded by downsizing to act more like small companies. Some large organizations now have separate work units whose purpose is to spark innovation. Individuals working in these units can focus their attention on creating new products that can then be developed by the company.

Opportunities for Women and Minorities

Small business is the portal through which many people enter the economic mainstream. Business ownership allows individuals, including women and minorities, to achieve financial success, as well as pride in their accomplishments. Figure 7.14 gives you an idea of how many American businesses are owned by women and minorities.

Business owners	2007	2018
Women-owned	37.5%	19.9%
Hispanic-owned	5.9%	5.8%
Asian-owned	5.6%	10.1%
Black-owned	3.6%	2.2%
American Indian and Alaska Native-owned	0.8%	0.4%
Native Hawaiian and other Pacific Islander-owned	0.2%	0.1%

Figure 7.14: Percent of all businesses owned by women and minorities.

What Industries Are Small Businesses In?

If you want to start a new business, you probably should avoid certain types of businesses. You'd have a hard time, for example, setting up a new company to make automobiles or aluminum, because you'd have to make tremendous investments in property, plant, and equipment, and raise an enormous amount of capital to pay your workforce. These large, up-front investments present barriers to entry.

Fortunately, plenty of opportunities are still available. Many types of businesses require reasonable initial investments, and not surprisingly, these are the ones that usually present attractive small business opportunities.

Industries by Sector

Let's define an **industry** as a group of companies that compete with one another to sell similar products. We'll focus on the relationship between a small business and the industry in which it operates, dividing businesses into two broad types of industries, or sectors: the goods-producing sector and the service-producing sector.

- The **goods-producing sector** includes all businesses that produce tangible goods. Generally speaking, companies in this sector are involved in manufacturing, construction, and agriculture.
- The **service-producing sector** includes all businesses that provide services but don't make tangible goods. They may be involved in retail and wholesale trade, transportation, finance, entertainment, recreation, accommodations, food service, and any number of other ventures.

About 20 percent of small businesses in the United States are concentrated in the goods-producing sector. The remaining 80 percent are in the service sector.[17] The high concentration of small businesses in the service-producing sector reflects the makeup of the overall US economy. Over the past 50 years, the service-producing sector has been growing at an impressive rate. In 1960, for example, the goods-producing sector accounted for 38 percent of GDP, the service-producing sector for 62 percent. By 2015, the balance had shifted dramatically, with the goods-producing sector accounting for only about 21 percent of GDP.[18]

Goods-Producing Sector

The largest areas of the goods-producing sector are construction and manufacturing. Construction businesses are often started by skilled workers, such as electricians, painters, plumbers, and home builders, and they generally work on local projects. Though manufacturing is primarily the domain of large businesses, there are exceptions.

How about making something out of trash? Daniel Blake never followed his mother's advice at dinner when she told him to eat everything on his plate. When he served as a missionary in Puerto Rico, Aruba, Bonaire, and Curacao after his first year in college, he noticed that the families he stayed with didn't either. But they didn't throw their uneaten food into the trash. Instead they put it on a compost pile and used the mulch to nourish their vegetable gardens and fruit trees. While eating at an all-you-can-eat breakfast buffet back home at Brigham Young University, Blake was amazed to see volumes of uneaten food in the trash. This triggered an idea: why not turn the trash into money? Two years later, he was running his company—EcoScraps—collecting 40 tons of food scraps a day from 75 grocers and turning it into high-quality potting soil that he sells online and to nurseries. His profit has reach almost half a million dollars on sales of $1.5 million.[19]

Service-Producing Sector

Many small businesses in this sector are **retailers**—they buy goods from other firms and sell them to consumers, in stores, by phone, through direct mailings, or over the Internet. In fact, entrepreneurs are turning increasingly to the Internet as a venue for start-up ventures. Take Tony Roeder, for example, who had a fascination with the red Radio Flyer wagons that many of today's adults had owned as children. In 1998, he started an online store through Yahoo! to sell red wagons from his home. In three years, he turned his online store into a million-dollar business.[20]

Other small business owners in this sector are **wholesalers**—they sell products to businesses that buy them for resale or for company use. A local bakery, for example, is acting as a wholesaler when it sells desserts to a restaurant, which then resells them to its customers. A small business that buys flowers from a local grower (the manufacturer) and resells them to a retail store is another example of a wholesaler.

A high proportion of small businesses in this sector provide professional, business, or personal services. Doctors and dentists are part of the service industry, as are insurance agents, accountants, and lawyers. So are businesses that provide personal services, such as dry cleaning and hairdressing.

David Marcks, for example, entered the service industry about 14 years ago when he learned that his border collie enjoyed chasing geese at the golf course where he worked. While geese are lovely to look at, they can make a mess of tees, fairways, and greens. That's where Marcks' company, Geese Police, comes in: Marcks employs specially trained dogs to chase the geese away. He now has 27 trucks, 32 border collies, and five offices. Golf courses account for only about 5 percent of his business, as his dogs now patrol corporate parks and playgrounds as well.[21] Figure 7.15 provides a more detailed breakdown of small businesses by industry.

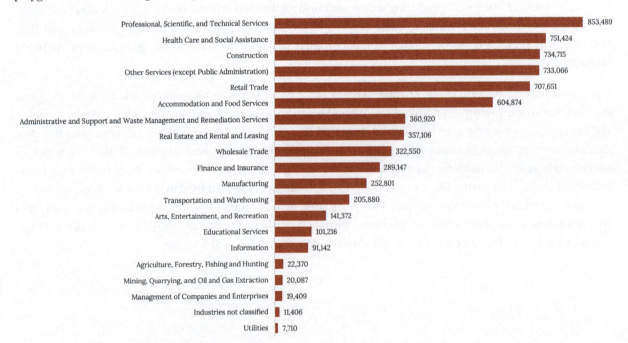

Figure 7.15: Number of small business establishments by industry, 2019.

Advantages and Disadvantages of Business Ownership

Do you want to be a business owner someday? Before deciding, you might want to consider the following advantages and disadvantages of business ownership.[22]

Advantages of Small Business Ownership

Being a business owner can be extremely rewarding. Having the courage to take a risk and start a venture is part of the American dream. Success brings with it many advantages:

- **Independence**. As a business owner, you're your own boss. You can't get fired. More importantly, you have the freedom to make the decisions that are crucial to your own business success.
- **Lifestyle**. Owning a small business gives you certain lifestyle advantages. Because you're in charge, you decide when and where you want to work. If you want to spend more time on non-work activities or with your family, you don't have to ask for the time off. Given today's technology, if it's important that you be with your family all day, you can run your business from your home.
- **Financial rewards**. In spite of high financial risk, running your own business gives you a chance to make more money than if you were employed by someone else. You benefit from your own hard work.
- **Learning opportunities**. As a business owner, you'll be involved in all aspects of your business. This situation creates numerous opportunities to gain a thorough understanding of the various business functions.
- **Creative freedom and personal satisfaction**. As a business owner, you'll be able to work in a field that you really enjoy. You'll be able to put your skills and knowledge to use, and you'll gain personal satisfaction from implementing your ideas, working directly with customers, and watching your business succeed.

Disadvantages of Small Business Ownership

As the little boy said when he got off his first roller-coaster ride, "I like the ups but not the downs!" Here are some of the risks you run if you want to start a small business:

- **Financial risk**. The financial resources needed to start and grow a business can be extensive. You may need to commit most of your savings or even go into debt to get started. If things don't go well, you may face substantial financial loss. In addition, there's no guaranteed income. There might be times, especially in the first few years, when the business isn't generating enough cash for you to live on.
- **Stress**. As a business owner, you are the business. There's a bewildering array of things to worry about—competition, employees, bills, equipment breakdowns, etc.. As the owner, you're also responsible for the well-being of your employees.

- **Time commitment.** People often start businesses so that they'll have more time to spend with their families. Unfortunately, running a business is extremely time-consuming. In theory, you have the freedom to take time off, but in reality, you may not be able to get away. In fact, you'll probably have less free time than you'd have working for someone else. For many entrepreneurs and small business owners, a 40-hour workweek is a myth. Vacations will be difficult to take and will often be interrupted. In recent years, the difficulty of getting away from the job has been compounded by cell phones, iPhones, Internet-connected laptops and iPads, and many small business owners have come to regret that they're always reachable.
- **Undesirable duties.** When you start up, you'll undoubtedly be responsible for either doing or overseeing just about everything that needs to be done. You can get bogged down in detail work that you don't enjoy. As a business owner, you'll probably have to perform some unpleasant tasks, like firing people.

In spite of these and other disadvantages, most small business owners are pleased with their decision to start a business. A survey conducted by the Wall Street Journal and Cicco and Associates indicates that small business owners and top-level corporate executives agree overwhelmingly that small business owners have a more satisfying business experience. Interestingly, the researchers had fully expected to find that small business owners were happy with their choices; they were, however, surprised at the number of corporate executives who believed that the grass was greener in the world of small business ownership.[23]

Starting a Business

Starting a business takes talent, determination, hard work, and persistence. It also requires a lot of research and planning. Before starting your business, you should appraise your strengths and weaknesses and assess your personal goals to determine whether business ownership is for you.[24]

Questions to Ask Before You Start a Business

If you're interested in starting a business, you need to make decisions even before you bring your talent, determination, hard work, and persistence to bear on your project.

Here are the basic questions you'll need to address:

- What, exactly, is my business idea? Is it feasible?
- What industry do I want to enter?
- What will be my competitive advantage?
- Do I want to start a new business, buy an existing one, or buy a franchise?
- What form of business organization do I want?

After making these decisions, you'll be ready to take the most important step in the entire process of starting a business: you must describe your future business in the form of a **business plan**—a document that identifies the goals of your proposed business and explains how these goals will be achieved. Think of a business plan as a blueprint for a proposed company: it shows how you intend to build the company and how you intend to make sure that it's sturdy. You must also take a second crucial step before you actually start up your business: You need to get **financing**—the money that you'll need to get your business off the ground.

The Business Idea

For some people, coming up with a great **business idea** is a gratifying adventure. For most, however, it's a daunting task. The key to coming up with a business idea is identifying something that customers want—or, perhaps more importantly, filling an **unmet need**. Your business will probably survive only if its purpose is to satisfy its customers—the ultimate users of its goods or services. In coming up with a business idea, don't ask, "What do we want to sell?" but rather, "What does the customer want to buy?"[25]

To come up with an innovative business idea, you need to be creative. If your idea is innovative enough, it may be considered **intellectual property,** a right that can be protected under the law. Prior **experience** accounts for the bulk of new business idea and also increases your chances of success. Take Sam Walton, the late founder of Wal-Mart. He began his retailing career at JCPenney and then became a successful franchiser of a Ben Franklin five-and-dime store. In 1962, he came up with the idea of opening large stores in rural areas, with low costs and heavy discounts. He founded his first Wal-Mart store in 1962, and when he died 30 years later, his family's net worth was $25 billion.[26]

Industry experience also gave Howard Schultz, a New York executive for a housewares company, his breakthrough idea. In 1981, Schultz noticed that a small customer in Seattle—Starbucks Coffee, Tea and Spice—ordered more coffeemaker cone filters than Macy's and many other large customers. So he flew across the country to find out why. His meeting with the owner-operators of the original Starbucks Coffee Co. resulted in his becoming part-owner of the company. Schultz's vision for the company far surpassed that of its other owners. While they wanted Starbucks to remain small and local, Schultz saw potential for a national business that not only

Figure 7.16: The original Starbucks store in Seattle, Washington.

sold world-class-quality coffee beans but also offered customers a European coffee-bar experience. After attempting unsuccessfully to convince his partners to try his experiment, Schultz left Starbucks and started his own chain of coffee bars, which he called Il Giornale (after an Italian newspaper). Two years later, he bought out the original owners and reclaimed the name Starbucks.[27]

Entrepreneurship and Small Business Development | 159

Ownership Options

As we've already seen, you can become a small business owner in one of three ways— by starting a new business, buying an existing one, or obtaining a franchise. Let's look more closely at the advantages and disadvantages of each option.

Starting from Scratch

The most common—and the riskiest—option is **starting from scratch**. This approach lets you start with a clean slate and allows you to build the business the way you want. You select the goods or services that you're going to offer, secure your location, and hire your employees, and then it's up to you to develop your customer base and build your reputation. This was the path taken by Andres Mason who figured out how to inject hysteria into the process of bargain hunting on the Web. The result is an overnight success story called Groupon.[28] Here is how Groupon (a blend of the words "group" and "coupon") works: A daily email is sent to 6.5 million people in 70 cities across the United States offering a deeply discounted deal to buy something or to do something in their city. If the person receiving the email likes the deal, he or she commits to buying it. But, here's the catch, if not enough people sign up for the deal, it is cancelled. Groupon makes money by keeping half of the revenue from the deal. The company offering the product or service gets exposure. But stay tuned: the "daily deals website isn't just unprofitable—it's bleeding hundreds of millions of dollars."[29] As with all start-ups cash is always a challenge.

Buying an Existing Business

If you decide to **buy an existing business**, some things will be easier. You'll already have a proven product, current customers, active suppliers, a known location, and trained employees. You'll also find it much easier to predict the business's future success.

There are, of course, a few bumps in this road to business ownership. First, it's hard to determine how much you should pay for a business. You can easily determine how much things like buildings and equipment are worth, but how much should you pay for the fact that the business already has steady customers?

In addition, a business, like a used car, might have performance problems that you can't detect without a test drive (an option, unfortunately, that you don't get when you're buying a business). Perhaps the current owners have disappointed customers; maybe the location isn't as good as it used to be. You might inherit employees that you wouldn't have hired yourself. Careful study called due diligence is necessary before going down this road.

Getting a Franchise

Lastly, you can buy a **franchise**. A **franchiser** (the company that sells the franchise) grants the **franchisee** (the buyer—you) the right to use a brand name and to sell its goods or services. Franchises market products in a variety of industries, including food, retail, hotels, travel, real estate, business services, cleaning services, and even weight-loss centers and wedding services. Figure 7.17 lists the top 10 franchises according to *Entrepreneur* magazine for 2015, 2020, and 2022.

Ranking	2015	2020	2022
1	Hampton by Hilton	Dunkin'	Taco Bell
2	Anytime Fitness	Taco Bell	The UPS Store
3	Subway	McDonald's	Popeyes Louisiana Kitchen
4	Jack in the Box	Sonic Drive-In	Jersey Mike's Subs
5	Supercuts	The UPS Store	Culver's
6	Jimmy John's Gourmet Sandwiches	Ace Hardware	Kumon
7	Servpro	Planet Fitness	Planet Fitness
8	Denny's	Jersey Mike's Subs	Servpro
9	Pizza Hut	Culver's	7-Eleven
10	7-Eleven	Pizza Hut	Tropical Smoothie Cafe

Figure 7.17: Entrepreneur's top franchises (2015, 2020, 2022).

As you can see from figure 7.18 below, the popularity of franchising has been growing quickly since 2011. Although the economic downturn decreased the number of franchises between 2008-11, note that the overall value of franchise outputs steadily increased. A new franchise outlet opens once every eight minutes in the United States, where one in ten businesses is now a franchise. Franchises employ eight million people (13 percent of the workforce) and account for 17 percent of all sales in the US ($1.3 trillion).[30]

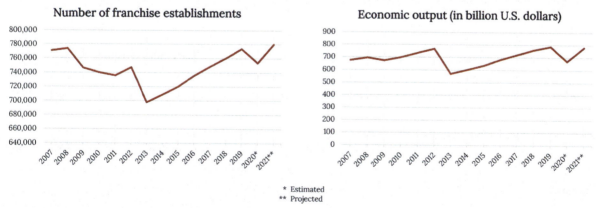

* Estimated
** Projected

Figure 7.18: The growth of franchising in the U.S.

Entrepreneurship and Small Business Development | 161

In addition to the right to use a company's brand name and sell its products, the franchisee gets help in picking a location, starting and operating the business, and benefits from advertising done by the franchiser. Essentially, the franchisee buys into a ready-to-go business model that has proven successful elsewhere, also getting other ongoing support from the franchiser, which has a vested interest in her success.

Coming with so many advantages, franchises can be very expensive. KFC franchises, for example, require a total investment of $1.3 million to $2.5 million each. This fee includes the cost of the property, equipment, training, start-up costs, and the franchise fee—a one-time charge for the right to operate as a KFC outlet. McDonald's is in the same price range ($1 million to $2.3 million). SUBWAY sandwich shops offer a more affordable alternative, with expected total investment ranging from $116,000 to $263,000.[31]

In addition to your initial investment, you'll have to pay two other fees on a monthly basis—a **royalty fee** (typically from 3 to 12 percent of sales) for continued support from the franchiser and the right to keep using the company's trade name, plus an advertising fee to cover your share of national and regional advertising. You'll also be expected to buy your products from the franchiser.[32]

But there are disadvantages. The cost of obtaining and running a franchise can be high, and you have to play by the franchiser's rules, even when you disagree with them. The franchiser maintains a great deal of control over its franchisees. For example, if you own a fast-food franchise, the **franchise agreement** will likely dictate the food and beverages you can sell; the methods used to store, prepare, and serve the food; and the prices you'll charge. In addition, the agreement will dictate what the premises will look like and how they'll be maintained. As with any business venture, you need to do your homework before investing in a franchise.

Launching a Business from the Inside

When someone mentions "entrepreneurship," many people equate the term to "start up," but entrepreneurial activity can also come from within established firms. However, it's often the case that the entrepreneurial spirit is not fully unleashed until an independent entity is formed around a venture.

That's exactly what happened in the case of Qualtrax, a company located in Blacksburg, Virginia.[33] The company was spawned from a need for customers of CCS, Inc. to become compliant with the requirements of the International Standards Organization. CCS (now known as Foxguard Solutions) employees developed a software tool to simplify ISO compliance audits, and the auditors were so impressed that they suggested marketing the tool more broadly. Over a period of nearly 20 years, the business grew to 10 dedicated employees, but Foxguard did not invest heavily in the software because the product was essentially a sideline business. Qualtrax shared sales and marketing resources with other business lines, so its growth was not necessarily a focal point for the company.

In 2011, CCS management appointed Amy Ankrum, an executive in their marketing department, to lead the Qualtrax business line with a simple mission in mind—determining whether Qualtrax could be scaled up or should be scaled down. Having the feeling that there was more to the business than had been achieved to date, Amy added Ryan Hagan as engineering manager for the software. Hagan quickly moved Qualtrax to an agile style of development, allowing for 5-6 new releases a year when annual releases had previously been the norm. This approach was much more responsive to customer needs, and in a business that depends on recurring revenue, it led to increased customer retention, which improved to over 95 percent each year. Revenue growth rates went up double digits.

Figure 7.19: Amy Ankrum at the Qualtrax headquarters in Blacksburg, Virginia.

In 2015, Qualtrax took its biggest leap of faith, moving out of Foxguard headquarters and becoming a separate legal entity. Ankrum located the offices near the campus of Virginia Tech, allowing the company to attract top-notch developers. The new location also allowed the company to take on its own culture—it's more like a start-up company now than it was 23 years ago when it started! Employees enjoy flexible hours, short walks to downtown lunches, and a brightly-lit, open, and collaborative space with the company values painted right on the walls.

The move to a separate entity also allowed the company to attract new investor funding which will be used to push the company into new markets, such as the utility industry. Much of the new investor group is local and made up of former executives with significant experience in Software-as-a-Service (SaaS) and Business-to-Business (B2B) relationships. These execs will offer expertise beyond what Qualtrax had in-house, and all involved share the objective of increasing job growth in the region.

Asked what was different before and after Qualtrax began its rapid growth, Ankrum said, "It takes focus for any business to reach its full potential." Since becoming its own company, Qualtrax has certainly enhanced that focus, and the new funding will allow them to offer ownership options to its now 26 employees. Qualtrax now dominates in quality and compliance software for a number of industries, including forensic crime labs. Thanks to the foresight of management, the company's best days most certainly lie ahead.

Why Some Businesses Fail and Where to Get Help

Why do Some Businesses Fail?

If you've paid attention to the occupancy of shopping malls over a few years, you've noticed that retailers come and go with surprising frequency. The same thing happens with restaurants—indeed, with all kinds of businesses. By definition, starting a business—small or large—is risky, and though many businesses succeed, a large proportion of them don't. One-third of small businesses that have employees go out of business within the first two years. As shown in figure 7.20, nearly half of small businesses have closed by the end of their fifth year, and 60-70 percent do not make it past their eighth year.[34]

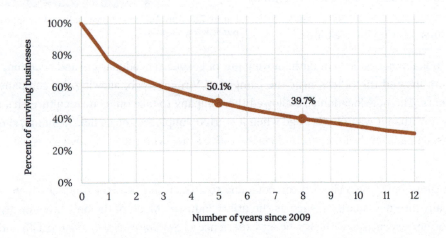

Figure 7.20: Long term survival rate of businesses in the U.S. (2009-2021).

As bad as these statistics on business survival are, some industries are worse than others. If you want to stay in business for a long time, you might want to avoid some of these risky industries. Even though your friends think you make the best pizza in the world, this doesn't mean you can succeed as a pizza parlor owner. Opening a restaurant or a bar is one of the riskiest ventures (and, therefore, start-up funding is hard to get).

You might also want to avoid the transportation industry. Owning a taxi might appear lucrative until you find out what a taxi license costs. It obviously varies by city, but in New York City the price tag is upward of $400,000. No wonder taxi companies are resisting Uber and Lyft with all the energy they can muster. And setting up a shop to sell clothing can be challenging. Your view of "what's in" may be off, and one bad season can kill your business. The same is true for stores selling communication devices: every mall has one or more cell phone stores so the competition is steep, and business can be very slow.[35]

Businesses fail for any number of reasons, but many experts agree that the vast majority of failures result from some combination of the following problems:

- **Bad business idea**. Like any idea, a business idea can be flawed, either in the conception or in the execution.
- **Cash problems**. Too many new businesses are underfunded. The owner borrows enough money to set up the business but doesn't have enough extra cash to operate during the start-up phase, when very little money is coming in but a lot is going out.
- **Managerial inexperience or incompetence**. Many new business owners have no experience in running a business; many have limited management skills. Knowing how to make or market a product doesn't necessarily mean knowing how to manage people or retain talented employees.
- **Lack of customer focus**. A major advantage of a small business is the ability to provide special attention to customers. But some small businesses fail to seize this advantage. Perhaps the owner doesn't anticipate customers' needs or keep up with changing markets or the customer-focused practices of competitors.
- **Inability to handle growth**. Growing sales is usually a good thing, but sometimes it can be a major problem. When a company grows, the owner's role changes. He or she needs to delegate work to others and build a business structure that can handle the increase in volume. Some owners don't make the transition and find themselves overwhelmed. In such cases, expansion actually damages the company.
- **Failure to adapt**. The external environment for a company can change dramatically. Companies that fail to keep up will not be around for long.

Help from the Small Business Administration

If you had your choice, which cupcake would you pick—vanilla Oreo, triple chocolate, or latte? In the last few years, cupcake shops are popping up in almost every city. Perhaps the bad economy has put people in the mood for small, relatively inexpensive treats.

Whatever the reason, you're fascinated with the idea of starting a cupcake shop. You have a perfect location, have decided what equipment you need, and have tested dozens of recipes (and eaten lots of cupcakes). You are set to go with one giant exception: you don't have enough savings to cover your start-up costs. You have made the round of most local banks, but they are all unwilling to give you a loan. So what do you do? Fortunately, there is help available. It is through your local Small Business Administration (SBA), which offers an array of programs to help current and prospective small business owners. The SBA won't actually loan you the money, but it will increase the likelihood that you will get funding from a local bank by guaranteeing the loan.

Here's how the SBA's loan guarantee program works: You apply to a bank for financing. A loan officer decides if the bank will loan you the money without an SBA guarantee. If the answer is no (because of some weakness in your application), the bank then decides if it will loan you the money if the SBA guarantees the loan. If the bank decides to do this, you get the money and make payments on the loan. If you default on the loan, the government reimburses the bank for its loss, up to the amount of the SBA guarantee.

Figure 7.21: Your new cupcake shop.

In the process of talking with someone at the SBA, you will discover other programs it offers that will help you start your business and manage your organization. For example, to apply for funding you will need a well-written business plan. Once you get the loan and move to the business start-up phase, you will have lots of questions that need to be answered. And you are sure you will need help in a number of areas as you operate your cupcake shop. Fortunately, the SBA can help with all of these management and technical-service tasks.

This assistance is available through a number of channels, including the SBA's extensive website, online courses, and training programs. A full array of individualized services is also available. The Small Business Development Center (SBDC) assists current and prospective small business owners with business problems and provides free training and technical information on all aspects of small business management.

These services are available at approximately 1,000 locations around the country, many housed at colleges and universities.[36]

If you need individualized advice from experienced executives, you can get it through the Service Corps of Retired Executives (SCORE). Under the SCORE program, a businessperson needing advice is matched with someone on a team of retired executives who work as volunteers. Together, the SBDC and SCORE help more than a million small businesspersons every year.[37]

 An interactive H5P element has been excluded from this version of the text. You can view it online here:
https://pressbooks.lib.vt.edu/fundamentalsofbusiness4e/?p=564#h5p-21

Chapter Video:

Corporate innovation and technology—solving customer challenges.

One or more interactive elements has been excluded from this version of the text. You can view them online here: https://www.youtube.com/watch?v=kMt4wqZfgmU

Key Takeaways

- Being **entrepreneurial** means you engage in a proactive process of overcoming constraints to create value in new ways usually in the form of a business
- Entrepreneurs can be single founders or co-founders that are part of a **founding team**
- Entrepreneurship tends to happen most in the **startup phase** of the **organization's lifecycle** and later during the **rebirth stage** when there is uncertainty present
- **Uncertainty** is one kind of knowledge problem that happens when you cannot know what action is likely to lead to a desired outcome as opposed to Risk which can be given a probability
- **Complexity** is another knowledge problem entrepreneurs experience because of the number of variables that make up a problem and the number of interactions between those variables that could influence outcomes.
- **Ambiguity** occurs when there isn't clarity for the entrepreneur around what is important or even what might happen.
- A related knowledge problem is e**quivocality** which occurs when there are multiple meanings or interpretations of what is important and what is possible that the entrepreneur must choose to pursue.
- All these knowledge problems surface as the entrepreneur seeks to **create value** for a group of customers
- There are different kinds of businesses that entrepreneurs start that vary in how they are funded (bootstrapping versus, debt financing, versus external investment), their goals (fiduciary responsibility, social and environmental responsibility, and lifestyle for founders), and the context or industry (health, digital, or corporate entrepreneurship) in which it happens.
- There are two main types of external investors. **Angel investors** invest their own money and **venture Capital** invests other people's money and expects high returns
- An **entrepreneurial ecosystem** refers to a community or network of people, spaces, and

Adapted from: OpenStax (CC BY). Access for free at https://www.youtube.com/watch?v=kMt4wqZfgmU

- available resources that interact around the creation of new ventures.
- **Coworking spaces** are open areas where entrepreneurs and business professionals can work out of that can be free or accessible through paying for a membership to get access.
- **Incubators** are offices that share common areas and support services that are rented out below the market rate to particular startup companies.
- **Accelerators** are investment programs that provide money, space, services, and some sort of training or mentoring to startups selected to participate in their program usually in exchange for equity and access to more investors on demo day.
- The process of starting a business requires the entrepreneur to reduce uncertainty around the customer and their problems in order to generate a solution that is unique and desirable that can be produced and sold in a sustainable and profitable system. This may require building a prototype, figuring out your customer acquisition cost (CAC), and understanding how much the lifetime value of a customer (LTV) is and how to find the right talent to create, capture and deliver value.

References

Figures

Figure 7.1: Entrepreneurial boundaries. Kindred Grey. 2022. CC BY 4.0. https://archive.org/details/7.1_20220804.

Figure 7.2: Facebook founder Mark Zuckerberg. Anthony Quintano. 2018. CC BY 2.0. https://commons.wikimedia.org/wiki/File:Mark_Zuckerberg_F8_2018_Keynote.jpg.

Figure 7.3: Collaborative teams yield the best results! Mario Gogh. 2018. Unsplash license. https://unsplash.com/photos/VBLHICVh-lI.

Figure 7.4: The organization life cycle. Kindred Grey. 2022. CC BY 4.0. https://archive.org/details/7.3_20220804.

Figure 7.5: Value creation. Kindred Grey. 2022. CC BY 4.0. https://archive.org/details/7.4-value-creation.

Figure 7.6: When entrepreneurship happens with the organization's lifecycle. Kindred Grey. 2022. CC BY 4.0. https://archive.org/details/7.5_20220804.

Figure 7.8: Glenn Feit, of grand prize winner QuickTech, pitches the team's product. Used with permission of Virginia Tech.

Figure 7.9: Different entrepreneurial journeys. Kindred Grey. 2022. CC BY 4.0. Includes photo by Romain Virtuel from Unsplash (Unsplash license), photo by Good Faces from Unsplash (Unsplash license), photo by Mikelya Fournier from Unsplash (Unsplash license), photo by Rock Staar from Unsplash (Unsplash license), and photo by Laura Chouette from Unsplash (Unsplash license). https://archive.org/details/7.7_20220804.

Figure 7.10: Establish partnerships that allow you to scale. Cytonn Photography. 2018. Unsplash license. https://unsplash.com/photos/n95VMLxqM2I.

Figure 7.11: Different types of funding for viral pathways. Village Capital's VIRAL Pathway. © Village Capital. 2017. Used under fair use. https://medium.com/village-capital/entrepreneurs-and-vcs-need-to-be-more-precise-in-the-way-they-talk-to-each-other-3e714e7a5245

Figure 7.12: Small business job gains and losses, 2000-2021 (in millions of jobs). Data from https://www.bls.gov/bdm/bdmfirmsize.htm#SIZE1.

Figure 7.13: Amazon annual revenue growth (2009-2021). Kindred Grey. 2022. CC BY 4.0. Includes Amazon logo from WikimediaCommons (public domain). Data from https://www.macrotrends.net/stocks/charts/AMZN/amazon/revenue. https://archive.org/details/7.3_20220804_202208.

Figure 7.14: Percent of all businesses owned by women and minorities. Data from https://www.census.gov/library/publications/2007/econ/2007-sbo-business-owners.html (2007) and https://www.census.gov/newsroom/press-releases/2021/annual-business-survey.html#:~:text=According%20to%20the%202019%20Annual,businesses%20were%20owned%20by%20women (2018).

Figure 7.15: Number of small business establishments by industry, 2019. Kindred Grey. 2022. CC BY 4.0. Data from https://www.census.gov/data/tables/2019/econ/susb/2019-susb-annual.html. https://archive.org/details/7.5_20220804_202208.

Figure 7.16: The original Starbucks store in Seattle, Washington. Backupboy. 2011. CC BY-SA 3.0. https://commons.wikimedia.org/wiki/File:1st_Starbucks_Seattle.jpeg.

Figure 7.18: The growth of franchising in the U.S. Kindred Grey. 2020. CC BY 4.0. Data from https://www.statista.com/statistics/190318/economic-output-of-the-us-franchise-sector/ and https://www.statista.com/statistics/190318/economic-output-of-the-us-franchise-sector/. https://archive.org/details/7.18_20220809.

Figure 7.19: Amy Ankrum at the Qualtrax headquarters in Blacksburg, Virginia. Stephen Skripak. 2017. CC BY NC SA 4.0.

Figure 7.20: Long term survival rate of businesses in the U.S. (2009-2021). Kindred Grey. 2022. CC BY 4.0. Data from Table 7 under "Total Private" https://www.bls.gov/bdm/bdmage.htm#Total. https://archive.org/details/7.10_20220804.

Figure 7.21: Your new cupcake shop. Meghan Rodgers. 2019. Unsplash license. https://unsplash.com/photos/QpeoWEazLlM.

Video

Video 1: Corporate innovation and technology—solving customer challenges. OpenStax. 2019. CC BY 4.0. https://www.youtube.com/watch?v=kMt4wqZfgmU.

Notes

1. Adapted from Marc J. Dollinger (2003). Entrepreneurship: Strategies and Resources, 3rd ed. Upper Saddle River, NJ: Prentice Hall. pp. 5–7.
2. Encyclopedia of World Biography (2006). "Marcia Kilgore: Entrepreneur and spa founder." Retrieved from: http://www.notablebiographies.com/newsmakers2/2006-Ei-La/Kilgore-Marcia.html
3. Jessica Bruder (2010). "The Rise Of The Serial Entrepreneur." Forbes. Retrieved from: http://www.forbes.com/2010/08/12/serial-entrepreneur-start-up-business-forbes-woman-entrepreneurs-management.html
4. Ibid.
5. U.S. Small Business Administration (2016). "Is Entrepreneurship For You?" Retrieved from: https://www.sba.gov/starting-business/how-start-business/entrepreneurship-you
6. Shari Waters (2016). "Top Four Reasons People Don't Start a Business." The Balance Small Businesses. Retrieved from: http://retail.about.com/od/startingaretailbusiness/tp/overcome_fears.htm
7. Townsend, D. M., Hunt, R. A., McMullen, J. S., & Sarasvathy, S. D. (2018). Uncertainty, knowledge problems, and entrepreneurial action. Academy of Management Annals, 12(2), 659-687.
8. Töytäri, P., & Rajala, R. (2015). Value-based selling: An organizational capability perspective. Industrial Marketing Management, 45, 101-112.
9. Kathleen Allen (2001). *Entrepreneurship for Dummies*. New York: Wiley. p. 14.
10. U.S. Small Business Administration (2016). "Qualifying as a Small Business." Retrieved from: https://www.sba.gov/contracting/getting-started-contractor/qualifying-small-business
11. SBA Office of Advocacy (2019). "2019 Small Business Profile". US Small Business Administration. Retrieved from https://cdn.advocacy.sba.gov/wp-content/uploads/2019/04/23142719/2019-Small-Business-Profiles-US.pdf
12. Brian Headd (2010). *An Analysis of Small Business and Jobs*. U.S. Small Business Administration, Office of Advocacy. Retrieved from: https://www.sba.gov/sites/default/files/files/an analysis of small business and jobs(1).pdf
13. Anthony Breitzman and Diana Hicks (2008). "An Analysis of Small Business Patents by Industry and Firm Size." Faculty Scholarship for the College of Science & Mathematics. Retrieved from: https://rdw.rowan.edu/csm_facpub/12
14. William J. Baumol (2005). "Small Firms: Why Market-Driven Innovation Can't Get Along without Them." U.S. Small Business Administration, Office of Advocacy.
15. Yahoo.com (2016). "Amazon.com Income Statement." Finance.yahoo.com. Retrieved from: http://finance.yahoo.com/q/is?s=AMZN Income Statement&annual
16. William J. Baumol (2005). "Small Firms: Why Market-Driven Innovation Can't Get Along without Them." U.S. Small Business Administration, Office of Advocacy.
17. U.S. Census Bureau (2012). "Estimates of Business Ownership by Gender, Ethnicity, Race, and Veteran Status: 2012." Retrieved from: http://www.census.gov/library/publications/2012/econ/2012-sbo.html#par_reference_25
18. Central Intelligence Agency (2016). "World Factbook." Retrieved from: https://www.cia.gov/library/publications/the-world-factbook/fields/2012.html
19. Ecoscraps (2016). "Our Story." Retrieved from: http://ecoscraps.com/pages/our-story
20. Isabel Isidro (2003). "How to Succeed Online with a Niche Business: Case of RedWagons.com." PowerHomeBiz.com. Retrieved from: http://www.powerhomebiz.com/online-business/success-online-business/succeed-online-niche-business-case-redwagons-com.htm
21. Isabel Isidro (2001). "Geese Police: A Real-Life Home Business Success Story." PowerHomeBiz.com. Retrieved from: http://www.powerhomebiz.com/working-from-home/success/geese-police-real-life-home-business-success-story.htm
22. Illinois Small Business Development Center at SIU (2016). "What are the Pros and Cons of Owning a Business?" Retrieved from: http://sbdc.siu.edu/frequently-asked-questions/index.html
23. Janean Chun (1997). "Type E Personality: What makes entrepreneurs tick?" Entrepreneur. Retrieved from: https://www.entrepreneur.com/article/13764
24. Kathleen Allen (2001). "Getting Started in Entrepreneurship" in *Entrepreneurship for Dummies*. New York: Wiley. p. 46.
25. Scott Thurm and Joann S. Lublin (2005). "Peter Drucker's Legacy Includes Simple Advice: It's All about the People." Wall Street Journal. Retrieved from: http://www.wsj.com/articles/SB113192826302796041

26. Peter Krass (1997). "Sam Walton: Running a Successful Business: Ten Rules that Worked for Me" in *The Book of Business Wisdom: Classic Writings by the Legends of Commerce and Industry.* New York: Wiley. pp. 225-230.
27. Howard Schultz and Dori Jones Yang (1997). *Pour Your Heart into It.* New York: Hyperion. pp. 24–109.
28. Christopher Steiner (2010). "Meet the Fastest Growing Company Ever." Forbes. Retrieved from: http://www.forbes.com/forbes/2010/0830/entrepreneurs-groupon-facebook-twitter-next-web-phenom.html
29. The Week (2011). "Groupon's 'Startling' Reversal of Fortune." Yahoo.com. Retrieved from: https://www.yahoo.com/news/groupons-startling-reversal-fortune-172800802.html
30. U.S. Census Bureau (2008). "2007 Economic Census: Franchise Statistics." Retrieved from: https://www.census.gov/econ/census/pdf/franchise_flyer.pdf
31. Hayley Peterson (2014). "Here's How Much It Costs To Open Different Fast Food Franchises In The US." Business Insider. Retrieved from: http://www.businessinsider.com/cost-of-fast-food-franchise-2014-11
32. Michael Seid and Kay Marie Ainsley (2002). "Franchise Fee—Made Simple." Entrepreneur. Retrieved from: https://www.entrepreneur.com/article/51174
33. Stephen Skripak (2017, February 22). Interview with Amy Ankrum.
34. U.S. Bureau of Labor Statistics (n.d.). Table 7: Survival of private sector establishments by opening year. Retrieved from: https://www.bls.gov/bdm/bdmage.htm#Total
35. Maureen Farrell (2007). "Risky Business: 44% of Small Firms Reach Year 4." Forbes. Retrieved from: http://www.msnbc.msn.com/id/16872553/ns/business-forbes_com/t/risky-business-small-firms-reach-year/#.Tl_xVY7CclA
36. U.S. Small Business Administration (2016). "Office of Small Business Development Centers: Entrepreneurial Development Services." Retrieved from: https://www.sba.gov/tools/local-assistance/districtoffices
37. U.S. Small Business Administration (2016). "SCORE.—Counselors to America's Small Businesses." Retrieved from: https://www.score.org/

8. Management and Leadership

Learning Objectives

- Identify the four interrelated functions of management: planning, organizing, leading, and controlling.
- Understand the process by which a company develops and implements a strategic plan.
- Explain how managers direct others and motivate them to achieve company goals.
- Describe the process by which a manager monitors operations and assesses performance.
- Explain what benchmarking is and its importance for managing organizations.
- Describe the skills needed to be a successful manager.

Noteworthy Management

Consider this scenario: you're halfway through the semester and ready for midterms. You open your class notes and declare them "pathetic." You regret scribbling everything so carelessly and skipping class so many times. That's when it hits you: what if there was a note-taking service on campus? When you were ready to study for a big test, you could buy complete and legible class notes. You've heard that there are class-notes services at some larger schools, but there's no such thing on your campus. So you ask yourself, why don't I start a note-taking business? Your upcoming set of exams may not be salvageable, but after that, you'd always have great notes. And in the process, you could learn how to manage a business (isn't that what majoring in business is all about?).

Figure 8.1: *How to become a successful manager.*

You might begin by hiring a bunch of students to take class notes. Then the note takers will e-mail them to your assistant, who'll get them copied (on a special type of paper that can't be duplicated). The last step will be assembling packages of notes and, of course, selling them. You decide to name your company "Notes-4-You."

It sounds like a great idea, but you're troubled by one question: why does this business need you? Do the note takers need a boss? Couldn't they just sell the notes themselves? This process could work, but it would work better if there was someone to oversee the operations: a manager—to make sure that the operations involved in preparing and selling notes were performed in both an effective and an efficient manner. You'd make the process **effective** by ensuring that the right things got done and that they all contributed to the success of the enterprise. You'd make the process **efficient** by ensuring that activities were performed in the right way and used the fewest possible resources.

What Do Managers Do?

The Management Process

The effective performance of your business will require solid **management**: the process of planning, organizing, leading, and controlling resources to achieve specific goals. A **plan** enables you to take your business concept beyond the idea stage. It does not, however, get the work done. For that to happen, you have to **organize** things effectively. You'll have to put people and other resources in place to make things happen. And because your note-taking venture is supposed to be better off with you in charge, you need to be a **leader** who can motivate your people to do well. Finally, to know whether things are in fact going well, you'll have to **control** your operations—that is, measure the results and compare them with the results that you laid out in your plan. Figure 8.2 summarizes the interrelationship between planning and the other functions that managers perform. This chapter will explore planning, leading, and controlling in some detail. Organizing is an especially complex topic, and will be discussed in Chapter 9.

Figure 8.2: The management process.

Planning

Without a plan, it's hard to succeed at anything. The reason is simple: if you don't know where you're going, you can't move forward. Successful managers decide where they want to be and then figure out how to get there; they set goals and determine the best way to achieve them. As a result of the planning process, everyone in the organization knows what should be done, who should do it, and how to do it.

Developing a Strategic Plan

Coming up with an idea—say, starting a note-taking business—is a good start, but it's only a start. Planning for it is a step forward. Planning begins at the highest level and works its way down through the organization. Step one is usually called **strategic planning**: the process of establishing an overall course of action. To begin this process, you should ask yourself a couple of very basic questions: why, for example, does the organization exist? What value does it create? Sam Walton posed these questions in the process of founding Wal-Mart: his new chain of stores would exist to offer customers the lowest prices with the best possible service.[1]

Once you've identified the purpose of your company, you're ready to take the remaining steps in the strategic-planning process:

- Write a mission statement that tells customers, employees, and others why your organization exists.
- Identify core values or beliefs that will guide the behavior of members of the organization.
- Assess the company's strengths, weaknesses, opportunities, and threats.
- Establish goals and objectives, or performance targets, to direct all the activities that you'll perform to achieve your mission.
- Develop and implement tactical and operational plans to achieve goals and objectives.

In the next few sections, we'll examine these components of the strategic-planning process.

Mission statement

As we saw in an earlier chapter, the **mission statement** describes the purpose of your organization—the reason for its existence. It tells the reader what the organization is committed to doing. It can be very concise, like the one from Mary Kay Inc. (the cosmetics company): "To enrich the lives of women around the world."[2] Or it can be as detailed as the one from Harley-Davidson: "We fulfill dreams inspired by the many roads of the world by providing extraordinary motorcycles and customer experiences. We fuel the passion for freedom in our customers to express their own individuality."[3]

A mission statement for Notes-4-You could be the following: "To provide high-quality class notes to college students." On the other hand, you could prepare a more detailed statement that explains what the company is committed to doing, who its customers are, what its focus is, what goods or services it provides, and how it serves its customers.

It is worth noting that some companies no longer use mission statements, preferring to communicate their reason for being in other manners.

Core values

Whether or not your company has defined a mission, it is important to identify what your organization stands for in terms of its values and the principles that will guide its actions. In Chapter 3 on Business Ethics and Social Responsibility, we explained that the small set of guiding principles that you identify as crucial to your company are known as **core values**—fundamental beliefs about what's important and what is and isn't appropriate in conducting company activities. Core values affect the overall planning processes and operations. At Volvo, three values—safety, quality, and environmental care—define the firm's "approach to product development, design and production."[4] Core values should also guide the behavior of every individual in the organization. At Coca-Cola, for instance, the values of leadership, collaboration, integrity, accountability, passion, diversity and quality tell employees exactly what behaviors are acceptable.[5] Companies communicate core values to employees and hold them accountable for putting them into practice by linking their values to performance evaluations and compensation.

In choosing core values for Notes-4-You, you're determined to be unique. After some thought, you settle on teamwork, trust, and dependability. Why these three? As you plan your business, you realize that it will need a workforce that functions as a team, trusts each other, and can be depended on to satisfy customers. In building your workforce, you'll seek employees who'll embrace these values.

Conduct a SWOT analysis

The next step in the strategic-planning process is to assess your company's fit with its environment. A common approach to environmental analysis is matching the strengths of your business with the opportunities available to it. It's called **SWOT analysis** because it calls for analyzing an organization's Strengths, Weaknesses, Opportunities, and Threats. It begins with an examination of **external factors** that could influence the company in either a positive or a negative way. These could include economic conditions, competition, emerging technologies, laws and regulations, and customers' expectations.

One purpose of assessing the external environment is to identify both **opportunities** that could benefit the company and **threats** to its success. For example, a company that manufactures children's bicycle helmets would view a change in federal law requiring all children to wear helmets as an opportunity. The news that two large sports-equipment companies were coming out with bicycle helmets would be a threat.

The next step is to evaluate the company's strengths and weaknesses, **internal factors** that could influence company performance in either a positive or negative way. **Strengths** might include a motivated workforce, state-of-the-art technology, impressive managerial talent, or a desirable location. The opposite of any of these strengths could signal a potential **weakness** (poor workforce, obsolete technology, incompetent management, or poor location). Armed with a good idea of internal strengths and weaknesses, as well as external opportunities and threats, managers will be better positioned to capitalize on opportunities and strengths. Likewise, they want to improve on any weak areas and protect the organization from external threats.

For example, Notes-4-You might say that by providing excellent service at a reasonable price while we're still small, it can solidify its position on campus. When the market grows due to increases in student enrollment, the company will have built a strong reputation and be in a position to grow. So even if a competitor comes to campus (a threat), the company expects to be the preferred supplier of class notes. This strategy will work only if the note-takers are dependable and if the process does not alienate the faculty or administration.

Set goals and objectives

Your mission statement affirms what your organization is generally committed to doing, but it doesn't tell you how to do it. So the next step in the strategic-planning process is establishing goals and objectives. **Goals** are major accomplishments that the company wants to achieve over a long period. **Objectives** are shorter-term performance targets that direct the activities of the organization toward the attainment of a goal. They should be clearly stated, achievable, and measurable: they should give target dates for the completion of tasks and stipulate who's responsible for taking necessary actions.[6]

An organization will have a number of goals and related objectives. Some will focus on financial measures, such as profit maximization and sales growth. Others will target operational efficiency or quality control. Still others will govern the company's relationships with its employees, its community, its environment, or all three.

Finally, goals and objectives change over time. As a firm reassesses its place in its business environment, it rethinks not only its mission but also its approach to fulfilling it. The reality of change was a major theme when the late McDonald's CEO Jim Cantalupo explained his goal to revitalize the company:

> "The world has changed. Our customers have changed. We have to change too. Growth comes from being better, not just expanding to have more restaurants. The new McDonald's is focused on building sales at existing restaurants rather than on adding new restaurants. We are introducing a new level of discipline and efficiency to all aspects of the business and are setting a new bar for performance."[7]

This change in focus was accompanied by specific performance objectives—annual sales growth of 3-5 percent and income growth of 6-7 percent at existing restaurants, plus a five-point improvement (based on customer surveys) in speed of service, friendliness, and food quality.

In setting strategic goals and performance objectives for Notes-4-You, you should keep things simple. Because you need to make money to stay in business, you could include a financial goal (and related objectives). Your mission statement promises "high-quality, dependable, competitively priced class notes," so you could focus on the quality of the class notes that you'll be taking and distributing. Finally, because your mission is to serve students, one goal could be customer oriented. Your list of goals and objectives might look like this:

- **Goal 1**: Achieve a 10 percent return on sales in your first five years.
- *Objective*: Sales of $20,000 and profit of $2,000 for the first 12 months of operation.
- **Goal 2**: Produce a high-quality product.
- *Objective*: First-year satisfaction scores of 90 percent or higher on quality of notes (based on survey responses on understandability, readability, and completeness).
- **Goal 3**: Attain 98 percent customer satisfaction by the end of your fifth year.
- *Objective*: Making notes available within two days after class, 95 percent of the time.

Tactical plans

The overall plan is broken down into more manageable, shorter-term components called **tactical plans**. These plans specify the activities and allocation of **resources** (people, equipment, money) needed to implement the strategic plan over a given period. Often, a long-range strategic plan is divided into several tactical plans; a five-year strategic plan, for instance, might be implemented as five one-year tactical plans.

Operational plans

The tactical plan is then broken down into various operational components that provide detailed action steps to be taken by individuals or groups to implement the tactical and strategic plans. **Operational plans** cover only a brief period—say, a month or two. At Notes-4-You, note-takers might be instructed to submit typed class notes five hours earlier than normal on the last day of the semester (an operational guideline). The goal is to improve the customer-satisfaction score on dependability (a tactical goal) and, as a result, to earn the loyalty of students through attention to customer service (a strategic goal).

Plan for contingencies and crises

Even with great planning, things don't always turn out the way they're supposed to. Perhaps your plans were flawed, or maybe something in the environment shifted unexpectedly. Successful managers anticipate and plan for the unexpected. Dealing with uncertainty requires contingency planning and crisis management.

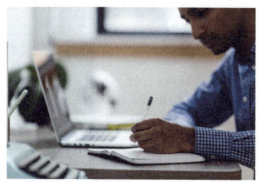

Figure 8.3: A note taker.

Contingency planning

With **contingency planning**, managers identify those aspects of the business that are most likely to be adversely affected by change. Then, they develop alternative courses of action in case an anticipated change does occur. You engage in contingency planning any time you develop a backup or fallback plan.

Crisis management

Organizations also face the risk of encountering crises that require immediate attention. Rather than waiting until such a crisis occurs and then scrambling to figure out what to do, many firms practice **crisis management**. Some, for instance, set up teams trained to deal with emergencies. Members gather information quickly and respond to the crisis while everyone else carries out his or her normal duties. The team also keeps the public, the employees, the press, and government officials informed about the situation and the company's response to it.[8]

Figure 8.4: A Wendy's restaurant.

An example of how to handle crisis management involves Wendy's. After learning that a woman claimed she found a fingertip in a bowl of chili she bought at a Wendy's restaurant in San Jose, California, the company's public relations team responded quickly. Within a few days, the company announced that the finger didn't come from an employee or a supplier. Soon after, the police arrested the woman and charged her with attempted grand larceny for lying about how the finger got in her bowl of chili and trying to extort $2.5 million from the company. But the crisis wasn't over for Wendy's. The incident was plastered all over the news as a grossed-out public sought an answer to the question, "Whose finger is (or was) it?" A $100,000 reward was offered by Wendy's to anyone with information that would help the police answer this question. The challenge Wendy's faced was how to entice customers to return to its 50 San Francisco-area restaurants (where sales had plummeted) while keeping a low profile nationally. Wendy's accomplished this objective by giving out free milkshakes and discount coupons to customers in the affected regions and, to avoid calling attention to the missing finger, by making no changes in its national advertising. The crisis-management strategy worked and the story died down (though it flared up temporarily when the police arrested the woman's husband, who allegedly bought the finger from a coworker who had severed it in an accident months earlier).[9]

Even with crisis-management plans in place, however, it's unlikely that most companies will emerge from a potentially damaging episode as unscathed as Wendy's did. For one thing, the culprits in the Wendy's case were caught, and the public was willing to forgive an organization it viewed as a victim. Given the current public distrust of corporate behavior, however, companies whose reputations have suffered due to questionable corporate judgment usually don't fare as well. These companies include the international oil company, BP, whose CEO, Tony Hayward, did a disastrous job handling the Gulf of Mexico crisis. A BP-controlled oil rig exploded in the Gulf of Mexico, killing eleven workers and creating the largest oil spill in US history. Hayward's lack of sensitivity will be remembered forever; particularly his response to a reporter's question on what he would tell those whose livelihoods were ruined: "We're sorry for the massive disruption it's caused their lives. There's no one who wants this over more than I do. I would like my life back." His comment was obviously upsetting to the families of the eleven men who lost their lives on the rig.[10] Then, there are the companies at which executives have crossed the line between the unethical to the downright illegal—Arthur Andersen, Enron, and Bernard L. Madoff Investment Securities, to name just a few. Given the high risk associated with a crisis, it should come as no surprise that contemporary managers spend more time anticipating crises and practicing their crisis-management responses.

Figure 8.5: BP's Deepwater Horizon oil spill in the Gulf of Mexico in 2010.

 An interactive H5P element has been excluded from this version of the text. You can view it online here: https://pressbooks.lib.vt.edu/fundamentalsofbusiness4e/?p=99#h5p-22

Leading

The third management function is **leading**—providing focus and direction to others and motivating them to achieve organizational goals. As owner and president of Notes-4-You, you might think of yourself as an orchestra leader. You have given your musicians (employees) their sheet music (plans). You've placed them in sections (departments) and arranged the sections (organizational structure) so the music will sound as good as possible. Now your job is to tap your baton and lead the orchestra so that its members make beautiful music together.[11]

Leadership Styles

It's fairly easy to pick up a baton, cue each section, and strike up the band; but it doesn't mean the music will sound good. What if your cues are ignored or misinterpreted or ambiguous? Maybe your musicians don't like your approach to making music and will just walk away. On top of everything else, you don't simply want to make music; you want to inspire your musicians to make great music. How do you accomplish this goal? How do you become an effective leader, and what style should you use to motivate others to achieve organizational goals?

Unfortunately, there are no definitive answers to questions like these. Over time, every manager refines his or her own **leadership style**, or way of interacting with and influencing others. Despite a vast range of personal differences, leadership styles tend to reflect one of the following approaches to leading and motivating people: the autocratic, the democratic (also known as participative), or the free rein.

- **Autocratic style**. Managers who have developed an autocratic leadership style tend to make decisions without soliciting input from subordinates. They exercise authority and expect subordinates to take responsibility for performing the required tasks without undue explanation.
- **Democratic style**. Managers who favor a democratic leadership style generally seek input from subordinates while retaining the authority to make the final decisions. They're also more likely to keep subordinates informed about things that affect their work.
- **Free-rein style**. In practicing a free rein leadership style, managers adopt a "hands-off" approach and provide relatively little direction to subordinates. They may advise employees but usually give them considerable freedom to solve problems and make decisions on their own.

At first glance, you'd probably not want to work for an autocratic leader. After all, most people don't like to be told what to do without having any input. Many like the idea of working for a democratic leader; it's flattering to be asked for your input. And though working in a free rein environment might seem a little unsettling at first, the opportunity to make your own decisions is appealing to many people. Each leadership style can be appropriate in certain situations.

To illustrate, let's say that you're leading a group of fellow students in a team project for your class. Are there times when it would be best for you to use an autocratic leadership style? What if your team was newly formed, unfamiliar with what needs to be done, under a tight deadline, and looking to you for direction? In this situation, you might find it appropriate to follow an autocratic leadership style (on a temporary basis) and assign tasks to each member of the group. In an emergency situation, such as a fire, or in the final seconds of a close ball game, there is generally not time for debate—the leader or coach must make a split second decision that demands an autocratic style.

But since most situations are non-emergency and most people prefer the chance to give input, the democratic leadership style is often favored. People are simply more motivated and feel more ownership of decisions (i.e., buy-in) when they have had a chance to offer input. Note that when using this style, the leader will still make the decision in most cases. As long as their input is heard, most people accept that it is the leader's role to decide in cases where not everyone agrees.

How about free rein leadership? Many people function most effectively when they can set their own schedules and do their work in the manner they prefer. It takes a great deal of trust for a manager to employ this style. Some managers start with an assumption of trust that is up to the employee to maintain through strong performance. In other cases, this trust must be earned over a period of time. Would this approach always work with your study group? Obviously not. It will work if your team members are willing and able to work independently and welcome the chance to make decisions. On the other hand, if people are not ready to work responsibly to the best of their abilities, using the free rein style could cause the team to miss deadlines or do poorly on the project.

The point being made here is that no one leadership style is effective all the time for all people or in all corporate cultures. While the democratic style is often viewed as the most appropriate (with the free rein style a close second), there are times when following an autocratic style is essential. Good leaders learn how to adjust their styles to fit both the situation and the individuals being directed.

Transformational Leadership

Theories on what constitutes effective leadership evolve over time. One theory that has received a lot of attention in the last decade contrasts two leadership styles: transactional and transformational. So-called **transactional leaders** exercise authority based on their rank in the organization. They let subordinates know what's expected of them and what they will receive if they meet stated objectives. They focus their attention on identifying mistakes and disciplining employees for poor performance. By contrast, **transformational leaders** mentor and develop subordinates, providing them with challenging opportunities, working one-on-one to help them meet their professional and personal needs, and encouraging people to approach problems from new perspectives. They stimulate employees to look beyond personal interests to those of the group.

So, which leadership style is more effective? You probably won't be surprised by the opinion of most experts. In today's organizations, in which team building and information sharing are important and projects are often collaborative in nature, transformational leadership has proven to be more effective. Modern organizations look for managers who can develop positive relationships with subordinates and motivate employees to focus on the interests of the organization. Leaders who can be both transactional and transformational are rare, and those few who have both capacities are very much in demand.[12]

An interactive H5P element has been excluded from this version of the text. You can view it online here: https://pressbooks.lib.vt.edu/fundamentalsofbusiness4e/?p=99#h5p-23

Controlling

Let's pause for a minute and reflect on the management functions that we've discussed so far—planning, organizing, and leading. As founder of Notes-4-You, you began by establishing plans for your new company. You defined its mission and set objectives, or performance targets, which you needed to meet in order to achieve your mission. Then, you organized your company by allocating the people and resources required to carry out your plans. Finally, you provided focus and direction to your employees and motivated them to achieve organizational objectives. Is your job finished? Can you take a well-earned vacation? Unfortunately, the answer is no: your work has just begun. Now that things are rolling along, you need to monitor your operations to see whether everything is going according to plan. If it's not, you'll need to take corrective action. This process of comparing actual to planned performance and taking necessary corrective action is called controlling.

A Five-Step Control Process

You can think of the **control function** as the five-step process outlined in figure 8.7. Let's see how this process might work at Notes-4-You. Let's assume that, after evaluating class enrollments, you estimate that you can sell 100 notes packages per month to students taking a popular sophomore-level geology course. So you set your standard at 100 units. At the end of the month, however, you look over your records and find that you sold only 80. In talking with your salespeople, you learn why you came up 20 packages short: it turns out that the copy machine broke down so often that packages frequently weren't ready on time. You immediately take corrective action by increasing maintenance on the copy machine.

Figure 8.6: Copy machine.

Now, let's try a slightly different scenario. Let's say that you still have the same standard (100 packages) and that actual sales are still 80 packages. In investigating the reason for the shortfall, you find that you overestimated the number of students taking the geology course. Calculating a more accurate number of students, you see that your original standard—estimated sales—was too high by 20 packages. In this case, you should adjust your standards to reflect expected sales of 80 packages.

In both situations, your control process has been helpful. In the first instance, you were alerted to a problem that cut into your sales. Correcting this problem would undoubtedly increase sales and, therefore, profits. In the second case, you encountered a defect in your planning and learned a good managerial lesson: plan more carefully.

01 Set the standard by which performance will be measured.

02 Measure performance.

03 Compare actual performance with the standard and identify any deviations from the standard.

04 Determine the reasons for the deviation.

05 Take corrective action if needed.

Figure 8.7: The control process.

Benchmarking

Benchmarking could be considered as a specialized kind of control activity. Rather than controlling a particular aspect of performance (say, defects for a specific product), benchmarking aims to improve a firm's overall performance. The process of benchmarking involves comparisons to other organizations' practices and processes with the objective of learning and improvement in both efficiency and effectiveness. Benchmarking exercises can be conducted in a number of ways:

- Organizations often monitor publicly available information to keep tabs on the competition. Annual reports, news articles, and other sources are monitored closely in order to stay aware of the latest developments. In academia, universities often use published rankings tables to see how their programs compare on the basis of standardized test scores, salaries of graduates, and other important dimensions.
- Organizations may also work directly with companies in unrelated industries in order to compare those functions of the business which are similar. A manufacture of aircraft would not likely have a great deal in common with a company making engineered plastics, yet both have common functions such as accounting, finance, information technology, and human resources. Companies can exchange ideas that help each other improve efficiency, and often at a very low cost to either.
- In order to compare more directly to competition without relying solely on publicly available data, companies may enter into benchmarking consortiums in which an outside consultant would collect key data from all participants, anonymize it, and then share the results with all participants. Companies can then gauge how they compare to others in the industry without revealing their own performance to others.

Managerial Skills

To be a successful manager, you'll have to master a number of skills. To get an entry-level position, you'll have to be technically competent at the tasks you're asked to perform. To advance, you'll need to develop strong interpersonal and conceptual skills. The relative importance of different skills varies from job to job and organization to organization, but to some extent, you'll need them all to forge a managerial career.

Throughout your career, you'll also be expected to communicate ideas clearly, use your time efficiently, and reach sound decisions.

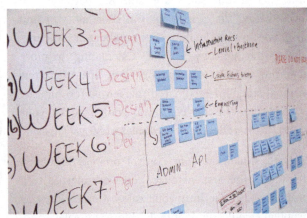

Figure 8.8: Managers are responsible for many things, including project timelines.

Technical Skills

You'll probably be hired for your first job based on your **technical skills**—the ones you need to perform specific tasks—and you'll use them extensively during your early career. If your college major is accounting, you'll use what you've learned to prepare financial statements. If you have a marketing degree and you join an ad agency, you'll use what you know about promotion to prepare ad campaigns. Technical skills will come in handy when you move up to a first-line managerial job and oversee the task performance of subordinates. Technical skills, though developed through job training and work experience, are generally acquired during the course of your formal education.

Interpersonal Skills

As you move up the corporate ladder, you'll find that you can't do everything yourself: you'll have to rely on other people to help you achieve the goals for which you're responsible. That's why **interpersonal skills**, also known as relational skills—the ability to get along with and motivate other people—are critical for managers in mid-level positions. These managers play a pivotal role because they report to top-level managers while overseeing the activities of first-line managers. Thus, they need strong working relationships with individuals at all levels and in all areas. More than most other managers, they must use "people skills" to foster teamwork, build trust, manage conflict, and encourage improvement.[13]

Conceptual Skills

Managers at the top, who are responsible for deciding what's good for the organization from the broadest perspective, rely on **conceptual skills**—the ability to reason abstractly and analyze complex situations. Senior executives are often called on to "think outside the box"—to arrive at creative solutions to complex, sometimes ambiguous problems. They need both strong analytical abilities and strong creative talents.

Communication Skills

Effective **communication skills** are crucial to just about everyone. At all levels of an organization, you'll often be judged on your ability to communicate, both orally and in writing. Whether you're talking informally or making a formal presentation, you must express yourself clearly and concisely. Talking too loudly, rambling, and using poor grammar reduce your ability to influence others, as does poor written communication. Confusing and error-riddled documents (including e-mails) don't do your message any good, and they will reflect poorly on you.[14]

Time-Management Skills

Managers face multiple demands on their time, and their days are usually filled with interruptions. Ironically, some technologies that were supposed to save time, such as voicemail and e-mail, have actually increased workloads. Unless you develop certain **time-management skills**, you risk reaching the end of the day feeling that you've worked a lot but accomplished little. What can managers do to ease the burden? Here are a few common-sense suggestions:

- Prioritize tasks, focusing on the most important things first.
- Set aside a certain time each day to return phone calls and answer e-mail.
- Delegate routine tasks.
- Don't procrastinate.
- Insist that meetings start and end on time, and stick to an agenda.
- Eliminate unnecessary paperwork.[15]

Decision-Making Skills

Every manager is expected to make decisions, whether alone or as part of a team. Drawing on your **decision-making skills** is often a process in which you must define a problem, analyze possible solutions, and select the best outcome. As luck would have it, because the same process is good for making personal decisions, we'll use a personal example to demonstrate the process approach to decision making. Consider the following scenario: you're upset because your midterm grades are much lower than you'd hoped. To make matters worse, not only are you in trouble academically, but also the other members of your business-project team are annoyed because you're not pulling your weight. Your lacrosse coach is very upset because you've missed too many practices, and members of the mountain-biking club of which you're supposed to be president are talking about impeaching you if you don't show up at the next meeting. And your significant other is feeling ignored.

A Six-Step Approach to Decision Making

Assuming that your top priority is salvaging your GPA, let's tackle your problem by using a six-step approach to solving problems that don't have simple solutions. We've summarized this model in figure 8.9[16]

Identify the problem you want to work on

Step one is getting to know your problem, which you can formulate by asking yourself a basic question: how can I improve my grades?

Gather relevant data

Step two is gathering information that will shed light on the problem. Let's rehash some of the relevant information that you've already identified: (a) you did poorly on your finals because you didn't spend enough time studying; (b) you didn't study because you went to see your girlfriend (who lives about three hours from campus) over the weekend before your exams (and on most other weekends, as a matter of fact); (c) what little studying you got in came at the expense of your team project and lacrosse practice; and (d) while you were away for the weekend, you forgot to tell members of the mountain-biking club that you had to cancel the planned meeting.

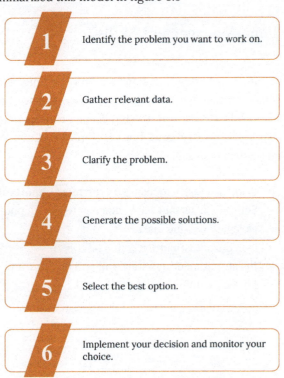

Figure 8.9: *The problem solving and decision making process.*

Clarify the problem

Once you review all the given facts, you should see that your problem is bigger than simply getting your grades up; your life is pretty much out of control. You can't handle everything to which you've committed yourself. Something has to give. You clarify the problem by summing it up with another basic question: what can I do to get my life back in order?

Generate possible solutions

Let's say that you've come up with the following possible solutions to your problem: (a) quit the lacrosse team, (b) step down as president of the mountain-biking club, (c) let team members do your share of work on the business project, and (d) stop visiting your significant other so frequently. The solution to your main problem—how to get your life back in order—will probably require multiple actions.

Select the best option

This is clearly the toughest part of the process. Working your way through your various options, you arrive at the following conclusions: (a) you can't quit the lacrosse team because you'd lose your scholarship; (b) you can resign your post in the mountain-biking club, but that won't free up much time; (c) you can't let your business-project team down (and besides, you'd just get a low grade); and (d) she wouldn't like the idea, but you could visit your girlfriend, say, once a month rather than once a week. So what's the most feasible (if not necessarily perfect) solution? Probably visiting your significant other once a month and giving up the presidency of the mountain-biking club.

Implement your decision and monitor your choice

When you call your girlfriend, she understands and is supportive. The vice president is happy to take over the mountain-biking club. After the first week, you're able to attend lacrosse practice, get caught up on your team business project, and catch up in all your other classes. The real test of your solution will be the results of the semester's finals.

Revisiting Qualtrax

In a previous chapter, we described the decisions made by Foxguard Solutions about its Qualtrax business, a new business venture developed inside the company. The decisions Foxguard made track quite well with the process described above. Consider the following:

- **Problem Identification**—Foxguard had a business line that wasn't an exact fit with its other business and was not performing up to the potential management believed it held.
- **Gather Relevant Data**—When Amy Ankrum was promoted, one of her first priorities was to determine what information would help her to understand the potential for the business and the resources needed to improve it.
- **Clarify the Problem**—Qualtrax had a definite market and potential to grow, but the parent company hadn't invested time/energy into doing that. Would more focus grow the business?
- **Generate Possible Solutions**—Management could have continued to try to grow the business in-house, sell it to another company, or spin it off
- **Select Best Option**—After a careful evaluation, management decided the spin-off was the best option to unleash the full potential of Qualtrax
- **Implement and Monitor**—The decision to spin-off Qualtrax could be measured on metrics such as growth in revenue, profits, and employee satisfaction. Based on the results to-date, it certainly seems like they made the right decision.

Managers and Information Technology

A trend having a major impact on managers is the proliferation of data and analytics in information technology. An increasing number of organizations are selling technology, and an increasing number are looking for cutting-edge technology to make and market the products and services they sell. One particularly useful type of technology is dashboard software. Much like the dashboard in a car, dashboard software gives managers a quick look into the relevant information they need to manage their companies. Most large companies are organized in divisions, and often each division relies on a particular type of application or database software. Dashboard software allows employees to access information from software they don't routinely use, for example, from an application used by a different division from their own. More important, however, is the ability of a dashboard to show up-to-the-minute information and to allow employees to see all the information they need—such as financial and performance data—on a single screen.

Such integrated functionality made dashboards extremely popular. A Gartner commentary suggests that companies put data and analytics at the heart of every company business decision.[17] Despite the increasing popularity of dashboard technology, the control tool has some drawbacks, such as focusing too intently on short-term results and ignoring the overall progress toward long-term goals. And some employees might bristle at being monitored as closely as dashboard tools allow.

Nonetheless, companies are seeing real results from implementing dashboard software. Robert Romanoff, a partner at the law firm of Levenfeld Romanoff in Chicago, uses dashboards that aggregate data from clients, strategic partners, and internal staff from the mailroom to the boardroom to improve what he calls the 3 Ps. The 3 Ps are process efficiency, project management, and strategic pricing.[18]

Adapted from: OpenStax *Introduction to Business* (CC BY). Access for free at https://openstax.org/books/introduction-business/pages/6-8-trends-in-management-and-leadership

Project Management

Project management is the use of specific knowledge, skills, tools, and techniques to deliver something of value to people and the marketplace. The development of a new product for a retail customer, the construction of a building, a merger and acquisition, a company's anniversary celebration, the expansion into a new geographic market—these are all examples of projects. As a student, you are assigned experiential learning projects. These academic projects, like business and industry projects, have a proposed outcome that typically include goals, objectives, deliverable tasks—also known as the project scope have a desired outcome with time constraints—a start date along with an expected finish date. In business, the project scope will also have an assigned budget and human resources. The role of a project manager is to plan, organize, facilitate resources and direct the completion of tasks for an organization so that specific projects are on time, on budget, and remain within scope.[19]

Applying Your Skills at Notes-4-You

So, what types of skills will managers at Notes-4-You need? To oversee note-taking and copying operations, **first-line managers** will require technical skills, probably in operations and perhaps in accounting. **Middle managers** will need strong interpersonal skills to maintain positive working relationships with subordinates and to motivate them. As president (the **top manager**), you'll need conceptual skills to solve problems and come up with creative ways to keep the business growing. And everyone will have to communicate effectively: after all, because you're in the business of selling written notes, it would look pretty bad if your employees wrote poorly. Finally, everyone will have to use time efficiently and call on problem-solving skills to handle the day-to-day crises that seem to plague every new company.

 An interactive H5P element has been excluded from this version of the text. You can view it online here: https://pressbooks.lib.vt.edu/fundamentalsofbusiness4e/?p=99#h5p-24

Chapter Videos

Roselinde Torres is an extremely accomplished leadership expert, and her TED Talk shares her insights on what it takes to be a great leader. If you have not seen TED Talks before, you will likely see a great many more before you graduate.

 One or more interactive elements has been excluded from this version of the text. You can view them online here: https://www.ted.com/talks/roselinde_torres_what_it_takes_to_be_a_great_leader

What makes a good leader?

 One or more interactive elements has been excluded from this version of the text. You can view them online here: https://www.youtube.com/watch?v=yLf2g2luL6A

Key Takeaways

- **Management** must include both **efficiency** (accomplishing goals using the fewest resources possible) and **effectiveness** (accomplishing goals as accurately as possible).
- The management process has four **functions**: **planning**, **organizing**, **leading**, and **controlling**.
- **Planning** for a business starts with **strategic planning**—the process of establishing an overall course of action.
- Management first identifies its **purposes**, creates a **mission statement**, and defines its **core values**.
- A **SWOT analysis** assesses the company's strengths and weaknesses and its fit with the external environment.
- **Goals and objectives**, or performance targets, are established to direct company actions, and **tactical plans** and **operational plans** implement objectives.
- A manager's **leadership style** varies depending on the manager, the situation, and the people being directed. There are several management styles.
    - An **autocratic** manager tends to make decisions without input and expects subordinates to follow instructions.
    - Managers who prefer a **democratic** style seek input into decisions.
    - A **free rein** manager provides no more guidance than necessary and lets subordinates make decisions and solve problems.
    - **Transactional** style managers exercise authority according to their rank in the organization, let subordinates know what's expected of them, and step in when mistakes are made.
    - **Transformational** style managers mentor and develop subordinates and motivate them to achieve organizational goals.
- The **control process** can be viewed as a five-step process: (1) establish standards, (2) **measure** performance, (3) **compare** actual performance with standards and identify any deviations, (4) **determine the reason** for deviations, and (5) **take corrective action** if needed.
- **Benchmarking** is a process for improving overall company efficiency and effectiveness by

> comparing performance to competitors.
> - Top managers need strong **conceptual skills**, while those at midlevel need good **interpersonal skills** and those at lower levels need **technical skills**.
> - All managers need strong **communication, decision-making,** and **time-management skills**.

References

Figures

Figure 8.1: How to become a successful manager. Kindred Grey. 2022. CC BY 4.0. https://archive.org/details/8.1_20220623.

Figure 8.2: The management process. Kindred Grey. 2022. CC BY 4.0. https://archive.org/details/8.2_20220623.

Figure 8.3: A note taker. Burst. 2018. CC0 license. https://www.pexels.com/photo/photo-of-man-using-laptop-374620/.

Figure 8.4: A Wendy's restaurant. Batu Gezer. 2020. Unsplash license. https://unsplash.com/photos/AGGhkGuVs2w.

Figure 8.5: BP's Deepwater Horizon oil spill in the Gulf of Mexico in 2010. DVIDSHUB. 2010. CC BY 2.0. https://commons.wikimedia.org/wiki/File:Flickr_-_DVIDSHUB_-_Oil_Spill.jpg.

Figure 8.6: Copy machine. Mahrous Houses. 2021. Unsplash license. https://unsplash.com/photos/5AoOejjRUrA.

Figure 8.7: The control process. Kindred Grey. 2022. CC BY 4.0. https://archive.org/details/8.7_20220623.

Figure 8.8: Managers are responsible for many things, including project timelines. Startup Stock Photos. 2015. CC0 license. https://www.pexels.com/photo/blue-printer-paper-7376/.

Figure 8.9: The problem solving and decision making process. Kindred Grey. 2022. CC BY 4.0. https://archive.org/details/8.9_20220623.

Videos

Video 1: What it Takes to be a Great Leader. TED. 2013. CC BY NC ND 4.0. https://www.ted.com/talks/roselinde_torres_what_it_takes_to_be_a_great_leader?language=en.

Video 2: What Makes A Good Leader. Brian Tracy. 2021. Copyrighted. https://www.youtube.com/watch?v=yLf2g2luL6A.

Notes

1. Wal Mart (2016). "Our Story." Retrieved from: http://corporate.walmart.com/our-story/our-history
2. Mary Kay (2016). "Corporate Careers: Discover what you love about Mary Kay." Retrieved from: http://www.marykay.com/en-US/About-Mary-Kay/EmploymentMaryKay
3. Harley Davidson (2016). "About Harley Davidson." Retrieved from: http://www.harley-davidson.com/content/h-d/en_US/company.html
4. Volvo Group (2016). "Volvo Group Global: Our Values." Retrieved from: http://www.volvogroup.com/group/global/en-gb/volvo group/ourvalues/Pages/volvovalues.aspx
5. Coca Cola Company (2016). "Our Company: Vision, Mission, and Values." Retrieved from: http://www.coca-colacompany.com/our-company/mission-vision-values
6. Scott Safranski and Ik-Whan Kwon (1991). "Strategic Planning for the Growing Business." U.S. Small Business Administration. Retrieved from: http://webharvest.gov/peth04/20041105092332/http://sba.gov/library/pubs/eb-6.pdf
7. Franchise Bison (2003). "McDonald's Announces Plans to Revitalize Its Worldwide Business and Sets New Financial Targets." Retrieved from: http://www.bison1.com/press_mcdonalds_04072003
8. Brian Perkins (2000). "Defining Crisis Management." Wharton Magazine. Retrieved from: http://whartonmagazine.com/issues/summer-2000/reunion-2000/
9. Matt Richtel (2005). "Wendy's Gets a Break, But Still Has Work Ahead of it." New York Times. Retrieved from: http://www.nytimes.com/2005/04/29/business/media/wendys-gets-a-break-but-still-has-work-ahead-of-it.html?_r=0
10. Jacqui Goddard (2010). "Embattled BP Chief: I Want my Life Back." The Times (London). Retrieved from: http://www.thetimes.co.uk/tto/news/article2534734.ece
11. John Reh (n.d.). "Management 101." About Money. Retrieved from: http://management.about.com/cs/generalmanagement/a/Management101.htm
12. Sarah Burke and Karen M. Collins, (2001). "Gender differences in leadership styles and management skills." Women In Management Review. pp. 244–257
13. Brian Perkins (2000). "Defining Crisis Management." Wharton Magazine. Retrieved from: http://whartonmagazine.com/issues/summer-2000/reunion-2000/
14. Brian L. Davis et al. (1992). *Successful Manager's Handbook: Development Suggestions for Today's Managers*. Minneapolis: Personnel Decisions Inc. p. 189.
15. Ibid.
16. Shari Caudron (1998). "Six Steps in Creative Problem Solving." Controller Magazine. p. 38; Caudron describes a systematic approach developed by Roger L. Firestien, president of Innovation Systems Group, Williamsville, NY.
17. "How Data Analytics Help in Making Business Decisions." *Gartner*, https://www.gartner.com/en/information-technology/insights/data-analytics.
18. Lawrence Gitman, et. al. (2018). Ch. 4 Summary of Learning Outcomes, *Introduction to Business*. (CC BY 4.0) OpenStax. Retrieved from: https://openstax.org/books/introduction-business/pages/4-summary-of-learning-outcomes. OpenStax *Introduction to Business* may be accessed for free at: https://openstax.org/books/introduction-business/pages/1-introduction.
19. Project Management Institute. (n.d.). What is Project Management | PMI. pmi.org. Retrieved from: https://www.pmi.org/about/learn-about-pmi/what-is-project-management

9. Structuring Organizations

Learning Objectives

- Identify the three levels of management and the responsibilities at each level.
- Discuss various options for organizing a business, and create an organization chart.
- Understand how specialization helps make organizations more efficient.
- Discuss the different ways that an organization can departmentalize.
- Explain other key terms related to this chapter such as chain of command, delegation of authority, and span of control.

Organizing

If you read our chapter on Management and Leadership, you will recall developing a strategic plan for your new company, Notes-4-You. Once a business has completed the planning process, it will need to organize the company so that it can implement that plan. A manager engaged in organizing allocates **resources** (people, equipment, and money) to achieve a company's **objectives**. Successful managers make sure that all the activities identified in the planning process are assigned to some person, department, or team and that everyone has the resources needed to perform assigned activities.

Levels of Management: How Managers Are Organized

A typical organization has several **layers of management**. Think of these layers as forming a pyramid like the one in figure 9.1, with top managers occupying the narrow space at the peak, first-line managers the broad base, and middle-managers the levels in between.

As you move up the pyramid, management positions get more demanding, but they carry more authority and responsibility (along with more power, prestige, and pay). Top managers spend most of their time in planning and decision making, while first-line managers focus on day-to-day operations. For obvious reasons, there are far more people with positions at the base of the pyramid than there are at the other two levels. Let's look at each management level in more detail.

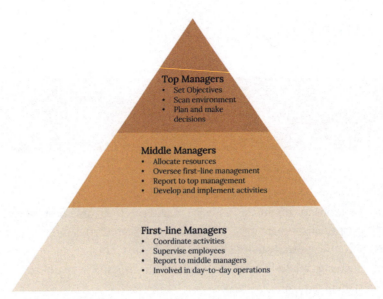

Figure 9.1: Levels of management.

Top Managers

Top managers are responsible for the health and performance of the organization. They set the objectives, or performance targets, designed to direct all the activities that must be performed if the company is going to fulfill its mission. Top-level executives routinely scan the external environment for opportunities and threats, and they redirect company efforts when needed. They spend a considerable portion of their time planning and making major decisions. They represent the company in important dealings with other businesses and government agencies, and they promote it to the public. Job titles at this level typically include chief executive officer (CEO), chief financial officer (CFO), chief operating officer (COO), president, and vice president.

Middle Managers

Middle managers are in the center of the management hierarchy: they report to top management and oversee the activities of first-line managers. They're responsible for developing and implementing activities and allocating the resources needed to achieve the objectives set by top management. Common job titles include operations manager, division manager, plant manager, and branch manager.

First-Line Managers

First-line managers supervise employees and coordinate their activities to make sure that the work performed throughout the company is consistent with the plans of both top and middle management. It's at this level that most people acquire their first managerial experience. The job titles vary considerably but include such designations as manager, group leader, office manager, foreman, and supervisor.

Let's take a quick survey of the management hierarchy at Notes-4-You. As president, you are a member of top management, and you're responsible for the overall performance of your company. You spend much of your time setting performance targets, to ensure that the company meets the goals you've set for it—increased sales, higher-quality notes, and timely distribution.

Several middle managers report to you, including your operations manager. As a middle manager, this individual focuses on implementing two of your objectives: producing high-quality notes and distributing them to customers in a timely manner. To accomplish this task, the operations manager oversees the work of two first-line managers—the note-taking supervisor and the copying supervisor. Each first-line manager supervises several non-managerial employees to make sure that their work is consistent with the plans devised by top and middle management.

Organizational Structure: How Companies Get the Job Done

Building an organizational structure engages managers in two activities: **job specialization** (dividing tasks into jobs) and **departmentalization** (grouping jobs into units). An organizational structure outlines the various roles within an organizational, which positions report to which, and how an organization will departmentalize its work. Take note than an organizational structure is an arrangement of positions that's most appropriate for your company at a specific point in time. Given the rapidly changing environment in which businesses operate, a structure that works today might be outdated tomorrow. That's why you hear so often about companies **restructuring**—altering existing organizational structures to become more competitive once conditions have changed. Let's now look at how the processes of specialization and departmentalization are accomplished.

Specialization

Organizing activities into clusters of related tasks that can be handled by certain individuals or groups is called **specialization**. This aspect of designing an organizational structure is twofold:

1. *Identify the activities that need to be performed* in order to achieve organizational goals.
2. *Break down these activities into tasks* that can be performed by individuals or groups of employees.

Specialization has several advantages. First and foremost, it leads to **efficiency**. Imagine a situation in which each department was responsible for paying its own invoices; a person handling this function a few times a week would likely be far less efficient than someone whose job was to pay the bills. In addition to increasing efficiency, specialization results in jobs that are easier to learn and roles that are clearer to employees. But the approach has disadvantages, too. Doing the same thing over and over sometimes leads to boredom and may eventually leave employees dissatisfied with their jobs. Before long, companies may notice decreased performance and increased absenteeism and turnover (the percentage of workers who leave an organization and must be replaced).

Departmentalization

The next step in designing an organizational structure is **departmentalization**—grouping specialized jobs into meaningful units. Depending on the organization and the size of the work units, they may be called divisions, departments, or just plain groups.

Traditional groupings of jobs result in different organizational structures, and for the sake of simplicity, we'll focus on two types—functional and divisional organizations.

Functional Organizations

A **functional organization** groups together people who have comparable skills and perform similar tasks. This form of organization is fairly typical for small to medium-size companies, which group their people by business functions: accountants are grouped together, as are people in finance, marketing and sales, human resources, production, and research and development. Each unit is headed by an individual with expertise in the unit's particular function. Examples of typical functions in a business enterprise include human resources, operations, marketing, and finance. Also, business colleges will often organize according to functions found in a business.

There are a number of advantages to the functional approach. The structure is simple to understand and enables the staff to specialize in particular areas; everyone in the marketing group would probably have similar interests and expertise. But homogeneity also has drawbacks: it can hinder communication and decision making between units and even promote interdepartmental conflict. The marketing department, for example, might butt heads with the accounting department because marketers want to spend as much as possible on advertising, while accountants want to control costs.

Divisional Organizations

Large companies often find it unruly to operate as one large unit under a functional organizational structure. Sheer size makes it difficult for managers to oversee operations and serve customers. To rectify this problem, most large companies are structured as **divisional organizations**. They are similar in many respects to stand-alone companies, except that certain common tasks, like legal work, tends to be centralized at the headquarters level. Each division functions relatively autonomously because it contains most of the functional expertise (production, marketing, accounting, finance, human resources) needed to meet its objectives. The challenge is to find the most appropriate way of structuring operations to achieve overall company goals. Toward this end, divisions can be formed according to products, customers, processes, or geography.

Product divisions

Product division means that a company is structured according to its product lines. General Motors, for example, has four product-based divisions: Buick, Cadillac, Chevrolet, and GMC.[1] Each division has its own research and development group, its own manufacturing operations, and its own marketing team. This allows individuals in the division to focus all their efforts on the products produced by their division. A downside is that it results in higher costs as corporate support services (such as accounting and human resources) are duplicated in each of the four divisions.

Customer divisions

Some companies prefer a **customer division** structure because it enables them to better serve their various categories of customers. Thus, Johnson & Johnson's 200 or so operating companies are grouped into three customer-based business segments: consumer business (personal-care and hygiene products sold to the general public), pharmaceuticals (prescription drugs sold to pharmacies), and professional business (medical devices and diagnostics products used by physicians, optometrists, hospitals, laboratories, and clinics).[2]

Process divisions

If goods move through several steps during production, a company might opt for a **process division** structure. This form works well at Bowater Thunder Bay, a Canadian company that harvests trees and processes wood into newsprint and pulp. The first step in the production process is harvesting and stripping trees. Then, large logs are sold to lumber mills and smaller logs are chopped up and sent to Bowater's mills. At the mill, wood chips are chemically converted into pulp. About 90 percent is sold to other manufacturers (as raw material for home and office products), and the remaining 10 percent is further processed into newspaper print. Bowater, then, has three divisions: tree cutting, chemical processing, and finishing (which makes newsprint).[3]

Geographical divisions

Geographical division enables companies that operate in several locations to be responsive to customers at a local level. Adidas, for example, is organized according to the regions of the world in which it operates. They have eight different regions, and each one reports its performance separately in their annual reports.[4]

Figure 9.2: Adidas' geographical divisions.

Summing Up Divisional Organizations

There are pluses and minuses associated with divisional organization. On the one hand, divisional structure usually enhances the ability to respond to changes in a firm's environment. If, on the other hand, services must be duplicated across units, costs will be higher. In addition, some companies have found that units tend to focus on their own needs and goals at the expense of the organization as a whole.

 An interactive H5P element has been excluded from this version of the text. You can view it online here: https://pressbooks.lib.vt.edu/fundamentalsofbusiness4e/?p=107#h5p-25

The Organization Chart

Once an organization has set its structure, it can represent that structure in an **organization chart**: a diagram delineating the interrelationships of positions within the organization. An example organization chart is shown in figure 9.3, using our "Notes-4-You" example from chapter 8.

Figure 9.3: An organizational chart for Notes-4-You.

Imagine putting yourself at the top of the chart, as the company's president. You would then fill in the level directly below your name with the names and positions of the people who work directly for you—your accounting, marketing, operations, and human resources managers. The next level identifies the people who work for these managers. Because you've started out small, neither your accounting manager nor your human resources manager will be currently managing anyone directly. Your marketing manager, however, will oversee one person in advertising and a sales supervisor (who, in turn, oversees the sales staff). Your operations manager will oversee two individuals—one to supervise note-takers and one to supervise the people responsible for making copies. The lines between the positions on the chart indicate the **reporting relationships**; for example, the Note-Takers Supervisor reports directly to the Operations Manager.

Although the structure suggests that you will communicate only with your four direct reports, this isn't the way things normally work in practice. Behind every formal communication network there lies a network of **informal communications**—unofficial relationships among members of an organization. You might find that over time, you receive communications directly from members of the sales staff; in fact, you might encourage this line of communication.

Now let's look at the chart of an organization that relies on a divisional structure based on goods or services produced—say, a theme park. The top layers of this company's organization chart might look like the one in figure 9.4A (left side of the diagram). We see that the president has two direct reports—a vice president in charge of rides and a vice president in charge of concessions. What about a bank that's structured according to its customer base? The bank's organization chart would begin like the one in figure 9.4B. Once again, the company's top manager has two direct reports, in this case a VP of retail-customer accounts and a VP of commercial-customer accounts.

Structuring Organizations | 199

Figure 9.4: Organizational charts for divisional structures.

Over time, companies revise their organizational structures to accommodate growth and changes in the external environment. It's not uncommon, for example, for a firm to adopt a functional structure in its early years. Then, as it becomes bigger and more complex, it might move to a divisional structure—perhaps to accommodate new products or to become more responsive to certain customers or geographical areas. Some companies might ultimately rely on a combination of functional and divisional structures. This could be a good approach for a credit card company that issues cards in both the United States and Europe. An outline of this firm's organization chart might look like the one in figure 9.5.

Figure 9.5: Organizational charts for functional and divisional structures.

Chain of Command

The vertical connecting lines in the organization chart show the firm's **chain of command**: the authority relationships among people working at different levels of the organization. That is to say, they show who reports to whom. When you're examining an organization chart, you'll probably want to know whether each person reports to one or more supervisors: to what extent, in other words, is there **unity of command**? To understand why unity of command is an important organizational feature, think about it from a personal standpoint. Would you want to report to more than one boss? What happens if you get conflicting directions? Whose directions would you follow?

There are, however, conditions under which an organization and its employees can benefit by violating the unity-of-command principle. Under a **matrix structure**, for example, employees from various functional areas (product design, manufacturing, finance, marketing, human resources, etc.) form teams to combine their skills in working on a specific project or product. This matrix organization chart might look like the one in the following figure.

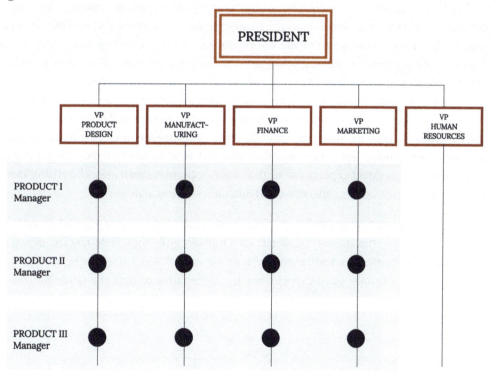

Figure 9.6: Example of a matrix structure.

Nike sometimes uses this type of arrangement. To design new products, the company may create product teams made up of designers, marketers, and other specialists with expertise in particular sports categories—say, running shoes or basketball shoes. Each team member would be evaluated by both the team manager and the head of his or her functional department.

Span of Control

Another thing to notice about a firm's chain of command is the number of layers between the top managerial position and the lowest managerial level. As a rule, new organizations have only a few layers of management—an organizational structure that's often called **flat**. Let's say, for instance, that a member of the Notes-4-You sales staff wanted to express concern about slow sales among a certain group of students. That person's message would have to filter upward through only two management layers—the sales supervisor and the marketing manager—before reaching the president.

As a company grows, however, it tends to add more layers between the top and the bottom; that is, it gets **taller**. Added layers of management can slow down communication and decision making, causing the organization to become less efficient and productive. That's one reason why many of today's organizations are restructuring to become flatter.

There are trade-offs between the advantages and disadvantages of flat and tall organizations. Companies determine which trade-offs to make according to a principle called **span of control**, which measures the number of people reporting to a particular manager. If, for example, you remove layers of management to make your organization flatter, you end up increasing the number of people reporting to a particular supervisor. If you refer back to the organization chart for Notes-4-You, you'll recall that, under your present structure, four managers report to you as the president: the heads of accounting, marketing, operations, and human resources. In turn, two of these managers have positions reporting to them: the advertising manager and sales supervisor report to the marketing manager, while the notetakers supervisor and the copiers supervisor report to the operations manager. Let's say that you remove a layer of management by getting rid of the marketing and operations managers. Your organization would be flatter, but what would happen to your workload? As president, you'd now have six direct reports rather than four: accounting manager, advertising manager, sales manager, notetaker supervisor, copier supervisor, and human resources manager.

So what's better—a narrow span of control (with few direct reports) or a wide span of control (with many direct reports)? The answer to this question depends on a number of factors, including frequency and type of interaction, proximity of subordinates, competence of both supervisor and subordinates, and the nature of the work being supervised. For example, you'd expect a much wider span of control at a nonprofit call center than in a hospital emergency room.

Delegating Authority

Given the tendency toward flatter organizations and wider spans of control, how do managers handle increased workloads? They must learn how to handle **delegation**—the process of entrusting work to subordinates. Unfortunately, many managers are reluctant to delegate. As a result, they not only overburden themselves with tasks that could be handled by others, but they also deny subordinates the opportunity to learn and develop new skills.

Responsibility and Authority

As owner of Notes-4-You, you'll probably want to control every aspect of your business, especially during the start-up stage. But as the organization grows, you'll have to assign responsibility for performing certain tasks to other people. You'll also have to accept the fact that **responsibility** alone—the duty to perform a task—won't be enough to get the job done. You'll need to grant subordinates the **authority** they require to complete a task—that is, the power to make the necessary decisions. (And they'll also need sufficient resources.) Ultimately, you'll also hold your subordinates accountable for their performance.

 An interactive H5P element has been excluded from this version of the text. You can view it online here: https://pressbooks.lib.vt.edu/fundamentalsofbusiness4e/?p=107#h5p-26

Centralization and Decentralization

If and when your company expands (say, by offering note-taking services at other schools), you'll have to decide whether most decisions should still be made by individuals at the top or delegated to lower-level employees. The first option, in which most decision making is concentrated at the top, is called **centralization**. The second option, which spreads decision making throughout the organization, is called **decentralization**.

Centralization has the advantage of consistency in decision-making. Since in a centralized model, key decisions are made by the same top managers, those decisions tend to be more uniform than if decisions were made by a variety of different people at lower levels in the organization. In most cases, decisions can also be made more quickly provided that top management does not try to control too many decisions. However, centralization has some important disadvantages. If top management makes virtually all key decisions, then lower-level managers will feel under-utilized and will not develop decision-making skills that would help them become promotable. An overly centralized model might also fail to consider information that only front-line employees have or might actually delay the decision-making process. Consider a case where the sales manager for an account is meeting with a customer representative who makes a request for a special sale price; the customer offers to buy 50 percent more product if the sales manager will reduce the price by 5 percent for one month. If the sales manager had to obtain approval from the head office, the opportunity might disappear before she could get approval—a competitor's sales manager might be the customer's next meeting.

An overly decentralized decision model has its risks as well. Imagine a case in which a company had adopted a geographically-based divisional structure and had greatly decentralized decision making. In order to expand its business, suppose one division decided to expand its territory into the geography of another division. If headquarters approval for such a move was not required, the divisions of the company might end up competing against each other, to the detriment of the organization as a whole. Companies that wish to maximize their potential must find the right balance between centralized and decentralized decision making.

An interactive H5P element has been excluded from this version of the text. You can view it online here: https://pressbooks.lib.vt.edu/fundamentalsofbusiness4e/?p=107#h5p-27

Key Takeaways

- Managers **coordinate the activities** identified in the planning process among individuals, departments, or other units and **allocate the resources** needed to perform them.
- Typically, there are **three levels of management**: **top managers**, who are responsible for overall performance; **middle managers**, who report to top managers and oversee lower-level managers; and **first-line managers**, who supervise employees to make sure that work is performed correctly and on time.
- Management must develop an **organizational structure**, or arrangement of people within the organization, that will best achieve company goals.
- The process begins with **specialization**—dividing necessary tasks into jobs; the principle of grouping jobs into units is called **departmentalization**.
- Units are then grouped into an appropriate organizational structure. **Functional** organization groups people with comparable skills and tasks; **divisional** organization creates a structure composed of self-contained units based on **product, customer, process**, or **geographical division**. Forms of organizational division are often combined.
- An organization's structure is represented in an **organization chart**—a diagram showing the interrelationships of its positions.
- This chart highlights the **chain of command**, or authority relationships among people working at different levels.
- It also shows the number of **layers** between the top and lowest managerial levels. An organization with few layers has a **wide span** of control, with each manager overseeing a large number of subordinates; with a **narrow span of control**, only a limited number of subordinates reports to each manager.

References

Figures

Figure 9.1: Levels of management. Kindred Grey. 2022. CC BY 4.0. https://archive.org/details/9.1_20220623.

Figure 9.2: Adidas' geographical divisions. Kindred Grey. 2022. CC BY-SA 3.0. Data from https://www.annualreports.com/HostedData/AnnualReports/PDF/OTC_ADDDF_2021.pdf. Added Adidas Logo by Unknown author from WikimediaCommons (public domain) and BlankMap-World-Continents-Coloured by Max Naylor from WikimediaCommons (CC BY-SA 3.0). https://archive.org/details/9.2_20220623.

Figure 9.3: An organizational chart for Notes-4-You. Kindred Grey. 2022. CC BY 4.0. Added Woman by verry poernomo from Noun Project (Noun Project license) and manager by Chrystina Angeline from Noun Project (Noun Project license). https://archive.org/details/9.3_20220623.

Figure 9.4: Organizational charts for divisional structures. Kindred Grey. 2022. CC BY 4.0. https://archive.org/details/9.4_20220623.

Figure 9.5: Organizational charts for functional and divisional structures. Kindred Grey. 2022. GNU General Public license. Added Blank map of the United States by Zntrip from WikimediaCommons (GNU General Public license) and Europe blank map by wiki-vr from WikimediaCommons (public domain). https://archive.org/details/9.5_20220623.

Figure 9.6: Example of a matrix structure. Kindred Grey. 2022. CC BY 4.0. https://archive.org/details/9.6_20220623.

Notes

1. Associated Press (2010). "General Motors Rebuilds with 4 Divisions." Augusta Chronicle. Retrieved from: http://chronicle.augusta.com/life/autos/2010-10-07/general-motors-rebuilds-4-divisions#
2. Johnson and Johnson (2016). "Company Structure." Retrieved from: http://www.jnj.com/about-jnj/company-structure
3. Lakehead University Faculty of Natural Resources Management (2016). "From the Forest to the Office and Home: Bowater—A Case Study in Newsprint and Kraft Pulp Production." Borealforest.org. Retrieved from: http://www.borealforest.org/paper/index.htm
4. Adidas Group (2015). "Adidas Group Annual Report 2015." Retrieved from: http://www.adidas-group.com/en/investors/financial-reports/#/2015/

10. Operations Management

Learning Objectives

- Define operations management and discuss the role of the operations manager in a manufacturing company.
- Describe the decisions and activities of the operations manager in overseeing the production process in a manufacturing company.
- Explain how to create and use both PERT and Gantt charts.
- Explain how manufacturing companies use technology to produce and deliver goods in an efficient, cost-effective manner.
- Describe the decisions made in planning the product delivery process in a service company.
- List the characteristics that distinguish service operations from manufacturing operations and identify the activities undertaken to manage operations in a service organization.
- Explain how manufacturing and service companies alike use total quality management and outsourcing to provide value to customers.

The Challenge: Producing Quality Jetboards

The product development process can be complex and lengthy. It took 16 years for Bob Montgomery and others at his company to develop the PowerSki Jetboard, and this involved thousands of design changes. It was worth it, though: the Jetboard was an exciting, engine-propelled personal watercraft—a cross between a high-performance surfboard and a competition water-ski/wakeboard that received extensive media attention and rave reviews. It was showered with honors, including Time magazine's "Best Invention of the Year" award.[1] Stories about the Jetboard appeared in more than 50 magazines around the world, and it was featured in several movies, over 25 TV shows, and on YouTube.[2]

Figure 10.1: The PowerSki Jetboard.

Montgomery and his team at PowerSki enjoyed taking their well-deserved bows for the job they did designing the product, but having a product was only the beginning for the company. The next step was developing a system that would produce high-quality Jetboards at reasonable prices. Before putting this system in place, PowerSki managers had to address several questions.

- What kind of production process should they use to make the Jetboards?
- How large should their production facilities be, and where should they be located?
- Where should they buy needed materials?
- What systems will be needed to control the production process and ensure a quality product?

Answering these and other questions helped PowerSki set up a manufacturing system through which it could accomplish the most important task that it had set for itself: efficiently producing quality Jetboards.

Operations Management in Manufacturing

Like PowerSki, every organization—whether it produces goods or provides services—sees Job 1 as furnishing customers with quality products. Thus, to compete with other organizations, a company must convert **resources** (materials, labor, money, information) into **goods or services** as efficiently as possible. The upper-level manager who directs this transformation process is called an **operations manager**. The job of **operations management** (OM) consists of all the activities involved in transforming a product idea into a finished product. In addition, operations managers are involved in planning and controlling the systems that produce goods and services. In other words, operations managers manage the process that transforms inputs into outputs. Figure 10.2 illustrates these traditional functions of operations management.

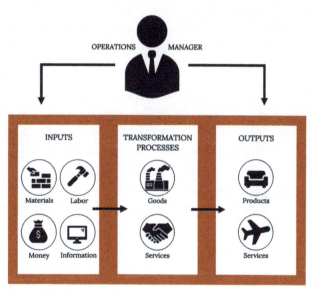

Figure 10.2: The transformation process.

Like PowerSki, all **manufacturers** set out to perform the same basic function: to transform resources into finished goods. To perform this function in today's business environment, manufacturers must continually strive to improve operational efficiency. They must fine-tune their production processes to focus on quality, to hold down the costs of materials and labor, and to eliminate all costs that add no value to the finished product. Making the decisions involved in the effort to attain these goals is another job of operations managers. Their responsibilities can be grouped as follows:

- **Production planning**. During production planning, managers determine how goods will be produced, where production will take place, and how manufacturing facilities will be laid out.
- **Production control**. Once the production process is under way, managers must continually schedule and monitor the activities that make up that process. They must solicit and respond to feedback and make adjustments where needed. At this stage, they also oversee the purchasing of raw materials and the handling of inventories.
- **Quality control**. The operations manager is directly involved in efforts to ensure that goods are produced according to specifications and that quality standards are maintained.

Let's take a closer look at each of these responsibilities.

Planning the Production Process

The decisions made in the planning stage have long-range implications and are crucial to a firm's success. Before making decisions about the operations process, managers must consider the goals set by marketing managers. Does the company intend to be a low-cost producer and to compete on the basis of price? Or does it plan to focus on quality and go after the high end of the market? Many decisions involve trade-offs. For example, low cost doesn't normally go hand in hand with high quality. All functions of the company must be aligned with the overall strategy to ensure success.

With these thoughts in mind, let's look at the specific types of decisions that have to be made in the production planning process. We've divided these decisions into those dealing with production methods, site selection, facility layout, and components and materials management.

An interactive H5P element has been excluded from this version of the text. You can view it online here:
https://pressbooks.lib.vt.edu/fundamentalsofbusiness4e/?p=117#h5p-28

Production-Method Decisions

The first step in production planning is deciding which type of **production process** is best for making the goods that your company intends to manufacture. In reaching this decision, you should answer such questions as:

- Am I making a one-of-a-kind good based solely on customer specifications, or am I producing high-volume standardized goods to be sold later?
- Do I offer customers the option of "customizing" an otherwise standardized good to meet their specific needs?

208 | Operations Management

One way to appreciate the nature of this decision is by comparing three basic types of processes or methods: make-to-order, mass production, and mass customization. The task of the operations manager is to work with other managers, particularly marketers, to select the process that best serves the needs of the company's customers.

Make-to-Order

At one time, most consumer goods, such as furniture and clothing, were made by individuals practicing various crafts. By their very nature, products were customized to meet the needs of the buyers who ordered them. This process, which is called a **make-to-order** strategy, is still commonly used by such businesses as print or sign shops that produce low-volume, high-variety goods according to customer specifications. This level of customization often results in a longer production and delivery cycle than other approaches.

Mass Production

By the early twentieth century, a new concept of producing goods had been introduced: **mass production** (or make-to-stock strategy), the practice of producing high volumes of identical goods at a cost low enough to price them for large numbers of customers. Goods are made in anticipation of future demand (based on forecasts) and kept in inventory for later sale. This approach is particularly appropriate for standardized goods ranging from processed foods to electronic appliances and generally result in shorter cycle times than a make-to-order process.

Mass Customization

There is at least one big disadvantage to mass production: customers, as one old advertising slogan put it, can't "have it their way." They have to accept standardized products as they come off assembly lines. Increasingly, however, customers are looking for products that are designed to accommodate individual tastes or needs but can still be bought at reasonable prices. To meet the demands of these consumers, many companies have turned to an approach called **mass customization**, which combines the advantages of customized products with those of mass production.

This approach requires that a company interact with the customer to find out exactly what the customer wants and then manufacture the good, using efficient production methods to hold down costs. One efficient method is to mass-produce a product up to a certain cut-off point and then to customize it to satisfy different customers.

One of the best-known mass customizers is Nike, which has achieved success by allowing customers to configure their own athletic shoes, apparel, and equipment through Nike's iD program. The Web has a lot to do with the growth of mass customization. Levi's, for instance, lets customers find a pair of perfect fitting jeans by going through an online fitting process. Oakley offers customized sunglasses, goggles, watches, and backpacks, while Mars, Inc. can make M&M's in any color the customer wants (say, school colors) as well as add text and even pictures to the candy.

Naturally, mass customization doesn't work for all types of goods. Most people don't care about customized detergents or paper products. And while many of us like the idea of customized clothes, footwear, or sunglasses, we often aren't willing to pay the higher prices they command.

Facilities Decisions

After selecting the best production process, operations managers must then decide where the goods will be manufactured, how large the manufacturing facilities will be, and how those facilities will be laid out.

Site Selection

In **site selection** (choosing a location for the business), managers must consider several factors:

- To minimize shipping costs, managers often want to locate plants close to suppliers, customers, or both.
- They generally want to locate in areas with ample numbers of skilled workers.
- They naturally prefer locations where they and their families will enjoy living.
- They want locations where costs for resources and other expenses—land, labor, construction, utilities, and taxes—are low.
- They look for locations with a favorable business climate—one in which, for example, local governments might offer financial incentives (such as tax breaks) to entice them to do business in their locales. For example, an enterprise zone is an area in which incentives are used to attract investments from private companies.

Managers rarely find locations that meet all these criteria. As a rule, they identify the most important criteria and aim at satisfying them. In deciding to locate in San Clemente, California, for instance, PowerSki was able to satisfy three important criteria: (1) proximity to the firm's suppliers, (2) availability of skilled engineers and technicians, and (3) favorable living conditions. These factors were more important than operating in a low-cost region or getting financial incentives from local government. Because PowerSki distributes its products throughout the world, proximity to customers was also unimportant.

Site Selection Example

In 2022, the LEGO Group, manufacturers of the iconic small toy bricks, announced that they had selected the state of Virginia for their next manufacturing plant. LEGO will invest over $1 billion to construct its first U.S. manufacturing with a new 1.7 million-square-foot precision manufacturing facility which will create over 1,760 new jobs. LEGO has other manufacturing plants in China, Vietnam, Mexico and the Czech Republic.

Niels B. Christiansen, CEO, the LEGO Group, said,

> "We were impressed with all that Virginia has to offer, from access to a skilled workforce, support for high-quality manufacturers, and great transport links. We appreciate support for our ambition to build a carbon-neutral run facility and construct a solar park and are looking forward to building a great team with support from the Virginia Talent Accelerator Program."

The LEGO Group is a family-owned company headquartered in Denmark and its products are sold in more than 130 countries worldwide.[3]

Figure 10.3: LEGO has announced they are opening a manufacturing plant in Virginia.

Capacity Planning

Now that you know where you're going to locate, you have to decide on the quantity of products that you'll produce. You begin by **forecasting** demand for your product, which isn't easy. To estimate the number of units that you're likely to sell over a given period, you have to understand the industry that you're in and estimate your likely share of the market by reviewing industry data and conducting other forms of research.

Once you've forecasted the demand for your product, you can calculate the **capacity requirements** of your production facility—the maximum number of goods that it can produce over a given time under normal working conditions. In turn, having calculated your capacity requirements, you're ready to determine how much investment in plant and equipment you'll have to make, as well as the number of labor hours required for the plant to produce at capacity.

Like forecasting, capacity planning is difficult. Unfortunately, failing to balance capacity and projected demand can be seriously detrimental to your bottom line. If you set capacity too low (and so produce less than you should), you won't be able to meet demand, and you'll lose sales and customers. If you set capacity too high (and turn out more units than you should), you'll waste resources and inflate operating costs.

Operations Management | 211

> An interactive H5P element has been excluded from this version of the text. You can view it online here:
> https://pressbooks.lib.vt.edu/fundamentalsofbusiness4e/?p=117#h5p-29

Managing the Production Process in a Manufacturing Company

Operations managers engage in the daily activities of materials management, which encompasses the activities of purchasing, inventory control, and work scheduling.

Purchasing and Supplier Selection

The process of acquiring the materials and services to be used in production is called **purchasing** (or procurement). For many products, the costs of materials make up about 50 percent of total manufacturing costs. Not surprisingly, materials acquisition gets a good deal of the operations manager's time and attention. As a rule, there's no shortage of vendors willing to supply materials, but the trick is finding the best suppliers. Operations managers must consider questions such as:

- Can the vendor supply the needed quantity of materials at a reasonable price?
- Is the quality good?
- Is the vendor reliable (will materials be delivered on time)?
- Does the vendor have a favorable reputation?
- Is the company easy to work with?

Getting the answers to these questions and making the right choices—a process known as **supplier selection**—is a key responsibility of operations management.

E-Procurement

Technology has changed the way businesses buy things. Through **e-procurement**, companies use the Internet to interact with suppliers. The process is similar to the one you'd use to find a consumer good—say, a high-definition TV—over the Internet. To choose a TV, you might browse the websites of manufacturers like Sony then shop prices and buy at Amazon, the world's largest online retailer.

If you were a purchasing manager using the Internet to buy parts and supplies, you'd follow basically the same process. You'd identify potential suppliers by going directly to private websites maintained by individual suppliers or to public sites that collect information on numerous suppliers. You could do your shopping through online catalogs, or you might participate in an online marketplace by indicating the type and quantity of materials you need and letting suppliers bid. Finally, just as you paid for your TV electronically, you could use a system called electronic data interchange (EDI) to process your transactions and transmit all your purchasing documents.

The Internet provides an additional benefit to purchasing managers by helping them communicate with suppliers and potential suppliers. They can use the Internet to give suppliers specifications for parts and supplies, encourage them to bid on future materials needs, alert them to changes in requirements, and give them instructions on doing business with their employers. Using the Internet for business purchasing cuts the costs of purchased products and saves administrative costs related to transactions. It's also faster for procurement and fosters better communications.

Inventory Control

If a manufacturer runs out of the materials it needs for production, then production stops. In the past, many companies guarded against this possibility by keeping large inventories of materials on hand. It seemed like the thing to do at the time, but it often introduced a new problem—wasting money. Companies were paying for parts and other materials that they wouldn't use for weeks or even months, and in the meantime, they were running up substantial storage and insurance costs. If the company redesigned its products, some parts might become obsolete before ever being used.

Most manufacturers have since learned that to remain competitive, they need to manage inventories more efficiently. This task requires that they strike a balance between two threats to productivity: losing production time because they've run out of materials and wasting money because they're carrying too much inventory. The process of striking this balance is called **inventory control**, and companies now regularly rely on a variety of inventory-control methods.

Just-in-Time Production

One method is called **just-in-time** (JIT) production: the manufacturer arranges for materials to arrive at production facilities just in time to enter the manufacturing process. Parts and materials don't sit unused for long periods, and the costs of "holding" inventory are significantly cut. JIT, however, requires considerable communication and cooperation between the manufacturer and the supplier. The manufacturer has to know what it needs and when. The supplier has to commit to supplying the right materials, of the right quality, at exactly the right time.

Material Requirements Planning

A software tool called **material requirements planning** (MRP), relies on sales forecasts and ordering lead times for materials to calculate the quantity of each component part needed for production and then determine when they should be ordered or made. The detailed sales forecast is turned into a master production schedule (MPS), which MRP then explodes into a forecast for the needed parts based on the bill of materials for each item in the forecast. A bill of materials is simply a list of the various parts that make up the end product. The role of MRP is to determine the anticipated need for each part based on the sales forecast and to place orders so that everything arrives just in time for production.

Graphical Tools: Gantt and PERT Charts

To control the timing of all operations, managers set up schedules: they select jobs to be performed during the production process, assign tasks to work groups, set timetables for the completion of tasks, and make sure that resources will be available when and where they're needed. There are a number of scheduling techniques. We'll focus on two of the most common—Gantt and PERT charts.

Gantt Charts

A **Gantt chart**, named after the designer, Henry Gantt, is an easy-to-use graphical tool that helps operations managers determine the status of projects. Let's say that you're in charge of making the "hiking bear" offered by the Vermont Teddy Bear Company. Figure 10.4 is a Gantt chart for the production of 100 of these bears. As you can see, it shows that several activities must be completed before the bears are dressed: the fur has to be cut, stuffed, and sewn; and the clothes and accessories must be made. Our Gantt chart tells us that by day six, all accessories and clothing have been made. The sewing and stuffing, however (which must be finished before the bears are dressed), isn't scheduled for completion until the end of day eight. As operations manager, you'll have to pay close attention to the progress of the sewing and stuffing operations to ensure that finished products are ready for shipment by their scheduled date.

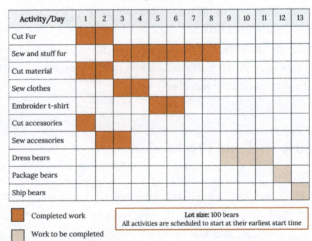

Figure 10.4: Example of a Gantt chart for a teddy bear.

PERT Charts

Gantt charts are useful when the production process is fairly simple and the activities aren't interrelated. For more complex schedules, operations managers may use **PERT charts**. PERT (which stands for Program Evaluation and Review Technique) is designed to diagram the activities required to produce a good, specify the time required to perform each activity in the process, and organize activities in the most efficient sequence. It also identifies a **critical path**: the sequence of activities that will entail the greatest amount of time. Figure 10.5 is a PERT diagram showing the process for producing one "hiker" bear at Vermont Teddy Bear.

Figure 10.5: Example of a PERT chart for a teddy bear.

Our PERT chart shows how the activities involved in making a single bear are related. It indicates that the production process begins at the cutting station. Next, the fur that's been cut for this particular bear moves first to the sewing and stuffing stations and then to the dressing station. At the same time that its fur is moving through this sequence of steps, the bear's clothes are being cut and sewn and its T-shirt is being embroidered. Its backpack and tent accessories are also being made at the same time. Note that fur, clothes, and accessories all meet at the dressing station, where the bear is dressed and outfitted with its backpack. Finally, the finished bear is packaged and shipped to the customer's house.

What was the critical path in this process? The path that took the longest amount of time was the sequence that included cutting, stuffing, dressing, packaging, and shipping—a sequence of steps taking 65 minutes. If you wanted to produce a bear more quickly, you'd have to save time on this path. Even if you saved the time on any of the other paths, you still wouldn't finish the entire job any sooner: the finished clothes would just have to wait for the fur to be sewn and stuffed and moved to the dressing station. We can gain efficiency only by improving our performance on one or more of the activities along the critical path.

The Technology of Goods Production

PowerSki founder and CEO Bob Montgomery spent 16 years designing the Jetboard and bringing it to production. At one point, in his efforts to get the design just right, he'd constructed 30 different prototypes. Montgomery thought that he could handle the designing of the engine without the aid of a computer. Before long, however, he realized that it was impossible to keep track of all the changes.

Computer-Aided Design

That's when Montgomery turned to computer technology for help and began using a **computer-aided design** (CAD) software package to design not only the engine but also the board itself and many of its components. The CAD program enabled Montgomery and his team of engineers to test the product digitally and work out design problems before moving to the prototype stage.

The sophisticated CAD software allowed Montgomery and his team to put their design paper in a drawer and to start building both the board and the engine on a computer screen. By rotating the image on the screen, they could even view the design from every angle. Having used their CAD program to make more than 400 design changes, they were ready to test the Jetboard in the water. During the tests, onboard sensors transmitted data to computers, allowing the team to make adjustments from the shore while the prototype was still in the water. Nowadays, PowerSki uses collaboration software to transmit design changes to the suppliers of the 340 components that make up the Jetboard. In fact, a majority of design work these days is done with the aid of computers, which add speed and precision to the process.

Computer-Aided Manufacturing

For many companies, the next step is to link CAD to the manufacturing process. A **computer-aided manufacturing** (CAM) software system determines the steps needed to produce the component and instructs the machines that do the work. Because CAD and CAM programs can "talk" with each other, companies can build components that satisfy exactly the requirements set by the computer-generated model. CAD/CAM systems permit companies to design and manufacture goods faster, more efficiently, and at a lower cost, and they're also effective in helping firms monitor and improve quality. CAD/CAM technology is used in many industries, including the auto industry, electronics, and clothing. If you have ever seen how a 3-D printer works, you have a pretty good idea of how CAM works too.

Figure 10.6: A 3-D printer.

Computer-Integrated Manufacturing

Figure 10.7: Robots at work in a BMW factory in Leipzig, Germany.

By automating and integrating all aspects of a company's operations, **computer-integrated manufacturing** (CIM) systems have taken the integration of computer-aided design and manufacturing to a higher level—and are in fact revolutionizing the production process. CIM systems expand the capabilities of CAD/CAM. In addition to design and production applications, they handle such functions as order entry, inventory control, warehousing, and shipping. In the manufacturing plant, the CIM system controls the functions of industrial robots—computer-controlled machines used to perform repetitive tasks that are also hard or dangerous for human workers to perform.

Operations Management for Service Providers

As the US economy has changed from a goods producer to a service provider over the last 60 years, the dominance of the manufacturing sector has declined substantially. Today, about 8.5 percent of US workers are employed in manufacturing,[4] in contrast to 30 percent in 1950.[5] Most of us now hold jobs in the **service sector**, which accounts for 80 percent of US jobs.[6] In 2013 Walmart was America's largest employer, followed by McDonald's, United Parcel Service (UPS), Target and Kroger. Not until we drop down to the ninth-largest employer—Hewlett Packard—do we find a company with a manufacturing component.[7]

Though the primary function of both manufacturers and service providers is to satisfy customer needs, there are several important differences between the two types of operations. Let's focus on three of them:

- **Intangibility**. Manufacturers produce tangible products—things that can be touched or handled, such as automobiles and appliances. Service companies provide intangible products, such as banking, entertainment, or education.
- **Customization**. Most manufactured goods are standardized. Services, by contrast, are often customized to satisfy the specific needs of a customer. For example, when you go to the hairdresser, you ask for a haircut that looks good on you because of the shape of your face and the texture of your hair.
- **Customer contact**. You could spend your entire working life assembling cars in Detroit and never meet a customer who bought a car that you helped to make. But if you were a restaurant server, you'd interact with customers every day. In fact, their satisfaction with your product would be determined in part by the service that you provided. Unlike manufactured goods, many services are bought and consumed at the same time.

Here is just one of the over twelve thousand Burger King restaurants across the globe. Not surprisingly, operational efficiency is just as important in service industries as it is in manufacturing. To get a better idea of the role of operations management in the service sector, we'll look closely at Burger King (BK), the world's fourth-largest restaurant chain.[8] BK has grown substantially since selling the first Whopper (for $0.37) almost half a century ago. The instant success of the fire-grilled burger encouraged the Miami founders of the company to expand by selling franchises.

Today, there are company-owned and independently-owned franchised BK restaurants in 100 countries, and they employ over 34,000 people.[9] More than 12 million customers visit BK each day.[10]

Operations Planning

When starting or expanding operations, businesses in the service sector must make a number of decisions quite similar to those made by manufacturers:

Figure 10.8: Burger King restaurant in Pattaya, Thailand.

- What services (and perhaps what goods) should they offer?
- Where will they locate their business, and what will their facilities look like?
- How will they forecast demand for their services?

Let's see how service firms like BK answer questions such as these.[11]

Operations Processes

Service organizations succeed by providing services that satisfy customers' needs. Companies that provide transportation, such as airlines, have to get customers to their destinations as quickly and safely as possible. Companies that deliver packages, such as FedEx, must pick up, sort, and deliver packages in a timely manner. Companies that provide both services and goods, such as Domino's Pizza, have a dual challenge: they must produce a quality good and deliver it satisfactorily.

Figure 10.9: Jimmy Johns uses a make-to-order approach.

Service providers that produce goods can adopt either a **make-to-order** or a **make-to-stock** approach to producing them. BK, which encourages patrons to customize burgers and other menu items, uses a make-to-order approach, building sandwiches one at a time. Meat patties, for example, go from the grill to a steamer for holding until an order comes in. Although many fast food restaurants have adopted the make-to-order model, a few continue to make-to-stock. For example, Dunkin' Donuts does not customize doughnuts, and so they do not have to wait for customer orders before making them.

Like manufacturers, service providers must continuously look for ways to improve **operational efficiency**. Throughout its 60-year history, BK has introduced a number of innovations that have helped make the company (as well as the fast-food industry itself) more efficient. BK, for example, was the first to offer drive-through service (which now accounts for over 50 percent of its sales)[12].

It was also a BK vice president, David Sell, who came up with the idea of moving the drink station from behind the counter so that customers could take over the time-consuming task of filling cups with ice and beverages. BK was able to cut back one employee per day at every one of its more than 11,000 restaurants. Material costs also went down because customers usually fill cups with more ice, which is cheaper than a beverage. Moreover, there were savings on supply costs because most customers don't bother with lids, and many don't use straws. On top of everything else, most customers liked the system (for one thing, it allowed them to customize their own drinks by mixing beverages), and as a result, customer satisfaction went up. Overall, the new process was a major success and quickly became the industry standard.

Facilities

When starting or expanding a service business, owners and managers must invest a lot of time in selecting a location, determining its size and layout, and forecasting demand. A poor location or a badly designed facility can cost customers, and inaccurate estimates of demand for products can result in poor service, excessive costs, or both.

Site Selection

Site selection is also critical in the service industry, but not for the same reasons as in the manufacturing industry. Service businesses need to be accessible to customers. Some service businesses, such as cable-TV providers, package-delivery services, and e-retailers, go to their customers. Many others, however—hotels, restaurants, stores, hospitals, and airports—have to attract customers to their facilities. These businesses must locate where there's a high volume of available customers. In picking a location, BK planners perform a detailed analysis of demographics and traffic patterns; the most important factor is usually traffic count—the number of cars or people that pass by a specific location in the course of a day. In the United States, where we travel almost everywhere by car, so BK looks for busy intersections, interstate interchanges with easy off and on ramps, or such "primary destinations" as shopping malls, tourist attractions, downtown business areas, or movie theaters. In Europe, where public transportation is much more common, planners focus on subway, train, bus, and trolley stops.

Once planners find a site with an acceptable traffic count, they apply other criteria. It must, for example, be easy for vehicles to enter and exit the site, which must also provide enough parking to handle projected dine-in business. Local zoning must permit standard signage, especially along interstate highways. Finally, expected business must be high enough to justify the cost of the land and building.

Size and Layout

In the service sector, most businesses must design their facilities with the customer in mind: they must accommodate the needs of their customers while keeping costs as low as possible. Let's see how BK has met this challenge.

For its first three decades, almost all BK restaurants were pretty much the same. They all sat on one acre of land (located "through the light and to the right"), had about 4,000 square feet of space, and held seating for 70 customers. All kitchens were roughly the same size. As long as land was cheap and sites were readily available, this system worked well. By the early 1990s, however, most of the prime sites had been taken, if not by BK itself, then by one of its fast-food competitors or other businesses needing a choice spot, including gas stations and convenience stores. With everyone bidding on the same sites, the cost of a prime acre of land had increased from $100,000 to over $1 million in a few short years.

To continue growing, BK needed to change the way it found and developed its locations. Planners decided that they had to find ways to reduce the size of a typical BK restaurant. For one thing, they could reduce the number of seats, because the business at a typical outlet had shifted over time from 90 percent inside dining to a 50-50 split between drive through and eat-in service.

David Sell (the same executive who had recommended letting customers fill their own drink cups) proposed to save space by wrapping Whoppers in paper instead of serving them in the cardboard boxes that took up more space. So BK switched to a single paper wrapper with the label "Whopper" on one side and "Cheese Whopper" on the other. To show which product was inside, employees just folded the wrapper in the right direction. Ultimately, BK replaced pallets piled high with boxes with just a few boxes of wrappers.

Ideas like these helped BK trim the size of a restaurant from 4,000 square feet to as little as 1,000. In turn, smaller facilities enabled the company to enter markets that were once cost prohibitive. Now BK could locate profitably in airports, food courts, strip malls, center-city areas, and even schools.

Capacity Planning

Estimating **capacity** needs for a service business isn't the same thing as estimating those of a manufacturer. Service providers can't store their products for later use: hairdressers can't "inventory" haircuts, and amusement parks can't "inventory" roller-coaster rides. Service firms have to build sufficient capacity to satisfy customers' needs on an "as-demanded" basis. Like manufacturers, service providers must consider many variables when estimating demand and capacity:

- How many customers will I have?
- When will they want my services (which days of the week, which times of the day)?
- How long will it take to serve each customer?
- How will external factors, such as weather or holidays, affect the demand for my services?

Forecasting demand is easier for companies like BK, which has a long history of planning facilities, than for brand-new service businesses. BK can predict sales for a new restaurant by combining its knowledge of customer-service patterns at existing restaurants with information collected about each new location, including the number of cars or people passing the proposed site and the effect of nearby competition.

Managing Operations

Overseeing a service organization puts special demands on managers, especially those running firms, such as hotels, retail stores, and restaurants, who have a high degree of contact with customers. Service firms provide customers with personal attention and must satisfy their needs in a timely manner. This task is complicated by the fact that demand can vary greatly over the course of any given day. Managers, therefore, must pay particular attention to employee work schedules and, in many cases, inventory management.

Managing service operations is about more than efficiency of service. It is about finding a balance between profitability, customer satisfaction and associate satisfaction, sometimes referred to as the **balanced scorecard**.

In his book titled *Moments of Truth*, Jan Carlzon, former Chief Executive Office of SAS Group, refers to those moments when an employee interacts with a customer.[13] Moments can range from calling a help line, checking in at an airline counter, the greeting from a hostess in a restaurant to having a maintenance problem resolved in a hotel guest room. The quality of staff a company hires, how they train their employees, and the focus management places on creating a culture of service will determine how successful the company is in service delivery and maximizing the impact of these moments of truth.

The Ritz-Carlton hotel company maximizes their moments of truth by living their motto, "We are Ladies and Gentleman serving Ladies and Gentleman." The Ritz-Carlton Three Steps of Service are:

1. A warm and sincere greeting. Use the guest's name.
2. Anticipation and fulfillment of the needs of each guest.
3. A fond farewell. Give a warm good-bye and use the guest's name.[14]

Ritz-Carlton reinforces this service culture daily in short meetings with all staff at the beginning of each shift.

> Southwest Airlines is recognized as an industry leader in service in the airline industry. The company defies various industry standards and relies on customer-centered leadership by offering low fares, not charging for bags and providing free entertainment. Staff focus on being swift and attentive to customer needs and Southwest is consistently recognized as the top airline for customer satisfaction.[15,16]

Scheduling

In manufacturing, managers focus on scheduling the activities needed to transform raw materials into finished goods. In service organizations, they focus on **scheduling** workers so that they're available to handle fluctuating customer demand. Each week, therefore, every BK store manager schedules employees to cover not only the peak periods of breakfast, lunch, and dinner, but also the slower periods in between. If he or she staffs too many people, labor cost per sales dollar will be too high. If there aren't enough employees, customers have to wait in lines. Some get discouraged, and even leave, and many may never come back.

Scheduling is made easier by information provided by a point-of-sale device built into every BK cash register. The register sends data on every sandwich, beverage, and side order sold by the hour, every hour of the day, every day of the week to a computer system that helps managers set schedules. To determine how many people will be needed for next Thursday's lunch hour, the manager reviews last Thursday's data, using sales revenue and a specific BK formula to determine the appropriate staffing level. Each manager can adjust this forecast to account for other factors, such as current marketing promotions or a local sporting event that will increase customer traffic.

Inventory Control

Businesses that provide both goods and services, such as retail stores and auto-repair shops, have the same **inventory control** problems as manufacturers: keeping levels too high costs money, while running out of inventory costs sales. Technology, such as the point-of-sale registers used at BK, makes the job easier. BK's system tracks everything sold during a given time and lets each store manager know how much of everything should be kept in inventory. It also makes it possible to count the number of burgers and buns, bags and racks of fries, and boxes of beverage mixes at the beginning or end of each shift. Because there are fixed numbers of supplies—say, beef patties or bags of fries—in each box, employees simply count boxes and multiply. In just a few minutes, the manager knows whether the inventory is correct (and should be able to see if any theft has occurred on the shift).

Producing for Quality

What do you do if your brand-new DVD player doesn't work when you get it home? What if you were late for a test because it took you 20 minutes to get a burger and fries at a drive-through window? Like most people, you'd probably be more or less disgruntled. As a customer, you're constantly assured that when products make it to market, they're of the highest possible quality, and you tend to avoid brands that have failed to live up to your expectations or to producers' claims.

But what is **quality**? According to the American Society for Quality, the term quality refers to "the characteristics of a product or service that bear on its ability to satisfy stated or implied needs."[17] When you buy a DVD player, you expect it to play DVDs. When you go to a drive-through window, you expect to be served in a reasonable amount of time. If your expectations are not met, you'll conclude that you're the victim of poor-quality.

Quality Management

Total quality management (TQM), or quality assurance, includes all the steps that a company takes to ensure that its goods or services are of sufficiently high quality to meet customers' needs. Generally speaking, a company adheres to TQM principles by focusing on three tasks:

1. Customer satisfaction
2. Employee involvement
3. Continuous improvement

Let's take a closer look at these three principles.

Customer Satisfaction

Companies that are committed to TQM understand that the purpose of a business is to generate a profit though **customer satisfaction**. Thus, they let their customers define quality by identifying desirable product features and then offering them. They encourage customers to tell them how to offer services that work the right way.

Armed with this knowledge, they take steps to make sure that providing quality is a factor in every facet of their operations—from design, to product planning and control, to sales and service. To get feedback on how well they're doing, many companies routinely use surveys and other methods to monitor customer satisfaction. By tracking the results of feedback over time, they can see where they need to improve.

Employee Involvement

Successful TQM requires that everyone in the organization, not simply upper-level management, commits to satisfying the customer. When customers wait too long at a drive-through window, it's the responsibility of a number of employees, not the manager alone. A defective DVD isn't solely the responsibility of the manufacturer's quality control department; it's the responsibility of every employee involved in its design, production, and even shipping. To get everyone involved in the drive for quality assurance, managers must communicate the importance of quality to subordinates and motivate them to focus on customer satisfaction. Employees have to be properly trained not only to do their jobs but also to detect and correct quality problems.

In many companies, employees who perform similar jobs work as teams, sometimes called **quality circles**, to identify quality, efficiency, and other work-related problems, to propose solutions, and to work with management in implementing their recommendations.

Continuous Improvement

An integral part of TQM is **continuous improvement**: the commitment to making constant improvements in the design, production, and delivery of goods and services.

Improvements can almost always be made to increase efficiency, reduce costs, and improve customer service and satisfaction. Everyone in the organization is constantly on the lookout for ways to do things better.

Statistical Process Control

Companies can use a variety of tools to identify areas for improvement. A common approach in manufacturing is called **statistical process control**. This technique monitors production quality by testing a sample of output to see whether goods in process are being made according to predetermined specifications. An example of a statistical process control method is Six Sigma. A **Six-Sigma** process is one in which 99.99966 percent of all opportunities to perform an operation are free of defects. This percentage equates to only 3.4 defects per million opportunities.

Assume for a moment that you work for Kellogg's, the maker of Raisin Bran cereal. You know that it's the company's goal to pack two scoops of raisins in every box of cereal.

How can you test to determine whether this goal is being met? You could use a statistical process control method called a sampling distribution. On a periodic basis, you would take a box of cereal off the production line and measure the amount of raisins in the box. Then you'd record that amount on a control chart designed to compare actual quantities of raisins with the desired quantity (two scoops). If your chart shows that several samples in a row are low on raisins, you'd take corrective action.

Outsourcing

PowerSki's Web site states that "PowerSki International has been founded to bring a new watercraft, the PowerSki Jetboard, and the engine technology behind it, to market."[18] That goal was reached in May 2003, when the firm emerged from a lengthy design period. Having already garnered praise for its innovative product, PowerSki was ready to begin mass-producing Jetboards. At this juncture, the management team made a strategic decision; rather than producing Jetboards in-house, they opted for **outsourcing**: having outside vendors manufacture the engines, fiberglass hulls, and associated parts. Assembly of the final product took place in a manufacturing facility owned by All American Power Sports in Moses Lake, Washington. This decision doesn't mean that the company relinquished control over quality; in fact, every component that goes into the PowerSki Jetboard is manufactured to exact specifications set by PowerSki. One advantage of outsourcing its production function is that the management team can thereby devote its attention to refining its product design and designing future products.

Outsourcing in the Manufacturing Sector

Outsourcing has become an increasingly popular option among manufacturers. For one thing, few companies have either the expertise or the inclination to produce everything needed to make a product. Today, more firms, like PowerSki, want to specialize in the processes that they perform best—and outsource the rest. Like PowerSki, they also want to take advantage of outsourcing by linking up with suppliers located in regions with lower labor costs. Outsourcing can be local, regional, or even international, and companies can outsource everything from parts for their products, like automobile manufacturers do, to complete manufacturing of their products, like Nike and Apple do.

Outsourcing in the Service Sector

Outsourcing is by no means limited to the manufacturing sector. Service providers also outsource many of their non-core functions. Some universities, for instance, outsource functions such as food services, maintenance, bookstore sales, printing, grounds keeping, security, and even residence operations. For example, there are several firms, like RGIS, who offer inventory services. They will send a team to your company to count your inventory for you. As RGIS puts it, "Our teams deliver the hands-on help needed to complete a wide variety of retail projects of all sizes, allowing your team to keep customer service as the number one priority."[19] Some software developers outsource portions of coding as a cost-saving measure. If you've ever had to get phone or chat assistance on your laptop, there's a good chance you spoke with someone in an outsourced call center. The center itself may have even been located offshore. This kind of arrangement can present unique challenges in quality control as differences in accents and the use of slang words can sometimes inhibit understanding. Nevertheless, in this era of globalization, expect the trend towards outsourcing offshore to continue.

 An interactive H5P element has been excluded from this version of the text. You can view it online here: https://pressbooks.lib.vt.edu/fundamentalsofbusiness4e/?p=117#h5p-30

Chapter Video

This video presents operations from multiple perspectives including manufacturing, restaurant food preparation, and brewing. Pay attention to the level of automation, which is a key aspect of operational decisions as labor gets more expensive.

 One or more interactive elements has been excluded from this version of the text. You can view them online here: https://www.youtube.com/watch?v=sL7hi5i9xMo

Key Takeaways

- **Operations management** oversees the process of transforming resources into goods and services.
- During **production planning**, managers determine how goods will be produced, where production will take place, and how manufacturing facilities will be laid out.
- In selecting the appropriate **production process**, managers consider three basic methods:
  - **make-to-order**
  - **mass production**
  - **mass customization**
- In **site selection** for a company's manufacturing operations, managers look for locations that minimize shipping costs, have an ample supply of skilled workers, provide a favorable community for workers and their families, offer resources at low cost, and have a favorable business climate.
- Commonly used inventory control methods include **just-in-time** (JIT) production, by which materials arrive just in time to enter the manufacturing process, and **material requirements planning** (MRP), a software tool to determine material needs.
- Gantt and PERT charts are two common tools used by operations managers.
  - A **Gantt chart** helps operations managers determine the status of projects.
  - **PERT charts** diagram the activities and time required and identify the **critical path**—the sequence of activities that will require the greatest amount of time.
- **Service firms** provide **intangible** products that are often customized to satisfy specific needs. Unlike manufactured goods, many services are bought and consumed at the same time.
- Estimating **capacity** needs for a service business is more difficult than for a manufacturer because service providers can't store their services for later use.
- Many companies deliver **quality** goods and services by adhering to principles of **total quality management** (TQM).
- **Outsourcing** can save companies money by using lower cost, specialized labor, located domestically or abroad.

References

Figures

Figure 10.1: The PowerSki Jetboard. Hydroforce Group LLC. 2016. Used with permission. https://web.archive.org/web/20160305123723/http://www.powerski.com/content/psi_index.php.

Figure 10.2: The transformation process. Kindred Grey. 2022. CC BY 4.0. Added build by Adrien Coquet from the Noun Project, Hammer by Nawicon from the Noun Project, Money Bag by Nawicon from the Noun Project, Computer by Adrien Coquet from the Noun Project, Factory by Abdul Wahhab from the Noun Project, Handshake by Susannanova from the Noun Project, manager by Chrystina Angeline from the Noun Project, Couch by Adrien Coquet from the Noun Project, Travel by Gregor Cresnar from the Noun Project (Noun Project license). https://archive.org/details/10.2_20220623.

Figure 10.3: LEGO has announced they are opening a manufacturing plant in Virginia. Alena Darmel. 2021. Pexels license. https://www.pexels.com/photo/a-person-playing-legos-7750841/.

Figure 10.4: Example of a Gantt chart for a teddy bear. Kindred Grey. 2022. CC BY 4.0. https://archive.org/details/10.3_20220623.

Figure 10.5: Example of a PERT chart for a teddy bear. Kindred Grey. 2022. CC BY 4.0. https://archive.org/details/10.4_20220623.

Figure 10.6: A 3-D printer. ZMorph All-in-One 3D Printers. 2019. Unsplash license. https://unsplash.com/photos/FB1vd3XT_zQ.

Figure 10.7: Robots at work in a BMW factory in Leipzig, Germany. BMW Werk Leipzig. 2005. CC BY-SA 2.0 DE. https://commons.wikimedia.org/wiki/File:BMW_Leipzig_MEDIA_050719_Download_Karosseriebau_max.jpg.

Figure 10.8: Burger King restaurant in Pattaya, Thailand. Kseniia Ilinykh. 2020. Unsplash license. https://unsplash.com/photos/geQbjXYkt9E.

Figure 10.9: Jimmy Johns uses a make-to-order approach. Kzoo Cowboy. 2018. CC BY 2.0. https://flic.kr/p/QzNjNW.

Video

Video 1: UniversityNow: Production and Operations Management Course Cover. Unowacademics. 2013. Copyrighted. https://www.youtube.com/watch?v=sL7hi5i9xMo&amp=&feature=youtu.be

Notes

1. Time Magazine (2001). "Best Inventions of 2001: Motorized Surfboard." Retrieved from: http://content.time.com/time/specials/packages/article/0,28804,1936165_1936240_1936351,00.html
2. Hydroforce Group LLC (2012). "Powerski Jetboards." Retrieved from: http://www.powerski.com/content/psi_index.php
3. Virginia Economic Development Partnership (2022, June 15) The LEGO Group to Establish U.S. Manufacturing Plant in Virginia, Creating Over 1,760 New Jobs. Retrieved from: https://www.vedp.org/press-release/2022-06/lego-group-chesterfield-county
4. National Association of Manufacturers (n.d.). 2021 United States Manufacturing Facts. Retrieved from: https://www.nam.org/state-manufacturing-data/2021-united-states-manufacturing-facts
5. Paul J. J. Payack and Edward M. L. Peters (2014). "Avoiding an American 'Lost Decade.'" Global Language Monitor. Retrieved from: http://www.languagemonitor.com/tag/percentage-of-the-non-farm-payroll-in-manufacturing/
6. U.S. Bureau of Labor Statistics (n.d.) Employment by Major Industry Sector. Retrieved from: https://www.bls.gov/emp/tables/employment-by-major-industry-sector.htm
7. Alexander E. M. Hess (2013). "The Ten Largest Employers in America." USA Today. Retrieved from: http://www.usatoday.com/story/money/business/2013/08/22/ten-largest-employers/2680249/
8. Hayley Fitzpatrick (2015). "The Top 20 Restaurant Chains." Business Insider. Retrieved from: http://www.businessinsider.com/top-restaurant-chains-in-the-world-2015-7
9. Restaurant Brands International Limited Partnership (2016). "2015 Form 10-K." Retrieved from: http://investor.rbi.com/~/media/Files/B/BurgerKing-IR/documents/10-k-rbi-lp-feb-26-2016.pdf
10. Burger King (2016). "About Us." Retrieved from: http://www.bk.com/about-bk
11. Information on Burger King was obtained from an interview with David Sell, former vice president of Central, Eastern, and Northern Europe divisions and president of Burger King France and Germany.
12. NPD (2012). "Drive-Thru Windows Still Put the Fast in Fast Food Restaurants, NPD Reports." Retrieved from: https://www.npd.com/wps/portal/npd/us/news/press-releases/pr_120530a/
13. Jan Carlzon (1987). *Moments of Truth*. Ballinger Publishing Company.
14. Ritz-Carlton Hotels (n.d.). Retrieved from: http://www.ritzcarlton.com/en/about/gold-standards
15. Morgan, B. (2021, June 3). Lessons from 10 Customer-Focused Leaders. Forbes. Retrieved from: https://www.forbes.com/sites/blakemorgan/2021/06/01/lessons-from-10-customer-focused-leaders/?sh=325b755b6c1f
16. Woodyard, C. (2020, May 27). Before Covid-19 Stopped the World, Southwest was Voted Best Airline in this Survey. USA Today. Retrieved from: https://www.usatoday.com/story/travel/airline-news/2020/05/27/southwest-airlines-tops-new-j-d-power-customer-satisfaction-study/5261907002/
17. American Society for Quality (n.d.). "Six Sigma Forum: Quality definition." Retrieved from: http://asq.org/sixsigma/quality-information/termsq-sixsigma.html
18. Powerski.com (2005). "About Powerski International." Retrieved from: http://www.powerski.com/aboutpsi.htm
19. RGIS (2015). "Retail: Why RGIS." Retrieved from: http://www.rgis.com/retail

11. Motivating Employees

> *Learning Objectives*
>
> - Define motivation, and understand why it is important in the workplace.
> - Understand the difference between intrinsic and extrinsic motivation.
> - Explain the major theories of motivation:
>   - Hierarchy-of-Needs theory
>   - Two-Factor theory
>   - Expectancy theory
>   - Equity theory

Motivation refers to an internally generated drive to achieve a goal or follow a particular course of action. Highly motivated employees focus their efforts on achieving specific goals. It's the manager's job, therefore, to motivate employees—to get them to try to do the best job they can. Motivated employees call in sick less frequently, are more productive, and are less likely to convey bad attitudes to customers and co-workers. They also tend to stay in their jobs longer, reducing turnover and the cost of hiring and training employees. But what motivates employees to do well? How does a manager encourage employees to show up for work each day and do a good job? Paying them helps, but many other factors influence a person's desire (or lack of it) to excel in the workplace. What are these factors, are they the same for everybody, and do they change over time? To address these questions, we'll examine four of the most influential theories of motivation: hierarchy-of-needs theory, two-factor theory, expectancy theory, and equity theory.

Intrinsic and Extrinsic Motivation

Before we begin our discussion of the various theories of motivation, it is important to establish the distinction between intrinsic and extrinsic motivation. Simply put, **intrinsic motivation** comes from within: the enjoyment of a task, the satisfaction of a job well done, and the desire to achieve are all sources of intrinsic motivation. On the other hand, **extrinsic motivation** comes about because of external factors such as a bonus or another form of reward. Avoiding punishment or a bad outcome can also be a source of extrinsic motivation; fear, it is said, can be a great motivator.

Hierarchy-of-Needs Theory

Psychologist Abraham Maslow's **hierarchy-of-needs theory** proposed that we are motivated by six initially unmet needs, arranged in the hierarchical order shown in figure 11.1, which also lists specific examples of each type of need in both the personal and work spheres of life. Look, for instance, at the list of personal needs in the middle column. At the bottom are **physiological needs** (such life-sustaining needs as food and shelter). Working up the hierarchy we experience **safety needs** (financial stability, freedom from physical harm), **social needs** (the need to belong and have friends), **esteem needs** (the need for self-respect and status), and **self-actualization needs** (the need to reach one's full potential or achieve some creative success). Late in his life, Maslow added **self-transcendence** to his model—the need to further a cause beyond the self.[1] There are two key things to remember about Maslow's model:

1. We must satisfy lower-level needs before we seek to satisfy higher-level needs.
2. Once we've satisfied a need, it no longer motivates us; the next higher need takes its place.

Maslow's hierarchy of needs	Personal fulfillment	Professional fulfillment
Highest: Self-transcendence	Devotion to a cause	Service to others
Self-actualization	Creative success and achievement	Challenging work, leadership, professional achievement
Esteem	Status and respect	Authority, titles, recognition
Social	Family and friendships	Team membership and social activities
Safety	Financial stability	Seniority/Job security
Lowest: Physiological	Food and shelter	Salary

Figure 11.1: Maslow's hierarchy of needs with examples.

Let's say, for example, that for a variety of reasons that aren't your fault, you're broke, hungry, and homeless. Because you'll probably take almost any job that will pay for food and housing (*physiological* needs), you go to work repossessing cars. Fortunately, your student loan finally comes through, and with enough money to feed yourself, you can go back to school and look for a job that's not so risky (a *safety* need). You find a job as a night janitor in the library, and though you feel secure, you start to feel cut off from your friends, who are active during daylight hours. You want to work among people, not books (a *social* need). So now you join several of your friends selling pizza in the student center. This job improves your social life, but even though you're very good at making pizzas, it's not terribly satisfying. You'd like something that your friends will respect enough to stop teasing you about the pizza job (an *esteem* need). So you study hard and land a job as an intern in the governor's office. On graduation, you move up through a series of government appointments and eventually run for state senator. As you're sworn into office, you realize that you've reached your full potential (a *self-actualization* need) and you comment to yourself, "It doesn't get any better than this."

Needs Theory and the Workplace

What implications does Maslow's theory have for business managers? There are two key points: (1) Not all employees are driven by the same needs, and (2) the needs that motivate individuals can change over time. Managers should consider which needs different employees are trying to satisfy and should structure rewards and other forms of recognition accordingly. For example, when you got your first job repossessing cars, you were motivated by the need for money to buy food. If you'd been given a choice between a raise or a plaque recognizing your accomplishments, you'd undoubtedly have opted for the money. As a state senator, by contrast, you may prefer public recognition of work well done (say, election to higher office) to a pay raise.

 An interactive H5P element has been excluded from this version of the text. You can view it online here: https://pressbooks.lib.vt.edu/fundamentalsofbusiness4e/?p=122#h5p-31

Two-Factor Theory

Another psychologist, Frederick Herzberg, set out to determine which work factors (such as wages, job security, or advancement) made people feel good about their jobs and which factors made them feel bad about their jobs. He surveyed workers, analyzed the results, and concluded that to understand employee *satisfaction* (or *dissatisfaction*), he had to divide work factors into two categories:

1. **Motivation factors.** Those factors that are strong contributors to job satisfaction
2. **Hygiene factors.** Those factors that are *not* strong contributors to satisfaction but that must be present to meet a worker's expectations and prevent job dissatisfaction

Figure 11.2 illustrates Herzberg's two-factor theory. Note that motivation factors (such as promotion opportunities) relate to *the nature of the work itself and the way the employee performs it*. Hygiene factors (such as physical working conditions) relate to *the environment in which it's performed*.

Two-Factor Theory and the Workplace

We'll ask the same question about Herzberg's model as we did about Maslow's: What does it mean for managers? Suppose you're a senior manager in an accounting firm, where you supervise a team of accountants, each of whom has been with the firm for five years. How would you use Herzberg's model to motivate the employees who report to you? Let's start with hygiene factors. Are salaries reasonable? What about working conditions? Does each accountant have his or her own workspace, or are they crammed into tiny workrooms? Are they being properly supervised or are they left on their own to sink or swim? If hygiene factors like these don't meet employees' expectations, they may be dissatisfied with their jobs.

Fixing problems related to hygiene factors may alleviate job *dissatisfaction*, but it won't necessarily improve anyone's job *satisfaction*. To increase satisfaction (and motivate someone to perform better), you must address motivation factors. Is the work itself challenging and stimulating? Do employees receive recognition for jobs well done? Will the work that an accountant has been assigned help him or her to advance in the firm? According to Herzberg, motivation requires a twofold approach: eliminating "dissatisfiers" and enhancing satisfiers.

Figure 11.2: Herzberg's two-factor-theory. Poor hygiene factors will increase job dissatisfaction while good motivators will increase satisfaction.

Expectancy Theory

MOTIVATION

EFFORT — Employees believe that effort will produce an acceptable performance

+

PERFORMANCE — Employees believe that acceptable performance will earn them the desired reward

+

REWARD — Employees value the offered reward

Figure 11.3: Expectancy theory.

Motivating Employees | 233

If you were a manager, wouldn't you like to know how your employees decide whether to work hard or goof off? Wouldn't it be nice to know whether a planned rewards program will have the desired effect—namely, motivating them to perform better in their jobs? These are the issues considered by psychologist Victor Vroom in his **expectancy theory**, which proposes that employees will work hard to earn rewards that they value and that they consider "attainable".

As you can see from figure 11.3, Vroom argues that an employee will be motivated to exert a high level of effort to obtain a reward under three conditions. The employee:

1. believes that his or her efforts will result in acceptable performance,
2. believes that acceptable performance will lead to the desired reward, and
3. values the reward.

Expectancy Theory and the Workplace

To apply expectancy theory to a real-world situation, let's analyze an automobile-insurance company with 100 agents who work from a call center. Assume that the firm pays a base salary of $2,000 a month, plus a $200 commission on each policy sold above ten policies a month. In terms of expectancy theory, under what conditions would an agent be motivated to sell more than ten policies a month?

1. The agent would have to believe that his or her efforts would result in policy sales (that, in other words, there's a positive link between effort and performance).
2. The agent would have to be confident that if he or she sold more than ten policies in a given month, there would indeed be a bonus (a positive link between performance and reward).
3. The bonus per policy—$200—would have to be of value to the agent.

Now let's alter the scenario slightly. Say that the company raises prices, thus making it harder to sell the policies. How will agents' motivation be affected? According to expectancy theory, motivation will suffer. Why? Because agents may be less confident that their efforts will lead to satisfactory performance. What if the company introduces a policy whereby agents get bonuses only if buyers don't cancel policies within 90 days? Now agents may be less confident that they'll get bonuses even if they do sell more than ten policies. Motivation will decrease because the link between performance and reward has been weakened. Finally, what will happen if bonuses are cut from $200 to $25? Obviously, the reward would be of less value to agents, and, again, motivation will suffer. The message of expectancy theory, then, is fairly clear: managers should offer rewards that employees value, set performance levels that they can reach, and ensure a strong link between performance and reward.

Equity Theory

What if you spent 30 hours working on a class report, did everything you were supposed to do, and handed in an excellent assignment (in your opinion). Your roommate, on the other hand, spent about five hours and put everything together at the last minute. You know, moreover, that he ignored half the requirements and never even ran his assignment through a spell-checker. A week later, your teacher returns the reports. You get a C and your roommate gets a B. In all likelihood, you'll feel that you've been treated unfairly relative to your roommate.

Your reaction makes sense according to the **equity theory of motivation**, which focuses on our perceptions of how fairly we're treated *relative to others*. Applied to the work environment, this theory proposes that employees analyze their contributions or **job inputs** (hours worked, education, experience, work performance) and their rewards or **job outcomes** (salary, bonus, promotion, recognition). Then they create a contributions/rewards ratio and compare it to those of other people. The basis of comparison can be any one of the following:

- Someone in a similar *position*.
- Someone holding a different position in the same *organization*.
- Someone with a similar *occupation*.
- Someone who shares certain *characteristics* (such as age, education, or level of experience).
- Oneself at another point in time.

When individuals perceive that the ratio of their contributions to rewards is comparable to that of others, they perceive that they're being treated fairly or **equitably**; when they perceive that the ratio is out of balance, they perceive **inequity**. Occasionally, people will perceive that they're being treated better than others. More often, however, they conclude that others are being treated better (and that they themselves are being treated worse). This is what you concluded when you saw your grade in the previous example. You've calculated your ratio of contributions (hours worked, research and writing skills) to rewards (project grade), compared it to your roommate's ratio, and concluded that the two ratios are out of balance.

Figure 11.4: *Equity theory. Inputs should balance with outcomes.*

What will an employee do if he or she perceives an inequity? The individual might try to bring the ratio into balance, either by decreasing inputs (working fewer hours, not taking on additional tasks) or by increasing outputs (asking for a raise). If this strategy fails, an employee might complain to a supervisor, transfer to another job, leave the organization, or rationalize the situation (e.g., deciding that the situation isn't so bad after all). Equity theory advises managers to focus on treating workers fairly, especially in determining compensation, which is, naturally, a common basis of comparison.

An interactive H5P element has been excluded from this version of the text. You can view it online here:
https://pressbooks.lib.vt.edu/fundamentalsofbusiness4e/?p=122#h5p-32

Key Takeaways

- **Motivation** describes an internally generated drive that propels people to achieve goals or pursue particular courses of action.
- There are four influential theories of motivation: hierarchy-of-needs theory, two-factor theory, expectancy theory, and equity theory:
    - **Hierarchy-of-needs** theory proposes that we're motivated by five unmet needs—physiological, safety, social, esteem, and self-actualization—and must satisfy lower-level needs before we seek to satisfy higher-level needs.
    - **Two-factor theory** divides work factors into **motivation factors** (those that are strong contributors to job satisfaction) and **hygiene factors** (those that, though not big contributors to satisfaction, must be present to prevent job dissatisfaction).
    - **Expectancy theory** proposes that employees work harder to obtain a reward when they value the reward, believe that their efforts will result in acceptable performance, and believe that acceptable performance will lead to a desired outcome or reward.
    - **Equity theory** focuses on our perceptions of how fairly we are treated relative to others. This theory proposes that employees create rewards ratios that they compare to those of others and will be less motivated when they perceive an imbalance in treatment.

References

Figures

Figure 11.1: Maslow's hierarchy of needs with examples. Mark E. Koltko-Rivera (2006). "Rediscovering the Later Version of Maslow's Hierarchy of Needs: Self-Transcendence and Opportunities for Theory, Research, and Unification." Review of General Psychology. Vol. 10. No. 4. pp. 302–317. Retrieved from: http://academic.udayton.edu/jackbauer/Readings 595/Koltko-Rivera 06 trans self-act copy.pdf.

Figure 11.2: Herzberg's two-factor-theory. Kindred Grey. 2022. CC BY 4.0. https://archive.org/details/11.2_20220623.

Figure 11.3: Expectancy theory. Kindred Grey. 2022. CC BY 4.0. https://archive.org/details/11.3_20220623.

Figure 11.4: Equity theory. Inputs should balance with outcomes. Kindred Grey. 2022. CC BY 4.0. Added Scales of Justice by Karen Arnold from Public Domain Pictures (CC0). https://archive.org/details/11.4_20220623.

Notes

1. Mark E. Koltko-Rivera (2006). "Rediscovering the Later Version of Maslow's Hierarchy of Needs: Self-Transcendence and Opportunities for Theory, Research, and Unification." Review of General Psychology. Vol. 10. No. 4. pp. 302–317. Retrieved from: http://academic.udayton.edu/jackbauer/Readings 595/Koltko-Rivera 06 trans self-act copy.pdf

12. Managing Human Resources

Learning Objectives

- Define human resource management and explain how managers develop and implement a human resource plan.
- Explain how companies train and develop employees, and discuss the importance of a diverse workforce.
- Identify factors that make an organization a good place to work, including competitive compensation and benefits packages.
- Explain how managers evaluate employee performance and retain qualified employees.

The Grounds of a Great Work Environment

Figure 12.1: Starbucks founder Howard Schultz.

Howard Schultz, founder and former CEO and Chairman of Starbucks Coffee Company, has vivid memories of his father slumped on the couch with his leg in a cast.[1] The ankle would heal, but his father had lost another job—this time as a driver for a diaper service. It was a crummy job; still, it put food on the table, and if his father couldn't work, there wouldn't be any money. Howard was seven, but he understood the gravity of the situation, particularly because his mother was seven months pregnant, and the family had no insurance.

This was just one of the many setbacks that plagued Schultz's father throughout his life—an honest, hard-working man frustrated by a system that wasn't designed to cater to the needs of common workers. He'd held a series of blue-collar jobs (cab driver, truck driver, factory worker), sometimes holding two or three at a time. Despite his willingness to work, he never earned enough money to move his family out of Brooklyn's federally-subsidized housing projects. Schultz's father died never having found fulfillment in his work life—or even a meaningful job. It was the saddest day of Howard's life.

As a kid, did Schultz ever imagine that one day he'd be the founder and chairman of an international coffee company? Of course not. But he did decide that if he was ever in a position to make a difference in the lives of people like his father, he'd do what he could. Remembering his father's struggles and disappointments, Schultz tried to make Starbucks the kind of company where he wished his father had worked. "Without even a high school diploma," Schultz admits, "my father probably could never have been an executive. But if he had landed a job in one of our stores or roasting plants, he wouldn't have quit in frustration because the company didn't value him. He would have had good health benefits, stock options, and an atmosphere in which his suggestions or complaints would receive a prompt, respectful response."[2]

Schultz is motivated by both personal and business considerations: "When employees have self-esteem and self-respect," he argues, "they can contribute so much more: to their company, to their family, to the world."[3] His founder's commitment continues today and is embedded in Starbucks' values: "Creating a culture of warmth and belonging, where everyone is welcome."[4] Those working at Starbucks are called partners because working for Starbucks is not just a job, it's a passion.[5]

Human Resource Management

Employees at Starbucks are vital to the company's success. They are its public face, and every dollar of sales passes through their hands.[6] They can make or break the company. If a customer has a positive interaction with an employee, the customer will come back. If an encounter is negative, the customer is probably gone for good. That's why it's crucial for Starbucks to recruit and hire the right people, train them properly, provide a motivating environment, and encourage them to stay with the company. Thus, the company works to provide satisfying jobs, a positive work environment, appropriate work schedules, and fair compensation and benefits. These activities are part of Starbucks's strategy to deploy human resources in order to gain competitive advantage. The process is called **human resource management** (HRM), which consists of all actions that an organization takes to attract, develop, and retain quality employees. Each of these activities is complex. Attracting talented employees involves the recruitment of qualified candidates and the selection of those who best fit the organization's needs. Development encompasses both new-employee orientation and the training and development of current workers. Retaining good employees means motivating them to excel, appraising their performance, compensating them appropriately, and doing what's possible to keep them.

Human Resource Planning

How does Starbucks make sure that its worldwide retail locations are staffed with just the right number of committed employees? How does Norwegian Cruise Lines make certain that when the Norwegian Dawn pulls out of New York harbor, it has a complete, fully trained crew on board to feed, entertain, and care for its passengers? Managing these tasks is a matter of **strategic human resource planning**—the process of developing a plan for satisfying an organization's human resources (HR) needs.

Figure 12.2: A Starbucks barista.

A strategic HR plan lays out the steps that an organization will take to ensure that it has the right number of employees with the right skills in the right places at the right times. HR managers begin by analyzing the company's mission, objectives, and strategies. Starbucks's objectives, for example, include "Creating a culture of warmth and belonging, where everyone is welcome" as well as fostering an environment in which employees treat both customers and each other with dignity and respect.[7] Thus, the firm's HR managers look for people who are "adaptable, self-motivated, passionate, creative team members."[8] The main goal of Norwegian Cruise Lines—to lavish passengers with personal attention—determines not only the type of employee desired (one with exceptionally good customer-relation skills and a strong work ethic) but also the number needed (one for every two passengers on the Norwegian Dawn).[9]

Job Analysis

To develop an HR plan, HR managers must be knowledgeable about the jobs that the organization needs performed. They organize information about a given job by performing a job analysis to identify the tasks, responsibilities, and skills that it entails, as well as the knowledge and abilities needed to perform it. Managers also use the information collected for the job analysis to prepare two documents:

- A **job description**, which lists the duties and responsibilities of a position
- A **job specification**, which lists the qualifications—skills, knowledge, and abilities—needed to perform the job

HR Supply and Demand Forecasting

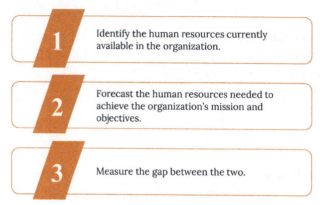

Figure 12.3: How to forecast hiring and firing needs.

Once they've analyzed the jobs within the organization, HR managers must **forecast** future hiring or job elimination needs (e.g. firings). This is the three-step process summarized below.

Starbucks, for instance, might find that it needs 300 new employees to work at stores scheduled to open in the next few months. Disney might determine that it needs 2,000 new cast members to handle an anticipated surge in visitors. Virgin Voyages might be short two dozen restaurant workers on one of its ships because of an unexpected increase in reservations.

After calculating the disparity between supply and future demand, HR managers must draw up plans for bringing the two numbers into balance. If the demand for labor is going to outstrip the supply, they may hire more workers, encourage current workers to put in extra hours, subcontract work to other suppliers, or introduce labor-saving initiatives. If the supply is greater than the demand, they may deal with overstaffing by not replacing workers who leave, encouraging early retirements, eliminating positions, or terminating employment.

Recruiting Qualified Employees

Armed with information on the number of new employees to be hired and the types of positions to be filled, the HR manager then develops a strategy for recruiting potential employees. **Recruiting** is the process of identifying suitable candidates and encouraging them to apply for openings in the organization.

Before going any further, we should point out that in recruiting and hiring, managers must comply with antidiscrimination laws; violations can have legal consequences. **Discrimination** occurs when a person is treated unfairly on the basis of a characteristic unrelated to ability. Under federal law, it's illegal to discriminate in recruiting and hiring on the basis of race, color, religion, sex, national origin, age, or disability. (The same rules apply to other employment activities, such as promoting, compensating, and terminating employees.)[10] The Equal Employment Opportunity Commission (EEOC) enforces a number of federal employment laws, including the following:

- Title VII of the Civil Rights Act of 1964, which prohibits employment discrimination based on race, color, religion, sex, or national origin. Sexual harassment is also a violation of Title VII.
- The Equal Pay Act of 1963, which protects both women and men who do substantially equal work from sex-based pay discrimination.

- The Age Discrimination in Employment Act of 1964, which protects individuals who are forty or older.
- Title I and Title V of the Americans with Disabilities Act of 1990, which prohibits employment discrimination against individuals with disabilities.[11]

In June 2020, the US Supreme Court, with a 6-3 decision, ruled that discrimination based on sex, should be understood to include sexual orientation and gender identity. This ruling provided the EEOC with additional enforcement under Title VII of the Civil Rights Act of 1964.[12]

Where to find candidates

The first step in recruiting is to find qualified candidates. Where do you look for them, and how do you decide whether they're qualified? Companies must assess not only the ability of a candidate to perform the duties of a job, but also whether he or she is a good "fit" for the company—i.e., how well the candidate's values and interpersonal style match the company's values and culture.

Internal versus external recruiting

Where do you find people who satisfy so many criteria? Basically, you can look in two places: inside and outside your own organization. Both options have pluses and minuses. Hiring internally sends a positive signal to employees that they can move up in the company—a strong motivation tool and a reward for good performance. In addition, because an internal candidate is a known quantity, it's easier to predict his or her success in a new position. Finally, it's cheaper to recruit internally. On the other hand, the company will probably have to fill the promoted employee's position. Going outside gives the hiring manager an opportunity to bring fresh ideas and skills into the company. In any case, it's often the only alternative, especially if no one inside the company has just the right combination of skills and experiences. Entry-level jobs are usually filled from the outside.

How to find candidates

Searching for new employees means publicizing the position. If looking internally in a small organization, employees can be alerted informally. In larger organizations, HR managers generally post openings on the internal corporate website or seek direct recommendations from various supervisors.

Recruiting people from outside is more complicated. Like marketing a product to buyers, the company promotes the virtues of working for the organization. Starbucks uses the following outlets to advertise openings:

- A dedicated section of the **corporate web site** ("Job Center," which lists openings, provides information about the Starbucks experience, and facilitates the submission of online applications)
- **College campus recruiting** (holding on-campus interviews and information sessions and participating in career fairs)
- **Internships** designed to identify future talent among college students
- Announcements on **employment web sites** like Monster.com, Vault.com, Glassdoor.com, and SimplyHired.com
- Newspaper **classified ads**
- Facebook and Twitter
- Local **job fairs**
- In-store recruiting posters
- Informative "business cards" for distribution to customers[13]

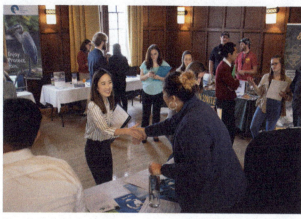

Figure 12.4: Students and recruiters at a college campus job fair.

Everything Starbucks does as a company bears on its ability to attract talent. Accordingly, everyone is responsible for recruiting, not just HR specialists. In fact, the best source of quality applicants is often the company's own labor force.[14]

The selection process

Recruiting gets people to apply for positions, but once you've received applications, you still have to select the best candidate—another complicated process.

The **selection process** entails gathering information on candidates, evaluating their qualifications, and choosing the right one. At the very least, the process can be time-consuming—particularly when you're filling a high-level position—and often involves several members of an organization.

Let's examine the selection process more closely by describing the steps that you'd take to become a special agent for the Federal Bureau of Investigation (FBI).[15] Most business students don't generally aspire to become FBI agents, but the FBI is quite interested in business graduates—especially if you have a major in accounting or finance. With one of these backgrounds, you'll be given priority in hiring. Why?

Unfortunately, there's a lot of white-collar crime that needs to be investigated, and people who know how to follow the money are well suited for the task.

Application

The first step in a new graduate being hired as an FBI accountant is applying for the job. Make sure you meet the minimum qualifications they advertise. To provide factual information on your education and work background, you'll submit an application, which the FBI will use as an initial screening tool.

Employment Tests

Next comes a battery of tests (a lot more than you'd take in applying for an everyday business position). Like most organizations, the FBI tests candidates on the skills and knowledge entailed by the job. Unlike most businesses, however, the FBI will also measure your aptitude, evaluate your personality, and assess your writing ability. You'll have to take a polygraph (lie-detector) test to determine the truthfulness of the information you've provided, uncover the extent of any drug use, and disclose potential security problems.

Interview

If you pass all these tests (with sufficiently high marks), you'll be granted an interview. It serves the same purpose as it does for business recruiters: it allows the FBI to learn more about you and gives you a chance to learn more about your prospective employer and your possible future in the organization. The FBI conducts structured interviews—a series of standard questions. You're judged on both your answers and your ability to communicate orally.

Physical Exam and Reference Checks

Let's be positive and say you passed the interview. What's next? You still have to pass a rigorous physical examination (including a drug test), as well as background and reference checks. Given its mission, the FBI sets all these hurdles a little higher than the average employer. Most businesses will ask you to take a physical exam, but you probably won't have to meet the fitness standards set by the FBI. Likewise, many businesses check references to verify that applicants haven't lied about (or exaggerated) their education and work experience. The FBI goes to great lengths to ensure that candidates are suitable for law-enforcement work.

Final Decision

The last stage in the process is out of your control. Will you be hired or not? This decision is made by one or more people who work for the prospective employer. For a business, the decision maker is generally the line manager who oversees the position being filled. At the FBI, the decision is made by a team at FBI headquarters.

Contingent Workers

Though most people hold permanent, full-time positions, there's a growing number of individuals who work at temporary or part-time jobs. Many of these are contingent workers hired to supplement a company's permanent workforce. Most of them are independent contractors, consultants, or freelancers who are paid by the firms that hire them. Others are on-call workers who work only when needed, such as substitute teachers. Still others are temporary workers (or "temps") who are employed and paid by outside agencies or contract firms that charge fees to client companies.

The Positives and Negatives of Temp Work

The use of contingent workers provides companies with a number of benefits. Because they can be hired and terminated easily, employers can better control labor costs. When things are busy, they can add temps, and when business is slow, they can release unneeded workers. Temps are often less expensive to employ than permanent workers, particularly because they rarely receive costly benefits. Employers can also bring in people with specialized skills and talents to work on special projects without entering into long-term employment relationships. Finally, companies can "try out" temps: if someone does well, the company can offer permanent employment; if the fit is less than perfect, the employer can easily terminate the relationship. There are downsides to the use of contingent workers, including increased training costs and decreased loyalty to the company. Also, many employers believe that because temps are usually less committed to company goals than permanent workers, productivity suffers.

 An interactive H5P element has been excluded from this version of the text. You can view it online here: https://pressbooks.lib.vt.edu/fundamentalsofbusiness4e/?p=131#h5p-33

Developing Employees

Because companies can't survive unless employees do their jobs well, it makes economic sense to train them and develop their skills. This type of support begins when an individual enters the organization and continues as long as he or she stays there.

New-Employee Orientation

Have you ever started your first day at a new job feeling upbeat and optimistic only to walk out at the end of the day thinking that maybe you've taken the wrong job? If this happens too often, your employer may need to revise its approach to orientation—the way it introduces new employees to the organization and their jobs. Starting a new job is a little like beginning college; at the outset, you may be experiencing any of the following feelings:

- Somewhat nervous but enthusiastic
- Eager to impress but not wanting to attract too much attention
- Interested in learning but fearful of being overwhelmed with information
- Hoping to fit in and worried about looking new or inexperienced[16]

The employer who understands these common feelings help newcomers adjust and avoid the pitfalls often associated with new-employee orientation:

- Failing to have a workspace set up for you
- Ignoring you or failing to supervise you
- Neglecting to introduce you to coworkers
- Swamping you with facts about the company[17]

A good employer will take things slowly, providing you with information about the company and your job on a need-to-know basis while making you feel as comfortable as possible. You'll get to know the company's history, traditions, policies, and culture over time. You'll learn more about salary and benefits and how your performance will be evaluated. Most importantly, you'll find out how your job fits into overall operations and what's expected of you.

Training and Development

It would be nice if employees came with all the skills they need to do their jobs. It would also be nice if job requirements stayed the same: once you've learned how to do a job, you'd know how to do it forever. In reality, new employees must be trained; moreover, as they grow in their jobs or as their jobs change, they'll need additional training. Unfortunately, training is costly and time-consuming.

How costly? Training magazine reported that businesses spent over $83 billion in 2019.[18] At Darden Restaurants, the parent company to restaurants such as Olive Garden and Red Lobster, training focuses on diversity skills.[19] What's the payoff? Why are such companies willing to spend so much money on their employees? Darden has been recognized by *Fortune* magazine as a "Diversity Champion," ranking it as one of the Top 20 employers on their list of diverse workforces.[20] At Booz Allen Hamilton, consultants specialize in finding innovative solutions to client problems, and their employer makes sure that they're up-to-date on all the new technologies by maintaining an Innovation Center to enable great ideas to converge and advance how they build value. They incorporate the community from design thinkers to entrepreneurs to engineers, crafting the insights and technology to solve the toughest problems of today and the future. This and their Ideas Festival and Innovation Hub allow the employees a chance to receive off-the-job training. This approach allows them to focus on learning without the distractions that would occur in the office.[21]

At Booz Allen Hamilton's technology "petting zoo," employees are receiving off-the-job training. This approach allows them to focus on learning without the distractions that would occur in the office. More common, however, is informal on-the-job training, which may be supplemented with formal training programs. This is the method, for example, by which you'd move up from mere coffee maker to a full-fledged "barista" if you worked at Starbucks.[22] You'd begin by reading a large spiral book (titled Starbucks University) on the responsibilities of the barista, pass a series of tests on the reading, then get hands-on experience in making drinks, mastering one at a time.[23] Doing more complex jobs in business will likely require even more training than is required to be a barista.

Diversity in the Workplace

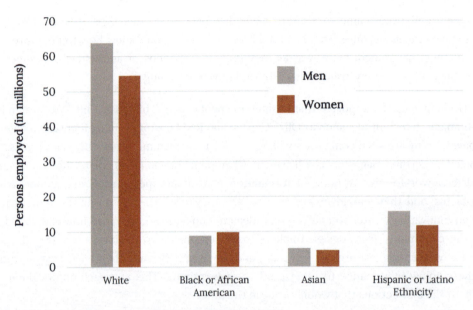

Figure 12.5: Employment by gender and ethnicity/race (2021).

The makeup of the US workforce has changed dramatically over the past 50 years. In the 1950s, more than 60 percent was composed of white males.[24] Today's workforce reflects the broad range of differences in the population—differences in gender, race, ethnicity, age, physical ability, religion, education, and lifestyle. As you can see in figure 12.5, more women and minorities have entered the workforce, and white males now make up 64 percent of the workforce.[25]

Most companies today strive for diverse workforces. HR managers work hard to recruit, hire, develop, and retain a diverse workforce. In part, these efforts are motivated by legal concerns: discrimination in recruiting, hiring, advancement, and firing is illegal under federal law and is prosecuted by the EEOC.[26] Companies that violate anti-discrimination laws are subject to severe financial penalties and also risk reputation damage. In November 2004, for example, the EEOC charged that recruiting policies at Abercrombie & Fitch, a national chain of retail clothing stores, had discriminated against minority and female job applicants between 1999 and 2004. The EEOC alleged that A&F had hired a disproportionate number of white salespeople, placed minorities and women in less visible positions, and promoted a virtually all-white image in its marketing efforts. Six days after the EEOC filed a lawsuit, the company settled the case at a cost of $50 million, but the negative publicity may hamper both recruitment and sales for some time.[27]

Reasons for building a diverse workforce go well beyond mere compliance with legal standards. It even goes beyond commitment to ethical standards. It's good business. People with diverse backgrounds bring fresh points of view that can be invaluable in generating ideas and solving problems. In addition, they can be the key to connecting with an ethnically diverse customer base. If a large percentage of your customers are Hispanic, it might make sense to have a Hispanic marketing manager. In short, capitalizing on the benefits of a diverse workforce means that employers should view differences as assets rather than liabilities. Forbes Magazine published 'America's Best Employers for Diversity 2022 List' and included the following:[28]

Figure 12.6: Models pose at the grand opening of an Abercrombie and Fitch store in Ireland, 2012.

Rank	Name	Industry	Headquarters
1	Progressive	Insurance	Mayfield, OH
2	VMware	IT, internet, software, and services	Palo Alto, CA
3	Booz Allen Hamilton	Professional services	McLean, VA
4	Cummins	Engineering, manufacturing	Columbus, IN
5	Interpublic Group (IPG)	Media and advertising	Ney York, NY
6	Adobe	IT, internet, software, and services	San Jose, CA
7	SAS Institute	IT, internet, software, and services	Cary, NC
8	Clorox	Packaged goods	Oakland, CA
9	TD Bank	Banking and financial services	Cherry Hill, NJ
10	Quicken Loans	Banking and financial services	Detroit, MI

Figure 12.7: Forbes' America's best employers for diversity 2022 list.

Perhaps many of us have heard the words – diversity, equity, inclusion – but what do they mean? How do we take these words and put them into action of awareness, understanding, respect and more? In addition, recently many organizations have added 'belonging' to their diversity strategy and practice – so what does that mean? According to The Office for Diversity, Equity, Inclusion, and Belonging (DEIB) at Virginia Tech's Pamplin College of Business, the acronym, DEIB, is defined as:

- Diversity (n): The visible and invisible characteristics and experiences that make people different. Everyone is diverse.
- Equity (v): Identifying and addressing imbalances and barriers that inhibit group and individual full engagement and success.
- Inclusion (v): The act of ensuring all groups and individuals have equitable access to resources and opportunities. Developing an understanding of unique needs and challenges are critical.
- Belonging (n): The nexus of diversity, equity and inclusion where all groups and individuals feel welcomed, valued, and are empowered to be active members in the community.[29]

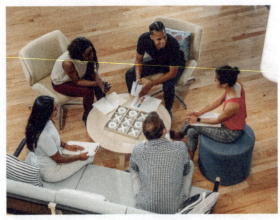

Figure 12.8: Diversity in the workplace.

Diversity, Equity, Inclusion and Belonging (DEIB) in Action

One leader in embracing diversity as an important part of their consumer business and corporate life is Capital One, an American bank holding company specializing in credit cards, auto loans, banking, and savings accounts, headquartered in McLean, Virginia with operations primarily in the United States. Based on the Capital One website, their commitment to diversity is specifically defined as:

"At Capital One, diversity, inclusion and belonging are valued at our core. We empower our associates to do great work by creating an inclusive culture—that values diverse perspectives, fosters collaboration and encourages innovative ideas—and a place where associates of all backgrounds can thrive by bringing their most authentic selves to work. We call this our Culture of Belonging, and it rests at the heart of our Diversity, and Inclusion & Belonging (DIB) efforts."[30]

Capital One encourages belonging by executing Business Resource Groups (BRGs). Capital One employees (aka associates) find places of connection through BRGs — voluntary, associate-led groups of individuals who join together based on common interests, backgrounds, demographics, identity or a passion for allyship. BRGs enrich the Capital One culture of belonging and deepen the understanding of diverse cultures, people and experiences. BRGs provide opportunities for leadership development, learning and connection as well as avenues to support Capital One's commitment to attract, develop and retain a diverse workforce. Over 60% of Capital One's global workforce belongs to one or more BRGs. In 2020, Capital One's seven BRGs launched virtual chapters and increased membership by 11%. BRGs hosted approximately 100 national events that year, engaging close to 40,000 associate attendees.[31]

As of March 2022, here is a list of the Capital One BRGs:

- CapAbilities : CapAbilities provides a community for associates who identify with having a disability, as well as caregivers and allies, and sustains active Advocacy Circles, including Autism Spectrum Connections and Gray Matter (with an emphasis on mental health and wellness). CapAbilities builds connections and removes barriers for people with disabilities within the workplace, marketplace and home.
- empowHER: empowHER elevates women and allies, and plays an important role attracting, engaging and developing tomorrow's leaders.
- ¡HOLA!: The mission of ¡HOLA! is to empower Hispanic and Latinx associates and allies to thrive both in and out of Capital One.
- Origins: Origins is our BRG for Asian and Pacific Islander associates and allies.
- Out Front: Out Front fosters open channels of communication and engagement among LGBTQ+ associates, leaders and allies across Capital One and focuses on raising awareness within and outside of Capital One as well as in our communities.
- Salute: Salute enables military, military spouse and veteran associates to thrive through associate engagement, active duty transition, recruiting, community engagement and reserve support.
- VOICES: VOICES helps build an environment where Black associates and allies are empowered to drive change, break barriers and make an impact across Capital One.
Tech-specific BRGs: Tech-specific BRGs enhance and complement the work of our Enterprise BRGs. Blacks in Tech, Hispanics in Tech, Women in Tech and Equality Allies are designed to meet the unique recruitment, development and community-building needs of our Tech associates, while also helping to develop a pipeline of future talent by instilling a love of technology in young girls and children of diverse backgrounds.[32]

What Makes a Great Place to Work?

Every year, the Great Places to Work Institute analyzes comments from thousands of employees and compiles a list of "The 100 Best Companies to Work for in America®," which is published in *Fortune* magazine. Having compiled its list for more than 20 years, the institute concludes that the defining characteristic of a great company to work for is trust between managers and employees. Employees overwhelmingly say that they want to work at a place where employees "trust the people they work for, have pride in what they do, and enjoy the people they work with."[33] They report that they're motivated to perform well because they're challenged, respected, treated fairly, and appreciated. They take pride in what they do, are made to feel that they make a difference, and are given opportunities for advancement.[34] The most effective motivators, it would seem, are closely aligned with Maslow's higher-level needs and Herzberg's motivating factors. The top ten companies are listed in figure 12.9.

Rank	Company
1	Cisco Systems
2	Hilton Worldwide Holdings
3	Wegmans Food Markets
4	Salesforce
5	Nvidia
6	Accenture
7	Rocket Companies
8	American Express
9	David Weekley Homes
10	Capital One Financial

Figure 12.9: Fortune's "Best companies to work for" (2022).

Job Redesign

The average employee spends more than 2,000 hours a year at work. If the job is tedious, unpleasant, or otherwise unfulfilling, the employee probably won't be motivated to perform at a very high level. Many companies practice a policy of job redesign to make jobs more interesting and challenging. Common strategies include job rotation, job enlargement, and job enrichment.

Job Rotation

Specialization promotes efficiency because workers get very good at doing particular tasks. The drawback is the tedium of repeating the same task day in and day out. The practice of job rotation allows employees to rotate from one job to another on a systematic basis, often but not necessarily cycling back to their original tasks. A computer maker, for example, might rotate a technician into the sales department to increase the employee's awareness of customer needs and to give the employee a broader understanding of the company's goals and operations. A hotel might rotate an accounting clerk to the check-in desk for a few hours each day to add variety to the daily workload. Through job rotation, employees develop new skills and gain experience that increases their value to the company. So great is the benefit of this practice that many companies have established rotational training programs that include scheduled rotations during the first 2-3 years of employment. Companies benefit because cross-trained employees can fill in for absentees, thus providing greater flexibility in scheduling, offer fresh ideas on work practices, and become promotion-ready more quickly.

Job Enlargement

Instead of a job in which you performed just one or two tasks, wouldn't you prefer a job that gave you many different tasks? In theory, you'd be less bored and more highly motivated if you had a chance at job enlargement—the policy of enhancing a job by adding tasks at similar skill levels. The job of sales clerk, for example, might be expanded to include gift-wrapping and packaging items for shipment. The additional duties would add variety without entailing higher skill levels.

Job Enrichment

Merely expanding a job by adding similar tasks won't necessarily "enrich" it by making it more challenging and rewarding. Job enrichment is the practice of adding tasks that increase both responsibility and opportunity for growth. It provides the kinds of benefits that, according to Maslow and Herzberg, contribute to job satisfaction: stimulating work, sense of personal achievement, self-esteem, recognition, and a chance to reach your potential.

Consider, for example, the evolving role of support staff in the contemporary office. Today, employees who used to be called "secretaries" assume many duties previously in the domain of management, such as project coordination and public relations. Information technology has enriched their jobs because they can now apply such skills as word processing, desktop publishing, creating spreadsheets, and managing databases. That's why we now use a term such as administrative assistant instead of secretary.[35]

Work/Life Quality

Building a career requires a substantial commitment in time and energy, and most people find that they aren't left with much time for non-work activities. Fortunately, many organizations recognize the need to help employees strike a balance between their work and home lives.[36] By helping employees combine satisfying careers and fulfilling personal lives, companies tend to end up with a happier, less-stressed, and more productive workforce. The financial benefits include lower absenteeism, turnover, and health care costs.

Alternative Work Arrangements

The accounting firm KPMG, which has made the list of the "100 Best Companies for Working Mothers" for 23 years,[37] is committed to promoting a balance between its employees' work and personal lives. KPMG offers a variety of work arrangements designed to accommodate different employee needs and provide scheduling flexibility.[38]

Flextime

Employers who provide for flextime set guidelines that allow employees to designate starting and quitting times. Guidelines, for example, might specify that all employees must work eight hours a day (with an hour for lunch) and that four of those hours must be between 10 a.m. and 3 p.m. Thus, you could come in at 7 a.m. and leave at 4 p.m., while coworkers arrive at 10 a.m. and leave at 7 p.m. With permission you could even choose to work from 8 a.m to 2 p.m., take two hours for lunch, and then work from 4 p.m. to 6 p.m.

Compressed Workweeks

Rather than work eight hours a day for five days a week, you might elect to earn a three-day weekend by working ten hours a day for four days a week.

Job Sharing

Under job sharing, two people share one full-time position, splitting the salary and benefits of the position as each handles half the job. Often they arrange their schedules to include at least an hour of shared time during which they can communicate about the job.

Telecommuting

Telecommuting means that you regularly work from home (or from some other non-work location). You're connected to the office by computer, fax, and phone. You save on commuting time, enjoy more flexible work hours, and have more opportunity to spend time with your family. A study of 5,500 IBM employees (one-fifth of whom telecommute) found that those who worked at home not only had a better balance between work and home life but also were more highly motivated and less likely to leave the organization.[39]

Though it's hard to count telecommuters accurately, Global Workplace Analytics estimates that, in 2016, "at least 3.7 million people (2.8 percent of the workforce) work from home at least half the time."[40] Telecommuting isn't for everyone. Working at home means that you have to discipline yourself to avoid distractions, such as TV, personal phone calls, and home chores and also not be impacted by feeling isolated from the social interaction in the workplace.

Family-Friendly Programs

In addition to alternative work arrangements, many employers, including KPMG, offer programs and benefits designed to help employees meet family and home obligations while maintaining busy careers. KPMG offers each of the following benefits.[41]

Dependent Care

Caring for dependents—young children and elderly parents—is of utmost importance to some employees, but combining dependent-care responsibilities with a busy job can be particularly difficult. KPMG provides on-site child care during tax season (when employees are especially busy) and offers emergency backup dependent care all year round, either at a provider's facility or in the employee's home. To get referrals or information, employees can call KPMG's LifeWorks Resource and Referral Service.

KPMG is by no means unique in this respect: more than 7 percent of US companies maintained on-site day care in 2012,[42] and 17 percent of all US companies offered child-care resources or referral services.[43]

Paid Parental Leave

The United States is one of only two countries in the world that does not guarantee paid leave to new mothers (or fathers), although California, Rhode Island and New Jersey are implementing state programs, and many employers offer paid parental leave as an employee benefit.[44] Any KPMG employee (whether male or female) who becomes a parent can take two weeks of paid leave. New mothers may also get time off through short-term disability benefits.

Caring for Yourself

Like many companies, KPMG allows employees to aggregate all paid days off and use them in any way they want. In other words, instead of getting, say, ten sick days, five personal days, and 15 vacation days, you get a total of 30 days to use for anything. If you're having personal problems, you can contact the Employee Assistance Program. If staying fit makes you happier and more productive, you can take out a discount membership at one of more than 9,000 health clubs. In fact, many employers, like North Carolina software company SAS, now have on-site fitness centers for employee use.[45]

Unmarried without Children

You've undoubtedly noticed by now that many programs for balancing work and personal lives target married people, particularly those with children. Single individuals also have trouble striking a satisfactory balance between work and non-work activities, but many single workers feel that they aren't getting equal consideration from employers.[46] They report that they're often expected to work longer hours, travel more, and take on difficult assignments to compensate for married employees with family commitments.

Needless to say, requiring singles to take on additional responsibilities can make it harder for them to balance their work and personal lives. It's harder to plan and keep personal commitments while meeting heavy work responsibilities. Frustration can lead to increased stress and job dissatisfaction. In several studies of stress in the accounting profession, unmarried workers reported higher levels of stress than any other group, including married people with children.[47]

With singles, as with married people, companies can reap substantial benefits from programs that help employees balance their work and non-work lives. PepsiCo, for example, offers a "concierge service," which maintains a dry cleaner, travel agency, convenience store, and fitness center on the premises of its national office in Purchase, New York.[48] Single employees seem to find these services helpful, but what they value most of all is control over their time. In particular, they want predictable schedules that allow them to plan social and personal activities. They don't want employers assuming that being single means that they can change plans at the last minute. It's often more difficult for singles to deal with last-minute changes because, unlike married coworkers, they don't have the at-home support structure to handle such tasks as tending to elderly parents or caring for pets.

An interactive H5P element has been excluded from this version of the text. You can view it online here:
https://pressbooks.lib.vt.edu/fundamentalsofbusiness4e/?p=131#h5p-34

Compensation and Benefits

Though paychecks and benefits packages aren't the only reasons why people work, they do matter. Competitive pay and benefits also help organizations attract and retain qualified employees. Companies that pay their employees more than their competitors generally have lower turnover. Consider, for example, The Container Store, which has appeared on Fortune magazine's list of "The 100 Best Companies to Work For."[49] The retail chain staffs its stores with fewer employees than its competitors but pays them more—in some cases, three times the industry average for retail workers. This strategy allows the company to attract extremely talented workers who, moreover, aren't likely to leave the company. Low turnover is particularly valuable in the retail industry because it depends on service-oriented personnel to generate repeat business. In addition to salary and wages, compensation packages often include other financial incentives, such as bonuses and profit-sharing plans, as well as benefits, such as medical insurance, vacation time, sick leave, and retirement accounts.

Wages and Salaries

The largest, and most important, component of a compensation package is the payment of wages or salary. If you're paid according to the number of hours you work, you're earning wages. Counter personnel at McDonald's, for instance, get wages, which are determined by multiplying an employee's hourly wage rate by the number of hours worked during the pay period. On the other hand, if you're paid for fulfilling the responsibilities of a position—regardless of the number of hours required to do it—you're earning a salary. The McDonald's manager gets a salary for overseeing the operations of the restaurant. He or she is expected to work as long as it takes to get the job done, without any adjustment in compensation.

Piecework and Commissions

Sometimes it makes more sense to pay workers according to the quantity of product that they produce or sell. Byrd's Seafood, a crab-processing plant in Crisfield, Maryland, pays workers on **piecework**: workers' pay is based on the amount of crabmeat that's picked from recently cooked crabs. (A good picker can produce 15 pounds of crabmeat an hour and earn about $100 a day.)[50] On the other hand, if you're working on **commission**, you're probably getting paid a percentage of the total dollar amount you sell. If you were a sales representative for an insurance company, like The Hartford, you'd get a certain amount of money for each automobile or homeowner policy you sold.[51]

Incentive Programs

In addition to regular paychecks, many people receive financial rewards based on performance, whether their own, their employer's, or both. Other incentive programs designed to reward employees for good performance include bonus plans and stock options.

Bonus plans

Texas Instruments' (TI) year-end bonuses—annual income given in addition to salary—are based on individual and company-wide performance. If the company has a profitable year, and if you contributed to that success, you'll get a bonus.[52] If the company doesn't do well, you may be out of luck—regardless of your personal performance, you might not receive a bonus.

Bonus plans have become quite common, and the range of employees eligible for bonuses has widened in recent years. In the past, bonus plans were usually reserved for managers above a certain level. Today, companies have realized the value of extending plans to include employees at virtually every level. The magnitude of bonuses still favors those at the top. High-ranking officers often get bonuses ranging from 30 percent to 50 percent of their salaries. Upper-level managers may get from 15 percent to 25 percent and middle managers from 10 percent to 15 percent. At lower levels, employees may expect bonuses from 3 percent to 5 percent of their annual compensation.[53]

Profit-sharing plans

Delta Airlines[54] and General Motors[55] both have profit-sharing arrangements with employees. Today, about 40 percent of all US companies offer some type of profit-sharing program.[56]

TI's plan is also pretty generous—as long as the company has a good year. Here's how it works. An employee's profit share depends on the company's operating profit for the year. If profits from operations reach 10 percent of sales, the employee gets a bonus worth 2 percent of his or her salary. In 2011, TI's operating profit was 22 percent, and employee bonuses were 7.9 percent of salary. But if operating profits are below 10 percent, nobody gets anything.[57]

Stock-option plans

The TI compensation plan also gives employees the right to buy shares of company stock at a 15 percent discount four times a year.[58] So, if the price of the stock goes up, the employee benefits. Say, for example, that the stock was selling for $30 a share when the option was granted in 2007. The employee would be entitled to buy shares at a price of $25.50, earning them an immediate 15 percent gain in value. Any increase in share price would add to that gain.[59]

At TI, stock options are used as an incentive to attract and retain top people.[60] Starbucks, by contrast, isn't nearly as selective in awarding stock options. At Starbucks, all employees can earn "Bean Stock"—the Starbucks employee stock-option plan. Both full- and part-time employees get Starbucks shares based on their earnings and their time with the company. If the company does well and its stock goes up, employees make a profit. Starbucks believes that Bean Stock pays off because employees are rewarded when the company does well, they have a stronger incentive to add value to the company (and so drive up its stock price). Starbucks has a video explaining their employee stock option program on this webpage.[61]

Benefits

Another major component of an employee's compensation package is benefits— compensation other than salaries, hourly wages, or financial incentives. Types of benefits include the following:

- Legally required benefits (Social Security and Medicare, unemployment insurance, workers' compensation)
- Paid time off (vacations, holidays, sick leave)
- Insurance (health benefits, life insurance, disability insurance)
- Retirement benefits

The cost of providing benefits is staggering. According to the US Bureau of Labor Statistics, it costs an average employer about 30 percent of a worker's salary to provide the same worker with benefits. If you include pay for time not worked (while on vacation or sick and so on), the percentage increases to 37 percent. The most money goes for paid time off (6.9 percent of salary costs), health care (8.1 percent), and retirement benefits (3.8 percent).[62]

Some workers receive only the benefits required by law while part-timers often receive no benefits at all.[63] Again, Starbucks is generous in offering benefits. The company provides benefits even to the part-timers who make up two-thirds of the company's workforce; anyone working at least 20 hours a week is eligible to participate in group medical coverage.[64]

Performance Appraisal

Employees generally want their managers to tell them three things: what they should be doing, how well they're doing it, and how they can improve their performance. Good managers address these issues on an ongoing basis. On a semiannual or annual basis, they also conduct formal performance appraisals to discuss and evaluate employees' work performance.

The Basic Three-Step Process

Appraisal systems vary both by organization and by the level of the employee being evaluated, but as you can see in figure 12.10, it's generally a three-step process:

1. Before managers can measure performance, they must set goals and performance expectations and specify the criteria (such as quality of work, quantity of work, dependability, initiative) that they'll use to measure performance.
2. At the end of a specified time period, managers complete written evaluations that rate employee performance according to the predetermined criteria.
3. Managers then meet with each employee to discuss the evaluation. Jointly, they suggest ways in which the employee can improve performance, which might include further training and development.

1. Set goals and performance expectations and specify the criteria that will be used to measure performance.

2. Complete a written evaluation that rates performance according to the stipulated criteria.

3. Meet with the employee to discuss the evaluation and suggest means of improving performance.

Figure 12.10: *Performance appraisal process.*

It sounds fairly simple, but why do so many managers report that, except for firing people, giving performance appraisals is their least favorite task?[65] To get some perspective on this question, we'll look at performance appraisals from both sides, explaining the benefits and identifying potential problems with some of the most common practices.

Among other benefits, formal appraisals provide the following:

- An opportunity for managers and employees to discuss an employee's performance and to set future goals and performance expectations.
- A chance to identify and discuss appropriate training and career-development opportunities for an employee.
- Formal documentation of the evaluation that can be used for salary, promotion, demotion, or dismissal purposes.[66]

As for disadvantages, most stem from the fact that appraisals are often used to determine salaries for the upcoming year. Consequently, meetings to discuss performance tend to take on an entirely different dimension: the manager may appear judgmental (rather than supportive), and the employee may get defensive. This adversarial atmosphere can make many managers not only uncomfortable with the task but also less likely to give honest feedback. (They may give higher marks in order to avoid delving into critical evaluations.) HR professionals disagree about whether performance appraisals should be linked to pay increases. Some experts argue that the connection eliminates the manager's opportunity to use the appraisal to improve an employee's performance. Others maintain that it increases employee satisfaction with the process and distributes raises on the basis of effort and results.[67]

360-Degree and Upward Feedback

Instead of being evaluated by one person, how would you like to be evaluated by several people—not only those above you in the organization but those below and beside you? The approach is called 360-degree feedback, and the purpose is to ensure that employees (mostly managers) get feedback from all directions—from supervisors, reporting subordinates, coworkers, and even customers. If it's conducted correctly, this technique furnishes managers with a range of insights into their performance in a number of roles.

Some experts, however, regard the 360-degree approach as too cumbersome. An alternative technique, called upward feedback, requires only the manager's subordinates to provide feedback. Computer maker Dell uses this approach as part of its manager-development plan. Every year, 40,000 Dell employees complete a survey in which they rate their supervisors on a number of dimensions, such as practicing ethical business principles and providing support in balancing work and personal life. Dell uses survey results for development purposes only, not as direct input into decisions on pay increases or promotions.[68]

Retaining Valuable Employees

When a valued employee quits, the loss to the employer can be serious. Not only will the firm incur substantial costs to recruit and train a replacement, but it also may suffer temporary declines in productivity and lower morale among remaining employees who have to take on heavier workloads. Given the negative impact of turnover—the permanent separation of an employee from a company—most organizations do whatever they can to retain qualified employees. Compensation plays a key role in this effort: companies that don't offer competitive compensation packages tend to lose employees. Other factors also come into play, such as training and development, as well as helping employees achieve a satisfying work/non-work balance. In the following sections, we'll look at a few other strategies for reducing turnover and increasing productivity.[69]

Creating a Positive Work Environment

Employees who are happy at work are more productive, provide better customer service, and are more likely to stay with the company. A study conducted by Sears, for instance, found a positive relationship between customer satisfaction and employee attitudes on ten different issues: a 5 percent improvement in employee attitudes results in a 1.3 percent increase in customer satisfaction and a 0.5 percent increase in revenue.[70]

Employee-Friendly Workplace

What sort of things improve employee attitudes? The 12,000 employees of software maker SAS Institute fall into the category of "happy workers." They choose the furniture and equipment in their offices, eat subsidized meals at one of three on-site restaurants, and enjoy other amenities like a 77,000 square-foot fitness center. They also have job security: no one's ever been laid off because of an economic downturn. The employee-friendly work environment helps SAS employees focus on their jobs and contribute to the attainment of company goals.[71] Not surprisingly, it also results in very low 3 percent turnover.

Recognizing Employee Contributions

Thanking people for work done well is a powerful motivator. People who feel appreciated are more likely to stay with a company than those who don't.[72] While a personal thank-you is always helpful, many companies also have formal programs for identifying and rewarding good performers. The Container Store rewards employee accomplishments in a variety of ways. For example, employees with 20 years of service are given a "dream trip"—one employee went on a seven day Hawaiian cruise.[73] The company is known for its supportive environment and in 2016 celebrated its seventeenth year on *Fortune*'s 100 Best Companies to Work For®.[74]

Involving Employees in Decision Making

Companies have found that involving employees in decisions saves money, makes workers feel better about their jobs, and reduces turnover. Some have found that it pays to take their advice. When General Motors asked workers for ideas on improving manufacturing operations, management was deluged with more than 44,000 suggestions during one quarter. Implementing a few of them cut production time on certain vehicles by 15 percent and resulted in sizable savings.[75]

Similarly, in 2001, Edward Jones, a personal investment company, faced a difficult situation during the stock-market downturn. Costs had to be cut, and laying off employees was one option. Instead, however, the company turned to its workforce for solutions. As a group, employees identified cost savings of more than $38 million. At the same time, the company convinced experienced employees to stay with it by assuring them that they'd have a role in managing it.[76]

Why People Quit

As important as such initiatives can be, one bad boss can spoil everything. The way a person is treated by his or her boss may be the primary factor in determining whether an employee stays or goes. People who have quit their jobs cite the following behavior by superiors:

- Making unreasonable work demands
- Refusing to value their opinions
- Failing to be clear about what's expected of subordinates
- Showing favoritism in compensation, rewards, or promotions[77]

Holding managers accountable for excessive turnover can help alleviate the "bad-boss" problem, at least in the long run. In any case, whenever an employee quits, it's a good idea for someone—other than the individual's immediate supervisor—to conduct an exit interview to find out why. Knowing why people are quitting gives an organization the opportunity to correct problems that are causing high turnover rates.

Involuntary Termination

Some companies employ a process called **Forced Ranking** to manage out their under-performers. In this approach, only a certain percentage of employees can receive a particular performance evaluation score, which forces some employees to the bottom of the distribution—sort of the opposite of a curved exam score. The employee pool in question is typically made up of those who do similar kinds of work. Ideally after being given some amount of time to improve, those who remain at the bottom of the performance distribution are then separated from the company. As you can imagine, this practice has caused a fair amount of controversy!

Before we leave this section, we should say a word or two about termination—getting fired. Though turnover—voluntary separations—can create problems for employers, they're not nearly as devastating as the effects of involuntary termination on employees. Losing your job is what psychologists call a "significant life change," and it's high on the list of "stressful life events" regardless of the circumstances. Sometimes, employers lay off workers because revenues are down and they must resort to downsizing—to cutting costs by eliminating jobs. Sometimes a particular job is being phased out, and sometimes an employee has simply failed to meet performance requirements.

Employment at Will

Is it possible for you to get fired even if you're doing a good job and there's no economic justification for your being laid off? In some cases, yes—especially if you're not working under a contract. Without a formal contract, you're considered to be employed at will, which means that both you and your employer have the right to terminate the employment relationship at any time. You can quit whenever you want, but your employer can also fire you whenever they want.

Fortunately for employees, over the past several decades, the courts have made several decisions that created exceptions to the employment-at-will doctrine.[78] Since managers generally prefer to avoid the expense of fighting wrongful discharge claims in court, many no longer fire employees at will. A good practice in managing terminations is to maintain written documentation so that employers can demonstrate just cause when terminating an employee. If it's a case of poor performance, the employee would be warned in advance that his or her current level of performance could result in termination and then be permitted an opportunity to improve performance. When termination is necessary, communication should be handled in a private conversation, with the manager explaining precisely why the action is being taken.

An interactive H5P element has been excluded from this version of the text. You can view it online here: https://pressbooks.lib.vt.edu/fundamentalsofbusiness4e/?p=131#h5p-35

Chapter Video

Southwest Airlines mission statement.

One or more interactive elements has been excluded from this version of the text. You can view them online here: https://www.youtube.com/watch?v=U3LDsUAU5CI

Key Takeaways

- The process of **human resource management** consists of actions that an organization takes to attract, develop, and retain quality employees.
- Human resource managers engage in **strategic human resource planning**—the process of developing a plan for satisfying the organization's human resource needs.
- The HR manager forecasts future hiring needs and begins the **recruiting** process to fill those needs.
- In recruiting and hiring, managers must comply with anti-discrimination laws enforced by the **Equal Employment Opportunity Commission** (EEOC). They cannot treat people unfairly on the basis of a characteristic unrelated to ability, such as race, color, religion, sex, national origin, age, or disability.
- HR managers also oversee employee training, from the first **orientation** to continuing **on-** or **off-the-job training**.
- Attracting a **diverse workforce** goes beyond legal compliance and ethical commitments, because a diverse group of employees can offer perspectives that may be valuable in generating ideas, solving problems, and connecting with an ethnically diverse customer base.
- Employees are motivated to perform well when they're challenged, respected, treated fairly, and appreciated.
- Some other factors that contribute to employee satisfaction include **job redesign** to make jobs more interesting and challenging, **job rotation,** which allows employees to rotate from one job to another, **job enlargement,** which enhances a job by adding tasks at similar skill levels, and **job enrichment,** which adds tasks that increase both responsibility and opportunity for growth.
- Many organizations recognize the need to help employees strike a balance between their work and home lives and offer a variety of work arrangements to accommodate different employee needs, such as **flextime** (flexible scheduling), **job sharing** (when two people share a job), and **telecommuting** (working from outside the office).
- Compensation includes pay and benefits. Workers who are paid by the hour earn **wages**, while those who are paid to fulfill the responsibilities of the job earn **salaries**. Some people receive **commissions** based on sales or are paid for output, based on a **piecework** approach.
- In addition employees can may receive year-end **bonuses**, participate in **profit-sharing plans**, or receive **stock options**.
- Managers conduct **performance appraisals** to evaluate work performance.
- **Turnover** is the permanent separation of an employee from a company and may happen if an employee is unsatisfied with their job, or because the organization is not satisfied with the employee. Sometimes, firms lay off workers, or **downsize**, to cut costs.

References

Figures

Figure 12.1: Starbucks founder Howard Schultz. Adam Bielawski. 2011. CC BY-SA 3.0. https://commons.wikimedia.org/wiki/File:Howard-Schultz_2011-04-12_photoby_Adam-Bielawski.jpg.

Figure 12.2: A Starbucks barista. Dmitriy Nushtaev. 2019. Unsplash license. https://unsplash.com/photos/wIBhj3G3hPA.

Figure 12.3: How to forecast hiring and firing needs. Kindred Grey. 2022. CC BY 4.0. https://archive.org/details/12.3_20220623.

Figure 12.4: Students and recruiters at a college campus job fair. University of Michigan School for Environment and Sustainability. 2019. CC BY 2.0. https://flic.kr/p/2heTunw.

Figure 12.5: Employment by gender and ethnicity/race (2021). Kindred Grey. 2022. CC BY 4.0. Data from https://www.bls.gov/cps/cpsaat10.pdf. https://archive.org/details/12.5_20220623.

Figure 12.6: White male models pose at the grand opening of an Abercrombie and Fitch store in Ireland, 2012. William Murphy. 2012. CC BY-SA 2.0. https://flic.kr/p/dpLH4e.

Figure 12.7: Forbes' America's best employers for diversity 2022 list. Data from https://www.forbes.com/best-employers-diversity/#2a8dff909b9e.

Figure 12.8: Diversity in the workplace. Kindel Media. 2021. Pexels license. https://www.pexels.com/photo/people-at-the-office-lobby-having-a-discussion-7688164/.

Figure 12.9: Fortune's "Best companies to work for" (2022). Data from https://fortune.com/best-companies/2022/.

Figure 12.10: Performance appraisal process. Kindred Grey. 2022. CC BY 4.0. https://archive.org/details/12.9_20220623.

Video

Video 1: Every. Single. One. Of. Us.. Southwest Airlines. 2022. Copyrighted. https://www.youtube.com/watch?v=U3LDsUAU5CI.

Notes

1. Introductory material on Howard Schultz and Starbucks comes from Howard Schultz and Dori Jones Yang (1997). *Pour Your Heart into It: How Starbucks Built a Company One Cup at a Time.* New York: Hyperion. pp. 3–8.
2. Ibid. p. 138.
3. Ibid. pp. 6-7
4. Starbucks (n.d.). "Mission Statement." Retrieved from https://www.starbucks.com/about-us/company-information/

mission-statement

5. Ibid.
6. Howard Schultz and Dori Jones Yang (1997). *Pour Your Heart into It: How Starbucks Built a Company One Cup at a Time.* New York: Hyperion. p. 125.
7. Starbucks (2016). "Working at Starbucks." Retrieved from: http://www.starbucks.com/careers/working-at-starbucks
8. Fortune (2007). "100 Top MBA Employers." Retrieved from: http://archive.fortune.com/magazines/fortune/mba100/2007/full_list/index.html
9. Cruise International (n.d.). "The Norwegian Dawn." Retrieved from: http://www.cruise-international.com/cruise-search/ShpDetailsQuery?nShp=290&nLine=18&nOperator=Norwegian Cruise Line
10. The U.S. Equal Employment Opportunity Commission (n.d.). "Prohibited Employment Policies/Practices." Retrieved from: https://www.eeoc.gov/laws/practices/index.cfm
11. The U.S. Equal Employment Opportunity Commission (n.d.). "Laws Enforced by the U.S. Equal Employment Opportunity Commission." Retrieved from: https://www.eeoc.gov/laws/statutes/index.cfm
12. Anthony Zurcher (2020). "US Supreme Court Backs Protection for LGBT workers." BBC News. Retrieved from: https://www.bbc.com/news/world-us-canada-53055632
13. Carolyn B. Thompson (n.d.). "In Focus: Target Your Recruitment Market." NetTemps.com. Retrieved from: http://www.net-temps.com/recruiters/infocus/article.htm?op=view&id=662#axzz4BVFt5rJY
14. David Lee (2006). "Your First Task as a Recruiter: Recruit Senior Management Onto Your Team." Humannature@work.com. Retrieved from: https://web.archive.org/web/20130529204750/http://www.humannatureatwork.com/Recruiting-Employees.htm
15. Federal Bureau of Investigation (n.d.). "Special Agents." FBI Jobs. Retrieved from: https://www.fbijobs.gov/special-agents; Federal Bureau of Investigation (n.d.). "How to Become a Special Agent." FBI Jobs. Retrieved from: https://www.fbijobs.gov/special-agents/how-become-special-agent
16. Adapted from Alan Price (2004). *Human Resource Management in a Business Context.* Hampshire, U.K.: Cengage EMEA. Retrieved from: http://www.bestbooks.biz/learning/induction.html
17. Susan M. Heathfield (2015). "Top Ten Ways to Turn Off a New Employee." About Money. Retrieved from: http://humanresources.about.com/library/weekly/aa022601a.htm
18. Training Magazine (2019). "2019 Training Industry Report." Retrieved from https://trainingmag.com/trgmag-article/2019-training-industry-report/.
19. Training magazine (2014). "2014 Top 125." Retrieved from: https://trainingmag.com/sites/default/files/2014_01_Training_Top_125_1.pdf
20. Ibid. p. 73.
21. Booz Allen Hamilton (n.d.). "Innovation Center." Retrieved from https://www.boozallen.com/about/innovation/washington-dc-innovation-center.html
22. Brooke Locascio (2004). "Working at Starbucks: More Than Just Pouring Coffee." Tea and Coffee Trade Online. Retrieved from: http://www.teaandcoffee.net/0104/coffee.htm
23. Howard Schultz and Dori Jones Yang (1997). *Pour Your Heart into It: How Starbucks Built a Company One Cup at a Time.* New York: Hyperion. pp. 250-251.
24. Judith Lindenberger and Marian Stoltz-Loike (2015). "Diversity in the Workplace." Zeromillion.com. Retrieved from: http://www.zeromillion.com/econ/workplace-diversity.html
25. Bureau of Labor Statistics (2021). "Labor Force Statistics from the Current Population Survey: Table 10 Employed Persons by Occupation, Race, Hispanic or Latino Ethnicity, and Sex." Retrieved from: http://www.bls.gov/cps/cpsaat10.pdf
26. U.S. Equal Employment Opportunity Commission (2009). "Federal Laws Prohibiting Job Discrimination: Questions and Answers." Retrieved from: http://www.eeoc.gov/facts/qanda.html
27. U.S. Equal Employment Opportunity Commission (2004). "EEOC Agrees to Landmark Resolution of Discrimination Case Against Abercrombie & Fitch." Retrieved from: https://www.eeoc.gov/eeoc/newsroom/release/11-18-04.cfm
28. Council, Jared. (2022, April 26). America's Best Employers for Diversity 2022. Forbes. Retrieved from: https://www.forbes.com/best-employers-diversity
29. Virginia Tech Pamplin College of Business, https://pamplin.vt.edu/deib/about.html
30. Home Page. Capital One. (n.d.). Retrieved from: https://www.capitalone.com/diversity/
31. Capital One. (2020). Forward Together - Capital One. Retrieved from: https://ecm.capitalone.com/WCM/diversity/cof_dibyearinreview-2020_external.pdf

32. Diversity. Capital One. (n.d.). Retrieved from: https://www.capitalone.com/diversity/business-resource-groups/
33. Great Place to Work Institute (2016). "What Is a Great Workplace?" Retrieved from: http://www.greatplacetowork.com/our-trust-approach/what-is-a-great-workplace
34. Jessica Rohman (2015). "15 Practice Areas Critical to Achieving a Great Workplace." Great Place to Work Institute. Retrieved from: http://www.greatplacetowork.com/events-and-insights/blogs-and-news/3040-15-practice-areas-critical-to-achieving-a-great-workplace
35. Sandra Kerka (1995). "The Changing Role of Support Staff." ERIC Clearinghouse on Adult, Career, and Vocational Education (ACVE) ARCHIVE Trends and Issues Alerts. Retrieved from: http://www.calpro-online.org/eric/docgen.asp?tbl=archive&ID=A019
36. Jeffrey Greenhaus, Karen Collins, and Jason Shaw (2003). "The Relationship between Work-Family Balance and Quality of Life." Journal of Vocational Behavior. Vol. 63. pp. 510–31.
37. Rivera, Candace. (2020, August 4). Proud to Be a Top 10 Company for Working Mothers. KPMG. Retrieved from: https://info.kpmg.us/news-perspectives/people-culture/proud-to-be-a-top-company-for-working-mothers.html
38. For further information or details about KPMG benefits, please visit http://us-jobs.kpmg.com/en/why-kpmg/benefits
39. WFC Resources Inc. (n.d.). "The Business Case for Telecommuting." Career/Life Alliances Services Inc. Retrieved from: http://www.clalliance.com/EXPO/docs/The_Business_Case_for_Telecommuting-WFCResources.pdf
40. Kate Lister (2016). "Latest Telecommuting Statistics." Global Workplace Analytics. Retrieved from: http://globalworkplaceanalytics.com/telecommuting-statistics
41. For further information or details about KPMG benefits, please visit http://us-jobs.kpmg.com/en/why-kpmg/benefits
42. Rana Florida (2012). "The Case For On-Site Day Care." Fast Company. Retrieved from: http://www.fastcompany.com/3036419/second-shift/the-case-for-onsite-daycare
43. Katherine Reynolds Lewis (2015). "What It Takes: Parental Support Trends at the Best Companies." Working Mother Magazine. Retrieved from: http://www.workingmother.com/what-it-takes-parental-support-trends-at-best-companies
44. Kate Gibson (2016). "Paid Parental Leave: Finally Coming to America?" CBS News Moneywatch. Retrieved from: http://www.cbsnews.com/news/paid-parental-leave-finally-coming-to-america/
45. Morley Safer and Rebecca Leung (2003). "Working The Good Life: SAS Provides Employees With Generous Work Incentives." CBS News/60 Minutes. Retrieved from: http://www.cbsnews.com/news/working-the-good-life/
46. Karen Collins and Elizabeth Hoover (1995). "Addressing the Needs of the Single Person in Public Accounting." Pennsylvania CPA Journal. p. 16.
47. Karen Collins and Larry Killough (1989). "Managing Stress in Public Accounting." Journal of Accountancy. Vol. 167. No.5. p. 92.
48. Glenn Withiam (1993). "American Concierges Set Service Standards." The Cornell Hotel and Restaurant Administration Quarterly. Vol. 34. No. 4. p. 26.
49. Great Place to Work Institute (2016). "Announcing the 2016 Fortune Best Companies to Work For." Retrieved from: http://reviews.greatplacetowork.com/rankings/2016-fortune-100-best-companies-to-work-for-list
50. Neil Learner (2000). "Ashore, a Way of Life Built Around the Crab." The Christian Science Monitor. Retrieved from: http://www.csmonitor.com/2000/0626/p15s1.html
51. The Hartford (2016). "Total Rewards: Competitive Compensation." Retrieved from: https://www.thehartford.com/careers/benefits
52. Texas Instruments (2012). "2012 Corporate Citizenship Report: Compensation." Retrieved from: http://www.ti.com/corp/docs/csr/2012/empwellbeing/payandbenefits/compensation.shtml
53. Jeff D. Opdyke (2004). "Getting a Bonus Instead of a Raise." Wall Street Journal. Retrieved from: http://www.wsj.com/articles/SB110427526449111461
54. Kristen Leigh Painter (2016). "Delta distributes .5 billion in profits to employees." Star Tribune. Retrieved from: http://www.startribune.com/delta-distributes-1-5-billion-in-profits-to-employees/368656151/
55. Greg Gardner (2016). "GM UAW workers to receive profit-sharing up to ,000." Detroit Free Press. Retrieved from: http://www.freep.com/story/money/cars/general-motors/2016/02/03/gm-uaw-workers-receive-profit-sharing-up-11000/79708340/
56. Lee Ann Obringer (2003). "How Employee Compensation Works." HowStuffWorks.com. Retrieved from: http://money.howstuffworks.com/benefits.htm
57. Texas Instruments (2012). "2012 Proxy Statement: Compensation discussion and analysis." p. 69. Retrieved from: http://www.ti.com/corp/docs/investor/proxy12/compensation_discussion_and_analysis.htm
58. Texas Instruments (2012). "2012 Corporate Citizenship Report: Compensation." Retrieved from: http://www.ti.com/corp/

docs/csr/2012/empwellbeing/payandbenefits/compensation.shtml

59. Ibid.
60. Ibid.
61. Starbucks (2016). "About Bean Stock." Retrieved from: http://starbucksbeanstock.com/en-us/welcome-en-us/about-bean-stock-en-us
62. Bureau of Labor Statistics (2016). "Employer Costs for Employee Compensation News Release." Retrieved from: http://www.bls.gov/news.release/ecec.nr0.htm
63. Bureau of Labor Statistics (2016). "Employee Benefits Survey, Private Industry Tables." Retrieved from: http://www.bls.gov/ncs/ebs/benefits/2015/ownership/prvt_all.pdf
64. Starbucks (2016). "Working at Starbucks." Retrieved from: http://www.starbucks.com/careers/working-at-starbucks
65. Susan Heathfield (2015). "Performance Appraisals Don't Work: The Traditional Performance Appraisal Process." About Money. Retrieved from: http://humanresources.about.com/od/performanceevals/a/perf_appraisal.htm
66. Bob Nelson and Peter Economy (2003). *Managing for Dummies*, 2nd ed. New York: Wiley. p. 140.
67. Archer North & Associates (2010). "Reward Issues." Performance-Appraisal.com. Retrieved from: http://www.performance-appraisal.com/rewards.htm
68. Dell, Inc. (2011). "2011 Corporate Responsibility Report: Listening, Inspiring, Sharing: Tell Dell." p. 37. Retrieved from: http://i.dell.com/sites/content/corporate/corp-comm/en/Documents/dell-fy11-cr-report.pdf
69. Gregory P. Smith (n.d.) "5 Tips to Attract, Keep and Motivate Your Employees." Businessknowhow.com. Retrieved from: http://www.businessknowhow.com/manage/attractworkforce.htm
70. Sue Shellenbarger (1998). "Companies Find It Pays To Be Nice to Employees." The Wall Street Journal. Retrieved from: http://www.wsj.com/articles/SB901063646490891000
71. Morley Safer and Rebecca Leung (2003). "Working The Good Life: SAS Provides Employees With Generous Work Incentives." CBS News/60 Minutes. Retrieved from: http://www.cbsnews.com/news/working-the-good-life/
72. Robert McGarvey (2004). "A Tidal Wave of Turnover." American Way. pp. 32–36.
73. The Container Store (2013). "What We Stand For: Organization with Heart—My 20-Year Trip." Retrieved from: http://standfor.containerstore.com/my-20-year-trip-2
74. The Container Store (2016). "What We Stand For: Organization with Heart—17 Years on FORTUNE's '100 Best' List." Retrieved from: http://standfor.containerstore.com/17-years-on-fortunes-100-best-list
75. Freda Turner (2002). "An Effective Employee Suggestion Program Has a Multiplier Effect." TheCEORefresher.com. Retrieved from: http://www.refresher.com/Archives/!ftmultiplier.html
76. Richard L. Daft and Dorothy Marcic (2006). *Understanding Management*, 6th Edition. Florence KY: Cengage Learning. p. 219.
77. Gregory P. Smith (n.d.). "Top Ten Reasons Why People Quit Their Jobs." Businessknowhow.com. Retrieved from: http://www.businessknowhow.com/manage/whyquit.htm
78. Charles Muhl (2001). "The Employment-at-Will Doctrine: Three Major Exceptions." Bureau of Labor Statistics Monthly Labor Review. Retrieved from: http://www.bls.gov/opub/mlr/2001/01/art1full.pdf

13. Union/Management Issues

Learning Objectives

- Explain why workers unionize and how unions are structured, and describe the collective-bargaining process.
- Discuss key terms associated with union and management issues, such as mediation and arbitration.
- Identify the tactics used by each side to support their negotiating positions: strikes, picketing, boycotting, and lockouts.

Labor Unions

As we saw in Chapter 11, Maslow believed that individuals are motivated to satisfy five levels of unmet needs (physiological, safety, social, esteem, and self-actualization). From this perspective, employees hope that full-time work will satisfy at least the two lowest-level needs: they want to be paid wages that are sufficient for them to feed, house, and clothe themselves and their families, and they expect safe working conditions and hope for some degree of job security.

Organizations also have needs: they need to earn profits that will satisfy their owners. They need to keep other stakeholders satisfied as well, which can cost money. Consider a metal-plating business that uses dangerous chemicals in its manufacturing processes; waste-water treatment is essential—and expensive. Sometimes, the needs of employees and employers are consistent: the organization can pay decent wages and provide workers with safe working conditions and job security while still making a satisfactory profit. At other times, there is a conflict—real, perceived, or a little bit of both—between the needs of employees and those of employers. In such cases, workers may be motivated to join a **labor union**—an organized group of workers that bargains with employers to improve its members' pay, job security, and working conditions.

Figure 13.1 graphs labor-union density—union membership as a percentage of payrolls—in the United States from 1930 to 2021. As you can see, there's been a steady decline since the middle part of the 1950s.[1]

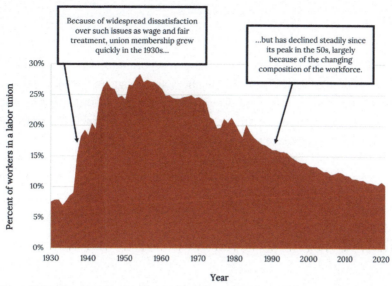

Figure 13.1: Union membership as a percentage of total employment (1930-2021).

Based on a 2022 report by the Bureau of Labor and Statistics (BLS), "In 2021, the number of wage and salary workers belonging to unions continued to decline (-241,000) to 14.0 million, and the percent who were members of unions—the union membership rate—was 10.3 percent. The rate was down from 10.8 percent in 2020—when the rate increased due to a disproportionately large decline in the total number of nonunion workers compared with the decline in the number of union members. The 2021 unionization rate is the same as the 2019 rate of 10.3 percent. In 1983, the first year for which comparable union data are available, the union membership rate was 20.1 percent and there were 17.7 million union workers."[2]

From the 1950s, only union membership among public workers (those employed by federal, state, and local governments, such as teachers, police, and firefighters) grew. In the 1940s, 10 percent of public workers and 34 percent of those in the private sector belonged to unions. Today, this has reversed: 36 percent of public workers and 7 percent of those in the private sector are union members.[3]

Why the decline in private sector unionization? Many factors come into play. The relatively weak economy has reduced the number of workers who have the confidence to go through a union organizing campaign; many workers are content just to have jobs and do not want to be seen as "rocking the boat." In addition, the United States has shifted from a manufacturing-based economy characterized by large, historically unionized companies to a service-based economy made up of many small firms that are harder to unionize.[4]

Union Structure

Unions have a pyramidal structure much like that of large corporations. At the bottom are **locals** that serve workers in a particular geographical area. Certain members are designated as **shop stewards** to serve as go-betweens in disputes between workers and supervisors. Locals are usually organized into **national unions** that assist with local contract negotiations, organize new locals, negotiate contracts for entire industries, and lobby government bodies on issues of importance to organized labor. In turn, national unions may be linked by a **labor federation**, such as the American Federation of Labor and Congress of Industrial Organizations (AFL–CIO), which provides assistance to member unions and serves as a principal political organ for organized labor.

Collective Bargaining

In a non-union environment, the employer makes largely unilateral, i.e., one-sided decisions on issues affecting its labor force, such as salary and benefits. Typically, employees are in no position to bargain for better deals. At the same time, however, employers have a vested interest in treating workers fairly. As we saw in Chapter 10, a reputation for treating employees well, for example, is a key factor in attracting talented people. Most employers want to avoid the costs involved in managing a unionized workforce; as a result, many offer generous pay and benefit packages in the hopes of keeping their workers happy—and un-unionized.

The process of setting pay and benefit levels is a lot different in a unionized environment. Union workers operate on a **contract** which usually covers some agreed-upon, multi-year period. When a given contract period begins to approach expiration, union representatives determine with members what they want in terms of salary increases, benefits, working conditions, and job security in their next contract. Union officials then tell the employer what its workers want and ask what they're willing to offer. When there's a discrepancy between what workers want and what management is willing to give—as there usually is—union officials serve as negotiators on behalf of their workforce, with the objective of extracting the best package of salary, benefits, and other conditions possible. The process of settling differences and establishing mutually agreeable conditions under which employees will work is called **collective bargaining**.

The Negotiation Process

Negotiations start when each side states its position and presents its demands. As in most negotiations, these opening demands simply stake out starting positions. Both parties usually expect some give-and-take and realize that the final agreement will fall somewhere between the two positions. If everything goes smoothly, a tentative agreement can be reached and then voted on by union members. If they accept the agreement, the process is complete and a contract is put into place to govern labor-management relations for a stated period. If workers reject the agreement, negotiators from both sides must go back to the bargaining table.

Mediation and Arbitration

If negotiations stall, the sides may call in outsiders. One option for engaging outside parties is called **mediation**, under which an impartial third party assesses the situation and makes recommendations for reaching an agreement. A mediator's advice can be accepted or rejected by either side. If mediation does not result in an agreement, because one or both sides are unwilling to accept the decision of the third party, they may opt instead for **arbitration**, under which the third party studies the situation and arrives at a **binding agreement**. The key difference between mediation and arbitration is the word "binding"—whatever the third party says goes, because both the union and management have agreed to accept the decision of the third party as a condition of entering into the arbitration process.

Grievance Procedures

Another difference between union and non-union environments is the handling of **grievances**—worker complaints on contract-related matters. When non-union workers feel that they've been treated unfairly, they can take up the matter with supervisors, who may or may not satisfy their complaints. When unionized workers have complaints (such as being asked to work more hours than stipulated under their contract), they can call on union representatives to resolve the problem, in conjunction with supervisory personnel, who are part of company management. If the outcome isn't satisfactory to the worker, the union can choose to take the problem to higher-level management on his or her behalf. If there is still no resolution, the union may submit the grievance to an arbitrator.

At times, labor and management can't resolve their differences through collective bargaining or formal grievance procedures. When this happens, each side may resort to a variety of tactics to win support for its positions and force the opposition to agree to its demands.

Union Tactics

Unions have several options at their disposal to pressure company management into accepting the terms and conditions union members are demanding. The tactics available to the union include striking, picketing, and boycotting. When they go on **strike**, workers walk away from their jobs and refuse to return until the issue at hand has been resolved. As undergraduates at Yale discovered when they arrived on campus in fall 2003, the effects of a strike can engulf parties other than employers and strikers: with 4,000 dining room workers on strike, students had to scramble to find food at local mini-markets. The strike—the eighth at the school since 1968—lasted 23 days, and in the end, the workers got what they wanted: better pension plans.[5]

Though a strike sends a strong message to management, it also has consequences for workers, who don't get paid when they're on strike. Unions often ease the financial pressure on strikers by providing cash payments, which are funded from the **dues** members pay to the unions. It is important to note that some unionized workers may not have the right to strike. For example, strikes by federal employees, such as air-traffic controllers, can be declared illegal if they jeopardize the public interest.

When you see workers parading with signs outside a factory or an office building (or even a school), they're probably using the tactic known as **picketing** (see figure 13.2). The purpose of picketing is informative—to tell people that a workforce is on strike or to publicize some management practice that is unacceptable to the union. In addition, because other union workers typically won't cross picket lines, marchers can sometimes interrupt the daily activities of the targeted organization. In April 2001, faculty at the University of Hawaii, unhappy about salaries, went on strike for 13 days. Initially, many students cheerfully headed for the beach, but before long, many more—particularly graduating seniors—began to worry about finishing the semester with the credits they needed to keep their lives on schedule.[6]

Figure 13.2: Chicago teachers picketing during a strike in 2019.

The final tactic available to unions is **boycotting**, in which union workers refuse to buy a company's products and try to get other people to follow suit. The tactic is often used by the AFL-CIO, which maintains a national "Don't Buy or Patronize" boycott list. In 2003, for example, at the request of two affiliates, the Actor's Equity Association and the American Federation of Musicians, the AFL-CIO added the road show of the Broadway musical *Miss Saigon* to the list. Why? The unions objected to the use of non-union performers who worked for particularly low wages and to the use of a "virtual orchestra," an electronic apparatus that can replace a live orchestra with software-generated orchestral accompaniment.[7]

Management Tactics

Management doesn't typically sit by passively, especially if the company has a position to defend or a message to get out. One available tactic is the **lockout**—closing the workplace to workers—though it's rarely used because it's legal only when unionized workers pose a credible threat to the employer's financial viability. If you are a fan of professional basketball, you may remember the NBA lockout in 2011 (older fans may remember a similar scenario that took place in 1999) which took place because of a dispute regarding the division of revenues and the structure of the salary cap.

Lockout tactics were also used in the 2011 labor dispute between the National Football League (NFL) and the National Football League Players Association when club owners and players failed to reach an agreement on a new contract. Prior to the 2011 season, the owners imposed a lockout, which prevented the players from practicing in team training facilities. Both sides had their demands: the players wanted a greater percentage of the revenues, which the owners were against. The owners wanted the players to play two additional regular season games, which the players were against. With the season drawing closer, an agreement was finally reached in July 2011 bringing the 130-day lockout to an end and ensuring that the 2011 football season would begin on time.[8]

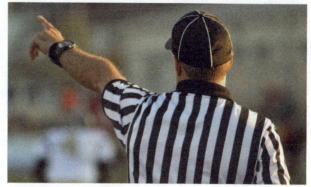

Figure 13.3: *In 2012, striking NFL referees were temporarily replaced by management.*

Another management tactic is replacing striking workers with **strikebreakers**—non-union workers who are willing to cross picket lines to replace strikers. Though the law prohibits companies from permanently replacing striking workers, it's often possible for a company to get a court injunction that allows it to bring in replacement workers. For example, the NFL employed replacement referees in 2012, a move which led to a number of very questionable calls on the field.[9]

Why Managers Often Resist Unionization Efforts

No union organizing campaign ever started with the premise that by unionizing, employees would receive lower wages or weaker benefit programs. To the contrary, unions approach prospective members with promises like higher pay, better health insurance, and more vacation time. Not surprisingly, then, business managers resist unions because they generally add to the cost of doing business. Higher costs can be addressed in several ways. Managers could accept lower profits, though such an outcome is unlikely given that owners/shareholders benefit from higher profits. They could raise prices and pass the higher costs along to customers, but doing so could hurt their competitiveness in the marketplace. Alternatively. they could find other ways to offset the increase in costs, but since managers are already supposed to be paying attention to costs, finding offsets can be quite difficult.

Another reason managers sometimes resist unionization is that unions often attempt to negotiate work rules that are to the benefit of their members. Business people who have worked in union environments have often complained of the lack of flexibility and the difficulty unions sometimes create in dealing with poor performing union employees. The grievance process can sometimes be long, cumbersome, and costly to administer.

Some companies find working with unions to be so unpleasant that they decide to voluntarily increase pay and benefits to preempt unions in advertising these benefits.

The Future of Unions

As we noted earlier, union membership in the United States has been declining for some time. So will membership continue to decline causing unions to lose even more power? The AFL–CIO is optimistic about union membership, pointing out recent gains in membership among women and immigrants, as well as health care workers, graduate students, and professionals.[10]

Convincing workers to unionize is still more difficult than it used to be and could become even harder in the future. Given their resistance to being unionized, employers have developed strategies for dissuading workers from unionizing—in particular, tactics for withholding job security. If unionization threatens higher costs for wages and benefits, management can resort to part-time or contract workers. They can also outsource work, eliminating jobs entirely. Many employers are now investing in technology designed to reduce the amount of human labor needed to produce goods or offer services. While it is impossible to predict the future, it is likely that unions and managers will remain adversaries for the foreseeable future.

 An interactive H5P element has been excluded from this version of the text. You can view it online here: https://pressbooks.lib.vt.edu/fundamentalsofbusiness4e/?p=136#h5p-36

Chapter Videos

There are two videos for this chapter, in order to present two opposing points of view as well as some useful history. Pay attention for the historical benefits we take for granted today but that came about as a result of efforts by unions. There are also two recent news interviews that provide the current perspective of Union Activity since 2021.

 One or more interactive elements has been excluded from this version of the text. You can view them online here: https://www.youtube.com/watch?v=tPqS-HdqnUg

 One or more interactive elements has been excluded from this version of the text. You can view them online here: https://www.youtube.com/watch?v=ewu-v36szlE

One or more interactive elements has been excluded from this version of the text. You can view them online here: https://www.youtube.com/watch?v=ui4hdoSGBQA

 One or more interactive elements has been excluded from this version of the text. You can view them online here: https://www.youtube.com/watch?v=hBWIDerD_fQ

Key Takeaways

- **Labor unions** are organized groups of workers that bargain with employers to improve members' pay, job security, and working conditions.
- When there's a discrepancy between what workers want in terms of salary increases, benefits, working conditions, and job security and what management is willing to give, the two sides engage in a process called **collective bargaining**.
- If negotiations break down, the sides may resort to **mediation** (in which an impartial third party makes recommendations for reaching an agreement) or **arbitration** (in which the third party imposes a binding agreement).
- When unionized workers feel that they've been treated unfairly, they can file **grievances**—complaints over contract-related matters that are resolved by union representatives and employee supervisors.
- If labor differences can't be resolved through collective bargaining or formal grievance procedures, each side may resort to a variety of tactics. The union can do the following:
  - Call a **strike** (in which workers leave their jobs until the issue is settled).
  - Organize **picketing** (in which workers congregate outside the workplace to publicize their position).
  - Arrange for **boycotting** (in which workers and other consumers are urged to refrain from buying an employer's products).
- Management may resort to a **lockout**—closing the workplace to workers—or call in **strikebreakers** (nonunion workers who are willing to cross picket lines to replace strikers).

References

Figures

Figure 13.1: Union membership as a percentage of total employment (1930-2021). Kindred Grey. 2022. CC BY 4.0. https://archive.org/details/13.1_20220623.

Figure 13.2: Chicago teachers picketing during a strike in 2019. Charles Edward Miller. 2019. CC BY-SA 2.0. https://commons.wikimedia.org/wiki/File:CICS_Teachers_and_Staff_Strike_Picket_Line_Chicago_Illinois_2-6-19_5808_%2833139353278%29.jpg.

Figure 13.3: In 2012, striking NFL referees were temporarily replaced by management. Nathan Shively. 2016. Unsplash license. https://unsplash.com/photos/MgIPNC8TG1c.

Videos

Video 1: Managing in a Union Environment. Thomson Reuters Compliance Learning. 2009. Copyrighted. https://www.youtube.com/watch?v=tPqS-HdqnUg.

Video 2: The Labor Movement in the United States. History. 2017. "Copyrighted. https://www.youtube.com/watch?v=ewu-v36szlE&amp=&feature=youtu.be.

Video 3: Unionizing in America: Next phase of pandemic realignment? CNBC Television. 2022. Copyrighted. https://www.youtube.com/watch?v=ui4hdoSGBQA.

Video 4: Amazon warehouse unionization is a big deal: Labor union chief Mary Kay Henry. CNBC Television. 2022. Copyrighted. https://www.youtube.com/watch?v=hBWIDerD_fQ.

Notes

1. Mayer, Gerald (2004). "Union Membership Trends in the United States." CRS Report for Congress. 1930-1982 Data Retrieved from: https://www.researchgate.net/publication/37157281_Union_Membership_Trends_in_the_United_States. 1983-2019 Data Retrieved from U.S. Bureau of Labor Statistics.
2. Bureau of Labor Statistics (Ed.). (2022, January 20). Union members - 2021 - bureau of labor statistics. bls.gov. Retrieved from: https://www.bls.gov/news.release/pdf/union2.pdf
3. Wikipedia (2016). "Labor Unions in the United States: Membership." Retrieved from: https://en.wikipedia.org/wiki/Labor_unions_in_the_United_States#Membership
4. Kris Maher (2010). "Union Membership Drops 10%." Wall Street Journal. Retrieved from: http://www.wsj.com/articles/SB10001424052748703822404575019350727544666; Steven Greenhouse (2011). "Union Membership in U.S. Fell to a 70-Year Low Last Year." New York Times. Retrieved from: http://www.nytimes.com/2011/01/22/business/22union.html
5. Steve Greenhouse (2003). "Yale's Labor Troubles Deepen as Thousands Go on Strike." New York Times. Retrieved from: http://www.nytimes.com/2003/03/04/nyregion/yale-s-labor-troubles-deepen-as-thousands-go-on-strike.html; Diane Scarponi (2003). "Pair of Yale Unions Approve Contract." Los Angeles Times. Retrieved from: http://articles.latimes.com/2003/sep/21/news/adna-yale21
6. Associated Press (2001). "Hawaii Professors End Strike." USA Today. Retrieved from: http://usatoday30.usatoday.com/

news/nation/2001-04-18-hawaii.htm

7. AFL–CIO (2003). "Statement by AFL-CIO President John Sweeney on 'Miss Saigon' Touring Show." AFL–CIO Press Releases. Retrieved from: http://ftp.workingamerica.org/Press-Room/Press-Releases/Statement-by-AFL-CIO-President-John-Sweeney-on-Mi
8. CNN Wire Staff (2011). "Players, Owners Sign Deal to End NFL Lockout." CNN. Retrieved from: http://edition.cnn.com/2011/SPORT/07/25/nfl.deal/
9. Michael Pearson (2012). "Sorry About That, NFL Chief Says About Replacements." CNN. Retrieved from: http://www.cnn.com/2012/09/27/sport/nfl-referees-deal/
10. Los Angeles County Federation of Labor, AFL-CIO (2011). "What Is a Union." Launionaflcio.org. Retrieved from: http://launionaflcio.org/what-is-a-union

14. Marketing: Providing Value to Customers

Learning Objectives

- Define the terms marketing, marketing concept, and marketing strategy.
- Outline the tasks involved in selecting a target market.
- Identify the four Ps of the marketing mix.
- Explain how to conduct marketing research.
- Discuss various branding strategies and explain the benefits of packaging and labeling.
- Describe the elements of the promotion mix.
- Explain how companies manage customer relationships.
- Identify the advantages and disadvantages of social media marketing.

A Robot with Attitude

Mark Tilden used to build robots for NASA that ended up being destroyed on Mars, but after seven years of watching the results of his work meet violent ends 36 million miles from home, he decided to specialize in robots for earthlings. He left the space world for the toy world and teamed up with Wow Wee Toys Ltd. to create "Robosapien," an intelligent robot with an attitude.[1] The 14-inch-tall robot, which is operated by remote control, has great moves. In addition to walking forward, backward, and turning, he dances, raps, and gives karate chops. He can pick up small objects and even fling them across the room, and he does everything while grunting, belching, and emitting other "bodily" sounds.

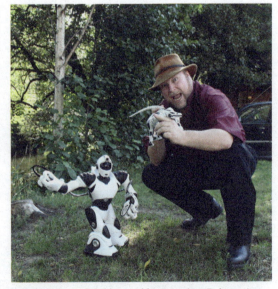

Figure 14.1: Mark Tilden and his creation, Robosapien.

Robosapien gave Wow Wee Toys a good head start in the toy robot market: in the first five months, more than 1.5 million Robosapiens were sold.[2] The company expanded the line to more than a dozen robotics and other interactive toys, including FlyTech Bladestar, a revolutionary indoor flying machine that won a Popular Mechanics magazine Editor's Choice Award in 2008).[3]

What does Robosapien have to do with marketing? The answer is fairly simple: though Mark Tilden is an accomplished inventor who has created a clever product, Robosapien wouldn't be going anywhere without the marketing expertise of Wow Wee. In this chapter, we'll look at the ways in which marketing converts product ideas like Robosapien into commercial successes.

What Is Marketing?

When you consider the functional areas of business—accounting, finance, management, marketing, and operations—marketing is the one you probably know the most about. After all, as a consumer and target of all sorts of advertising messages, you've been on the receiving end of marketing initiatives for most of your life. What you probably don't appreciate, however, is the extent to which marketing focuses on providing value to the customer. According to the American Marketing Association, "Marketing is the activity, set of institutions, and processes for creating, communicating, delivering, and exchanging offerings that have value for customers, clients, partners, and society at large."[4]

In other words, marketing isn't just advertising and selling. It includes everything that organizations do to satisfy customer needs:

- Coming up with a product and defining its features and benefits.
- Setting its price.
- Identifying its target market.
- Making potential customers aware of it.
- Getting people to buy it.
- Delivering it to people who buy it.
- Managing relationships with customers after it has been delivered.

Think about a typical business—a local movie theater, for example. It's easy to see how the person who decides what movies to show is involved in marketing: he or she selects the product to be sold. It's even easier to see how the person who puts ads in the newspaper works in marketing: he or she is in charge of advertising—making people aware of the product and getting them to buy it. What about the ticket seller and the person behind the counter who gets the popcorn and soda or the projectionist? Are they marketing the business? Absolutely. The purpose of every job in the theater is satisfying customer needs, and as we've seen, identifying and satisfying customer needs is what marketing is all about. Marketing is a team effort involving everyone in the organization.

If everyone is responsible for marketing, can the average organization do without an official marketing department? Not necessarily: most organizations have marketing departments in which individuals are actively involved in some marketing-related activity—product design and development, pricing, promotion, sales, and distribution. As specialists in identifying and satisfying customer needs, members of the **marketing department** manage—plan, organize, lead, and control—the organization's overall marketing efforts.

The Marketing Concept

Figure 14.2 is designed to remind you that to achieve company profitability goals, you need to start with three things:

1. Find out what customers or potential customers need.
2. Develop products to meet those needs.
3. Engage the entire organization in efforts to satisfy customers.

Figure 14.2: The marketing concept leads to company profit.

At the same time, you need to achieve organizational goals, such as profitability and growth. This basic philosophy—satisfying customer needs while meeting organizational goals—is called the **marketing concept**, and when it's effectively applied, it guides all of an organization's marketing activities.

The marketing concept puts the customer first: as your most important goal, satisfying the customer must be the goal of everyone in the organization. But this doesn't mean that you ignore the bottom line; if you want to survive and grow, you need to make some profit. What you're looking for is the proper balance between the commitments to customer satisfaction and company survival. Consider the case of Medtronic, a manufacturer of medical devices, such as pacemakers and defibrillators. The company boasts more than 50 percent of the market in cardiac devices and is considered the industry standard setter.[5] Everyone in the organization understands that defects are intolerable in products that are designed to keep people alive. Thus, committing employees to the goal of zero defects is vital to both Medtronic's customer base and its bottom line. "A single quality issue," explains CEO Arthur D. Collins Jr., "can deep-six a business."[6]

Selecting a Target Market

Businesses earn profits by selling goods or providing services. It would be nice if everybody in the marketplace was interested in your product, but if you tried to sell it to everybody, you'd probably spread your resources too thin. You need to identify a specific group of consumers who should be particularly interested in your product, who would have access to it, and who have the means to buy it. This group represents your **target market**, and you need to aim your marketing efforts at its members.

Identifying Your Market

How do marketers identify target markets? First, they usually identify the overall market for their product—the individuals or organizations that need a product and are able to buy it. This market can include either or both of two groups:

1. A **consumer market**—buyers who want the product for personal use
2. An **industrial market**—buyers who want the product for use in making other products

You might focus on only one market or both. A farmer, for example, might sell blueberries to individuals on the consumer market and, on the industrial market, to bakeries that will use them to make muffins and pies.

Segmenting the Market

The next step in identifying a target market is to divide the entire market into smaller portions, or **market segments**—groups of potential customers with common characteristics that influence their buying decisions. An especially narrow market segment is known as a **niche market**, for example, extreme luxury goods that less than 1 percent of people can afford. Let's look at some of the most useful categories in detail.

Demographic segmentation

Demographic segmentation divides the market into groups based on such variables as age, marital status, gender, ethnic background, income, occupation, and education.

Age, for example, will be of interest to marketers who develop products for children, retailers who cater to teenagers, colleges that recruit students, and assisted-living facilities that promote services among the elderly. Lifetime Television for Women targets female viewers, while Telemundo networks targets Hispanics. When Hyundai offers recent college graduates a $400 bonus towards leasing or buying a new Hyundai, the company's marketers are segmenting the market according to education level.[7]

Geographic segmentation

Geographic segmentation—dividing a market according to such variables as climate, region, and population density (urban, suburban, small-town, or rural)—is also quite common. Climate is crucial for many products: snow shovels would not sell in Hawaii. Consumer tastes also vary by region. That's why McDonald's caters to regional preferences, offering a breakfast of Spam and rice in Hawaii,[8] tacos in Arizona, and lobster rolls in Massachusetts.[9] Outside the United States, menus diverge even more widely (you can get seaweed burgers or, if you prefer, seasoned seaweed fries in Japan).[10]

Figure 14.3: A McDonald's gracoro burger in Japan. It contains shrimp, macaroni, and white sauce.

Likewise, differences between urban and suburban life can influence product selection. For example, it's a hassle to parallel park on crowded city streets. Thus, Toyota engineers have developed a product especially for city dwellers. The Japanese version of the Prius, Toyota's hybrid gas-electric car, can automatically parallel park itself. Using computer software and a rear-mounted camera, the parking system measures the spot, turns the steering wheel, and swings the car into the space (making the driver—who just sits there—look like a master of parking skills).[11] After its success in the Japanese market, the self-parking feature was brought to the United States.

Behavioral segmentation

Dividing consumers by such variables as attitude toward the product, user status, or usage rate is called **behavioral segmentation**. Companies selling technology-based products might segment the market according to different levels of receptiveness to technology. They could rely on a segmentation scale developed by Forrester Research that divides consumers into two camps: technology optimists, who embrace new technology, and technology pessimists, who are indifferent, anxious, or downright hostile when it comes to technology.[12]

Some companies segment consumers according to user status, distinguishing among nonusers, potential users, first-time users, and regular users of a product. Depending on the product, they can then target specific groups, such as first-time users. Credit-card companies use this approach when they offer membership points to potential customers in order to induce them to get their card.

Psychographic segmentation

Psychographic segmentation classifies consumers on the basis of individual lifestyles as they're reflected in people's interests, activities, attitudes, and values. Do you live an active life and love the outdoors? If so, you may be a potential buyer of hiking or camping equipment or apparel. If you're a risk taker, you might catch the attention of a gambling casino. The possibilities are limited only by the imagination.

Clustering Segments

Typically, marketers determine target markets by combining, or "**clustering**," segmenting criteria. What characteristics does Starbucks look for in marketing its products? Three demographic variables come to mind: age, geography, and income. Buyers are likely to be males and females ranging in age from about 25 to 40 (although college students, aged 18 to 24, are moving up in importance). Geography is a factor as customers tend to live or work in cities or upscale suburban areas. Those with relatively high incomes are willing to pay a premium for Starbucks specialty coffee and so income—a socioeconomic factor—is also important.

 An interactive H5P element has been excluded from this version of the text. You can view it online here: https://pressbooks.lib.vt.edu/fundamentalsofbusiness4e/?p=152#h5p-37

The Marketing Mix

After identifying a target market, your next step is developing and implementing a marketing program designed to reach it. As figure 14.4 shows, this program involves a combination of tools called the **marketing mix**, often referred to as the "**four Ps**" of marketing:

1. Developing a **product** that meets the needs of the target market
2. Setting a **price** for the product
3. Distributing the product—getting it to a **place** where customers can buy it
4. **Promoting** the product—informing potential buyers about it

Pricing will be covered in more detail in its own dedicated chapter.

Figure 14.4: The marketing mix.

Marketing: Providing Value to Customers | 285

Developing a Product

The development of Robosapien was a bit unusual for a company that was already active in its market.[13] Generally, product ideas come from people within the company who understand its customers' needs. Internal engineers are then challenged to design the product. In the case of Robosapien, the creator, Mark Tilden, had conceived and designed the product before joining Wow Wee Toys. The company gave him the opportunity to develop the product for commercial purposes, and Tilden was brought on board to oversee the development of Robosapien into a product that satisfied Wow Wee's commercial needs.

Robosapien is not a "kid's toy," though kids certainly love its playful personality. It's a home-entertainment product that appeals to a broad audience—children, young adults, older adults, and even the elderly. It's a big gift item, and it has developed a following of techies and hackers who take it apart, tinker with it, and even retrofit it with such features as cameras and ice skates.

Conducting Marketing Research

Before settling on a strategy for Robosapien, the marketers at Wow Wee did some homework. First, to zero in on their target market, they had to find out what various people thought of the product. More precisely, they needed answers to questions like the following:

- Who are our potential customers?
- What do they like about Robosapien? What would they change?
- How much are they willing to pay for it?
- Where will they expect to buy it?
- How can we distinguish it from competing products?
- Will enough people buy Robosapien to return a reasonable profit for the company?

The last question would be left up to Wow Wee management, but, given the size of the investment needed to bring Robosapien to market, Wow Wee couldn't afford to make the wrong decision. Ultimately, the company was able to make an informed decision because its marketing team provided answers to key questions through **marketing research**—the process of collecting and analyzing the data that are relevant to a specific marketing situation. This data had to be collected in a systematic way. Market research seeks two types of data:

1. Marketers generally begin by looking at **secondary data**—information already collected, whether by the company or by others, that pertains to the target market.
2. With secondary data in hand, they're prepared to collect **primary data**—newly collected information that addresses specific questions.

Secondary data can come from inside or outside the organization. Internally available data includes sales reports and other information on customers. External data can come from a number of sources. The US Census Bureau, for example, posts demographic information on American households (such as age, income, education, and number of members), both for the country as a whole and for specific geographic areas.

Population data helped Wow Wee estimate the size of its potential US target market. Other secondary data helped the firm assess the size of foreign markets in regions around the world, such as Europe, the Middle East, Latin America, Asia, and the Pacific Rim. This data helped position the company to sell Robosapien in 85 countries, including Canada, England, France, Germany, South Africa, Australia, New Zealand, Hong Kong, and Japan.

Using secondary data that is already available (and free) is a lot easier than collecting your own information. Unfortunately, however, secondary data didn't answer all the questions that Wow Wee was asking in this particular situation. To get these answers, the marketing team had to conduct primary research, working directly with members of their target market. First they had to decide exactly what they needed to know, then determine who to ask and what methods would be most effective in gathering the information.

We know what they wanted to know—we've already listed example questions. As for whom to talk to, they randomly selected representatives from their target market. There is a variety of tools for collecting information from these people, each of which has its advantages and disadvantages. To understand the marketing-research process fully, we need to describe the most common of these tools:

- **Surveys**. Sometimes marketers mail questionnaires to members of the target market. The process is time consuming and the response rate generally low. Online surveys are easier to answer and so get better response rates than other approaches.
- **Personal interviews**. Though time consuming, personal interviews not only let you talk with real people but also let you demonstrate the product. You can also clarify answers and ask open-ended questions.
- **Focus groups**. With a focus group, you can bring together a group of individuals (perhaps 6 to 10) and ask them questions. A trained moderator can explain the purpose of the group and lead the discussion. If sessions are run effectively, you can come away with valuable information about customer responses to both your product and your marketing strategy.

Wow Wee used focus groups and personal interviews because both approaches had the advantage of allowing people to interact with Robosapien. In particular, focus-group sessions provided valuable opinions about the product, proposed pricing, distribution methods, and promotion strategies.

Researching your target market is necessary before you launch a new product, but the benefits of marketing research don't extend merely to brand-new products. Companies also use it when they're deciding whether or not to refine an existing product or develop a new marketing strategy for an existing product. Kellogg's, for example, conducted online surveys to get responses to a variation on its Pop-Tarts brand—namely, Pop-Tarts filled with a mixture of traditional fruit filling and yogurt. Marketers had picked out four possible names for the product and wanted to know which one kids and mothers liked best. They also wanted to know what they thought of the product and its packaging. Both mothers and kids liked the new Pop-Tarts (though for different reasons) and its packaging, and the winning name for the product launched in the spring of 2011 was "Pop-Tarts Yogurt Blasts." The online survey of 175 mothers and their children was conducted in one weekend by an outside marketing research group.[14]

 An interactive H5P element has been excluded from this version of the text. You can view it online here: https://pressbooks.lib.vt.edu/fundamentalsofbusiness4e/?p=152#h5p-38

Branding

Armed with positive feedback from their research efforts, the Wow Wee team was ready for the next step: informing buyers—both consumers and retailers—about their product. They needed a **brand**—some word, letter, sound, or symbol that would differentiate their product from similar products on the market. They chose the brand name Robosapien, hoping that people would get the connection between homo sapiens (the human species) and Robosapien (the company's coinage for its new robot "species"). To prevent other companies from coming out with their own "Robosapiens," they took out a **trademark**: a symbol, word, or words legally registered or established by use as representing a company or product. Trademarking requires registering the name with the US Patent and Trademark Office. Though this approach—giving a unique brand name to a particular product—is a bit unusual, it isn't unprecedented. Mattel, for example, established a separate brand for Barbie, and Anheuser-Busch sells beer under the brand name Budweiser. Note, however, that the more common approach, which is taken by such companies as Microsoft, Dell, and Apple, calls for marketing all the products made by a company under the company's brand name.

Branding Strategies

Companies can adopt one of three major strategies for branding a product:

1. With **private branding** (or private labeling), a company makes a product and sells it to a retailer who in turn resells it under its own name. A soft-drink maker, for example, might make cola for Wal-Mart to sell as its Sam's Choice Cola.
2. With **generic branding**, the maker attaches no branding information to a product except a description of its contents. Customers are often given a choice between a brand-name prescription drug or a cheaper generic drug with the same formula.
3. With **manufacturer branding**, a company sells one or more products under its own brand names. Adopting a **multiproduct-branding** approach, it sells many products under one brand name. Food-maker ConAgra sells soups, frozen treats, and complete meals under its *Healthy Choice* label. Using a **multibranding** approach, the company assigns different brand names to products covering different segments of the market. Automakers often use multibranding. The Volkswagen group of brands also includes Audi and Lamborghini.

> Branding is used in hotels to allow chains (Marriott, Hyatt, Hilton) to offer hotel brands that meet various customers' travel needs while still maintaining their loyalty to the chain. The same customer who would choose an Extended Stay hotel with a full kitchen when on a long term assignment might stay at a convention hotel when attending a trade show and then stay in a resort property when traveling with their family. By segmenting different types of hotel locations, amenities, room sizes and décor, hotel chains can meet the needs of a wide variety of travelers. In the past decade "soft" branding has become common to allow unique hotels to take advantage of being part of a chain reservation system and loyalty program. For example, Marriott now has over 260 affiliated independent hotels in its Autograph Collection which is up from 100 in 2016.[15]
>
> | Type of hotel | Marriott | Hilton | Hyatt |
> |---|---|---|---|
> | **Luxury** | Ritz Carlton
JW Marriott | Waldorf Astoria
Conrad | Park Hyatt
Andaz |
> | **Independent** | Autograph Collection | Curio Collection | Unbound Collection |
> | **Full service** | Marriott
Renaissance
Gaylord | Hilton
Canopy
Doubletree | Hyatt |
> | **Select service** | Courtyard by Marriott
AC Hotels | Hilton Garden Inn
Hampton Inn | Hyatt Place |
> | **Extended stay** | Residence Inn | Homewood Suites | Hyatt House |
>
> Figure 14.5: Major hotel chains and their brands.

> Loyalty programs are heavily used in the hospitality industry, especially airlines and hotels, as part of their Customer Relationship Management programs. Loyalty programs are often targeted to high value business travelers with less price sensitivity. They achieve loyalty status and perks while traveling as well as earning points to use for personal travel rewards. Once a loyalty program member obtains elite status with significant associated perks such as guaranteed room availability, airport club lounge access, etc., the customer is much less likely to use other brands.

Building Brand Equity

Wow Wee went with the multibranding approach, deciding to market Robosapien under the robot's own brand name. Was this a good choice? The answer would depend, at least in part, on how well the product sells. Another consideration is the impact on Wow Wee's other brands. If Robosapien fared poorly, its failure would not reflect badly on Wow Wee's other products. On the other hand, if customers liked Robosapien, they would have no reason to associate it with other Wow Wee products. In this case, Wow Wee wouldn't gain much from its **brand equity**—any added value generated by favorable consumer experiences with Robosapien. To get a better idea of how valuable brand equity is, think for a moment about the effect of the name Dell on a product. When you have a positive experience with a Dell product—say, a laptop or a printer—you come away with a positive opinion of the entire Dell product line and will probably buy more Dell products. Over time, you may even develop brand loyalty: you may prefer—or even insist on—Dell products. Not surprisingly, brand loyalty can be extremely valuable to a company. Because of customer loyalty, Apple's brand tops Interbrand's *Best Global Brands* ranking with a value of over $170 billion. Google's brand is valued at $120 billion, the Coca-Cola brand is estimated at more than $78 billion, and Microsoft and IBM round out the top five, with brands valued at over $65 billion each.[16]

Packaging and Labeling

Packaging can influence a consumer's decision to buy a product or pass it up. Packaging gives customers a glimpse of the product, and it should be designed to attract their attention, with consideration given to color choice, style of lettering, and many other details. Labeling not only identifies the product but also provides information on the package contents: who made it and where or what risks are associated with it (such as being unsuitable for small children).

How has Wow Wee handled the packaging and labeling of Robosapien? The robot is 14 inches tall, and is also fairly heavy (about seven pounds), and because it's made out of plastic and has movable parts, it's breakable. The easiest, and least expensive, way of packaging it would be to put it in a square box of heavy cardboard and pad it with Styrofoam. This arrangement would not only protect the product from damage during shipping but also make the package easy to store. However, it would also eliminate any customer contact with the product inside the box (such as seeing what it looks like). Wow Wee, therefore, packages

Figure 14.6: Robosapien in its package.

Robosapien in a container that is curved to his shape and has a clear plastic front that allows people to see the whole robot. Why did Wow Wee go to this much trouble and expense? Like so many makers of so many products, it has to market the product while it's still in the box.

Meanwhile, the labeling on the package details some of the robot's attributes. The name is highlighted in big letters above the descriptive tagline "A fusion of technology and personality." On the sides and back of the package are pictures of the robot in action with such captions as "Dynamic Robotics with Attitude" and "Awesome Sounds, Robo-Speech & Lights." These colorful descriptions are conceived to entice the consumer to make a purchase because its product features will satisfy some need or want.

Packaging can serve many purposes. The Robosapien package attracts attention to the product's features. For other products, packaging serves a more functional purpose. Nabisco packages some of its snacks—Oreos, Chips Ahoy, and Lorna Doone's—in "100 Calorie Packs." The packaging makes life simpler for people who are keeping track of calories.

 An interactive H5P element has been excluded from this version of the text. You can view it online here: https://pressbooks.lib.vt.edu/fundamentalsofbusiness4e/?p=152#h5p-39

Marketing: Providing Value to Customers | 291

Place

A great deal is involved in getting a product to the place in which it is ultimately sold. If you're a fast food retailer, for example, you'll want your restaurants to be in high-traffic areas to maximize your potential business. If your business is selling beer, you'll want it to be offered in bars, restaurants, grocery stores, convenience stores, and even stadiums. Placing a product in each of these locations requires substantial negotiations with the owners of the space, and often the payment of slotting fees, an allowance paid by the manufacturer to secure space on store shelves.

Retailers are marketing intermediaries that sell products to the eventual consumer. Without retailers, companies would have a much more difficult time selling directly to individual consumers, no doubt at a substantially higher cost. The most common types of retailers are summarized in figure 14.7 below. You will likely recognize many of the examples provided. It is important to note that many retailers do not fit neatly into only one category. For example, WalMart, which began as a discount store, has added groceries to many of its outlets, also placing it in competition with supermarkets.

Type of retailer	Description	Examples
Category killer	Sells a wide variety of products of a particular type, selling at a low price due to their large scale	Dick's Sporting Goods
Convenience store	Offers food, beverages, and other products, typically in individual servings, at a higher price, and geared to fast service	7-Eleven
Department store	Offers a wide assortment of products grouped into different departments (e.g., jewelry, apparel, perfume)	Nordstrom, Macy's
Discount store	Organized into departments, but offer a range of merchandise generally seen as lower quality and at a much lower price	Target, Walmart
Specialty store	Offers goods typically confined to a narrow category; high level of personal service and higher prices than other retailers	Local running shops or jewelry stores
Supermarket	Offers mostly consumer staples such as food and other household items	Kroger, Food Lion
Warehouse club stores	Offers a wide variety of products in a warehouse-style setting; sells many products in bulk; usually requires membership fee	Costco, Sam's Club

Figure 14.7: The most common types of retailers, with examples.

Of course, in an age where e-commerce is taking an increasing share of the retail spending dollar, "place" is not always a physical location that the customer visits. Products ordered online ship from manufacturers to distribution centers and then directly on to the end customer without passing through a traditional retail outlet. An emerging trend in retailing is **showrooming** in which a customer visits a traditional retailer, gets familiar with particular items available, and then orders the item online, often from an unrelated online retailer. The term comes from the fact that the traditional retail outlet has served only as a showroom—a place to view the product, as opposed to a place where the sale is made. As shopping habits change, retailers have been challenged to keep their space relevant and attractive to the ultimate consumer.

Promoting a Product

Your **promotion mix**—the means by which you communicate with customers—may include advertising, personal selling, sales promotion, and publicity. These are all tools for telling people about your product and persuading potential customers to buy it. Before deciding on an appropriate promotional strategy, you should consider a few questions:

- What's the main purpose of the promotion?
- What is my target market?
- Which product features should I emphasize?
- How much can I afford to invest in a promotion campaign?
- How do my competitors promote their products?

To promote a product, you need to imprint a clear image of it in the minds of your target audience. What do you think of, for instance, when you hear "Ritz-Carlton"? What about "Motel 6"? They're both hotel chains, that have been quite successful in the hospitality industry, but they project very different images to appeal to different clienteles. The differences are evident in their promotions. The Ritz-Carlton web site describes "luxury hotels" and promises that the chain provides "the finest personal service and facilities throughout the world."[17] Motel 6, by contrast, characterizes its facilities as "discount hotels" and assures you that you'll pay "the lowest price of any national chain."[18]

Promotional Tools

We'll now examine each of the elements that can go into the promotion mix—advertising, personal selling, sales promotion, and publicity. Then we'll see how Wow Wee incorporated them into a promotion mix to create a demand for Robosapien.

Advertising

Advertising is paid, non-personal communication designed to create an awareness of a product or company. Ads are everywhere—in print media (such as newspapers, magazines, the Yellow Pages), on billboards, in broadcast media (radio and TV), and on the Internet. It's hard to escape the constant barrage of advertising messages; it's estimated that the average consumer is confronted by about 5,000 ad messages each day (compared with about 500 ads a day in the 1970s).[19] For this very reason, ironically, ads aren't as effective as they used to be. Because we've learned to tune them out, companies now have to come up with innovative ways to get through to

Figure 14.8: Digital advertising is everywhere you look!

potential customers. A New York Times article[20] claims that "anywhere the eye can see, it's likely to see an ad." Subway turnstiles are plastered with ads for GEICO auto insurance, Chinese food containers are decorated with ads for Continental Airways, and parking meters display ads for Campbell's Soup[21] Advertising is still the most prevalent form of promotion.

The choice of **advertising media** depends on your product, target audience, and budget. A popular vacation destination selling spring-break getaways to college students might post flyers on campus bulletin boards or run ads on social media platforms. The co-founders of Nantucket Nectars found radio ads particularly effective. Rather than pay professionals, they produced their own ads themselves.[22] As unprofessional as this might sound, the ads worked, and the business grew.

Personal Selling

Personal selling refers to one-on-one communication with customers or potential customers. This type of interaction is necessary in selling large-ticket items, such as homes, and it's also effective in situations in which personal attention helps to close a sale, such as sales of cars and insurance policies.

Figure 14.9: Personal selling at Best Buy.

Many retail stores depend on the expertise and enthusiasm of their salespeople to persuade customers to buy. Home Depot has grown into a home-goods giant in large part because it fosters one-on-one interactions between salespeople and customers. The real difference between Home Depot and everyone else isn't the merchandise; it's the friendly, easy-to-understand advice that sales people give to novice homeowners, according to one of its cofounders.[23] Best Buy's knowledgeable sales associates make them "uniquely positioned to help consumers navigate the increasing complexity of today's technological landscape," according to CEO Hubert Joly.[24]

Sales Promotion

It's likely that at some point, you have purchased an item with a coupon or because it was advertised as a buy-one-get-one special. If so, you have responded to a **sales promotion**—one of the many ways that sellers provide incentives for customers to buy. Sales promotion activities include not only those mentioned above but also other forms of discounting, sampling, trade shows, in-store displays, and even sweepstakes. Some promotional activities are targeted directly to consumers and are designed to motivate them to purchase now. You've probably heard advertisers make statements like "limited time only" or "while supplies last." If so, you've encountered a sales promotion directed at consumers. Other forms of sales promotion are directed at dealers and intermediaries. Trade shows are one example of a dealer-focused promotion. Mammoth centers such as McCormick Place in Chicago host enormous events in which manufacturers can display their new products to retailers and other interested parties. At food shows, for example, potential buyers can sample products that manufacturers hope to launch to the market. Feedback from prospective buyers can even result in changes to new product formulations or decisions not to launch.

Figure 14.10: Sales promotion in a retail store.

Marketing: Providing Value to Customers | 295

Publicity and Public Relations

Figure 14.11: AirPods.

Free **publicity**—say, getting your company or your product mentioned or pictured in a newspaper or on TV—can often generate more customer interest than a costly ad. When Dr. Dre and Jimmy Iovine were finalizing the development of their Beats headphones, they sent a pair to LeBron James. He liked them so much he asked for 15 more pairs, and they "turned up on the ears of every member of the 2008 US Olympic basketball team when they arrived in Shanghai. 'Now that's marketing,' says Iovine."[25] It wasn't long before the pricey headphones became a must-have fashion accessory for everyone from celebrities to high school students.

Consumer perception of a company is often important to a company's success. Many companies, therefore, manage their public relations in an effort to garner favorable publicity for themselves and their products. When the company does something noteworthy, such as sponsoring a fundraising event, the public relations department may issue a press release to promote the event. When the company does something negative, such as selling a prescription drug that has unexpected side effects, the public relations department will work to control the damage to the company. Each year the Hay Group and Korn Ferry survey more than 1,000 company top executives, directors, and industry leaders in twenty countries to identify companies that have exhibited exceptional integrity or commitment to corporate social responsibility. The rankings are publishes annually as Fortune magazine's "World's Most Admired Companies.®"[26] Topping the list in 2022 are Apple, Amazon, Microsoft, Pfizer and Walt Disney.[27]

Marketing Robosapien

Now let's look more closely at the strategy that Wow Wee pursued in marketing Robosapien in the United States. The company's goal was ambitious: to promote the robot as a must-have item for kids of all ages. As we know, Wow Wee intended to position Robosapien as a home-entertainment product, not as a toy. The company rolled out the product at Best Buy, which sells consumer electronics, computers, entertainment software, and appliances. As marketers had hoped, the robot caught the attention of consumers shopping for TV sets, DVD players, home and car audio equipment, music, movies, and games. Its $99 price tag was a little lower than the prices of other merchandise, and that fact was an important asset: shoppers were willing to treat Robosapien as an impulse item—something extra to pick up as a gift or as a special present for children, as long as the price wasn't too high.

Meanwhile, Robosapien was also getting lots of free publicity. Stories appeared in newspapers and magazines around the world, including the New York Times, the Times of London, Time magazine, and National Parenting magazine. Commentators on The Today Show, The Early Show, CNN, ABC News, and FOX News all covered it. The product received numerous awards, and experts predicted that it would be a hot item for the holidays.

At Wow Wee, Marketing Director Amy Weltman (who had already had a big hit with the Rubik's Cube) developed a gala New York event to showcase the product. From mid- to late August, actors dressed in six-foot robot costumes roamed the streets of Manhattan, while the 14-inch version of Robosapien performed in venues ranging from Grand Central Station to city bars. Everything was recorded, and film clips were sent to TV stations.

Figure 14.12: *Robosapien*.

The stage was set for expansion into other stores. Macy's ran special promotions, floating a 24-foot cold-air robot balloon from its rooftop and lining its windows with armies of Robosapien's. Wow Wee trained salespeople to operate the product so that they could help customers during in-store demonstrations. Other retailers, including The Sharper Image, Spencer's, and Toys "R" Us, carried Robosapien, as did e-retailers such as Amazon.com. The product was also rolled out (with the same marketing flair) in Europe and Asia.

When national advertising hit in September, all the pieces of the marketing campaign came together—publicity, sales promotion, personal selling, and advertising. Wow Wee ramped up production to meet anticipated fourth-quarter demand and waited to see whether Robosapien would live up to commercial expectations.

Interacting with Customers

Customer-Relationship Management

Customers are the most important asset that any business has. Without enough good customers, no company can survive. Firms must not only attract new customers but also retain current customers. In fact, repeat customers are more profitable. It's estimated that it costs as much as five times more to attract and sell to a new customer than to an existing one.[28] Repeat customers also tend to spend more, and they're much more likely to recommend you to other people.

Retaining customers is the purpose of **customer-relationship management**—a marketing strategy that focuses on using information about current customers to nurture and maintain strong relationships with them. The underlying theory is fairly basic: to keep customers happy, you treat them well, give them what they want, listen to them, reward them with discounts and other loyalty incentives, and deal effectively with their complaints.

Take Caesars Entertainment Corporation, which operates more than 50 casinos under several brands, including Caesars, Harrah's, Bally's, and Horseshoe. Each year, it sponsors the World Series of Poker with a top prize in the millions. Caesars gains some brand recognition when the 22-hour event is televised on ESPN, but the real benefit derives from the information cards filled out by the 7,000 entrants who put up $10,000 each. Data from these cards is fed into Caesars database, and almost immediately every entrant starts getting special attention, including party invitations, free entertainment tickets, and room discounts. The program is all part of Harrah's strategy for targeting serious gamers and recognizing them as its best customers.[29]

Sheraton Hotels uses a softer approach to entice return customers. Sensing that its resorts needed both a new look and a new strategy for attracting repeat customers, Sheraton launched its "Year of the Bed" campaign; in addition to replacing all its old beds with luxurious new mattresses and coverings, it issued a "service promise guarantee"—a policy that any guest who's dissatisfied with his or her Sheraton stay will be compensated. The program also calls for a customer-satisfaction survey and discount offers, both designed to keep the hotel chain in touch with its customers.[30]

Another advantage of keeping in touch with customers is the opportunity to offer them additional products. Amazon.com is a master at this strategy. When you make your first purchase at Amazon.com, you're also making a lifelong "friend"—one who will suggest (based on what you've bought before) other things that you might like to buy. Because Amazon.com continually updates its data on your preferences, the company gets better at making suggestions.

Social Media Marketing

In the last several years, the popularity of **social media marketing** has exploded. You already know what social media is—Facebook, Twitter, Instagram, TikTok, LinkedIn, YouTube, and any number of other online sites that allow you to network, share your opinions, ideas, photos, etc. Social media marketing is the practice of including social media as part of a company's marketing program.

Why do businesses use social media marketing? Before responding, ask yourself these questions: how much time do I spend watching TV? When I watch TV, do I sit through the ads? Do I read newspapers or magazines and flip right past the ads? Now, put yourself in the place of Brady Brewer, chief marketing officer of Starbucks. Does it make sense for him to spend millions of dollars to place an ad for Starbucks on TV or in a newspaper or magazine? Or should he instead spend the money on social media marketing initiatives that have a high probability of connecting to Starbucks's market?

For companies like Starbucks, the answer is clear. The days of trying to reach customers through ads on TV, in newspapers, or in magazines are over. Most television watchers skip over commercials, and few Starbucks's customers read newspapers or magazines, and even if they do, they don't focus on the ads. Social media marketing provides a number of advantages to companies, including enabling them to[31],[32]

- create brand awareness;
- connect with customers and potential customers by engaging them in two-way communication;
- establishing the brand as a thought leader;
- being relevant or staying top of mind when users log in to their accounts;
- increasing visitors to the website;
- build brand loyalty by providing opportunities for a targeted audience to participate in company-sponsored activities, such as contests;
- offer and publicize incentives, such as special discounts or coupons;
- gather feedback and ideas on how to improve products and marketing initiatives;
- allow customers to interact with each other and spread the word about a company's products or marketing initiatives; and
- take advantage of low-cost marketing opportunities by being active on social sites.

To get an idea of the power of social media marketing, think of the ALS Ice Bucket Challenge. According to the ALS Association: "the ALS Ice Bucket Challenge started in the summer of 2014 and became the world's largest global social media phenomenon. More than 17 million people uploaded their challenge videos to Facebook; these videos were watched by 440 million people a total of 10 billion times."[33] The ALS Association raised $115 million in six weeks (their usual annual budget was only $20 million).[34]

Figure 14.13: *The ALS ice bucket challenge in action.*

Marketing: Providing Value to Customers | 299

Brand	Campaign	Reason why	What	Result
Zoom	Virtual background contest	Increase brand awareness	Zoom asked their community to share a picture or video using its virtual background feature. Every month three winning entries were awarded branded items as prizes, which are announced on their social channels	Zoom leveraged the power of a contest and giveaway to drive engagement across their social media channels
Planters	The death of Mr. Peanut (#RIPPeanut)	Increase brand awareness and follow social trend	In perhaps the most unique social media marketing stunt of 2020, Planters said goodbye to their beloved Mr. Peanut. The #RIPPeanut campaign was inspired by the internet's response to the death of Iron Man. It aimed to repeat the same level of engagement on social media that Tony Stark's death caused in Avengers	Planters took a risk by playing off of the popularity of a movie icon while utilizing satirical, never-before-seen content to bring forward a 114-year-old brand. The tweet garnered nearly 50,000 retweets.
Dove	In the #PassTheCrown marketing campaign, Dove believes that everyone should be able to embrace their natural hair without judgment.	This campaign was to continue around its core values of inclusivity, natural beauty, and positive body image	Dove teamed up with National Urban League, Color of Change, and Western Centre to end race-based hair discrimination in the U.S.	Grew an audience of loyal followers and micro-influencers around the world that came into action when called upon

Figure 14.14: Top social media campaigns of 2021.

Figure 14.15: A woman on Zoom.

Advertisers Jump on Podcasts and Videos

Podcasts are basically blogs with a multimedia file. The trend developed when a new version of iTunes software made it easy for people to create their own podcasts and post them on a website. There are more than 8,000 podcasters in the United States. Besides individuals, companies are beginning to do their own podcasts as well as posting videos from the company on YouTube as another marketing channel. For listeners, the advantage of a podcast is convenience. Companies now have the ability to use streaming video, which potential customers can download to their mobile devices; for example, ABC News offering a digital version of its programming. The customers' favorite programs download automatically from the internet, usually free of charge, and they can listen to the programs any time they wish. They can also listen wherever they wish, if they have a mobile device to receive the downloads.

Gimlet Media is one of the nation's largest podcasters, offering material from nearly 40 different stations as podcasts. At first ad-free, Gimlet's podcasts are done for direct-to-consumer companies like Blue Apron, as well as for traditional advertisers like Pepsi and Ford. Gimlet now includes a short advertisement before the programming—short enough that people won't fast-forward through it. Gimlet also received a $5 million investment from advertising giant WPP, a clear sign that the business community sees a bright future in podcasts.[35]

Pet owners can go to http://www.purina.com and opt in to receive Purina's podcasts. The products will offer advice ranging from animal training to pet insurance to nutrition for older pets. Weekly tips will also be sent on things such as how to help your dog lose weight. Owners spend close to $25 billion a year on pet food. The aim of the podcasts is to build brand loyalty with a soft sell.[36]

Videos have become another important promotions channel. Literally hundreds of thousands of videos can be viewed on YouTube, the top video-hosting site on the internet. Many people now log in to YouTube to watch videos on a particular product and how the product can be used. Entrepreneurs and other small-business owners have made extensive use of YouTube to provide value to their customers by creating and uploading informational videos that highlight their products.[37]

Social Media Marketing Challenges

The main challenge of social media marketing is that it can be very time consuming. It takes determination and resources to succeed. Small companies often lack the staff to initiate and manage social media marketing campaigns.[38] Even large companies can find the management of media marketing initiates overwhelming. A recent study of 1,700 chief marketing officers indicates that many are overwhelmed by the sheer volume of customer data available on social sites, such as Facebook and Twitter.[39] This is not surprising given that in 2016, Facebook had more than 1.6 billion active users and more than 2.9 billon by 2022.[40,41]

Adapted from: OpenStax *Introduction to Business* (CC BY).
Access for free at https://openstax.org/books/introduction-business/pages/12-10-trends-in-social-media

The marketing officers recognize the potential value of this data but are not always capable of using it. A chief marketing officer in the survey described the situation as follows: "The perfect solution is to serve each consumer individually. The problem? There are billions of them."[42] In spite of these limitations, 82 percent of those surveyed plan to increase their use of social media marketing over the next 3 to 5 years. To understand what real-time information is telling them, companies will use analytics software, which is capable of analyzing unstructured data. This software is being developed by technology companies, such as IBM, and advertising agencies.

The bottom line: what is clear is that marketing, and particularly advertising, has changed forever. As Simon Pestridge, Nike's global director of marketing for Greater China, said about Nike's marketing strategy, "We don't do advertising any more. Advertising is all about achieving awareness, and we no longer need awareness. We need to become part of people's lives, and digital allows us to do that."[43]

A New Marketing Model

The 4 P's have served marketers well for generations, but new innovations can disrupt even the most established concepts. A new framework is taking hold in marketing—the **4 C's**. In this model, each of the C words replaces one of the P's, flipping the model from the perspective of the marketer to that of the customer. In the new model:

1. **Consumer** replaces Product: Products solve a need for a customer; by focusing on the consumer in the 4 C's model, the point of view changes to a customer-based perspective and also allows for the inclusion of services, which are purchased about as often as physical products.
2. **Convenience** rather than Place: Both words speak to the same point—where can my customers obtain my product or service? But in an age where so many products and services are sourced online, the word "convenience" incorporates more than just a physical location, as was implied by the word "place."
3. **Cost** takes the place of Price: From the standpoint of the buyer, the price charged by the seller becomes their cost. Moving to the word "cost" results in seeing things from the perspective of the customer, consistent with other aspects of the model.
4. **Communication** replaces Promotion: In its most basic form, promotion is about informing potential customers so that they will recognize the value in a product or service and part with the funds necessary to obtain it. However, the word "promotion" also has taken on the context of a deal or discount. By moving to the word "communication," the new model incorporates all forms of reaching customers, whether through advertising, coupons, social media campaigns, and many others.

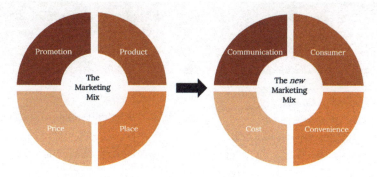

Figure 14.16: The new marketing mix (the 4 C's).

The 4 C's framework appears to be gaining traction, and it may eventually replace the 4 P's altogether. If so, we will no doubt find ourselves rewriting this entire chapter!

 An interactive H5P element has been excluded from this version of the text. You can view it online here: https://pressbooks.lib.vt.edu/fundamentalsofbusiness4e/?p=152#h5p-40

Chapter Video

Marketing is unfortunately not always truthful or entirely accurate. This video features some examples of misleading advertising which persists in business because it often works.

 One or more interactive elements has been excluded from this version of the text. You can view them online here: https://www.youtube.com/watch?v=M-HrTC8QCbM

Key Takeaways

- **Marketing** is a set of processes for creating, communicating, and delivering value to customers and for improving customer relationships.
- A **target market** is a specific group of consumers who are particularly interested in a product, would have access to it, and are able to buy it.
- Target markets are identified through **market segmentation**—finding specific subsets of the overall market that have common characteristics that influence buying decisions.
- Markets can be segmented on a number of variables including **demographics**, **geographics**, **behavior**, and **psychographics** (or lifestyle variables).
- Developing and implementing a marketing program involves a combination of tools called the **marketing mix**: **product**, **price**, **place**, and **promotion**.
- Before settling on a marketing strategy, marketers often do **marketing research** to collect and analyze relevant data.
- Methods for collecting primary data include **surveys**, **personal interviews**, and **focus groups**.
- To protect a **brand** name, companies register trademarks with the US Patent and Trademark Office.
- There are three major **branding strategies**:
    - With **private branding**, the maker sells a product to a retailer who resells it under its own name.
    - Under **generic branding**, a no-brand product contains no identification except for a description of the contents.
    - Using **manufacturer branding**, a company sells products under its own brand names.
- When consumers have a favorable experience with a product, it builds **brand equity**.
    - If consumers are loyal to it over time, it enjoys **brand loyalty**.
- **Retailers** are intermediaries that sell to the end consumer. Types of retailers include **category killers**, **convenience stores**, **department stores**, **discount stores**, **specialty stores**, **supermarkets**, **and warehouse club stores**.
- The **promotion mix** includes all the tools for telling people about a product and persuading potential customers to buy it. It can include **advertising**, **personal selling**, **sales promotion**, and **publicity**.

References

Figures

Figure 14.1: Mark Tilden and his creation, Robosapien. Eirik Newth. 2006. CC BY 2.0. https://flic.kr/p/mKf2n.

Figure 14.2: The marketing concept leads to company profit. Kindred Grey. 2022. CC BY 4.0. https://archive.org/details/14.2_20220627.

Figure 14.3: A McDonald's gracoro burger in Japan. It contains shrimp, macaroni, and white sauce. 毒島みるく. 2021. Public domain. https://commons.wikimedia.org/wiki/File:Gracoro_of_McDonald%27s_Japan.jpg.

Figure 14.4: The marketing mix. Kindred Grey. 2022. CC BY 4.0. https://archive.org/details/14.4_20220627.

Figure 14.6: Robosapien in its package. Jim Trottier. 2009. CC BY-SA 2.0. https://flic.kr/p/73fDon.

Figure 14.8: Digital advertising is everywhere you look! Joshua Earle. 2017. Unsplash license. https://unsplash.com/photos/X_roZ7toBJY.

Figure 14.9: Personal selling at Best Buy. Intel Free Press. 2012. CC BY-SA 2.0. https://flic.kr/p/drsHhs.

Figure 14.10: Sales promotion in a retail store. charlesdeluvio. 2019. Unsplash license. https://unsplash.com/photos/OtC8kRzlbqo.

Figure 14.11: AirPods. Aaina Sharma. 2017. Unsplash license. https://unsplash.com/photos/rl2MXeP6sss.

Figure 14.12: Robosapien. jonobacon. 2007. CC BY 2.0. https://flic.kr/p/CP6gZ.

Figure 14.13: The ALS ice bucket challenge in action. Major Tom Agency. 2019. Unsplash license. https://unsplash.com/photos/mgS73ggL8RU.

Figure 14.14: Recent social media marketing campaigns. Table data adapted from https://www.meltwater.com/en/blog/best-social-media-marketing-examples.

Figure 14.15: A woman on Zoom. Anna Shvets. 2020. Pexels license. https://www.pexels.com/photo/people-on-a-video-call-4226262/.

Figure 14.16: The new marketing mix (the 4 C's). Kindred Grey. 2022. CC BY 4.0. https://archive.org/details/14.15_20220627.

Video

Top 10 Misleading Marketing Tactics. WatchMojo. 2014. Copyrighted. https://www.youtube.com/watch?v=M-HrTC8QCbM

Notes

1. WowWee Toys (n.d.). "Robosapien: A Fusion of Technology and Personality." Retrieved from: http://wowwee.com/robosapien-x
2. Michael Taylor (2004). "Innovative Toy Packs a Punch." South China Morning Post (Hong Kong). Retrieved from: http://www.scmp.com/article/478240/innovative-toy-packs-punch
3. WowWee Toys (n.d.). "Our Story." Retrieved from: http://wowwee.com/about/company-history
4. American Marketing Association (2013). "Definition of Marketing." Retrieved from: https://www.ama.org/AboutAMA/Pages/Definition-of-Marketing.aspx
5. Funding Universe (n.d.). "Medtronic Inc. History." Retrieved from: http://www.fundinguniverse.com/company-histories/medtronic-inc-history/
6. Michael Arndt (2004). "High Tech—and Handcrafted." Bloomberg. Retrieved from: http://www.bloomberg.com/news/articles/2004-07-04/high-tech-and-handcrafted
7. Hyundai Motor America (2016). "Special Programs: College Graduate Program." Hyundai USA. Retrieved from: https://www.hyundaiusa.com/financial-tools/college-grad-program.aspx
8. Pacific Business News (2002). "McDonald's Test Markets Spam." The Business Journals. Retrieved from: http://www.bizjournals.com/pacific/stories/2002/06/10/daily22.html
9. Svenske chef (2002). "The Super McDonalds." Halfbakery. Retrieved from: http://www.halfbakery.com/idea/The_20Super_20McDonalds
10. Tucker S. Cummings (2010). "Interesting Menu Items from McDonalds in Asia." Weird Asia News. Retrieved from: http://www.weirdasianews.com/2010/03/23/blank-interesting-menu-items-mcdonalds-asia/
11. Time (2003). "Best Inventions 2003: Hybrid Car." Retrieved from: http://content.time.com/time/specials/packages/article/0,28804,1935038_1935083_1935719,00.html
12. James L. McQuivey and Gina Fleming (2012). "Segmenting Customers by Technology PreferenceMaking Technographics® Segmentation Work." Forrester. Retrieved from: https://www.forrester.com/report/Segmenting Customers By Technology Preference/-/E-RES72761
13. Information in this section was obtained through an interview with the director of marketing at Wow Wee Toys Ltd. conducted on July 15, 2004.
14. Brendan Light (2004). "Kellogg's Goes Online for Consumer Research." Packaging Digest. Retrieved from": http://www.packagingdigest.com/kellogg-s-goes-online-consumer-research
15. Marriott Hotels. (2022, May 11). Autograph Collection Hotels. Retrieved from: https://web.archive.org/web/20220511211356/https://hotel-development.marriott.com/brands/autograph-collection
16. Interbrand (2016). "Rankings." Interbrand.com. Retrieved from: http://interbrand.com/best-brands/best-global-brands/2015/ranking/
17. The Ritz-Carlton Hotel Company LLC (2016). "Gold Standards." Retrieved from: http://www.ritzcarlton.com/en/about/gold-standards
18. G6Hospitality LLC (2015). "Corporate Profile." Motel 6. Retrieved from: https://www.motel6.com/en/faq.html
19. Caitlin A. Johnson (2009). "Cutting Through Advertising Clutter." CBS News. Retrieved from: http://www.cbsnews.com/stories/2006/09/17/sunday/main2015684.shtml
20. Louise Story (2007). "Anywhere the Eye Can See, It's Likely to See an Ad." New York Times. Retrieved from: http://www.nytimes.com/2007/01/15/business/media/15everywhere.html?pagewanted=all
21. Seth Godin (1999). *Permission Marketing: Turning Strangers into Friends, and Friends into Customers.* New York: Simon & Schuster. p. 31.
22. Paul Gough (2002). "Nantucket Nectars: New Flavors, Old Ad Strategy." Media Post. Retrieved from: http://www.mediapost.com/publications/article/2812/nantucket-nectars-new-flavors-old-ad-strategy.html?edition=
23. Kevin J. Clancy (2001). "Sleuthing, Not Slashing, for Growth." Across the Board. Vol. 38. No. 5. p. 9.
24. Daphne Howland (2016). "Best Buy CEO: Customer Service Key to Battling Amazon." Retail Dive Retrieved from: http://www.retaildive.com/news/best-buy-ceo-customer-service-key-to-battling-amazon/419812/
25. Burt Helm (2014). "How Dr. Dre's Headphones Company Became a Billion-Dollar Business." Inc. Retrieved from: http://www.inc.com/audacious-companies/burt-helm/beats.html

26. Fortune Editors. (Ed.). (2022, February 1). World's most admired companies. Fortune. Retrieved from: https://fortune.com/worlds-most-admired-companies/
27. Ibid.
28. Alex Lawrence (2012). "Five Customer Retention Tips for Entrepreneurs." Forbes. Retrieved from: http://www.forbes.com/sites/alexlawrence/2012/11/01/five-customer-retention-tips-for-entrepreneurs/#56de8ec717b0
29. Stephanie Fitch (2004). "Stacking the Deck." Forbes. Retrieved from: http://www.forbes.com/forbes/2004/0705/132.html
30. Hotel News Resource (2004). "Sheraton Hotels Lure Travelers With the Promise of a Good Night's Sleep in New Million Television and Print Ad Campaign." Retrieved from: http://www.hotelnewsresource.com/article10706.html
31. Seth Godin (1999). *Permission Marketing: Turning Strangers into Friends, and Friends into Customers.* New York: Simon & Schuster. pp. 40-52.
32. Stacy McLachlan and Christina Newberry. (2021). 22 Benefits of Social Media for Business. Hootsuite. Retrieved from: https://blog.hootsuite.com/social-media-for-business
33. ALS Association (n.d.). "ALS Ice Bucket Challenge – FAQ." Retrieved from: http://www.alsa.org/about-us/ice-bucket-challenge-faq.html?referrer=https://www.google.com/
34. Ibid.
35. Peter Kafka, "Podcast Network Gimlet Media Has Raised Another $5 Million—This Time from Ad Giant WPP," *Recode*, https://www.recode.net, September 6, 2017.
36. "U.S. Pet Food Market Size & Share Is Expected to Reach USD 30.01 Billion in 2022: Zion Market Research," https://globenewswire.com, May 22, 2017; "How Purina Made Fetch Happen [Again]," *Medium.com*, https://medium.com, April 5, 2017.
37. Lawrence Gitman, et. al. (2018). Trends in Social Media. *Introduction to Business*. OpenStax. (CC BY 4.0) Retrieved from: https://openstax.org/books/introduction-business/pages/12-10-trends-in-social-media. OpenStax *Introduction to Business* may be accessed for free at: https://openstax.org/books/introduction-business/pages/1-introduction.
38. Susan Ward (2016). "What is Social Network Marketing?" The Balance Small Business. Retrieved from: http://sbinfocanada.about.com/od/socialmedia/g/socmedmarketing.htm
39. Georgina Prodhan (2011). "Marketers Struggle to Harness Social Media – Survey." Reuters. Retrieved from: http://www.reuters.com/article/socialmedia-ibm-idUSL5E7LA3JO20111011
40. Statista (2016). "Number of Monthly Active Facebook Users Worldwide as of 1st Quarter 2016 (in Millions)." Retrieved from: http://www.statista.com/statistics/264810/number-of-monthly-active-facebook-users-worldwide/
41. Facebook: Global Daily Active Users 2022. Statista. (2022, July 28). Retrieved from: https://www.statista.com/statistics/346167/facebook-global-dau/#:~:text=Facebook%20audience%20reach&text=The%20number%20of%20monthly%20active,to%20be%2076.84%20by%20202
42. Georgina Prodhan (2011). "Marketers Struggle to Harness Social Media – Survey." Reuters. Retrieved from: http://www.reuters.com/article/socialmedia-ibm-idUSL5E7LA3JO20111011
43. Johan Ronnestam (n.d.). "Simon Pestridge from Nike Makes Future Advertising Sound Simple." Ronnestam. Retrieved from: http://www.ronnestam.com/simon-pestridge-from-nike-make-future-advertising-sound-simple/

15. Pricing Strategy

Learning Objectives

- Identify pricing strategies that are appropriate for new and existing products.
- Understand the stages of the product life cycle.

Pricing a Product

As introduced in a previous chapter, one of the four Ps in the marketing mix is **price**. Pricing is such an important aspect of marketing that it merits its own chapter. Pricing a product involves a certain amount of trial and error because there are so many factors to consider. If a product or service is priced too high, many people simply won't buy it. Or your company might even find itself facing competition from some other supplier that thinks it can beat your price. On the other hand, if you price too low, you might not make enough profit to stay in business. Let's look at several pricing options that were available to those marketers at Wow Wee who were responsible for pricing Robosapien, an example we introduced earlier. We'll begin by discussing two strategies that are particularly applicable to products that are being newly introduced.

New Product Pricing Strategies

When Robosapien was introduced to the market, it had little direct competition in its product category. True, there were some "toy" robots available, but they were not nearly as sophisticated. Sony offered a pet dog robot called Aibo, but its price tag of $1,800 was really high. Even higher up the price-point scale was the $3,600 iRobi robot made by the Korean company Yujin Robotics to entertain kids and even teach them foreign languages. Parents could also monitor kids' interactions with the robot through its video-camera eyes; in fact, they could even use the robot to relay video messages telling kids to shut it off and go to sleep.[1]

Figure 15.1: Sony's robot dog, Aibo.

Skimming and Penetration Pricing

Because Wow Wee was introducing an innovative product in an emerging market with few direct competitors, it considered one of two pricing strategies:

1. With a **skimming strategy**, Wow Wee would start off with the highest price that keenly interested customers would pay. This approach would generate early profits, but when competition enters—and it will, because at high prices, healthy profits can be made in the market—Wow Wee would have to lower its price. Even without competition, they would likely lower prices gradually to bring in another group of consumers not willing to pay the initial high price.
2. Using **penetration pricing**, Wow Wee would initially charge a low price, both to discourage competition and to grab a sizable share of the market. This strategy might give the company some competitive breathing room (potential competitors won't be attracted to low prices and modest profits). Over time, as its dominating market share discourages competition, Wow Wee could push up its prices.

Other Pricing Strategies

In their search for the best price level, Wow Wee's marketing managers could consider a variety of other approaches, such as cost-based pricing, demand-based pricing, prestige pricing, and odd-even pricing. Any of these methods could be used not only to set an initial price but also to establish long-term pricing levels.

Before we examine these strategies, let's pause for a moment to think about the pricing decisions that you have to make if you're selling goods for resale by retailers. Most of us think of price as the amount that we—consumers—pay for a product. But when a manufacturer (such as Wow Wee) sells goods to retailers, the price it gets is not what we the consumers will pay for the product. In fact, it's a lot less.

Here's an example. Say you buy a shirt at the mall for $40 and that the shirt was sold to the retailer by the manufacturer for $20. In this case, the retailer would have applied a **mark-up** of 100 percent to this shirt, or in other words $20 mark-up is added to the $20 cost to arrive at its price (hence a 100 percent markup) resulting in a $40 sales price to the consumer. Mark-up allows the retailer to cover its costs and make a profit.

Cost-Based Pricing

Using **cost-based pricing**, Wow Wee's accountants would figure out how much it costs to make Robosapien and then set a price by adding a profit to the cost. If, for example, it cost $40 to make the robot, Wow Wee could add on $10 for profit and charge retailers $50. Cost-based pricing has a fundamental flaw—it ignores the value that consumers would place on the product. As a result, it is typically only employed in cases where something new or customized is being developed where the cost and value cannot easily be determined before the product is developed. A defense contractor might use cost-based pricing for a new missile system, for example. The military might agree to pay costs plus some agreed amount of profit to create the needed incentives for the contractor to develop the system. Building contractors might also use cost-based pricing to protect themselves from unforeseen changes in a project: the client wanting a home addition would get an estimate of the cost and have an agreement for administrative fees or profit, but if the client changes what they want, or the contractor has unexpected complications in the project, the client will pay for the additional costs.

Demand-Based Pricing

Let's say that Wow Wee learns through market research how much people are willing to pay for Robosapien. Following a **demand-based pricing** approach, it would use this information to set the price that it charges retailers. If consumers are willing to pay $120 retail, Wow Wee would charge retailers a price that would allow retailers to sell the product for $120. What would that price be? If the 100 percent mark-up example applied in this case, here's how we would arrive at it: $120 consumer selling price minus a $60 markup by retailers means that Wow Wee could charge retailers $60. Retailer markup varies by product category and by retailer, so this example is just to illustrate the concept.

 An interactive H5P element has been excluded from this version of the text. You can view it online here: https://pressbooks.lib.vt.edu/fundamentalsofbusiness4e/?p=163#h5p-41

Dynamic Pricing

In the hospitality industry, the supply of available rooms or seats is fixed; it cannot be changed easily. Moreover, once the night is over or the flight has departed, you can no longer sell that room or seat. This fact combined with the variation in demand for rooms or flights on certain days or times (think holidays or special events), has led to **dynamic pricing**. Revenue management, and the growth of online travel agencies (OTA's) like Hotwire, Expedia, and Priceline are methods of maximizing revenue for a given night or flight. Hotels and airlines use sophisticated **revenue management** tools to forecast demand and adjust the availability of various price points. Online travel agents like Hotwire publicize last-minute availability with special rates so that unsold rooms or flights can attract customers and still earn revenue. This approach allows hotels and airlines to maximize revenue opportunities for high demand times such as university graduations and holidays, and also for special events like the Super Bowl or the Olympics. Losses are minimized during low-demand times because unused capacity is offered at a discount, attracting customers who might not have considered traveling at off peak times.

Prestige Pricing

Some people associate a high price with high quality—and, in fact, there generally is a correlation. Thus, some companies adopt a **prestige-pricing** approach—setting prices artificially high to foster the impression that they're offering a high-quality product.

Competitors are reluctant to lower their prices because it would suggest that they're lower-quality products. Let's say that Wow Wee finds some amazing production method that allows it to produce Robosapien at a fraction of its current cost. It could pass the savings on by cutting the price, but it might be reluctant to do so: what if consumers equate low cost with poor quality?

Odd-Even Pricing

Do you think $9.99 sounds cheaper than $10? If you do, you're part of the reason that companies sometimes use **odd-even pricing**—pricing products a few cents (or dollars) under an even number. Retailers, for example, might price Robosapien at $99 (or even $99.99) if they thought consumers would perceive it as less than $100.

Figure 15.2: Odd-even pricing; it's less than $6.00!

Loss Leaders

Have you ever seen items in stores that were priced so low that you wondered how the store could make any money? There's a good chance they weren't—the store may have been using a **loss leader** strategy—pricing an item at a loss to draw customers into the store. Once there, store managers hope that the customer will either buy accessories to go along with the new purchase or actually select a different item not priced at a loss. You might have visited the store to buy a specially-priced laptop and ended up leaving with a more expensive one that had a faster processor. Or perhaps you bought the HDTV that was advertised, but then also bought a new surge protector and a streaming player. In either case, you did exactly what the store hoped when they priced the advertised item at a loss.

Bundling

Perhaps you are one of the many customers of a cable television provider that also buys their high-speed internet and/or their phone service. Or when you stop by your favorite fast-food outlet for lunch, maybe you sometimes buy the combo of burger, fries, and a drink. If you do, you've experienced the common practice of a **bundling** strategy—pricing items as a group, or bundle, at a discount to the cost of buying the items separately. Bundling has significant advantages to both buyers and sellers. Obviously, buyers receive the discount. Sellers, on the other hand, can sell more goods and services with this approach. Perhaps you would have settled for a water instead of a soft drink, but the combo price made the soft drink just a few cents more. Without bundling, that soft drink might not have been sold. Bundling is also used by insurance companies when they offer their customers growing discounts for combining automobile, home, life, and other policies together. This provides business efficiencies for the insurance companies as the primary customer data is typically the same and provides the customer overall savings and a single point of contact for their insurance needs.

If the sale involves some kind of recurring service—like the previously-mentioned example of cable—bundling can also result in higher levels of customer retention. If you decided one day that you wanted to replace automobile insurance, for example, you might well find that the discount from moving to another insurance provider was far less than you expected, because unbundled from your other insurance plans, the price for your renters insurance for example could take a substantial jump. If so, like many others who have likely considered making this move, you might find it in your best interests to stick with the original bundled package, no matter how trapped or frustrated you might feel as a result.

The Concept of Mark-Up

Inherent in any pricing strategy is the need to make money—no business would last long selling items or services below cost. A *mark-up* is simply the amount added to the cost of a product in order to cover indirect costs and provide a profit. For example, if a producer of packaged cookies sold them to convenience stores for 40 cents a unit, and the convenience store resold them for 60 cents, the store would have taken a 20 cent mark-up on the cookies. Mark-up can also be calculated in percentage terms, in which case the percentage is determined from the original cost. In our cookie example, the mark-up is 50 percent—20 cents of mark-up divided by the 40 cents that the convenience store paid for them. While the concept of mark-up is most commonly used in a retail setting, it can be applied in any case in which an item is resold by an intermediary that links the producer to the ultimate consumer.

  An interactive H5P element has been excluded from this version of the text. You can view it online here: https://pressbooks.lib.vt.edu/fundamentalsofbusiness4e/?p=163#h5p-42

The Product Life Cycle

Sport utility vehicles (SUVs) are among the most popular categories of passenger car on US roads. Offering an elevated view of the road, the safety that comes with size, spacious interior and cargo areas, and often superior handling performance in bad weather—especially 4-wheel-drive SUVs—it is no wonder that American consumers have bought tens of millions of these vehicles. For a long time, SUV sales followed close to the classical pattern of what is known as the product life cycle.

Figure 15.3: *Honda, a top automotive manufacturer.*

Figure 15.4: *Product life cycle.*

Yet in 2009, when the economy faltered due to the financial crisis and oil prices surged from about $40 a barrel to nearly $80,[2] many pundits declared the SUV to be in permanent decline. In fact, the data appeared to support this contention.

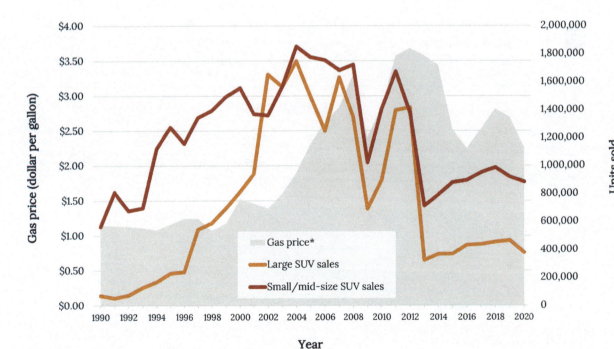

Figure 15.5: *SUV sales by size (1990-2020). *Gas prices are not adjusted for inflation.*

314 | Pricing Strategy

As you can see from the figure, SUV sales did in fact decline, rather dramatically. But SUV sales are too critical to the profitability of the major automakers for them to just watch their cash flows disappear.[3] Instead, the automakers redesigned their products, including an increased emphasis on smaller SUVs. In fact, the Honda CR-V and the Toyota RAV4, two of the smaller SUV's on the market, now battle each other for the crown of top-selling SUV in the United States.[4] Many consumers adapted their budgets to compensate for higher oil prices. Sales, particularly of mid-sized SUVs, roared back in 2010, with sales of large SUV's showing a similar, but smaller, upward trend too.

While their new designs certainly helped to reinvigorate sales, more recently automakers have gotten a somewhat unexpected additional boost from declining oil prices. For all their benefits, SUVs are not the most fuel efficient cars on the market. But as consumers began to pay less at the pump, the cost of operating SUVs declined, and SUV sales have continued to be strong. Automakers continue to invest in new models—for example, German automaker Volkswagen introduced a new 5-seat, mid-sized SUV at the Detroit auto show in January, 2015. The company is assembling a group of about 200 experts, including representatives of its dealer network, to help it better cater its offerings to the American market.[5]

Many products tend to follow the classical product life cycle pattern of figure 15.4. Let's take a closer look at the product life cycle and see what we can learn from it. The graph is a simplified depiction of the product life cycle concept. Many products never make it past the introduction stage. Some products avoid or reverse decline by reinventing themselves. In part, reinvention is what the SUV market has experienced, in addition to the boost it has received from lower gas prices.

The Life Cycle and the Changing Marketing Mix

As a product or brand moves through its life cycle, the company that markets it will shift its marketing-mix strategies. Figure 15.6 summarizes the market and industry features of each stage. Let's see how the mix might be changed to address the differences from one stage to the next.

Stage	Introduction	Growth	Maturity	Decline
Price levels	Depends on choice of introductory strategy	Converges as competitors enter market	Initially high but tend to decline as growth disappears	Initially declines but may rise as competitors exit
Number of competitors	Few	Rapidly rising	Begins to decline through consolidation	Few or one
Industry profits	Negative	Rising	Highest	Declining
Customers	Few—Innovators only	Rising—Early adopters	High/Stable, begins to drop late in cycle	Declining
Objectives	Awareness and adoption	Gain market share	Defend share and maximize profits	Milk remaining value, minimize investment

Figure 15.6: The product life cycle: characteristics of each stage.

Pricing Strategy | 315

Introduction Stage

At the start of the **introduction stage**, people—other than those who work in the industry—are likely to be completely unaware that a product even exists. Building awareness is a key to adoption of the product. Companies invest in advertising to make consumers aware of their offerings and the benefits of becoming a customer. For many products, the early adopters are people who value newness and innovation. If a company faces only limited competition, it might use a skimming approach to pricing because people who want to be among the first to have the product will generally be willing to pay a higher price (recall that "skimming" means that the company will set initial prices high, and only those consumers who feel especially excited about the product will buy it). The company will then lower prices to appeal to the next layer of consumers—those who wanted the product but were unwilling to pay the high introductory price. The company will continue to gradually lower prices, in effect taking off layer after layer of potential customers until the product is priced low enough to be afforded by the mass market.

Figure 15.7: VR headset.

If the company has or expects a lot of competition, though, it may decide to use penetration pricing and capture a lot of market share, which may discourage some potential competitors from entering the market at all. The higher the price levels in a market, the more likely it is that new competitors will want to enter.

During the introductory stage, the industry as whole will sell only a relatively small quantity of the product, so competitors will distribute the product through just a few channels. Most retailers charge what is called a "slotting fee"—a payment the manufacturer makes to persuade the retailer to stock the item. If the product fails, they do not offer refunds on these charges, so producers will want to be confident that a product will draw enough customers before they pay these fees and so may limit its initial distribution. Because sales at this stage are low while advertising and other costs are high, all competitors tend to lose money during this stage.

Growth Stage

As the competitors in an industry focus on building sales, successful products will enter a stage of rapid customer adoption, which is not surprisingly called the **growth stage** in the product life cycle. Depending on how innovative and attractive a product is, the industry might reach the growth stage relatively quickly—or it could take many months or even longer for that point to arrive, if it happens at all. In order for industry sales to increase rapidly, advertising costs will generally be very high during the growth stage. If competition appears, companies may respond by lowering prices to retain their market shares. Competitors will also be looking for channels in which to distribute their products. Where possible, they will try to establish exclusive arrangements with distributors, at least for a period of time, so that their product may be the only one available in a product category at a particular retail outlet. During the growth stage, it is also important for companies to invest in making improvements to their products so as to maintain any advantage they may have established over their competitors. Since sales are rising rapidly during the growth stage, many products begin to turn a profit here, even though they are still investing heavily in advertising, establishing distribution, and refining the product itself.

Figure 15.8: Apple watch.

Maturity Stage

If a product survives the growth stage, it will probably remain in the **maturity stage** for a long time. Sales still grow in the initial part of this stage, though at a decreasing rate. Later in the maturity stage, sales will plateau and eventually begin to move in a slightly downward direction. By this stage, if not sooner, competitors will have settled on a strategy intended to deliver them a sustainable competitive advantage—either by being the low cost producer of a product, or by successfully differentiating their product from the competition. Since at least one competitor will generally move towards a low-cost strategy, after initially peaking, price levels begin to decline during the maturity stage. Price wars may even occur, but profits still tend to be strong because sales volume remains high.

Figure 15.9: iPhones.

As the product becomes outdated, the company may make changes in keeping with changing consumer preferences, but usually not as rapidly as in the earlier stages of the life of a product. Branding becomes a key aspect of success in the maturity stage, particularly for those companies seeking to differentiate their products as their source of competitive advantage. Also during the maturity stage, industry consolidation is high; in other words, larger competitors will buy up smaller competitors in order to find synergies and build share and scale economies. Some models of the product life cycle reflect a stage called "**shakeout**," which occurs towards the end of the growth and the beginning of the maturity stages. The term shakeout reflects this trend towards industry consolidation. Some competitors survive and others get "shaken out," either by going out of business or by being acquired by a stronger competitor.

Decline Stage

At some point, virtually every product will reach the **decline stage**, the point at which sales drop significantly. New innovations, changes in consumer tastes, regulations, and other forces from the macro-level business environment can change the outlook for a product almost overnight. Products with a very short life cycle are known as "fads." They may move through the entire product life cycle in a matter of months. Many products, particularly those which have experienced a long period in maturity, may stay in the decline phase for years. Ironically, price levels during the decline stage may actually increase, which occurs because the number of competitors is few—in fact, there may be only one remaining, giving that company great pricing power over the few

Figure 15.10: A landline phone. While many households have switched to using cell phones, landlines are still used in office settings.

consumers who still want or need the product. New product development is usually very limited, unless a company believes that innovation can restart growth in the category, as we saw with new SUV models. Also, advertising is typically limited or non-existent—those who need the product are likely to know about it already. So while it may seem counter-intuitive, many companies make a lot of money while they are riding the downward shape of the product life cycle curve during the decline stage.

An interactive H5P element has been excluded from this version of the text. You can view it online here:
https://pressbooks.lib.vt.edu/fundamentalsofbusiness4e/?p=163#h5p-43

Key Takeaways

- There are several pricing strategies appropriate for different product and market situations:
    - A new product can be introduced with a **skimming strategy**—starting off with a high price that keenly interested customers are willing to pay. The alternative is a **penetration strategy,** charging a low price, both to keep out competition and to grab as much market share as possible.
    - With **cost-based pricing**, a company determines the cost of making a product and then sets a price by adding a profit to the cost.
    - With **demand-based pricing**, marketers set the price that they think consumers will pay.
    - Companies use **prestige pricing** to capitalize on the common association of high price and quality, setting an artificially high price to substantiate the impression of high quality.
    - Finally, with **odd-even pricing**, companies set prices at such figures as $9.99 (an odd amount), counting on the common impression that it sounds cheaper than $10 (an even amount).
- The stages of development and decline that products go through over their lives is called the **product life cycle**.
- The stages a product goes through are **introduction**, **growth**, **maturity**, and **decline**. A process called **shakeout** occurs during the transition between growth and maturity, resulting in fewer competitors remaining in the market.
- As a product moves through its life cycle, the company that markets it will shift its marketing-mix strategies.

References

Figures

Figure 15.1: Sony's robot dog, Aibo. Morgan. 2010. CC BY 2.0. https://en.wikipedia.org/wiki/File:AIBO_ERS-111_-_July_2010.jpg.

Figure 15.2: Odd-even pricing; it's less than $6.00! Thom Milkovic. 2017. Unsplash license. https://unsplash.com/photos/9q9QLH4yYLY.

Figure 15.3: Honda, a top automotive manufacturer. Tabea Schimpf. 2018. Unsplash license. https://unsplash.com/photos/O7WzqmeYoqc.

Figure 15.4: Product life cycle. Kindred Grey. 2022. CC BY 4.0. https://archive.org/details/15.4_20220627.

Figure 15.5: SUV sales by size (1990-2020). *Gas prices are not adjusted for inflation. Kindred Grey. 2022. CC BY 4.0. Data from https://www.energy.gov/eere/vehicles/fact-915-march-7-2016-average-historical-annual-gasoline-pump-price-1929-2015 [Gas prices (1990-1994)]; https://www.eia.gov/dnav/pet/hist/LeafHandler.ashxn=PET&s=EMM_EPM0_PTE_NUS_DPG&f=A [Gas prices (1994-2021)]; https://www.bts.gov/archive/publications/national_transportation_statistics/table_01_21 [Sales data (1990-2012)]; Wards Automotive Yearbook [Sales data (2013-2021)]. https://archive.org/details/15.5_20220627.

Figure 15.7: VR headset. Hammer & Tusk. 2016. Unsplash license. https://unsplash.com/photos/3kB63Vz7xVg.

Figure 15.8: Apple watch. Lloyd Dirks. 2017. Unsplash license. https://unsplash.com/photos/0vsk2_9dkqo.

Figure 15.9: iPhones. Daniel Romero. 2019. Unsplash license. https://unsplash.com/photos/wMTBGjh314M.

Figure 15.10: A landline phone. While many households have switched to using cell phones, landlines are still used in office settings. Julian Hochgesang. 2020. Unsplash license. https://unsplash.com/photos/Dkn8-zPIbwo.

Notes

1. Cliff Edward (2004). "Ready to Buy a Home Robot?" Business Week. Retrieved from: http://www.bloomberg.com/news/articles/2004-07-18/ready-to-buy-a-home-robot
2. Ron Scherer (2009). "Oil Prices Top a Barrel - Double the Cost of a Year Ago." Christian Science Monitor. Retrieved from: http://www.csmonitor.com/USA/2009/1224/Oil-prices-top-78-a-barrel-double-the-cost-of-a-year-ago
3. Eric Mayne (2005). "Big 3 SUV Blitz Could Backfire." Detroit News.
4. Kelsey Mays (2016). "Top 10 Best-Selling Cars: February 2016." Cars.com. Retrieved from: https://www.cars.com/articles/top-10-best-selling-cars-february-2016-1420683940927/
5. Andreas Cremer (2015). "VW Aims to Tune in to Local Tastes in Latest U.S. Turnaround Plan." Reuters. Retrieved from: http://www.reuters.com/article/autoshow-volkswagen-idUSL6N0UR0NR20150112

16. Hospitality and Tourism

Learning Objectives

- Understand what tourism is: definition, components, and importance.
- Understand the economic, social, and environmental benefits and costs of tourism.
- Define hospitality and the pineapple tradition.
- Identify the types of hotel categories and how they are determined.
- Examine the different categories of food service operations.
- Understand the different types of events, meetings, and conventions.

Tourism

The tourism industry is often cited as the largest industry in the world, contributing 10 percent of the world's GDP. In 2016 there were over 1.2 billion international tourists: that's a substantial economic impact and movement of goods and services![1] Tourism is also considered an export and is unique in that the consumers come to the product where it is consumed on-site. Before we dig any deeper, let's explore what the term "tourism" means.

Figure 16.1: Tourists gather at the Eiffel Tower.

Definition of Tourism

There are a number of ways tourism can be defined. The United Nations World Tourism Organization (UNWTO) embarked on a project from 2005 to 2007 to create a common glossary of terms for tourism. It defines tourism as follows:

> A social, cultural and economic phenomenon which entails the movement of people to countries or places outside their usual environment for personal or business/professional purposes. These people are called visitors (which may be either tourists or excursionists; residents or non-residents) and tourism has to do with their activities, some of which imply tourism expenditure.[2]

In other words, **tourism** is the movement of people for a number of purposes (whether business or pleasure). It is important to understand the various groups and constituencies involved in this movement. Of course it includes the tourist, but also the vast array of businesses providing goods and services for the tourist, the government and political structure of a destination, and the local residents of the destination community itself. Each of these components are necessary parts of a successful tourism destination and operate within private and public sectors, the built environment, and the natural environment. All these come together to create the processes, activities, and outcomes of tourism.

If it all seems a little overwhelming, it might be helpful to break tourism down into broad industry groups, each of which will be covered in this chapter:

- Accommodation and Lodging
- Food and Beverage Services (F & B)
- Recreation and Entertainment
- Convention & Event Management
- Travel Services
- Private Clubs

Benefits and Costs of Tourism

Tourism impacts can be grouped into three main categories: economic, social, and environmental. These impacts are analyzed using data gathered by businesses, governments, and industry organizations. Some impacts gain more attention than others. It is also important to recognize that different groups and constituencies are impacted differently.

Economic Impacts of Tourism

The tourism industry has a huge economic impact that continues to expand to new markets and destinations. According to the UNWTO, in 2016 "The total export value from international tourism amounted to US$ 1.5 trillion."[3] Regions with the highest growth in terms of tourism dollars earned (2016 vs 2015) are Africa, Asia and the Pacific, the Americas Europe. Only the Middle East posted negative growth at the time of the report. As well, the UNWTO's *Tourism 2030 Vision* report predicts that international arrivals will reach nearly 1.8 billion by 2030.[4] Figure 16.2 provides additional information about the impact of tourism worldwide. The global pandemic of 2020 which limited or in some cases ceased any citizen travel has had a direct and significant impact on global tourism, as outlined in Figure 16.2.

Figure 16.2: The impact of global tourism before and after the pandemic.

Positive impacts from the prior economic boom include robust foreign exchange, increases in income, and GDP growth. Tourism can also offer diverse employment opportunities, can be developed with local products, and is often compatible with other economic activities within a destination. Tourism often injects money into the community that leads to secondary economic development as well. For example, successful resorts may create the need for a commercial laundry facility or a pet boarding business.

However, there are also negative impacts. Property values may increase to the point of unaffordability for local residents, and the seasonality of the tourism industry may create a feast-or-famine economy. As with any economy, if too many resources are focused on just one industry, communities may be vulnerable to any unexpected economic, social, or environmental changes. One example is the New Jersey shore after the devastation of Hurricane Sandy in 2012. The tourism industry was severely impacted, leaving no economic fallback for local residents.

Social Impacts of Tourism

In addition to the economic benefits of tourism development, positive social impacts include an increase in amenities (e.g., parks, recreation facilities), investment in arts, culture, heritage and tradition, celebration of indigenous communities, and community pride. Tourism also has the potential to break down language, socio-cultural, religious, and political barriers. When developed conscientiously, tourism can, and does, contribute to a positive quality of life for residents and promotes a positive image of the destination.

However, as identified by the United Nations Environment Programme, negative social impacts of tourism can include: change or loss of indigenous identity and values; culture clashes; changes in family structure; conflict within the community for the tourism dollar; and ethical issues, including an increase in sex tourism, crime, gambling, and/or the exploitation of child workers.[5]

Environmental Impacts of Tourism

Tourism relies on, and greatly impacts, the natural environment in which it operates. In some destinations, there is a great appreciation of the environmental resources as the source of the tourism industry, and as such there are environmental protection policies and plans in place. Tourism has helped to save many delicate ecosystems and their flora and fauna. Preservation of these important resources benefits not only the tourist but also the local residents as well.

Even though many areas of the world are conserved in the form of parks and protected areas, tourism development can still have severe negative economic impacts. According to The United Nations Environment Programme, these can include the depletion of natural resources (water, forests, etc.), pollution (air pollution, noise, sewage, waste and littering), and physical impacts (construction activities, marina development, trampling, loss of biodiversity, and spread of disease).[6]

The environmental impacts of tourism can reach beyond local areas and have an effect on the global ecosystem. One example is increased air travel, which is often identified as a major contributor to climate change.

Whether positive or negative, tourism is a force for change around the world, and the industry is transforming at a staggering rate.

 An interactive H5P element has been excluded from this version of the text. You can view it online here: https://pressbooks.lib.vt.edu/fundamentalsofbusiness4e/?p=183#h5p-44

Accommodation and Lodging

The Hospitality Industry

When looking at tourism it is important to consider the term hospitality. Some define **hospitality** as "the business of helping people to feel welcome and relaxed and to enjoy themselves."[7] Simply put, the **hospitality industry** is the combination of the accommodation and food and beverage groupings, collectively making up the largest segment of the industry.

The pineapple has long been the symbol of hospitality. The Caribs, indigenous people of the Lower Antilles in the Caribbean, first used it as such a symbol. The Spaniards knew they were welcome if a pineapple was placed at the entrance to the village. This symbolism spread across Europe and North America where it became the custom to carve the shape of a pineapple into the columns of residences.[8] It is now common to see the image of the pineapple as a sign of welcome, warmth and hospitality.

Figure 16.3: The Pineapple Hotel in Liverpool.

The types of employees and resources required to run an accommodation business—whether it be a hotel, motel, or even a campground—are quite similar. All these businesses need staff to check in guests, provide housekeeping, employ maintenance workers, and provide a place for people to sleep. As such, they can be grouped together under the heading of **accommodation and lodging**. Figure 16.4 summarizes the various groupings within the industry.

Category	Examples
Accommodations and lodging	Hotels and motels Resorts Campgrounds/Cabins AirBnB/Home Away Timeshare
Recreation and entertainment	Gaming Theme parks Adventure and outdoor recreation
Travel services	Travel agents/OTAs Airlines Cruise ships Rail/Bus Car EcoTourism
Food and beverage services	Restaurants Catering Institutional
Conventions and event management	Meetings Expositions Social and special events
Clubs	City Private country clubs

Figure 16.4: The scope of the hospitality industry.

Hotel Types

Hotels are typically referred to by hotel type or other classifications. Hotel type is determined primarily by how it will function and what amenities will be included within the property. Size, location, service levels and type of business or targeted market segments are additional classifications. Industry also classifies hotels by chain scale ... separating hotels into categories determined by their average daily rates. Various ownership structures and brand affiliations also differentiate hotels.

Classifications

Hotels may be classified on a number of different variables. **Type of Hotel:** There are numerous classifications by hotel type including all-inclusive hotels, all-suite properties, B&B/Inns, boutique, convention/conference centers, condo hotels, resort, extended stay, full service, casino, limited service and timeshare properties. **Size and Complexity:** A hotel can be classified by the number of guest rooms it has; hotel sizes can range from a small boutique hotel with fewer than 50 rooms to a large resort hotel with more than 1,000 rooms. The complexity of the hotel is determined by the volume and number of additional revenue generating functions such as the square feet of available conference space, number of F&B operations and additional services and amenities like pools, fitness centers, spas, golf, etc. **Location:** The location of a hotel can also determine the type of guest served. An airport hotel may be very different from a city-center property in an urban environment, or a remote island resort or a small quaint bed and breakfast located on top of a mountain. Hotels that specialize in conferences, may locate near entertainment destinations like Las Vegas or Disney theme parks to provide pre-post conference activities for attendees. **Service Level:** The level of service provided is also a key variable, ranging from an inexpensive budget or economy hotel, (Limited or Focused Service Hotels) which may have limited services and amenities, to upscale and luxury hotels (Full Service Hotels) with many services and a wide range of amenities. **Market Segmentation:** Figure 16.5 outlines the characteristics of specific hotel types that have evolved to match the needs of a particular traveler segment. As illustrated, hotels adapt and diversify depending on the markets they desire and need to drive occupancy levels and generate revenues. Some hotels will specialize in a specific market segment, but in today's competitive environment, most hotels will target a combination of these segments.

Market segment	Traveler type	Characteristics
Commercial	Individual business travel	- High-volume corporate accounts in city or airport properties - Stronger demand Monday through Thursday
Leisure	Leisure travelers—family, tourists	- Purpose for travel includes sightseeing, recreation, or visiting friends and relatives - Stronger demand Friday and Saturday nights and all week during holidays and the summer
Meetings and groups	Corporate groups, associations, social, military, education, religious, and fraternal groups (aka, SMERF)	- Includes meetings, seminars, trade shows, conventions, and gatherings of over 10 people - Peak convention demand is typically spring and fall in most locations - Proximity to a conference center and meeting and banquet space increase this market
Extended stay	Business and leisure	- Often offers kitchen facilities and living room spaces - Bookings are typically more than five nights - Often business related (e.g., extended health care, construction projects, corporate projects) - Leisure demand driven by a variety of circumstances including family visiting relatives, home renovations, snowbirds escaping winter

Figure 16.5: Types of hotel market segments and their key characteristics.

There are several other industry related organizations, such as Forbes and AAA which provide **Consumer Ratings** for individual hotels … another form of classifying a property. Forbes has traditionally awarded one to five "Stars" and AAA, one to five "Diamond" ratings. Additionally, many social media applications like Trip Advisor offer hotel property ratings to consumers.

Chain Scale: Smith Travel Research (STR) is an organization that provides the lodging industry with global data benchmarking, analytics and marketplace insights. STR classifies the lodging industry into six chain scale segments according to their respective brand Average Daily Rate (ADR). The six segments are defined as **Luxury**; **Upper Upscale**; **Upscale**; Mid-Scale with F&B (**Upper Mid-Scale**); Mid-Scale without F&B (**Mid-Scale**) and **Economy.** Through STR's 30—plus years of service to the hospitality industry—they have developed vital benchmarking performance solutions, established market trend transparency and provided data used by the investment community to support hotel development projects. Their core product, the STAR report, provides hotel owners and operators with comparative performance data between their property and a defined set of market competitors and allows you to follow trends in hotel occupancy, average daily rate (ADR) and revenue per available room (RevPar). Developers, investors, industry analysts, hotel brands and management companies all utilize STR data when determine what type of hotel to build and what location would provide maximum opportunity for success.

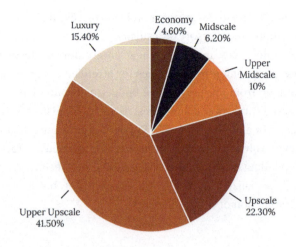

Figure 16.6: Example of a hotel market segmentation by STR's Chain Scale.

The type of ownership, brand affiliation and management are also very important variables in the classification of hotels. Owners may manage their own hotels independently but in today's competitive environment, they would likely sign a Franchise Agreement with a nationally recognized brand as well as a Management Contract with a hotel management company to manage the property. A hotel chain such as Marriott, Hilton, Hyatt or IHG (Intercontinental Hotel Group) is comprised of multiple brands: Marriott, following their recent merger with Starwood currently has 30 different hotel brands, with each name representing a different level of price, service or targeted market segments.

Branding Decision

Selecting a brand affiliation is one of the most significant decisions hotel owners must make.[9] The brand affiliation selected will largely determine the cost of hotel development or conversion of an existing property to meet the standards of the new brand. The affiliation will also determine a number of things about the ongoing operation including the level of services and amenities offered, cost of operation, marketing opportunities or restrictions, and the competitive position in the marketplace. For these reasons, owners typically consider several branding options before choosing to operate independently or to adopt a brand affiliation.

Franchise Agreements

Another managerial and ownership structure is franchising. A hotel franchise enables individuals or investment companies (the franchisee) to build or purchase a hotel and then buy or lease a brand name to become part of a chain of hotels using the franchisor's hotel brand, image, loyalty program, goodwill, procedures, cost controls, marketing, and reservations systems.[10]

Figure 16.7: The San Diego Marriott.

A franchisee becomes part of a network of properties that use a central reservations system with access to electronic distribution channels, regional and national marketing programs, central purchasing, revenue management support, and brand operating standards. A franchisee also receives training, support, and advice from the franchisor and must adhere to regular inspections, audits, and reporting requirements.

Selecting a franchise structure may reduce investment risk by enabling the franchisee to associate with an established hotel company. Franchise fees can be substantial, and a franchisee must be willing to adhere to the contractual obligations with the franchisor.[11] Franchise fees typically include an initial fee paid with the franchise application and continuing fees paid during the term of the agreement. These fees are usually a percentage of revenue but can be set at a fixed fee. The total percentage of sales ranges significantly for hotels from 3.3–14.7 percent with a median of 11.8 percent.[12]

Management Contracts

It is common for ownership to utilize a **management contract**, which is a service offered by a management company to manage a hotel or resort for its owners. Owners have two main options for the structure of a management contract. One is to enter into a management agreement with an independent third-party hotel management company to manage the hotel. There are hundreds of these companies, but some of the large organizations include Aimbridge, Benchmark Hospitality, Crescent Hotels, Interstate Hotels, and White Lodging. A slightly different option is for owners to select a single company to provide both the brand and the expertise to manage the property. Marriott, Hilton, and Hyatt, are companies that provide this second option to owners.

Figure 16.8: The Inn at Virginia Tech, managed by Benchmark Hospitality.

Hospitality and Tourism | 329

Food and Beverage Services

Figure 16.9: Fine dining.

The **food and beverage** sector is commonly known to industry professionals by its initials F&B. The F&B sector grew from simple origins to meet the basic needs for food and beverage services to increasing demand for unique experiences and broader options. As the interests of the public became more diverse, so too did the offerings of the F&B sector. The increasing awareness and demand for organic, sustainable, local or craft options as well as special dietary needs in food and beverage continue to challenge this industry. In addition, in order to better attract and serve a diverse array of diners, the F&B industry now consists of a variety of segments. The following is a discussion of each.

Quick-Service Restaurants

Figure 16.10: Subway is a quick-service restaurant.

Formerly known as fast-food restaurants, examples of **quick-service restaurants**, or QSRs, include Chick-fil-A, Subway, and Pizza Hut. This prominent portion of the food sector generally caters to both residents and visitors, and it is represented in areas that are conveniently accessed by both. Brands, chains, and franchises dominate the QSR landscape. While the sector has made steps to move away from the traditional "fast-food" image and style of service, it is still dominated by both fast food and food fast; in other words, food that is purchased and prepared quickly, and generally consumed quickly as well.

Fast-Casual Restaurants

Fast-Casual restaurants focus on higher quality ingredients than QSR's and provide made-to-order food in an environment that does not include table service. Customers usually queue and order at a counter. The seating area is more upscale and comfortable. Examples would include Chipotle Mexican Grill, Panera and Jason's Deli.

Figure 16.11: Panera is a fast-casual restaurant.

Full-Service Restaurants

Full-service restaurants are perhaps the most fluid of the F&B operation types, adjusting and changing to the demands of the marketplace. Consumer expectations are higher here than with QSRs.[13] The menus offered are varied, but in general reflect the image of the restaurant or consumer's desired experience. Major segments include fine dining, family/casual, ethnic, and upscale casual.

Fine dining restaurants are characterized by highly trained chefs preparing complex food items, exquisitely presented. Meals are brought to the table by experienced servers with sound food and beverage knowledge in an upscale atmosphere with table linens, fine china, crystal stemware, and silver-plate cutlery. The table is often embellished with fresh flowers and candles. In these businesses, the average check, which is the total sales divided by number of guests served, is quite high (often reviewed with the cost symbols of three or four dollar signs: $$$ or $$$$.) Examples include the Inn at Little Washington, Ruth's Chris Steakhouse and Capitol Grille.

Figure 16.12: A fine-dining restaurant in the Netherlands.

Casual restaurants serve moderately-priced to upscale food in a more casual atmosphere. Casual dining comprises a market segment between fast casual establishments and fine dining restaurants. Casual dining restaurants often have a full bar with separate bar staff, a larger beer menu and a limited wine menu. This segment is full of chains such as Chili's, Outback, Red Robin and Cracker Barrel as well as many independent restaurants in regional or local markets.

Family restaurants offer affordable menu items that span a variety of customer tastes. They also have the operational flexibility in menu and restaurant layout to welcome large groups of diners. An analysis of menus in family/casual restaurants reveals a high degree of operational techniques such as menu item cross-utilization, where a few key ingredients are repurposed in several ways. Both chain and independent restaurant operators flourish in this sector. Examples of chains in this category would be Golden Corral, Cici's Pizza and Ponderosa Steakhouse.

Ethnic restaurants typically reflect the owner's cultural identity, Vietnamese, Cuban, Thai, etc. The growth and changing nature of this sector reflects the acceptance of various ethnic foods within our communities. Ethnic restaurants generally evolve along two routes: toward remaining authentic to the cuisine of the country of origin or toward larger market acceptance through modifying menu items.[14] Examples would be P.F. Chang's, Tara Thai or Pei Wei.

 An interactive H5P element has been excluded from this version of the text. You can view it online here: https://pressbooks.lib.vt.edu/fundamentalsofbusiness4e/?p=183#h5p-45

Wineries, Cideries, Local Craft Beer, and Distilleries

The **beverage industry** continues to evolve as well with a strong focus on local craft beers, wines, cider and distilling. Wineries exist in almost every state, with over 300 in Virginia as of 2022.[15] Wine, bourbon, cider trails and brew pub crawls, etc. are used to generate awareness and create experiences for customers. Wineries often use event space or festivals to take advantage of the beauty of the winery and supplement their revenues.

Alcohol sales, in many ways, have continued to evolve as a unique source of tourism revenue across the United States and around the world. From wine tours in Napa, California to scotch whisky tastings in Edinburgh, Scotland consumers are seeking different tastes as a part of their travels. Alcohol producers range from small first-generation entrepreneurs to wineries that have carried a family name for decades. The size of operation can also vary considerably from small wineries that produce very small batches to huge corporations, like Constellation Brands, that control and sell multiple brands of wine, beer and liquor from producers around the world. Constellation Brands – www.cbrands.com

Wineries

Figure 16.13: Afton Mountain Vineyards, VA.

Wine and wineries have attracted consumer dollars and consumer interest for hundreds of years. Consumers not only purchase wine to taste, but many also purchase wine to collect and even use as an investment. With respect to tourism, wineries are uniquely positioned to provide a special consumer experience. Wineries are often on beautiful, well-manicured farms with elaborate tasting rooms and event venues. Growers, as a part of their story or sales pitch, will review the local terroir. The "terroir" is the blend of culture, climate, soil and terrain factors that allow for the unique growing conditions of one or more grape varieties, from which the wine is made. [16]

Because of the dependency on climate, the industry is constantly evolving due to climate change. New varietals are introduced in areas where they could not grow even 50 years ago. An interesting example is the recent popularity of the "British Sparkler". Across the English Channel, French wine and champagne brands are well-known. However, in recent years, British wine growers have been able to create exceptional sparkling wines from similar chalky soil and the same Chardonnay varietal. [17]

Cideries and Industry Legislation

The Craft Beverage Modernization and Reform Act of 2015 (CBMA) was a huge shot in the arm for entrepreneurs in the beverage industry. Overall, this act loosened the alcohol control laws permitting growers, brewers and distillers to distribute product easier. [18], [19] A portion of this act was referred to as the "Cider Act" as it enabled farmers to open Cider tasting rooms and more easily distribute canned and bottled product.[20] Multiple states like Connecticut followed suit in easing state alcohol tax and control laws. [21] Cider was the fastest growing segment of the beverage industry between 2013-2014, with a growth rate of over 75%, stealing market share from wine and beer.[22] Another version of the CBMA was passed in 2019 further extending consumer access to cider.

Local Craft Beer

In most parts of the world the offering of a cold beer goes hand in hand with hospitality. While a few global corporations do control large portions of world-wide distribution, in the United States there has been a steady growth in American Craft beer, in recent decades. The combination of the growing popularity of home brewing clubs in the 1970's and 1980's, combined with the use of the internet to share and promote brews in the 1990's and then the easing of alcohol distribution laws has created the craft brewing category. Total breweries in the United States including Regional Craft, Microbreweries, Taprooms, Brewpubs and large commercial breweries have grown from 4847 in 2015 to 8884 in 2020, according to the Brewers Association www.brewersassocaition.org. These brewery categories vary mainly based on size of production and the percent of beverage sales vs. onsite food sales. [23]

Figure 16.14: *Beer being brewed in steam-fired kettles in a Brazillian brewery.*

Craft beer makers typically pick from three very different growth strategies. The first strategy is more personal and closer to the rebel mentality of many craft beer makers. These brewers strive to leverage local resources and develop new local traditions to promote their products. Many of these brewers self-distribute their product, if it is sold outside of the brewery tasting rooms. Nearly every mid-size city in the country has an example this localized strategy. Big Lick Brewing in Roanoke, VA is an ideal example of this approach.

The second strategy is the "grow and sell" plan. A successful local brewer may fall into this plan, with a little luck, or it may be a strategy from the start to help support large scale growth. In this strategy the success of the brewer grows from a local market to a regional market. Their beer is distributed by one or more distributors who is aligned with a large national brewer. The national brewer takes note of the regional brewer growth and rather than compete directly, they purchase the regional brewer; they buy their competitor. For the smaller brewer this deal is often significant and it represents an ideal retirement strategy. The acquisition of Devils Back Bone by Anheuser Busch/Inbev is a good example. [24]

The third strategy is rarer. In this case the local brewer has more access to resources and is able to grow the brand on a large scale, moving from local to regional to a national brand, on their own. To help propel the growth of this brand it must be exceptional. To distribute the beer outside of the local market this brewer will develop multiple relationships with distributors to help support strategic growth, as market share and production grow. Sierra Nevada out of Chico, CA is one of the few such beer brands that has been able to thread this needle.

Distilleries and Mixology

Like wine and beer, distilled spirits often are a reflection of the local culture and geography. In the United States as of August 2021 there were 2290 craft sprit producers with about a third of those focused on whisky production. [25] Consumer brand preferences run strong in many categories and liquor is no exception. Craft distillers strive to create powerful branding, to not just sell the next drink, but to create customers for life. These branding programs share the brands history, geography, chemistry and culture with customers as part of an educational tasting experience. The Makers Mark Ambassador program and its sprawling distillery operation, with multiple tasting rooms, is a perfect example.

In the last few years, tequila has been the spirits category with the best growth. In 2020 it was North America's fastest growing alcoholic beverage category with 5.7 billion dollars in annual sales. [26] Celebrity endorsements along with changing consumer demographics has helped fuel the growth in this category. According to US Census Reports, Hispanic and Latino demographic growth was 23% between the 2010 and 2020 census.[27] This change in consumer demographics certainly modified the overall market composition and created new opportunities for some distillers.

The evolving industry

The COVID pandemic has let the "genie out of the bottle" in more ways than one. Restaurant owners appealed to lawmakers for some flexibility in providing alcohol to customers, in the name of saving industry jobs, and in 2019 another revision of a Craft Beverage Modernization Act 2019 was passed.[28] Many states took alcohol control laws a step further, in favor of retailer and bar owners, and permitted cocktails to go as a new legal revenue stream for business owners. Multiple states have since made the changes permanent, while some continue to have the laws on the books, as a temporary relief strategy, during the pandemic. [29]

Institutional Food Service

Institutional food service is large scale and often connected to governmental (National Parks) or corporate level organizations. Often run under a predetermined contract, the institutional F&B sector includes:

- Hospitals
- Educational institutions
- Prisons and other detention facilities
- Corporate staff cafeterias
- National Park restaurants and concessions
- Cruise ships
- Airports and other transportation terminals and operations

Examples of companies who focus on Institutional Food Service are Compass, Sodexho, Aramark.

Accommodation Food Service

This sector includes hotel restaurants and bars, room service, and self-serve dining operations (such as a breakfast room). Hotel restaurants are usually open to the public and reliant on this public patronage in addition to business from hotel guests. Collaborations between hotel and restaurant chains have seen reliable pairings such as the combination of Shula's Steakhouse and Marriott Hotels.

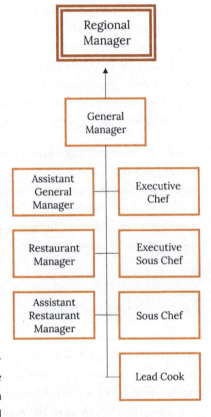

Figure 16.15: Restaurant industry career path.

Restaurant Industry Profitability and Cost Control

According to the National Restaurant Association, QSRs have the highest pre-tax profit margin at 6.6 percent, while full-service restaurants have a margin of 6.1 percent. There will be significant variances from these percentages at individual locations, even within the same brand.[30]

Restaurant operating expenses	% of total revenue (full-service)	% of total revenue (QSR)
Cost of food and beverage sales	33%	33%
Salaries and wages (including benefits)	33%	28%
Fixed costs (rent, taxes, property insurance, etc.)	6%	3%

Figure 16.16: Restaurant operating expenses as a percent of revenue.

336 | Hospitality and Tourism

A number of costs influence the profitability of an F&B operation. Some of the key operating expenses (as a percentage of revenue) are detailed in figure 16.16[31], above, where food cost and salaries & wages are the two major expenses, each accounting for approximately a third of the total. Other expenses include rental and leasing of venue, utilities, advertising, and depreciation of assets. These percentages represent averages, and will vary greatly by sector and location.

Cost control and containment is essential for all F&B businesses. Demanding particular attention are the labor, food, and beverage costs, also known as the operator's primary costs. In addition to these big ticket items, there is the cost of reusable operating supplies such as cutlery, glassware, china, and linen in full-service restaurants.

Recreation and Entertainment

Recreation

Recreation can be defined as the pursuit of leisure activities during one's spare time[32] and can include vastly different activities such as golfing, sport fishing, and rock climbing. Defining recreation as it pertains to tourism, however, is more challenging.

Let's start by exploring some recreation-based terms that are common in the tourism industry. Outdoor recreation can be defined as "outdoor activities that take place in a natural setting, as opposed to a highly cultivated or managed landscape such as a playing field or golf course."[33] This term is typically applied to outdoor activities in which individuals engage close to their community. When these activities are further away, and people must travel some distance to participate in them, they are often described as "adventure tourism". According to the United Nations World Tourism Organization (UNWTO), adventure tourism is "a trip that includes at least two of the following three elements: physical activity, natural environment, and cultural immersion."[34]

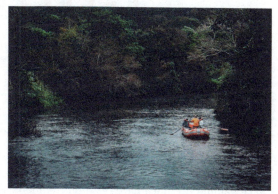

Figure 16.17: Adventure tourism: whitewater rafting in Argentina.

Ultimately, categorization is based on a combination of several factors, including manner of engagement in the activity (risk exposure, experience requirement, group or solo activity), the distance travelled to access the activity, and the type of environment (proximity to nature, level of challenge involved) in which the activity occurs.

According to the 2021 Global Adventure Tourism Market Report, the global adventure travel market is expecting an elevation of $2.02 billion (in U.S. dollars) by 2030 and is witnessing a compound annual growth rate of 10.7 percent from 2020-30.[35]

Entertainment

Entertainment is a very broad category which overlaps with many of the areas discussed elsewhere in this chapter, like hotels and accommodation. Two major types of entertainment that we'll discuss here are gaming and theme parks.

Gaming

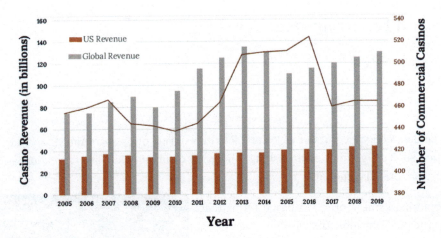

Figure 16.18: U.S. and global casino revenues (2005-2019).

Gaming has grown significantly in the United States and globally. The number of casinos in the United States has been growing since 2010, as shown in figure 16.18. Casinos are found all over the United States in major cities, riverboats, and on Native American lands. However, US casino revenue has been relatively flat, while global gaming revenues have been on the increase, largely due to Asian market growth. Most casinos involve other facets of the Hospitality industry such as lodging, F&B, golf, entertainment, spas, etc., but they also have the added challenges of casino operations.

Theme Parks

Theme parks have a long history dating back to the 1500's in Europe, and have evolved ever since. Today, it is hard not to compare any amusement park destination to Disneyland and Disney World. Opened in 1955 in sunny California, Disneyland set the standard for theme parks. Theme parks outside of California and Florida are often highly seasonal operations challenged with significant staffing and training requirements each year.

Figure 16.19: Disney is one of the most well-known theme parks.

Convention and Event Management

A **convention** is a large meeting of people with similar interests who meet for a period of at least a few days to discuss their field. An **event** is a gathering at a given place and time, usually of some importance, often celebrating or commemorating a special occasion.

Both conventions and events can be extremely complex projects, which is why, over time, the role of meeting planners has taken on greater importance. The development of education, training programs, and professional designations such as CMPs (Certified Meeting Planners), CSEP (Certified Special Events Professional), and CMM (Certificate in Meeting Management) has led to increased credibility in this business and demonstrates the importance of the sector to the economy.

Meeting planners may be independent contractors hired to facilitate the planning process, work directly for the company full time to coordinate their meeting, or work for hotels, conference centers and event venues directly.

- The various tasks involved in meeting and event planning include:
- Conceptualizing/theming
- Site inspection & selection
- Logistics and planning
- Human resource management
- Security
- Marketing and public relations
- Budgeting and financial management
- Sponsorship procurement
- Management and evaluation

Event Categories

Mega-Events

A **mega-event** is a large scale, highly prestigious event such as the Olympic Games, the FIFA World Cup, or a global economic summit. These events typically gain tremendous media coverage and have major economic impacts on the host location, both positive and negative. High levels of tourism (1 million visitors) associated with a mega-event brings revenue, but the revenue may be outweighed by substantial capital and social costs incurred by the host. The events are often awarded to host destinations through a bidding process and gain tremendous media coverage.

Figure 16.20: The Bejing olympics is an example of a mega-event.

Special Events

A **special event** is a one-time or infrequent specific ritual, presentation, performance, or celebration. Special events are planned and created to mark a special occasion, such as a presidential inauguration or the Queen of England's 90th birthday. Like mega-events, there may be significant media coverage and economic impact for the host city or destination.

Hallmark Events

A **hallmark event** is a unique event that is often identified with the location where it is held, like Carnival in Rio de Janeiro or Oktoberfest in Munich. Hallmark events contribute significant economic benefits and even can create a competitive advantage for the host city or destination that attracts tourists.

Festival

A **festival** is a themed public celebration that conveys, through a kaleidoscope of activities, certain meaning to participants and spectators. Festivals are often celebrations of community or culture and feature music, dance, or dramatic performances. Examples include Lollapalooza, the Cannes Film Festival, and Junkanoo in the Bahamas.

Figure 16.21: Mardi Gras in New Orleans, 2018.

Local Community Events

A local **community event** is generated by and for locals; although it may attract tourists, its main audience is the local community. The community may experience measurable economic impacts, as might happen at The Steppin' Out Street Fair in Blacksburg (think hotel stays and eating out). Fundraisers and community picnics are also examples in this category.

Meetings and Conventions

The tourism industry also has a long history of creating, hosting, and promoting meetings and conventions that draw business travelers. In fact, Convention and Visitor Bureau's (CVB's) work hard to attract these meetings and conventions to their city to drive economic benefit for hotels, restaurants, entertainment venues, etc.

There are several types of such events

Conventions generally have very large attendance, and are held on a regular schedule but in different locations. They also often require a bidding process. Political conventions are one such example.

Association Meetings or Conferences are held regionally and nationally for hundreds of associations or events focused on specific themes. Examples would be the National Restaurant Association Annual Convention, ComicCon, or the National Auto Show.

Corporate Meetings will vary significantly in size and purpose and include regional or national sales meetings, shareholder meetings, training sessions, or celebrations. The location will vary depending on the nature of the meeting. They may be held at an airport property, a traditional corporate meeting facility or even an upscale resort.

Trade Shows and **Trade Fairs** can be stand-alone events, or adjoin a convention or conference.

Seminars, **Workshops**, and **Retreats** are examples of smaller-scale events.

As meeting planners have become more creative, meeting and convention delegates have been more demanding about meeting sites. No longer are hotel meeting rooms and convention centers the only type of location used; non-traditional venues have adapted and become competitive in offering services for meeting planners. These include architectural spaces such as airplane hangars, warehouses, or rooftops and experiential venues such as aquariums, museums, and galleries.[36]

Travel Services

Transportation and travel services are another large element of the tourism industry. This area includes cruise ships, airlines, rail, car rentals, and even ride sharing such as Uber and Lyft. Each of these segments is impacted significantly by fuel costs, safety issues, load factors and government regulation.

Cruises

If you've ever been on a cruise, you are in good company. According to CLIA (Cruise Lines International Association), 23 million passengers were expected to go on a cruise worldwide on 62 member lines in 2015.[37] The industry employs over 900,000 people.[38]

Figure 16.22: Cruise ship near St. Thomas, U.S. Virgin Islands.

Over 55 percent of the world's cruise passengers are from North America, and the leading destinations (based on ship deployments), according to CLIA are:[39]

- The Caribbean (36 percent)
- The Mediterranean (20 percent)
- Northern Europe (11 percent)
- Australia/New Zealand (6 percent)
- Alaska (6 percent)
- Asia (5 percent)
- South America (3 percent)

Travel Services

The **travel services sector** is made up of a complex web of relationships between a variety of suppliers, tourism products, destination marketing organizations, tour operators, and travel agents, among many others. Under the North American Industry Classification System (NAICS), the travel services industry group includes "establishments primarily engaged in travel arrangement and reservation services. Examples ... are tourist and travel agencies; travel tour operators and wholesale operators; convention and visitors' bureaus; airline, bus, railroad and steamship ticket offices; sports and theatrical ticket offices; and airline, hotel and restaurant reservation offices."[40] Tourism services support industry development and the delivery of guest experiences.

Travel Agencies

A **travel agency** is a business that operates as the intermediary between the travel industry (supplier) and the traveler (purchaser). Part of the role of the travel agency is to market prepackaged travel tours and holidays to potential travelers. The agency can further function as a broker between the traveler and hotels, car rentals, and tour companies.[41] Travel agencies can be small and privately owned or part of a larger entity.

Online Travel Agencies (OTAs)

Online travel agents (OTAs) are companies that aggregate accommodations and transportation options and allow users to choose one or many components of their trip based on price or other incentives. Examples of OTAs include Booking.com, Expedia.com, Hotwire.com, and Kayak.com. OTAs are gaining popularity with the travelling public. Revenue of leading online travel agencies (OTAs) worldwide rose in 2021 over the previous year, after dropping sharply in 2020 due to the coronavirus (COVID-19) pandemic. Despite the substantial increase, however, the figures did not catch up yet with pre-pandemic levels. Overall, Booking was the OTA recording the highest revenue in 2021, generating nearly 11 billion U.S. dollars. Expedia placed second on the ranking, with roughly 8.6 billion U.S. dollars that year.[42]

Tour Operators

A **tour operator** packages all or most of the components of an offered trip and then sells them to the traveler. These packages can also be sold through retail outlets or travel agencies.[43] Tour operators work closely with hotels, transportation providers, and attractions in order to purchase large volumes of each component and package these at a better rate than the traveler could by purchasing individually.

Destination Marketing Organizations (DMOs)

Destination marketing organizations (DMOs) include national tourism boards, state/provincial tourism offices, and community convention and visitor bureaus around the world. DMOs promote "the long-term development and marketing of a destination, focusing on convention sales, tourism marketing and service"[44].

Country Clubs

Country clubs are another part of the Hospitality industry with a very different service strategy focusing on serving members who will develop relationships with the staff compared to a more transactional service interaction in lodging, restaurants or airlines.

Country clubs do not focus as strongly on profit as they do on maximizing member satisfaction, retention and growth while maintaining an attractive fee structure. Country (or city) clubs, will typically have restaurant and bar operations, catered events and other amenities such as golf, tennis, pool, fitness facilities, etc. Depending on the type of club, family and youth events are important to maintain and grow membership.

Figure 16.23: *The Old Course at Half Moon Bay, CA.*

Strong customer service, culinary, event management and general management skills are necessary to be successful in clubs.

Chapter Video

As in any other fast-moving industry, the landscape in Hospitality and Tourism is always changing. This video explores 10 of the more important current trends impacting the industry.

 One or more interactive elements has been excluded from this version of the text. You can view them online here: https://www.youtube.com/watch?v=SJ8Momwv7Qk

Hospitality and Tourism | 345

> **Key Takeaways**
>
> - The **Tourism** industry is the largest industry in the world with significant benefit and costs to a region. The global competition for the tourism dollar is significant within the US and between countries.
> - **Hotels** vary significantly in size, quality, purpose, chain affiliation, and ownership. The complexity of the operation and leadership vary as well.
> - **Food and Beverage** is made up of a wide variety of restaurant types from QSR, Fast Casual, Fine Dining and Ethnic. **Institutional food service in business**, hospitals, education, parks and concessions are a significant part of the Food and Beverage industry.
> - The evolution of tastes and consumer expectations in food and beverage continue to provide opportunity and challenges in the industry for ethnic sustainable, organic, local, craft, and other unique experiences.

References

Portions of this chapter were adapted from Westcott, Morgan (Ed) *Introduction to Tourism and Hospitality in BC*. CC BY 4.0. https://opentextbc.ca/introtourism. Available for free at: http://open.bccampus.ca.

Figures

Figure 16.1: Tourists gather at the Eiffel Tower. Siebe Warmoeskerken. 2018. Unsplash license. https://unsplash.com/photos/mxNrtFzOd-I.

Figure 16.2: The impact of global tourism before and after the pandemic. Kindred Grey. 2022. CC BY 4.0. Data from https://wttc.org/Portals/0/Documents/Reports/2021/Global%20Economic%20Impact%20and%20Trends%202021.pdf [international spending, GDP, and jobs]; https://data.worldbank.org/indicator/BX.GSR.TRVL.ZS [global service exports]. https://archive.org/details/16.2_20220627.

Figure 16.3: The Pineapple Hotel in Liverpool. Rodhullandemu. 2012. CC BY-SA 3.0. https://commons.wikimedia.org/wiki/File:Pineapple,_Park_Road,_Liverpool.jpg.

Figure 16.6: Example of a hotel market segmentation by STR's Chain Scale. Kindred Grey. 2022. CC BY 4.0. https://archive.org/details/16.6_20220627.

Figure 16.7: The San Diego Marriott. Christina Hsu. 2009. CC BY-NC-SA 2.0. https://flic.kr/p/6KZ5Cv.

Figure 16.8: The Inn at Virginia Tech, managed by Benchmark Hospitality. Anastasia Cortes. 2016. Public domain. Provided by Steve Skripak.

Figure 16.9: Fine dining. Delightin Dee. 2021. Unsplash license. https://unsplash.com/photos/_WI3DGseB3g.

Figure 16.10: Subway is a quick-service restaurant. Szymon12455. 2018. Unsplash license. https://unsplash.com/photos/-jv94-xYy-E.

Figure 16.11: Panera is a fast-casual restaurant. Mike Mozart. 2014. CC BY 2.0. https://commons.wikimedia.org/wiki/File:Panera_Bread_(13883443466).jpg.

Figure 16.12: A fine-dining restaurant in the Netherlands. Ronan Kruithof. 2019. Unsplash license. https://unsplash.com/photos/PCE0T5i4pDI.

Figure 16.13: Afton Mountain Vineyards, VA. Kevin Oliver. 2017. CC BY-NC-ND 2.0. https://flic.kr/p/V9h6v5.

Figure 16.14: Beer being brewed in steam-fired kettles in a Brazillian brewery. Roberta keiko Kitahara Santana. 2019. Unsplash license. https://unsplash.com/photos/RfL3l-I1zhc.

Figure 16.15: Restaurant industry career path. Kindred Grey. 2022. CC BY 4.0. https://archive.org/details/16.15_202206.

Figure 16.16: Restaurant operating expenses as a percent of revenue. Adapted from National Restaurant Association (2016). Restaurant Operations Report 2016 Edition. Washington, D.C.

Figure 16.17: Adventure tourism: whitewater rafting in Argentina. Jonatan Lewczuk. 2018. Unsplash license. https://unsplash.com/photos/hN7jhC_YWk0.

Figure 16.18: U.S. and global casino revenues (2005-2019). (2005-2015) Data Retrieved from: https://gaming.unlv.edu/reports/national_annual_revenues.pdf; 2016 data retrieved from: https://web.archive.org/web/20170301070205/http://gaming.unlv.edu/reports/national_monthly.pdf; 2017 data retrieved from: https://www.americangaming.org/resources/state-of-the-states-2018-the-aga-survey-of-the-commercial-casino-industry/; 2018 data retrieved from: https://web.archive.org/web/20190201140714/https://gaming.unlv.edu/reports/national_monthly.pdf; 2019 data retrieved from: https://abcnews.go.com/Entertainment/wireStory/us-commercial-casinos-won-436-billion-2019-37-71069042; Global revenue data retrieved from: https://www.statista.com/statistics/271577/global-casino-gaming-market-revenue/; Number of commercial casinos data retrieved from: https://www.statista.com/statistics/187972/number-of-us-commercial-casinos-since-2005/.

Figure 16.19: Disney is one of the most well-known theme parks. Bastien Nvs. 2020. Unsplash license. https://unsplash.com/photos/g3CR0UJ1CyM.

Figure 16.20: The Bejing olympics is an example of a mega-event. zhang kaiyv. 2021. Unsplash license. https://unsplash.com/photos/VAnriQouDIw.

Figure 16.21: Mardi Gras in New Orleans, 2018. Cayetano Gil. 2018. Unsplash license. https://unsplash.com/photos/T0tb5Olqkis.

Figure 16.22: Cruise ship near St. Thomas, U.S. Virgin Islands. Peter Hansen. 2017. Unsplash license. https://unsplash.com/photos/MeGmdPNe36w.

Figure 16.23: The Old Course at Half Moon Bay, CA. Cristina Glebova. 2022. Unsplash license. https://unsplash.com/photos/ihZwGiVMUCY.

Notes

1. World Tourism Organization UNWTO (2015). "Why Tourism?" Retrieved from: http://www2.unwto.org/content/why-tourism
2. United Nations Statistics Division (2010, December). "Tourism as an Internationally Traded Service and Beyond." Newsletter of the Interagency Task Force on Statistics of International Trade in Services. No. 6. p. 1. Retrieved from: http://unstats.un.org/unsd/tradeserv/tfsits/newsletter/TFSITS_newsletter_6.pdf
3. World Tourism Organization UNWTO (2015). "Exports from International Tourism Rise 4% in 2015." Retrieved from: http://media.unwto.org/press-release/2016-05-03/exports-international-tourism-rise-4-2015
4. Association of Bhutanese Tour Operators (2010). "UNWTO Tourism Vision 2020 Forecast Released." Retrieved from: http://www.abto.org.bt/2010/06/unwto-tourism-2020-vision-forecast-released/
5. United Nations Environment Programme (2016). "Negative Socio-Cultural Impacts from Tourism." Retrieved from: http://www.unep.org/resourceefficiency/Business/SectoralActivities/Tourism/FactsandFiguresaboutTourism/ImpactsofTourism/Socio-CulturalImpacts/NegativeSocio-CulturalImpactsFromTourism/tabid/78781/Default.aspx
6. United Nations Environment Programme (2016). "Tourism's Three Main Impact Areas." Retrieved from: http://www.unep.org/resourceefficiency/Business/SectoralActivities/Tourism/TheTourismandEnvironmentProgramme/FactsandFiguresaboutTourism/ImpactsofTourism/EnvironmentalImpacts/TourismsThreeMainImpactAreas/tabid/78776/Default.aspx
7. Discover Hospitality (2015). "What is Hospitality?" Retrieved from: https://web.archive.org/web/20150814071021/http://discoverhospitality.com.au/what-is-hospitality
8. L. P. Coyle (1982). "Pineapple" in *World Encyclopedia of Food*. New York: Facts on File. p. 517.
9. C. Crandell, K. Dickinson, and G. I. Kanter (2004). "Negotiating the hotel management contract" In *Hotel Asset Management: Principles & Practices*. East Lansing, MI: University of Denver and American Hotel & Lodging Educational Institute.
10. S. Rushmore (2005). "What Does a Hotel Franchise Cost?" Canadian Lodging Outlook. Retrieved from: www.hotel-online.com/News/PR2005_4th/Oct05_FranchiseCost.html
11. Ibid.; N. Migdal (n.d.). "Franchise Agreements vs. Management Agreements: Which One Do I Choose?" Hotel Business Review. Retrieved from: hotelexecutive.com/business_review/2101/test-franchise-agreements-vs-management-agreements-which-one-do-i-choose
12. Stephen Rushmore Jr., Erin S. Bagley (2014). "2014 United States Hotel Franchise Fee Guide." HVS. Retrieved from: http://www.hvs.com/article/7097/2014-united-states-hotel-franchise-fee-guide/
13. H. G. Parsa, K. R. Lord, S. Putrevu, and J. Kreeger (2015). "Corporate Social and Environmental Responsibility in Services; Will Consumers Pay for It?" Journal of Retailing and Consumer Services. Vol. 22. pp. 250-260.
14. A. H. Mak, M. Lumbers, A. Eves, and R. C. Change (2012). "Factors Influencing Tourist Food Consumption." International Journal of Hospitality Management. Vol. 31. No. 3. pp. 928-936.
15. Virginia is for Wine Lovers. (n.d.) Virginia is for Lovers. Retrieved from: https://www.virginia.org/things-to-do/food-and-drink/wineries
16. Kathleen Willcox, July 6, 2017, "Climate change is putting English Sparkling Wine on the Map" Retrieved from https://www.vinepair.com/articles
17. Craft Beverage Modernization and Tax Reform Act of 2015, S. 1562, 114th Cong. (2015). Retrieved from: https://www.congress.gov/bill/114th-congress/senate-bill/1562/text
18. Wyden, Ron (2015). One Pager Craft Beverage Modernization and Tax Reform Act of 2015. Retrieved from: https://www.wyden.senate.gov/imo/media/doc/One%20Pager.pdf
19. CIDER Act, H. R. 600, 114th Cong. (2015). Retrieved from: https://www.congress.gov/bill/114th-congress/house-bill/600/text
20. Pazniokas, Mark and Moore, Maya. (2019) CT Legislature Passes Law to Help Beer, Cider Makers, Hartford Business

Journal. Retrieved from: https://www.hartfordbusiness.com/article/ct-legislature-passes-law-to-help-beer-cider-makers

21. Jaken Emen, "What the Country's New Cider Act Means for You" Retrieved from: https://www.eater.com/2016/1/28/10854324/new-us-cider-act
22. Brewers Association (n.d.), For Small & Independent Craft Brewers, Brewers Association. Retrieved from: https://www.brewersassociation.org
23. Hudson Lindenberger, June 16, 2021 , "Alcohol Consumption In the US Saw Its Most Significant Volume Gain in Almost Two Decades" Retrieved from: https://www.forbes.com/sites/hudsonlindenberger/2021/06/16/alcohol-consumption-in-the-united-states-saw-its-most-significant-volume-gain-in-almost-two-decades-in-2020/?sh=5b55ed8b724d
24. Maisey, Jeff (2016, May 19). Devil of a Deal, Virginia Craft Beer. Retrieved from: https://virginiacraftbeer.com/devil-of-a-deal
25. Maker's Mark Ambassador Program (n.d.) Maker's Mark Ambassador Experience. Retrieved from: https://www.makersmark.com/ambassadors
26. Fortune Business Insights (n.d.). Tequila Market Share, Size & COVID-19 Impact Analysis. Report ID: FBI104172. Retrieved from: https://www.fortunebusinessinsights.com/tequila-market-104172
27. U.S. Census Bureau, (2021, August 12). 2020 Census Illuminates Racial and Ethnic Composition of the Country. Retrieved from: https://www.census.gov/library/stories/2021/08/improved-race-ethnicity-measures-reveal-united-states-population-much-more-multiracial.html
28. Pete Johnson, P. (2020, November 17). Craft Beverage Modernization and tax reform act. Brewers Association. Retrieved from: https://www.brewersassociation.org/current-issues/craft-beverage-modernization-and-tax-reform-act-24
29. Lucas, A. (2021, June 1). To-Go Cocktails Will Stick Around in at Least 20 States After the Pandemic. CNBC. Retrieved from: https://www.cnbc.com/2021/05/28/to-go-cocktails-will-stick-around-in-at-least-20-states-after-covid.html
30. American Restaurant Association and Deloitte Development LLC (2016). *2016 Restaurant Operations Report*. Washington, D.C.: National Restaurant Association. p. 5.
31. Ibid.
32. J. Tribe (2011). *The Economics of Recreation, Leisure, and Tourism*, 4th ed. Oxford, England: Elsevier.
33. Tourism BC (2013). "2009/2010 Outdoor Recreation Study." Destination British Columbia. Retrieved from: http://www.destinationbc.ca/getattachment/Research/Research-by-Activity/All-Research-by-Activity/Outdoor-Recreation-Study-2009-2010,-January-2013/Outdoor-Recreation-for-Distribution-14Jan13-FINAL-DRAFT-(2).pdf.aspx
34. United Nations World Tourism Organization (2014). *Global Report on Adventure Tourism*. UNWTO and the Adventure Tourism Trade Association. p. 12. Retrieved from: http://cf.cdn.unwto.org/sites/all/files/pdf/final_1global_report_on_adventure_tourism.pdf
35. Publisher. (2021, August 16). Adventure Travel is Trending Upward. Leisure Group Travel. Retrieved from: https://leisuregrouptravel.com/adventure-travel-is-trending-upward/
36. K. Colston (2014, April 24). "Non-Traditional Event Venues – Endless Entertainment." Retrieved from: http://helloendless.com/non-traditional-event-venues/
37. CLIA (2016). *CLIA 2015 Annual Report: One Voice: Advancing Our Industry Together*. Cruise Lines International Association. p. 10. Retrieved from: http://www.cruising.org/docs/default-source/market-research/clia_2015_annualreport_web.pdf?sfvrsn=0
38. Ibid.
39. CLIA (2015). *CLIA 2015 Cruise Industry Outlook: Cruising to New Horizons and Offering Travelers More*. Cruise Lines International Association. p. 28. Retrieved from: http://www.cruising.org/docs/default-source/research/2015-cruise-industry-outlook.pdf
40. Government of Canada (2014). "NAICS 2007: 5615 Travel Arrangement and Reservation Services." Statistics Canada. Retrieved from: http://stds.statcan.gc.ca/naics-scian/2007/cs-rc-eng.asp?criteria=5615
41. C. Goeldner and B. Ritchie (2003). *Tourism: Principles, Practices, Philosophies*, 9th ed. Hoboken, New Jersey: John Wiley & Sons, Inc.
42. Published by Statista Research Department, & 24, M. (2022, May 24). Revenue of Leading OTAs Worldwide 2021. Statista. Retrieved from: https://www.statista.com/statistics/934995/revenue-of-leading-otas-worldwide/
43. C. Goeldner and B. Ritchie (2003). *Tourism: Principles, Practices, Philosophies*, 9th ed. Hoboken, New Jersey: John Wiley & Sons, Inc.
44. The Destination Marketing Association International (2014). "The value of DMOs." Retrieved from: http://www.destinationmarketing.org/value-dmos

17. Accounting and Financial Information

Learning Objectives

- Define accounting and explain the differences between managerial accounting and financial accounting.
- Identify some of the users of accounting information and explain how they use it.
- Explain the function of the income statement.
- Explain the function of the balance sheet.
- Calculate a break-even point given the necessary information.
- Evaluate a company's performance using financial statements and ratio analysis.
- Define finance and how the role of the financial manger impacts a firm's overall strategy.
- Explain the key differences between debt and equity, and understand the major types and features of long-term debt.

Apple Inc. is the most valuable company in the world. This statement is based on market value, which in April 2022 was roughly $2.9 trillion.[1] Although markets can fluctuate, sometimes wildly, if you are reading this chapter for a course only months later, it is unclear whether Apple will have retained or ceded its leadership position to Microsoft, which has taken the leadership position multiple times since 2018.

You may wonder what kind of information is used to make these determinations. How does the market know that Apple should be valued more than $500 billion higher than Microsoft, for example?[2] Do investors just make their decisions on instinct? Well, some do, but it's not a formula for sustained success. In most cases, in deciding how much to pay for a company, investors rely on published accounting and financial information released by publicly-traded companies. This chapter will introduce you to the subject of accounting and financial information so you can begin to get an understanding for how the valuation process works.

Figure 17.1: Amazon's headquarters in Seattle, Washington.

The Role of Accounting

Accounting is often called "the language of business" because it communicates so much of the information that owners, managers, and investors need to evaluate a company's financial performance. These people are stakeholders in the business—they're interested in its activities because they're affected by them. The financial futures of owners and other investors may depend heavily on strong financial performance from the business, and when performance is poor, managers may be replaced or laid off in a downsizing. In fact, a key purpose of accounting is to help stakeholders make better business decisions by providing them with financial information. You shouldn't try to run an organization or make investment decisions without accurate and timely financial information, and it is the accountant who prepares this information. More importantly, accountants make sure that stakeholders understand the meaning of financial information, and they work with both individuals and organizations to help them use financial information to deal with business problems. Actually, collecting all the numbers is the easy part. The hard part is analyzing, interpreting, and communicating the information. Of course, you also have to present everything clearly while effectively interacting with people from every business discipline. In any case, we're now ready to define **accounting** as the process of measuring and summarizing business activities, interpreting financial information, and communicating the results to management and other decision makers.

Fields of Accounting

Accountants typically work in one of two major fields. **Management accountants** provide information and analysis to decision makers inside the organization in order to help them run it. **Financial accountants** furnish information to individuals and groups both inside and outside the organization in order to help them assess its financial performance. Their primary focus, however, is on external parties. In other words, management accounting helps you keep your business running while financial accounting tells the outside world how well you're running it.

Management Accounting

Management accounting, also known as managerial accounting, plays a key role in helping managers carry out their responsibilities. Because the information that it provides is intended for use by people who perform a wide variety of jobs, the format for reporting information is flexible. Reports are tailored to the needs of individual managers, and the purpose of such reports is to supply relevant, accurate, timely information that will aid managers in making decisions. In preparing, analyzing, and communicating such information, accountants work with individuals from all the functional areas of the organization—human resources, operations, marketing, etc.

Figure 17.2: *The role of managerial accounting.*

Financial Accounting

Financial accounting is responsible for preparing the organization's **financial statements**—including the **income statement**, the **statement of owner's equity**, the **balance sheet**, and the **statement of cash flows**—that summarize a company's past performance and evaluate its current financial condition. If a company is traded publicly on a stock market such as the NASDAQ, these financial statements must be made public, which is not true of the internal reports produced by management accountants. In preparing financial statements, financial accountants adhere to a uniform set of rules called **generally accepted accounting principles** (GAAP)—the basic principles for financial reporting issued by an independent agency called the **Financial Accounting Standards Board** (FASB). Users want to be sure that financial statements have been prepared according to GAAP because they want to be sure that the information reported in them is accurate. They also know that when financial statements have been prepared by the same rules, they can be compared from one company to another.

While companies headquartered in the United States follow US-based GAAP, many companies located outside the United States follow a different set of accounting principles called **International Financial Reporting Standards** (IFRS). These multinational standards, which are issued by the International Accounting Standards Board (IASB), differ from US GAAP in a number of important ways, but we're not at the point yet of exploring these sometimes fine distinctions. Bear in mind, however, that, according to most experts, a single set of worldwide standards will eventually emerge to govern the accounting practices of both US and non-US companies.

Who Uses Financial Accounting Information?

The users of managerial accounting information are pretty easy to identify—basically, they're a firm's managers. We need to look a little more closely, however, at the users of financial accounting information, and we also need to know a little more about what they do with the information that accountants provide them.

Owners and Managers

In summarizing the outcomes of a company's financial activities over a specified period of time, financial statements are, in effect, report cards for owners and managers. They show, for example, whether the company did or didn't make a profit and furnish other information about the firm's financial condition. They also provide some information that managers and owners can use in order to take corrective action, though reports produced by management accountants offer a much greater level of depth.

Investors and Creditors

Investors and **creditors** furnish the money that a company needs to operate, and not surprisingly, they want to know how that business is performing. Because they know that it's impossible to make smart investment and loan decisions without accurate reports on an organization's financial health, they study financial statements to assess a company's performance and to make decisions about continued investment.

According to the world's most successful investor, Warren Buffett, the best way to prepare yourself to be an investor is to learn all the accounting you can. Buffet, chairman and CEO of Berkshire Hathaway, a company that invests in other companies, turned an original investment of $10,000 into a net worth of $96 billion as of 2022.[3] in four decades, and he did it, in large part, by paying close attention to financial accounting reports.

Figure 17.3: Warren Buffet, presidential medal of freedom recipient in 2011.

Figure 17.4: The role of financial accounting.

Government Agencies

Businesses are required to furnish financial information to a number of government agencies. Publicly-owned companies, for example—the ones whose shares are traded on a stock exchange—must provide annual financial reports to the **Securities and Exchange Commission** (SEC), a federal agency that regulates stock trades and which is charged with ensuring that companies tell the truth with respect to their financial positions. Companies must also provide financial information to local, state, and federal taxing agencies, including the Internal Revenue Service (IRS).

Other Users

A number of other external users have an interest in a company's financial statements. Suppliers, for example, need to know if the company to which they sell their goods is having trouble paying its bills or may even be at risk of going under. Employees and labor unions are interested because salaries and other forms of compensation are dependent on an employer's performance.

Figures 17.2 and 17.4 illustrate the main users of management and financial accounting and the types of information produced by accountants in the two areas. In the rest of this chapter, we'll learn how to prepare a set of financial statements and how to interpret them. We'll also discuss issues of ethics in the accounting communities and career opportunities in the accounting profession.

 An interactive H5P element has been excluded from this version of the text. You can view it online here: https://pressbooks.lib.vt.edu/fundamentalsofbusiness4e/?p=190#h5p-46

Understanding Financial Statements

We hope that, so far, at least one thing is clear: If you're in business, you need to understand financial statements. The law no longer allows high-ranking executives to plead ignorance or fall back on delegation of authority when it comes to responsibility for a firm's financial reporting. In a business environment tainted by episodes of fraudulent financial reporting and other corporate misdeeds, top managers are now being held responsible for the financial statements issued by the people who report to them. Top managers need to know how well the company is performing. Financial information helps managers identify signs of impending trouble before it is too late.

The Function of Financial Statements

Put yourself in the place of Connie in figure 17.5, who runs Connie's Confections out of her home. She loves what she does, and she feels that she's doing pretty well. In fact, she has an opportunity to take over a nearby store at very reasonable rent, and she can expand by getting a modest bank loan and investing some more of her own money. So it's decision time for Connie: She knows that the survival rate for start-ups isn't very good, and before taking the next step, she'd like to get a better idea of whether she's actually doing well enough to justify the risk. The basic financial statements will give her some answers.

Since this book is for an introductory course, we will focus our attention on the income statement and balance sheet only, even though we mentioned other financial statements earlier in the chapter.

Toying with a Business Idea

To bring this concept closer to home, let's assume that you need to earn money while you're in college and that you've decided to start a small business. Your business will involve selling stuff to other college students, and to keep things simple, we'll assume that you're going to operate on a "cash" basis: you'll pay for everything with cash, and everyone who buys something from you will pay in cash.

You may have at least a little cash on you right now—some currency, or paper money, and coins. In accounting, however, the term **cash** refers to more than just paper money and coins. It also refers to the money that you have in checking and savings accounts and includes items that you can deposit in these accounts, such as money orders and different types of checks.

Your first task is to decide exactly what you're going to sell. You've noticed that with homework, exams, social commitments, and the hectic lifestyle of the average college student, you and most of the people you know always seem to be under a lot of stress. Sometimes you wish you could just lie back between meals and bounce a ball off the wall. And that's when the idea hits you: Maybe you could make some money by selling a product called the "Stress-Buster Play Pack." Here's what you have in mind: you'll buy small toys and other fun stuff—instant stress relievers—at a local dollar store and pack them in a rainbow-colored plastic treasure chest labeled "Stress-Buster."

Figure 17.5: Three financial statements that can help business owners keep track of sales, assets, cash flow, and many other things.

The Accounting Equation

To begin keeping track of your company financially, you'll first need to understand the fundamental accounting equation:

Assets = Liabilities + Owner's Equity

Think of assets as things *owned* by your business—cash in the bank, product inventory, etc. And think of liabilities as the amounts *owed*—perhaps you've had a job where your pay check came a couple of weeks after you did the work; during that unpaid window, the amount due to you was a liability to your employer. *Owner's equity* represents the value of the firm according to your financial statements; obviously it is good to own more than you owe.

This simple but important equation highlights the fact that a company's **assets** came from somewhere: either from investments made by the owners (**owner's equity**) or from loans (**liabilities**). This means that the asset section of the balance sheet on the one hand and the liability and owner's-equity section on the other must be equal, or **balance**.

Let's say you have $200 in cash and borrow $400 from your parents or other relatives, and plan to buy a month's worth of plastic treasure chests and toys. After that, you'll use the cash generated from sales of Stress-Buster Play Packs to replenish your supply. You open a bank account for your new business and create your opening financial statement—the **balance sheet.**

The Balance Sheet

A **balance sheet** reports the following information:

- **Assets**: the resources from which it expects to gain some future benefit
- **Liabilities**: the debts that it owes to outside individuals or organizations
- **Owner's equity**: the investment in the business

At the time you open the account, your balance sheet would look like this:

Stress-Buster Company
Balance sheet
As of September 1, 2022

Assets	
Cash	**$600**
Liabilities and owner's equity	
Liabilities	$400
Owner's equity	$200
Total liabilities and owner's equity	**$600**

Figure 17.6: Stress-Buster's balance sheet as of September 1, 2022.

The amount you owe your relatives is a liability to you, and your own investment of $200 in the business is represented by your owner's equity.

Now it is time to start buying toys, repackaging them, and selling your Stress-Busters. Each plastic chest will cost $1.00, and you'll fill each one with a variety of five simple toys, all of which you can buy for $1.00 each.

You plan to sell each Stress-Buster Play Pack for $10 from a rented table stationed outside a major dining hall. Renting the table will cost you $20 a month. In order to make sure you can complete your school work, you decide to hire fellow students to staff the table at peak traffic periods. They'll be on duty from noon until 2:00 p.m. each weekday except Fridays, and you'll pay them a generous $7.50 an hour. Wages, therefore, will cost you $240 a month (2 hours × 4 days × 4 weeks = 32 hours × $7.50). Finally, you'll run ads in the college newspaper at a monthly cost of $40. Thus your total monthly costs will amount to $300 ($20 + $240 + $40).

The Income Statement

Let's say that during your first month, you sell 100 play packs. Not bad, you say to yourself, but did I make a profit? To find out, you prepare an income statement showing **revenues**, or sales, and **expenses**—the costs of doing business. You divide your expenses into two categories:

- **Cost of goods sold**: the total cost of the goods that you've sold
- **Operating expenses**: the costs of operating your business except for the costs of things that you've sold.

Now you need to do some subtracting:

- The difference between sales revenue and cost of goods sold is your **gross profit**, also known as **gross margin**.
- The difference between gross profit and operating expenses is your **net income** or **profit**, which is the proverbial "bottom line." Note we've assumed you're making money, but businesses can also have a net loss.

Figure 17.7 is your income statement for the first month. (Remember that we've made things simpler by handling everything in cash.)

Stress-Buster company income statement (Month ended: September 30, 2022)	
Sales (100 x $10.00)	$1,000
Less cost of goods sold (100 x $6)	$600
Gross profit (100 x ($10 - $6))	**$400**
Less operating expenses	
Salaries	$240
Advertising	$40
Table rental	$20
	$300
Net income (profit) ($400 - $300)	**$100**

Figure 17.7: Stress-Buster's income statement for September 2022.

Did You Make Any Money?

What does your income statement tell you? It has provided you with four pieces of valuable information:

- You sold 100 units at $10 each, bringing in **revenues** or **sales** of $1,000.
- Each unit that you sold cost you $6—$1 for the treasure chest plus 5 toys costing $1 each. So your **cost of goods sold** is $600 (100 units × $6 per unit).
- Your **gross profit**—the amount left after subtracting cost of goods sold from sales—is $400 (100 units × $4 each).
- After subtracting **operating expenses** of $300—the costs of doing business other than the cost of products sold—you generated a positive **net income** or **profit** of $100.

Whereas your **balance sheet** tells you what you have *at a specific point in time*, your **income statement** tells you how much income you earned *over some period of time*, in this case, the month of September.

 An interactive H5P element has been excluded from this version of the text. You can view it online here: https://pressbooks.lib.vt.edu/fundamentalsofbusiness4e/?p=190#h5p-47

Companies prepare financial statements on at least a 12-month basis—that is, for a **fiscal year** which ends on December 31 or some other logical date, such as June 30 or September 30. Fiscal years can vary because companies generally pick a fiscal-year end date that coincides with the end of a peak selling period; thus a crabmeat processor might end its fiscal year in October, when the crab supply has dwindled. Most companies also produce financial statements on a quarterly or monthly basis. For Stress-Buster, you'll want to prepare them monthly to stay on top of how your new business is doing. Let's prepare a new balance sheet to how things have changed by the end of the month.

Recall that Stress-Buster earned $100 during the month of September and that you decided to leave these earnings in the business. This $100 profit increases two items on your balance sheet: the assets of the company (its cash) and your investment in it (its owner's equity). Figure 17.8 shows what your balance sheet will look like on September 30. You now have $700 in cash: $400 that you borrowed plus $300 that you've invested in the business (your original $200 investment plus the $100 profit from the first month of operations, which you've kept in the business).

Stress-Buster company balance sheet (As of September 30, 2022)	
Assets	
Cash ($600 original + $100 earned)	$700
Liabilities and owner's equity	
Liabilities	$400
Owner's equity ($200 invested by owner + $100 profits retained)	$300
Total liabilities and owner's equity	$700

Figure 17.8: Stress-Buster's balance sheet at the end of September 2022.

A Quick Word about Credit

Because the money you borrowed came from your trusting relatives, they loaned it to you on the basis of you signing a simple note promising to pay it back. Such a loan is considered *unsecured credit*. But what if you had borrowed the money from a bank? The banker would probably have required *collateral*, which is property or some other asset that would become the property of the lender if you failed to pay. If you know someone who had a car loan, you probably know that if the loan went unpaid, the bank could repossess the car. This type of loan is called *secured credit*, because the bank makes it with the security that if the borrower cannot or will not pay, they can take possession of the collateral, sell it, and recover their money that way.

Breakeven Analysis

Let's take a short detour to see how Stress Buster's financial information might be put to use. As you look at your first financial statements, you might ask yourself: is there some way to figure out the level of sales you need to avoid losing money—to "break even"? This can be done using **breakeven analysis**. To break even (have no profit or loss), your total sales revenue must exactly equal all your expenses (both variable and fixed). **Variable costs** depend on the quantity produced and sold; for example, each Stress-Buster includes the treasure chest and the toys inside. **Fixed costs** don't change as the quantity sold changes; for example, you'll pay for your advertising whether you sell Stress-Busters or not. The balance between revenue and expenses will occur when gross profit equals all other (fixed) costs. To determine the level of sales at which this will occur, you need to do the following (using data from the previous example):

1. Determine your total fixed costs:

    ◦ Fixed costs = $240 salaries + $40 advertising + $20 table = $300

2. Identify your variable costs on a per-unit basis:

    ◦ Variable cost per unit = $6 ($1 for the treasure chest and $5 for the toys)

3. Determine your **contribution margin** per unit: selling price per unit—variable cost per unit:

    ◦ Contribution margin = $10 selling price—$6 variable cost per unit = $4

4. Calculate your breakeven point in units: fixed costs / contribution margin per unit:

    ◦ Breakeven in units = $300 fixed costs / $4 contribution margin per unit = 75 units

Your calculation means that if you sell 75 units, you'll end up with zero profit (or loss) and will exactly break even. To test your calculation, you can prepare a what-if income statement for

75 units in sales (your breakeven number). The resulting statement is shown in figure 17.9.

Of course you want to do better than just break even, so you could modify this analysis to a targeted level of profit by adding that amount to your fixed costs and repeating the calculation. Breakeven analysis is rather handy. It enables you to determine the level of sales that you must reach to avoid losing money and the level of sales that you have to reach to earn a certain profit. Such information will be vital to planning your business.

Stress-Buster company income statement (Month ended: September 30, 2022) At break even level of sales = 75 units		
Sales (75 x $10.00)		$750
Less cost of goods sold (75 x $6)		$450
Gross profit ($75 x ($10 - $6))		**$300**
Less operating expenses		
Salaries	$240	
Advertising	$40	
Table rental	$20	
	$300	
Net income (profit) ($300 - $300)		$0

Figure 17.9: Stress-Buster's breakeven income statement.

Now that you know a bit about financial statements, we'll spend a little time talking about how financial statements are used to help owners, managers, investors, and creditors assess a firm's performance and financial strength. You can glean a wealth of information from financial statements, but first you need to learn a few basic principles for "unlocking" it.

Financial Statement Analysis

Types of Financing Used by Companies

Before we go any further, let's outline two basic forms of financing—i.e., how do companies get the money they need in order to operate? One way is to borrow the money, which is known as *debt financing*. A business might take a loan from a commercial bank, or it might issue bonds which pay a particular rate of interest over a set period of time. At the end of the life of the bond, the borrower would repay the *principal*, i.e., the amount borrowed, to the holders of those bonds. Another form of financing would be to sell an ownership stake in the company, which is known as *equity financing*. Many business owners are reluctant to part with an ownership stake in the

Figure 17.10: Financial analysts at work.

company because they then have to share the profits with those who have purchased a share of the company. However, lenders will only provide so much financing before they begin to get concerned about the borrower's ability to repay, so in practice, most businesses use some combination of debt and equity financing to fund the operations of the company.

Trend Analysis from the Income Statement

Now let's look at some of the things we can learn from analyzing financial statements. Figure 17.11 is an abbreviated financial statement for Apple for 2021 taken directly from their website. You will note that instead of showing only the current year's results, the company has shown data for the prior two years as well.

From this relatively simple exhibit, considerable information about Apple's performance can be obtained. For example:

- Apple sales grew at 33 percent from 2020 to 2021, not bad for a company with such a large base of sales already.
- Net income as a percent of sales (a ratio also known as return on sales) was 21.6 percent—or in other words, for every $5 in sales, Apple turned more than $1 of it into profit. That is substantial!

Many other calculations are possible from Apple's data, and we will look at a few more as we explore ratio analysis.

Apple Inc.—Consolidated Statement of Operations (Income Statement)

	2019	2020	2021
Net sales	$260,174	$274,515	$365,817
Cost of sales	$161,782	$169,559	$212,981
Gross margin	$98,392	$104,956	$152,836
Total operating expenses:	$34,462	$38,668	$43,887
Research and development	$16,217	$18,752	$21,914
Selling, general and administrative	$18,245	$19,916	$21,973
Operating income	$63,930	$66,288	$108,949
Other income/(expense), net	$1,807	$803	$258
Income before provision for income taxes	$65,737	$67,091	$109,207
Provision for income taxes	$10,481	$9,680	$14,527
Net income	$55,256	$57,411	$94,680
Earnings per share:			
Basic	$2.99	$3.31	$5.67
Diluted	$2.97	$3.28	$5.61
Shares used in computing earnings per share:			
Basic	$18,471,336	$17,352,119	$16,701,272
Diluted	$18,595,651	$17,528,214	$16,864,919
Cash dividends declared per common share	$0.75	$0.795	$0.85

Figure 17.11: Apple's statement of operations, 2021. (In millions, except number of shares which are reflected in thousands and per share amounts.)

Ratio Analysis

How do you compare Apple's financial results with those of other companies in your industry or with the other companies whose stock is available to investors? And what about your balance sheet? Are there relationships on this statement that also warrant investigation? These issues can be explored by using **ratio analysis**, a technique for evaluating a company's financial performance.

Remember that a ratio is just one number divided by another, with the result expressing the relationship between the two numbers. It's hard to learn much from just one ratio, or even a number of ratios covering the same period. Rather, the deeper value in ratio analysis lies in looking at the trend of ratios over time and in comparing the ratios for several time periods with those of other companies. There are a number of different ways to categorize financial ratios.

Here's one set of categories:

- **Profitability ratios** tell you how much profit is made relative to the amount invested (return on investment) or the amount sold (return on sales).
- **Liquidity ratios** tell you how well positioned a company is to pay its bills in the near term. Liquidity refers to how quickly an asset can be turned into cash. For example, share of stock is substantially more liquid than a building or a machine.
- **Debt ratios** look at how much borrowing a company has done in order to finance the operations of the business. The more borrowing, the more risk a company has taken on, and so the less likely it would be for new lenders to approve loan applications.
- **Efficiency ratios** tell you how well your assets are being managed.

We could employ many different ratios, but we'll focus on a few key examples.

Profitability Ratios

Earlier we looked at the **return on sales** for Apple. Another profitability ratio on which the financial markets focus is **earnings per share**, also known as EPS. This ratio divides net income by the number of shares of stock outstanding. According to the earlier exhibit, Apple increased its EPS from $3.31 in 2020 to $5.67 in 2021, which indicates growth of about 71 percent—excellent for a company that is already among the world's largest. Well-paid analysts will spend hours to understand how these results were achieved every time Apple issues new financial statements.

Liquidity Ratios

Liquidity ratios are one element of measuring the financial strength of a company. They assess its ability to pay its current bills. A key liquidity ratio is called the **current ratio**. It simply examines the relationship between a company's **current assets** and its **current liabilities**. On September 27, 2021 (remember that balance sheets reflect a point in time), Apple had $121.4 billion in current assets and $106.3 billion in current liabilities. Simply, what this means is that Apple has more money on hand than they need to pay their bills. When a company has a current ratio greater than one, they are in good shape to pay their bills; companies selling to Apple on credit would not need to worry that it is likely to run out of money.

Apple, Inc.—Consolidated Balance Sheets

	2020	2021
Assets		
Current assets:		
Cash and cash equivalents	$38,016	$38,466
Marketable securities	$52,927	$31,368
Accounts receivable, net	$16,120	$18,503
Inventories	$4,061	$5,219
Vendor non-trade receivables	$21,325	$14,533
Other current assets	$11,264	$13,376
Total current assets	$143,713	$121,465
Non-current assets:		
Marketable securities	$100,887	$134,539
Property, plant and equipment, net	$36,766	$37,815
Other non-current assets	$42,522	$43,339
Total non-current assets	$180,175	$215,693
Total assets	$323,888	$337,158
Liabilities and Shareholders' Equity		
Current liabilities:		
Accounts payable	$42,296	$40,127
Other current liabilities	$42,684	$45,660
Deferred revenue	$6,643	$7,595
Commercial paper	$4,996	$5,000
Term debt	$8,773	$8,003
Total current liabilities	$105,392	$106,385
Non-current liabilities:		
Term debt	$98,667	$108,642
Other non-current liabilities	$54,490	$52,953
Total non-current liabilities	$153,157	$161,595
Total liabilities	$258,549	$267,980
Commitments and contingencies		
Shareholders' equity		
Common stock and additional paid-in capital, $0.00001 par value: 50,400,000 shares authorized; 16,686,305 and 16,976,763 shares issued and outstanding, respectively	$50,779	$54,203
Retained earnings	$14,966	$15,261
Accumulated other comprehensive income/(loss)	(406)	(286)
Total shareholders' equity	$65,339	$69,178
Total liabilities and shareholders' equity	$323,888	$337,158

Figure 17.12: Apple's balance sheet, 2021. (In millions, except number of shares which are reflected in thousands and par value.)

Apple's current ratio:

$$\frac{\$121.4 \; billion}{\$106.3 \; billion} = 1.14 > 1$$

Now, let's look quickly at something that is not part of the ratio; look down one line on the balance sheet to long-term marketable securities and see that Apple owns $31.3 billion. While they are long term and so not part of the current ratio, these securities are still easily convertible to cash. So Apple has far more cushion than the current ratio reflects, even though it reflected a healthy financial position already.

Debt Ratios

Apple's debt to equity ratio:

$$\frac{\$267.9 \; billion}{\$69.1 \; billion} = 3.87$$

A key debt ratio, which tells us how the company is financed, is the **debt-to-equity ratio**, which calculates the relationship between funds acquired from creditors (**debt**) and funds invested by owners (**equity**). For this ratio calculation, we use Apple's *total liabilities*, not just the line on the balance sheet that says long-term debt, because in effect, Apple is borrowing from those who it owes but has not yet paid. Apple's total liabilities at the end of its 2021 fiscal year were $267.9 billion versus owner's equity of $69.1 billion, a ratio of 3.87, which means Apple has borrowed more than it has invested in the business.

To some investors, that high level of debt might seem alarming. But remember that Apple has $31.3 billion invested in marketable securities. If it wished to do so, Apple could sell some of those securities and pay down its debts, thus improving its ratio. It's likely that anyone thinking about lending money to Apple and seeing these figures would be confident that Apple has the ability to pay back what they borrow.

Efficiency and Effectiveness Ratios

There are many more ratios which we could apply to Apple to more completely understand its performance. Yet going deeper into ratios would be beyond the scope of an introductory business course. If you continue your study of business, you will get ample exposure to these ratios in your accounting and finance courses. So we'll leave the rest for another day.

 An interactive H5P element has been excluded from this version of the text. You can view it online here: https://pressbooks.lib.vt.edu/fundamentalsofbusiness4e/?p=190#h5p-48

Careers in Financial Management[4]

Exploring business careers

Profile: Vicki Saunders, Venture Capitalist and Entrepreneur

Many women dream of starting their own business. But this involves a large investment of time, dedication, creativity—and money. Even the best ideas fall flat without strong financial backing and fiscal management. Most start-ups don't have a chief financial officer, let alone an unlimited amount of cash to fund their owners' dreams.

According to a recent report, there are more than 11 million woman-owned businesses in the United States that employ close to 9 million people and generate more than $1.6 trillion in revenues. And revenues have increased for these businesses more than 35% over the last decade compared to 27% among all U.S. companies. Despite these impressive statistics, less than 4 percent of venture capital funding goes to this group of entrepreneurs. That's where Vicki Saunders and SheEO, her venture capital start-up, come into the picture.

Adapted from: OpenStax *Introduction to Business* (CC BY). Access for free at https://openstax.org/books/introduction-business/pages/16-introduction

Saunders, who describes herself as a serial entrepreneur, previously cofounded and ran four different business ventures. She believes that the funding universe for women entrepreneurs needs to be fixed and offers her plan via SheEO, a platform to enlist women "activators" to invest money to create a pool of capital distributed to select woman-owned businesses in the form of 0% interest loans that are paid back within five years. The activators are more than just investors, however. Saunders envisions these women as being a crucial part of the businesses in which they invest, by providing operational support, resources for suppliers and other vendors, and a solid networking opportunity for everything from legal support to cultivating new customers. In a recent campaign called Radical Generosity, $1,000 was raised from each of 500 women, and that pool of $500,000 was split among five woman-led businesses.

In year three of the funding venture in 2017, SheEO funded 15 companies and invested $1.5 million. SheEO has funded entrepreneurs working on a variety of businesses, including artificial intelligence, hardware for people with disabilities, food, and education. While SheEO currently operates in four regions, Canada, Los Angeles, San Francisco, and Colorado, Saunders's goals for funding woman-led businesses are lofty. By 2020, Saunders hopes to have a million investors and a billion dollars to fund 10,000 entrepreneurs. But her ultimate goal is to change the culture around how investors support businesses—all businesses. According to Saunders, activating women on behalf of other women will change the world.[5,6,7,8,9,10,11]

In today's fast-paced global economy, managing a firm's finances is more complex than ever. For financial managers, a thorough command of traditional finance activities—financial planning, investing money, and raising funds—is only part of the job. Financial managers are more than number crunchers. As part of the top management team, chief financial officers (CFOs) need a broad understanding of their firm's business and industry, as well as leadership ability and creativity. They must never lose sight of the primary goal of the financial manager: to maximize the value of the firm to its owners.

Financial management—spending and raising a firm's money—is both a science and an art. The science part is analyzing numbers and flows of cash through the firm. The art is answering questions such as these: Is the firm using its financial resources in the best way? Aside from costs, why choose a particular form of financing? How risky is each option? Another important concern for both business managers and investors is understanding the basics of securities markets and the securities traded on them, which affect both corporate plans and investor pocketbooks. About 52 percent of adult Americans now own stocks, compared to just 25 percent in 1981.[12]

How do finance and the financial manager affect the firm's overall strategy?

Any company, whether it's a small-town bakery or General Motors, needs money to operate. To make money, it must first spend money—on inventory and supplies, equipment and facilities, and employee wages and salaries. Therefore, finance is critical to the success of all companies. It may not be as visible as marketing or production, but management of a firm's finances is just as much a key to the firm's success.

Financial management—the art and science of managing a firm's money so that it can meet its goals—is not just the responsibility of the finance department. All business decisions have financial consequences. Managers in all departments must work closely with financial personnel. If you are a sales representative, for example, the company's credit and collection policies will affect your ability to make sales. The head of the IT department will need to justify any requests for new computer systems or employee laptops.

Revenues from sales of the firm's products should be the chief source of funding. But money from sales doesn't always come in when it's needed to pay the bills. Financial managers must track how money is flowing into and out of the firm (see figure 17.14). They work with the firm's other department managers to determine how available funds will be used and how much money is needed. Then they choose the best sources to obtain the required funding.

Figure 17.13: Managers, IT employees, and sales representatives working together to manage a firm's financials.

For example, a financial manager will track day-to-day operational data such as cash collections and disbursements to ensure that the company has enough cash to meet its obligations. Over a longer time horizon, the manager will thoroughly study whether and when the company should open a new manufacturing facility. The manager will also suggest the most appropriate way to finance the project, raise the funds, and then monitor the project's implementation and operation.

Financial Management is closely related to accounting. In most firms, both areas are the responsibility of the vice president of finance or CFO. But the accountant's main function is to collect and present financial data. Financial managers use financial statements and other information prepared by accountants to make financial decisions. Financial managers focus on **cash flows**, the inflows and outflows of cash. They plan and monitor the firm's cash flows to ensure that cash is available when needed.

Adapted from: OpenStax *Introduction to Business* (CC BY). Access for free at https://openstax.org/books/introduction-business/pages/16-1-the-role-of-finance-and-the-financial-manager

The Financial Manager's Responsibilities and Activities

Financial managers have a complex and challenging job. They analyze financial data prepared by accountants, monitor the firm's financial status, and prepare and implement financial plans. One day they may be developing a better way to automate cash collections, and the next they may be analyzing a proposed acquisition. The key activities of the financial manager are:

- **Financial planning**: Preparing the financial plan, which projects revenues, expenditures, and financing needs over a given period.
- **Investment** (spending money): Investing the firm's funds in projects and securities that provide high returns in relation to their risks.
- **Financing** (raising money): Obtaining funding for the firm's operations and investments and seeking the best balance between debt (borrowed funds) and equity (funds raised through the sale of ownership in the business).

The Goal of the Financial Manager

How can financial managers make wise planning, investment, and financing decisions? The main goal of the financial manager is to maximize the value of the firm to its owners. The value of a publicly owned corporation is measured by the share price of its stock. A private company's value is the price at which it could be sold.

To maximize the firm's value, the financial manager has to consider both short- and long-term consequences of the firm's actions. Maximizing profits is one approach, but it should not be the only one. Such an approach favors making short-term gains over achieving long-term goals. What if a firm in a highly technical and competitive industry did no research and development? In the short run, profits would be high because research and development is very expensive. But in the long run, the firm might lose its ability to compete because of its lack of new products.

Adapted from: OpenStax *Introduction to Business* (CC BY). Access for free at https://openstax.org/books/introduction-business/pages/16-1-the-role-of-finance-and-the-financial-manager

This is true regardless of a company's size or point in its life cycle. At Corning, a company founded more than 160 years ago, management believes in taking the long-term view and not managing for quarterly earnings to satisfy Wall Street's expectations. The company, once known to consumers mostly for kitchen products such as Corelle dinnerware and Pyrex heat-resistant glass cookware, is today a technology company that manufactures specialized glass and ceramic products. It is a leading supplier of Gorilla Glass, a special type of glass used for the screens of mobile devices, including the iPhone, the iPad, and devices powered by Google's Android operating system. The company was also the inventor of optical fiber and cable for the telecommunications industry. These product lines require large investments during their long research and development (R&D) cycles and for plant and equipment once they go into production.[13]

Figure 17.14: *How cash flows through a business.*

This can be risky in the short term, but staying the course can pay off. In fact, Corning recently announced plans to develop a separate company division for Gorilla Glass, which now has more than 20 percent of the phone market—with over 200 million devices sold. In addition, its fiber-optic cable business is back in vogue and thriving as cable service providers such as Verizon have doubled down on upgrading the fiber-optic network across the United States. As of 2017, Corning's commitment to repurposing some of its technologies and developing new products has helped the company's bottom line, increasing revenues in a recent quarter by more than 16 percent.[14]

As the Corning situation demonstrates, financial managers constantly strive for a balance between the opportunity for profit and the potential for loss. In finance, the opportunity for profit is termed return; the potential for loss, or the chance that an investment will not achieve the expected level of return, is risk. A basic principle in finance is that the higher the risk, the greater the return that is required. This widely accepted concept is called the risk-return trade-off. Financial managers consider many risk and return factors when making investment and financing decisions. Among them are changing patterns of market demand, interest rates, general economic conditions, market conditions, and social issues (such as environmental effects and equal employment opportunity policies).

 An interactive H5P element has been excluded from this version of the text. You can view it online here: https://pressbooks.lib.vt.edu/fundamentalsofbusiness4e/?p=190#h5p-58

Adapted from: OpenStax *Introduction to Business* (CC BY). Access for free at https://openstax.org/books/introduction-business/pages/16-1-the-role-of-finance-and-the-financial-manager

Chapter Video: The Difference Between Accounting and Finance

Zach De Gregorio, CPA, explains the difference in these two functional areas of business.

 One or more interactive elements has been excluded from this version of the text. You can view them online here: https://www.youtube.com/watch?v=_8bAY-Tspd4

Key Takeaways

- **Accounting** is the process of measuring and summarizing business activities, interpreting financial information, and communicating the results to management and other decision makers.
- **Managerial accounting** deals with information produced for internal users, while **financial accounting** deals with external reporting.
- The **income statement** captures sales and expenses over a period of time and shows how much a firm made or lost in that period.
- The **balance sheet** reflects the financial position of a firm at a given point in time, including its assets, liabilities, and owner's equity. It is based on the following equation: assets – liabilities = owner's equity.
- **Breakeven analysis** is a technique used to determine the level of sales needed to break even—to operate at a sales level at which you have neither profit nor loss.
- **Ratio analysis** is used to assess a company's performance and financial condition over time and to compare one company to similar companies or to an overall industry.
- Categories of ratios include **profitability ratios**, **liquidity ratios**, **debt ratios**, and **efficiency and effectiveness ratios**.

References

Figures

Figure 17.1: Amazon's headquarters in Seattle, Washington. طططه. 2019. CC BY-SA 4.0. https://commons.wikimedia.org/wiki/File:AmazonTowers1-3.jpg.

Figure 17.2: The role of managerial accounting. Kindred Grey. 2022. CC BY 4.0. Includes manager by Andre from Noun Project, Woman by
verry poernomo from Noun Project, and manager by Chrystina Angeline from Noun Project (Noun Project license). https://archive.org/details/17.2_20220627.

Figure 17.3: Warren Buffet, presidential medal of freedom recipient in 2011. Medill DC. 2011. CC BY 2.0. https://flic.kr/p/9iudpv.

Figure 17.4: The role of financial accounting. Kindred Grey. 2022. CC BY 4.0. Includes manager by Andre from Noun Project and Woman by
verry poernomo from Noun Project (Noun Project license). https://archive.org/details/17.4_20220627.

Figure 17.5: Three financial statements that can help business owners keep track of sales, assets, cash flow, and many other things. Kindred Grey. 2022. CC BY 4.0. Includes image by Pinar Kucuk from Unsplash (Unsplash license). https://archive.org/details/17.5_20220627.

Figure 17.10: Financial analysts at work. Pavel Danilyuk. 2021. Pexels license. https://www.pexels.com/photo/man-and-woman-working-at-the-office-7654120/.

Figure 17.11: Apple's statement of operations, 2021. (In millions, except number of shares which are reflected in thousands and per share amounts.) Data from https://s2.q4cdn.com/470004039/files/doc_financials/2021/q4/_10-K-2021-(As-Filed).pdf.

Figure 17.12: Apple's balance sheet, 2021. (In millions, except number of shares which are reflected in thousands and par value.) Data from https://www.apple.com/newsroom/pdfs/FY21_Q2_Consolidated_Financial_Statements.pdf.

Figure 17.13: Managers, IT employees, and sales representatives working together to manage a firm's financials. fauxels. 2019. Pexels license. https://www.pexels.com/photo/people-discuss-about-graphs-and-rates-3184292/.

Figure 17.14: How cash flows through a business. Kindred Grey. 2022. CC BY 4.0. Adapted from Rice University, OpenStax, under CC BY 4.0 license. https://archive.org/details/17.13.

Video

Video 1: The difference between accounting and finance. Zach De Gregorio. 2015. Copyrighted. https://www.youtube.com/watch?v=_8bAY-Tspd4.

Notes

1. Most Valuable Companies in the World. The Week UK. (n.d.). Retrieved from: https://www.theweek.co.uk/business/companies/955282/worlds-most-valuable-companies
2. Ibid.
3. Forbes Magazine. (n.d.). Warren Buffett. Forbes. Retrieved from: https://www.forbes.com/profile/warren-buffett
4. Text in the remainder of this chapter is adapted from © OpenStax, Chapter 16 Understanding Financial Management and Securities Markets, *Introduction to Business*. (CC BY) OpenStax and is freely available at https://openstax.org/books/introduction-business/pages/16-introduction
5. SHEEO (n.d.), "About Us," https://sheeo.world/about-us
6. Emma Hinchliffe, "SheEO Has a Plan to Build a $1 Billion Fund for Female Founders," Mashable, Retrieved from https://mashable.com/article/sheeo-investing-female-founders
7. Catherine McIntyre, (2016). "How Vicki Saunders Plans to Get a Million Women Involved in Venture Capital," Canadian Business, Retrieved from https://archive.canadianbusiness.com/innovation/sheeo-radical-generosity-vicki-saunders
8. Kimberly Weisul, (2016). "Venture Capital Is Broken. These Women Are Trying to Fix It," Inc., Retrieved from https://www.inc.com/magazine/201611/kimberly-weisul/new-face-of-funding.html
9. Geri Stengel, (2017). "Women Become Financiers to Disrupt the Funding Landscape for Entrepreneurs," Forbes, Retrieved from https://www.forbes.com/sites/geristengel/2017/10/18/women-become-financiers-to-disrupt-the-funding-landscape-for-entrepreneurs
10. Kathleen Chaykowski, (2017). "Meet the Top Women Investors in VC in 2017," Forbes, Retrieved from https://www.forbes.com/sites/kathleenchaykowski/2017/04/18/top-women-midas-2017-venture-capital
11. Jill Richmond, (2016). "Everything May Be Broken But This CEO's Glasses Are a Rose Hue," Forbes, Retrieved from https://www.forbes.com/sites/jillrichmond/2016/12/16/everything-may-be-broken-but-this-ceos-glasses-are-a-rose-hue
12. Danielle Kurtzleben, "While Trump Touts Stock Market, Many Americans Are Left Out of the Conversation," NPR, http://www.npr.org, March 1, 2017.
13. Gary P. Pisano, "You Need an Innovation Strategy," *Harvard Business Review*, https://hbr.org, accessed October 10, 2017.
14. Panos Mourdoukoutas, "Corning Beats Apple," *Forbes*, https://www.forbes.com, July 9, 2017.

18. Personal Finances

Learning Objectives

- Develop strategies to avoid being burdened with debt.
- Explain how to manage monthly income and expenses.
- Define personal finances and financial planning.
- Explain the financial planning life cycle.
- Discuss the advantages of a college education in meeting short- and long-term financial goals.
- Explain compound interest and the time value of money.
- Discuss the value of getting an early start on your plans for saving.

The World of Personal Credit

Do you sometimes wonder where your money goes? Do you worry about how you'll pay off your student loans? Would you like to buy a new car or even a home someday and you're not sure where you'll get the money? If these questions seem familiar to you, you could benefit from help in managing your personal finances, which this chapter will seek to provide.

Figure 18.1: Credit cards.

Let's say that you're 28 and single. You have a good education and a good job—you're pulling down $60,000 working with a local accounting firm. You have $6,000 in a retirement savings account, and you carry three credit cards. You plan to buy a condo in two or three years, and you want to take your dream trip to the world's hottest surfing spots within five years. Your only big worry is the fact that you're $70,000 in debt, due to student loans, your car loan, and credit card debt. In fact, even though you've been gainfully employed for a total of six years now, you haven't been able to make a dent in that $70,000. You can afford the necessities of life and then some, but you've occasionally wondered if you're ever going to have enough income to put something toward that debt.[1]

Now let's suppose that while browsing through a magazine in the doctor's office, you run across a short personal-finances self-help quiz. There are six questions:

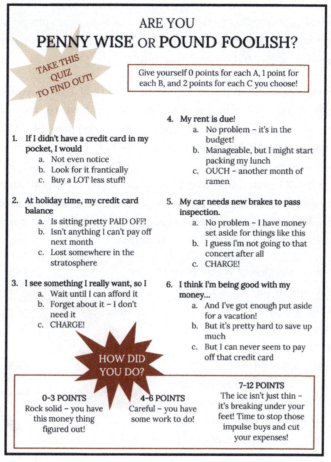

Figure 18.2: Financial quiz.

You took the quiz and answered with a B or C to a few questions, and are thereby informed that you're probably jeopardizing your entire financial future.

Personal-finances experts tend to utilize the types of questions on the quiz: if you answered B or C to any of the first three questions, you have a problem with splurging; if any questions from four through six got a B or C, your monthly bills are too high for your income.

Building a Good Credit Rating

So, you have a financial problem. According to the quick test you took, you splurge and your bills are too high for your income. If you get in over your head and can't make your loan or rent payments on time, you risk hurting your **credit rating**—your ability to borrow in the future.

How do potential lenders decide whether you're a good or bad credit risk? If you're a poor credit risk, how does this affect your ability to borrow, or the rate of interest you have to pay? Whenever you use **credit**, those from whom you borrow (retailers, credit card companies, banks) provide information on your debt and payment habits to three national **credit bureaus**: Equifax, Experian, and TransUnion. The credit bureaus use the information to compile a numerical credit score, called a **FICO score**; it ranges from 300–850, with the majority of people falling in the 600–700 range. In compiling the score, the credit bureaus consider five criteria: **payment history**—paying your bills on time (the most important), **total amount owed**, **length of your credit history**, **amount of new credit you have**, and **types of credit you use**. The credit bureaus share their score and other information about your credit history with their subscribers.[2]

So what does this do for you? It depends. If you pay your bills on time and don't borrow too heavily, you'd likely have a high FICO score and lenders would like you, probably giving you reasonable interest rates on the loans you requested. But if your FICO score is low, lenders won't likely lend you money (or would lend it to you at high interest rates). A low FICO score can even affect your chances of renting an apartment or landing a particular job. So it's very important that you do everything possible to earn and maintain a high credit score.

Figure 18.3: FICO credit score range.

As a young person, though, how do you build a credit history that will give you a high FICO score? Based on feedback from several financial experts, Emily Starbuck Gerson and Jeremy Simon of CreditCards.com compiled the list in figure 18.4 of ways students can build good credit.[3]

Figure 18.4: How to build good credit as a student.

If you meet the qualifications to obtain your own credit card, look for a card with a low interest rate and no annual fee.

 An interactive H5P element has been excluded from this version of the text. You can view it online here: https://pressbooks.lib.vt.edu/fundamentalsofbusiness4e/?p=199#h5p-49

Secured vs. Unsecured Credit

On some types of loans, the lender (likely a bank) will require the borrower to offer collateral in order to be approved for the loan. Anyone who has taken out a car loan or bought a house using a mortgage loan has likely pledged the car or the home as a way to ensure the bank that they will be repaid—if the borrower fails to repay, the bank can repossess the car or foreclose on the house, taking ownership of it temporarily and reselling it in order to recover the amount of the loan. In these cases, the car or the house serve as collateral—security pledged to the lender in order to make it more likely that the amount of the loan will be repaid. Loans that involve this type of security are referred to as secured loans or secured credit.

Not all types of loans involve collateral. For example, many families take out student loans when their children go off to college. Credit cards are a form of loan as well. Neither case involves collateral; the lender makes the loans based, at least in part, on the credit worthiness of the borrower. When no collateral is involved, the loans are called *unsecured*. Since the bank takes more risk in lending when no collateral can be pledged, unsecured loans will often require higher interest rates in order for it to be worth the bank taking the risk in making this type of loan.

A Few More Words about Debt

What should you do to turn things around—to start getting out of debt? According to many experts, you need to take two steps:

1. Cut up your credit cards and start living on a cash-only basis.
2. Do whatever you can to bring down your monthly bills.

Although credit cards can be an important way to build a credit rating, many people simply lack the financial discipline to handle them well. If you see yourself in that statement, then moving to a pay-as-you go basis, i.e., cash or debit card only, may be for you. Be honest with yourself; if you can't handle credit, then don't use it.

Bringing Down Those Monthly Bills

So what can you can to bring down your monthly bills? If you want to take a gradual approach, one financial planner suggests that you perform the following "exercises" for one week:[4]

- Keep a written record of everything you spend and total it at week's end.
- Keep all your ATM receipts and count up the fees.
- Take $100 out of the bank and don't spend a penny more.
- Avoid gourmet coffee shops.

You'll probably be surprised at how much of your money can quickly become somebody else's money. If, for example, you spend $4 every day for one cup of coffee at a coffee shop, you're laying out nearly $1,400 a year just for coffee. If you use your ATM card at a bank other than your own, you'll probably be charged a fee that can be nearly as high as $5.[5]

If you withdraw cash from an ATM twice a week, you could be racking up $500 in annual fees. Another idea—eat out as a reward, not as a rule. A sandwich or leftovers from home can be just as tasty and can save you $6 to $10 a day, even more than our number for coffee! In 2013, the website *DailyWorth* asked three women to try to cut their spending in half. After tracking her spending, one participant discovered that she had spent $175 eating out in just one week; do that for a year and you'd spend over $9,000![6] If you think your cable bill is too high, consider alternatives like *PlaystationVue* or *Sling*. Changing channels is a bit different, but the savings can be substantial.

Figure 18.5: These can really add up quickly!

You may or may not be among the American consumers who buy 35 million cans of Bud Light each day, or 150,000 pounds of Starbucks coffee, or 2.4 million Burger King hamburgers. Yours may not be one of the 70 percent of US households with an unopened consumer-electronics product lying around.[7] Bottom line: If at age 28 you have a good education and a good job, a $60,000 income, and a $70,000 debt (by no means an implausible scenario) there's a very good reason why you should think hard about controlling your debt. Your level of indebtedness will be a key factor in your ability—or inability—to reach your long-term financial goals, such as home ownership, a dream trip, and, perhaps most importantly, a reasonably comfortable retirement.

Financial Planning

Before we go any further, we need to nail down a couple of key concepts. First, just what, exactly, do we mean by personal finances? Finance itself concerns the flow of money from one place to another, and your personal finances concern your money and what you plan to do with it as it flows in and out of your possession. Essentially, then, personal finance is the application of financial principles to the monetary decisions that you make either for your individual benefit or for that of your family.

Second, as we suggested earlier, monetary decisions work out much more beneficially when they're planned rather than improvised. Thus our emphasis on financial planning—the ongoing process of managing your personal finances in order to meet goals that you've set for yourself or your family.

Financial planning requires you to address several questions, some of them relatively simple:

- What's my annual income?
- How much debt do I have, and what are my monthly payments on that debt?

Others will require some investigation and calculation:

- What's the value of my assets?
- How can I best budget my annual income?

Still others will require some forethought and forecasting:

- How much wealth can I expect to accumulate during my working lifetime?
- How much money will I need when I retire?

The Financial Planning Life Cycle

Another question that you might ask yourself—and certainly would do if you worked with a professional in financial planning—is, "How will my financial plans change over the course of my life?" Figure 18.6 illustrates the financial life cycle of a typical individual—one whose financial outlook and likely outcomes are probably a lot like yours.[8] As you can see, our diagram divides this individual's life into three stages, each of which is characterized by different life events (such as beginning a family, buying a home, planning an estate, retiring).

Figure 18.6: The financial life cycle.

At each stage, there are recommended changes in the focus of the individual's financial planning:

- Stage 1 focuses on building wealth.
- Stage 2 shifts the focus to the process of preserving and increasing wealth that one has accumulated and continues to accumulate.
- In Stage 3, the focus turns to the process of living on (and, if possible, continuing to grow) one's saved wealth after retirement.

At each stage, of course, complications can set in—changes in such conditions as marital or employment status or in the overall economic outlook, for example. Finally, as you can also see, your financial needs will probably peak somewhere in stage 2, at approximately age 55, or 10 years before typical retirement age.

 An interactive H5P element has been excluded from this version of the text. You can view it online here: https://pressbooks.lib.vt.edu/fundamentalsofbusiness4e/?p=199#h5p-50

Choosing a Career

Until you're on your own and working, you're probably living on your parents' wealth right now. In our hypothetical life cycle, financial planning begins in the individual's early 20s. If that seems like rushing things, consider a basic fact of life: this is the age at which you'll be choosing your career—not only the sort of work you want to do during your prime income-generating years, but also the kind of lifestyle you want to live. What about college? Most readers of this book, of course, have decided to go to college. If you haven't yet decided, you need to know that college is an extremely good investment of both money and time.

Figure 18.7 summarizes the findings of a study conducted by the US Census Bureau.[9] A quick review shows that course of the financial life cycle, families headed by those college graduates will earn about $1.6 million more[10] than families headed by high school graduates. (With better access to health care—and, studies show, with better dietary and health practices—college graduates will also live longer. And so will their children.)[11]

Education	Average income	Percentage increase over previous level
Less than a high school diploma	$32,188	–
High school diploma, no college	$40,612	26%
Some college, no degree	$45,604	12%
Associate degree	$48,776	7%
Bachelor's degree	$67,860	39%
Master's degree	$80,340	18%
Doctoral degree	$98,020	22%
Professional degree	$98,436	0.4%

Figure 18.7: Average earnings by education level.

What about the student-loan debt that so many people accumulate? For every $1 that you spend on your college education, you can expect to earn about $35 during the course of your financial life cycle.[12] At that rate of return, you should be able to pay off your student loans (unless, of course, you fail to practice reasonable financial planning).

Naturally, there are exceptions to these average outcomes. You'll find some college graduates stocking shelves at 7-Eleven, and you'll find college dropouts running multibillion-dollar enterprises. Microsoft cofounder Bill Gates dropped out of college after two years, as did his founding partner, Paul Allen. Though exceptions to rules (and average outcomes) certainly can be found, they fall far short of disproving them: in entrepreneurship as in most other walks of adult life, the better your education, the more promising your financial future. One expert in the field puts the case for the average person bluntly: educational credentials "are about being employable, becoming a legitimate candidate for a job with a future. They are about climbing out of the dead-end job market."[13]

Time Is Money

The fact that you have to choose a career at an early stage in your financial life cycle isn't the only reason that you need to start early on your financial planning. Let's assume, for instance, that it's your eighteenth birthday and that on this day you take possession of $10,000 that your grandparents put in trust for you. You could, of course, spend it; in particular, it would probably cover the cost of flight training for a private pilot's license—something you've always wanted but were convinced that you couldn't afford right away. Your grandfather, of course, suggests that you put it into some kind of savings account. If you just wait until you finish college, he says, and if you can find a savings plan that pays 5 percent interest, you'll have the $10,000 plus about another $2,000 for something else or to invest.

The total amount you'll have—$12,000—piques your interest. If that $10,000 could turn itself into $12,000 after sitting around for four years, what would it be worth if you actually held on to it until you did retire—say, at age 65? A quick trip to the Internet to find a compound-interest calculator informs you that, 47 years later, your $10,000 will have grown to $104,345 (assuming a 5 percent interest rate). That's not really enough for retirement on, but it would be a good start. On the other hand, what if that four years in college had paid off the way you planned, so that once you get a good job you're able to add, say, another $10,000 to your retirement savings account every year until age 65? At that rate, you'll have amassed a nice little nest egg of slightly more than $1.6 million.

Compound Interest

In your efforts to appreciate the potential of your $10,000 to multiply itself, you have acquainted yourself with two of the most important concepts in finance. As we've already indicated, one is the principle of compound interest, which refers to the effect of earning interest on your interest.

Let's say, for example, that you take your grandfather's advice and invest your $10,000 (your principal) in a savings account at an annual interest rate of 5 percent. Over the course of the first year, your investment will earn $500 in interest and grow to $10,500. If you now reinvest the entire $10,500 at the same 5 percent annual rate, you'll earn another $525 in interest, giving you a total investment at the end of year 2 of $11,025. And so forth. And that's how you can end up with $81,496.67 at age 65.

Time Value of Money

You've also encountered the principle of the time value of money—the principle whereby a dollar received in the present is worth more than a dollar received in the future. If there's one thing that we've stressed throughout this chapter so far, it's the fact that most people prefer to consume now rather than in the future. If you borrow money from me, it's because you can't otherwise buy something that you want at the present time. If I lend it to you, I must forego my opportunity to purchase something I want at the present time. I will do so only if I can get some compensation for making that sacrifice, and that's why I'm going to charge you interest. And you're going to pay the interest because you need the money to buy what you want to buy now. How much interest should we agree on? In theory, it could be just enough to cover the cost of my lost opportunity, but there are, of course, other factors. Inflation, for example, will have eroded the value of my money by the time I get it back from you. In addition, while I would be taking no risk in loaning money to the US government, I am taking a risk in lending it to you. Our agreed-on rate will reflect such factors.[14]

Finally, the time value of money principle also states that a dollar received today starts earning interest sooner than one received tomorrow. Let's say, for example, that you receive $2,000 in cash gifts when you graduate from college. At age 23, with your college degree in hand, you get a decent job and don't have an immediate need for that $2,000. So you put it into an account that pays 10 percent compounded and you add another $2,000 ($167 per month) to your account every year for the next 11 years.[15] The orange line in figure 18.8 graphs how much your account will earn each year and how much money you'll have at certain ages between 24 and 67.

As you can see, you'd have nearly $52,000 at age 36 and a little more than $196,000 at age 50; at age 67 you'd be just a bit short of $1 million. The yellow line in the graph shows what you'd have if you hadn't started saving $2,000 a year until you were age 36. As you can also see, you'd have a respectable sum at age 67, but less than half of what you would have accumulated by starting at age 23. More important, even to accumulate that much, you'd have to add $2,000 per year for a total of 32 years, not just 12.

Here's another way of looking at the same principle. Suppose that you're 20 years old, don't have $2,000, and don't want to attend college full-time. You are, however, a hard worker and a conscientious saver, and one of your financial goals is to accumulate a $1 million retirement nest egg. As a matter of fact, if you can put $33 a month into an account that pays 12 percent interest compounded,[16] you can have your $1 million by age 67. That is, if you start at age 20. As you can see from figure 18.9, if you wait until you're 21 to start saving, you'll need $37 a month. If you wait until you're 30, you'll have to save $109 a month, and if you procrastinate until you're 40, the ante goes up to $366 a month.[17] Unfortunately in today's low interest rate environment, finding 10–12 percent return is not likely. Nevertheless, these figures illustrate the significant benefit of saving early.

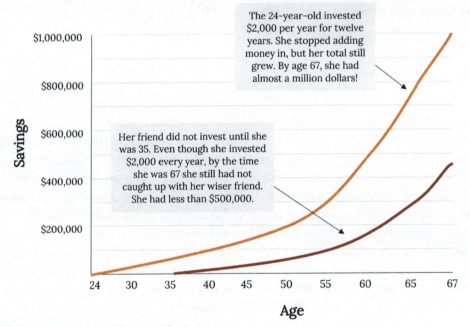

Figure 18.8: *The power of compound interest.*

The reason should be fairly obvious: a dollar saved today not only starts earning interest sooner than one saved tomorrow (or 10 years from now) but also can ultimately earn a lot more money in the long run. Starting early means in your 20s—early in stage 1 of your financial life cycle. As one well-known financial advisor puts it, "If you're in your 20s and you haven't yet learned how to delay gratification, your life is likely to be a constant financial struggle."[18]

How to save a million dollars by age 67

Make your first payment at age:	And this is what you'll have to save each month:
20	$33
21	$42
23	$47
24	$53
25	$60
26	$67
27	$76
28	$85
30	$109
35	$199
40	$366
50	$1,319
60	$6,253

Figure 18.9: What Does It Take to Save a Million Dollars?

Suppose you want to save or invest—do you know how or where to do so? You probably know that your branch bank can open a savings account for you, but interest rates on such accounts can be pretty unattractive. Investing in individual stocks or bonds can be risky, and usually require a level of funds available that most students don't have. In those cases, mutual funds can be quite interesting. A mutual fund is a professionally managed investment program in which shareholders buy into a group of diversified holdings, such as stocks and bonds. Companies like Vanguard and Fidelity offer a range of investment options including indexed funds, which track with well-known indices such as the Standard & Poors 500, a.k.a. the S&P 500. Minimum investment levels in such funds can actually be within the reach of many students, and the funds accept electronic transfers to make investing more convenient. One key to keep in mind when investing is **diversification**—a fancy way of saying not to put all your eggs in one basket. We'll leave a more detailed discussion of investment vehicles to your more advanced courses.

 An interactive H5P element has been excluded from this version of the text. You can view it online here: https://pressbooks.lib.vt.edu/fundamentalsofbusiness4e/?p=199#h5p-51

Chapter Videos

If you ask graduates who came before you what they wish they had known when they were first out of school, many would probably say, "how to handle my personal finances." While these two videos and this chapter won't make you financially literate, hopefully they will whet your appetite to learn more.

 One or more interactive elements has been excluded from this version of the text. You can view them online here: https://www.youtube.com/watch?v=ToyLXa0ULaM

 One or more interactive elements has been excluded from this version of the text. You can view them online here: https://www.youtube.com/watch?v=pysohj7GsBI

Key Takeaways

- Credit worthiness is measured by the **FICO score**—or **credit rating**—which can range from 300–850. The average ranges from 680–719.
- To maintain a satisfactory score, pay your bills on time, borrow only when necessary, and pay in full whenever you do borrow.
- Eighty-one percent of financial planners recommend eating out less as a way to reduce your expenses.
- **Personal finance** is the application of financial principles to the monetary decisions that you make.
- **Financial planning** is the ongoing process of managing your personal finances in order to meet your goals, which vary by stage of life.
- **Time value of money** is the principle that a dollar received in the present is worth more than a dollar received in the future due to its potential to earn interest.
- **Compound interest** refers to the effect of earning interest on your interest. It is a powerful way to accumulate wealth.

References

Figures

Figure 18.1: Credit cards. Avery Evans. 2020. Unsplash license. https://unsplash.com/photos/RJQE64NmC_o.

Figure 18.2: Financial quiz. Kindred Grey. 2022. CC BY 4.0. https://archive.org/details/18.2_20220627.

Figure 18.3: FICO credit score range. Kindred Grey. 2022. CC BY 4.0. https://archive.org/details/18.3_20220627.

Figure 18.4: How to build good credit as a student. Kindred Grey. 2022. CC BY 4.0. https://archive.org/details/18.4_20220627.

Figure 18.5: These can really add up quickly! Gema Saputera. 2020. Unsplash license. https://unsplash.com/photos/7Gm1Jwt1uYA.

Figure 18.6: The financial life cycle. Kindred Grey. 2022. CC BY 4.0. https://archive.org/details/18.6_20220627.

Figure 18.7: Average earnings by education level. Data from https://www.bls.gov/careeroutlook/2021/data-on-display/education-pays.htm.

Figure 18.8: The power of compound interest. Kindred Grey. 2022. CC BY 4.0. https://archive.org/details/18.8_20220627.

Videos

Video 1: What College Students Need to Know About Money! Cambridge Credit Counseling Corp. 2010. Copyrighted. https://www.youtube.com/watch?v=ToyLXa0ULaM

Video 2: Compound Interest. Reserve Bank of New Zealand. 2012. Copyrighted. https://www.youtube.com/watch?v=pysohj7GsBI

Notes

1. This vignette is adapted from a series titled USA TODAY's Financial Diet. Go to http://usatoday30.usatoday.com/money/perfi/basics/financial-diet-digest-2005.htm and use the embedded links to follow the entire series.
2. Colin Robertson (2015). "Credit Score Range – Where Do You Fit In?" Thetruthaboutcreditcards.com. Retrieved from: http://www.thetruthaboutcreditcards.com/credit-score-range/.
3. Emily Starbuck Gerson and Jeremy M. Simon (2016). "10 Ways Students Can Build Good Credit." CreditCards.com. Retrieved from: http://www.creditcards.com/credit-card-news/help/10-ways-students-get-good-credit-6000.php
4. USA Today and Elissa Buie (2005). "Exercise 1: Start Small, Watch Progress Grow." USA Today. Retrieved from: http://usatoday30.usatoday.com/money/perfi/basics/2005-04-14-financial-diet-excercise1_x.htm
5. Darla, Mercado. (2019, October 2). ATM Bank Fees Hit a Record High - And It's Draining Your Cash. CNBC. Retrieved from: https://www.cnbc.com/2019/10/02/atm-bank-fees-hit-a-record-high-and-its-draining-your-cash.html

6. Cynthia Ramnarace (2013). "Could You Cut Your Spending in Half?" Daily Worth. Retrieved from: https://www.dailyworth.com/posts/2046-could-you-cut-your-spending-in-half/2
7. Michael Arrington (2008). "Ebay Survey Says Americans Buy Crap They Don't Want." Tech Crunch. Retrieved from: https://techcrunch.com/2008/08/21/ebay-survey-says-americans-buy-crap-they-dont-want/
8. Timothy J. Gallager and Joseph D. Andrews Jr. (2003). *Financial Management: Principles and Practice*, 3rd ed. Upper Saddle River, NJ: Prentice Hall. pp. 34, 196.
9. U.S. Census Bureau (2015). "PINC-03. Educational Attainment-People 25 Years Old and Over, by Total Money Earnings, Work Experience, Age, Race, Hispanic Origin, and Sex." Retrieved from: http://www.census.gov/data/tpeople who graduate from high school can expect to enjoy average annual earnings about 28 percent higher than those of people who don't, and those who go on to finish college can expect to generate 76 percent more annual income than high school graduates who didn't attend college. Over theables/time-series/demo/income-poverty/cps-pinc/pinc-03.html
10. Katherine Hansen (2016). "What Good is a College Education Anyway? The Value of a College Education." Quintessential Live Career. Retrieved from: https://www.livecareer.com/quintessential/college-education-value
11. Ibid.
12. Ibid.
13. Ibid.
14. Timothy J. Gallager and Joseph D. Andrews Jr. (2003). *Financial Management: Principles and Practice*, 3rd ed. Upper Saddle River, NJ: Prentice Hall. pp. 34, 196.
15. The 10 percent rate is not realistic in today's economic market and is used for illustrative purposes only.
16. Again, this interest rate is unrealistic in today's market and is used for illustrative purposes only.
17. Arthur J. Keown (2007). *Personal Finance: Turning Money into Wealth*, 4th ed. Upper Saddle River, NJ: Pearson Education. p. 23.
18. AllFinancialMatters (2006). "An Interview with Jonathan Clements – Part 2." Retrieved from: http://allfinancialmatters.com/2006/02/10/an-interview-with-jonathan-clements-part-2/

19. Technology in Business

Learning Objectives

- Discuss how information technology has transformed business and managerial decision-making.
- Explain why computer networks are an important part of today's information technology systems.
- Describe the types of systems that make up a typical company's management information system.
- Explain how technology management and planning help companies optimize their information technology systems.
- Describe the best ways to protect computers and the information they contain.
- Explore and understand the leading trends in information technology.
- Understand the importance and role of cyber security and the impact on companies and personal information if not practiced.

Exploring Business Careers: John Daly, Daly Investment Management, LLC

When meeting with a Daly Investment[1] financial consultant, most likely you are thinking about money, *your* money. Whether you seek a short-term investment or a retirement nest egg, money will be your focus. You probably will not be thinking about the technological infrastructure required to transmit information throughout a multibillion dollar, nationwide institution such as TD Ameritrade—information that often is private and financial in nature. Luckily for you, however, the company is led by financial advisor John Daly, who works with TD Ameritrade to support his company's technology needs.

Adapted from: OpenStax *Introduction to Business* (CC BY). Access for free at https://openstax.org/books/introduction-business/pages/13-introduction

After successful careers at Charles Schwab and Morgan Stanley, Daly knew when he started his own firm he would need IT support so that he could ensure the security of the funds he managed for his customers while focusing on the financial aspects of managing their finances. In addition to providing a financial trading platform for individual investors, TD Ameritrade has a robust set of **software as a service** (SaaS) cloud-based tools that allow Daly to focus on his core competencies rather than having to hire, train, and maintain a complex set of IT resources that his clients can trust.

Given the size of the assets it manages, TD Ameritrade's **management information system** (MIS) is necessarily large. TD Ameritrade's open architecture environment enables financial advisors like John Daly to select the technology they want to use. The lesson is that Daly could act as an entrepreneur and start his own firm while providing information technology with the scale that customers expect and providing the personal service that is often missing when dealing with larger organizations.[234]

This chapter focuses on the role of information technology (IT) in business, examining the details of MIS organization, as well as the challenges companies encounter in an increasingly technological world. As John Daly learned, harnessing the power of information technology gives a company a significant competitive advantage.

Transforming Businesses through Information

Information technology (IT) includes the equipment and techniques used to manage and process information. Information is at the heart of all organizations. Without information about the processes of and participants in an organization—including orders, products, inventory, scheduling, shipping, customers, suppliers, and employees—a business cannot operate.

In less than 70 years, we have shifted from an industrial society to a knowledge-based economy driven by information. Businesses depend on information technology for everything from running daily operations to making strategic decisions. Computers are the tools of this information age, performing extremely complex operations as well as everyday jobs such as word processing and creating spreadsheets. The pace of change has been rapid since the personal computer became a fixture on most office desks. Individual units became part of small networks, followed by more sophisticated enterprise-wide networks. figures 19.1 and 19.2 summarize the types of computer equipment and software, respectively, most commonly used in business management information systems today.

Computer type	Description	Comments
Tablets	Self-contained computers in which applications (apps) can reside. These devices can also be linked into a network over which other programs can be accessed.	Increasing power, speed, and memory accessed via the cloud make these tablets the dominant computer for many business processes.
Desktop personal computers (PC)	Self-contained computers on which software can reside. These PCs can also be linked into a network over which other programs can be accessed.	Increasing power, speed, memory, and storage make these commonly used for many business processes. Can handle text, audio, video, and complex graphics.
Laptop computers	Portable computers similar in power to desktop computers.	Smaller size and weight make mobile computing easier for workers.
Minicomputers	Medium-sized computers with multiple processors, able to support from four to about 200 users at once.	The distinction between the larger minicomputers and smaller mainframes is blurring.
Miniframe computers	Large machines about the size of a refrigerator; can simultaneously run many different programs and support hundreds or thousands of users.	Extremely reliable and stable, these are used by companies and governments to process large amounts of data. They are more secure than PCs.
Servers	Greatest storage capacity and processing speeds.	These are subject to crashes and can be upgraded and repaired while operating.
Supercomputers	Most powerful computers, now capable of operating at speeds of 280 trillion calculations per second.	Companies can rent time to run projects from special supercomputer centers.

Figure 19.1: Business computing equipment.

Adapted from: OpenStax *Introduction to Business* (CC BY). Access for free at https://openstax.org/books/introduction-business/pages/13-introduction

Application type	Description
Word processing software	Used to write, edit, and format documents such as letters and reports. Spelling and grammar checkers, mail merge, tables, and other tools simplify document preparation.
Spreadsheet software	Used for preparation and analysis of financial statements, sales forecasts, budgets, and similar numerical and statistical data. Once the mathematical formulas are keyed into the spreadsheet, the data can be changed and the solution will be recalculated instantaneously.
Database management programs	Serve as electronic filing cabinets for records such as customer lists, employee data, and inventory information. Can sort data based on various criteria to create different reports.
Graphics and presentation programs	Create tables, graphs, and slides for customer presentations and reports. Can add images, video, animation, and sound effects.
Desktop publishing software	Combines word processing, graphics, and page layout software to create documents. Allows companies to design and produce sales brochures, catalogs, advertisements, and newsletters in-house.
Communications programs	Translate data into a form for transmission and transfer it across a network to other computers. Used to send and retrieve data and files.
Integrated software suites	Combine several popular types of programs, such as word processing, spreadsheet, database, graphics presentation, and communications programs. Component programs are designed to work together.
Groupware	Facilitates collaborative efforts of workgroups so that several people in different locations can work on one project. Supports online meetings and project management (scheduling, resource allocation, document and e-mail distribution, etc.).
Financial software	Used to compile accounting and financial data and create financial statements and reports.

Figure 19.2: Business computing software.

Although most workers spend their days at powerful desktop computers, other groups tackle massive computational problems at specialized supercomputer centers. Tasks that would take years on a PC can be completed in just hours on a supercomputer. With their ability to perform complex calculations quickly, supercomputers play a critical role in national security research, such as analysis of defense intelligence; scientific research, from biomedical experiments and drug development to simulations of earthquakes and star formations; demographic studies such as analyzing and predicting voting patterns; and weather and environmental studies. Businesses, too, put supercomputers to work by analyzing big data to gain insights into customer behavior, improving inventory and production management and for product design.[5]

The speed of these special machines has been rising steadily to meet increasing demands for greater computational capabilities, and the next goal is quadrillions of computations per second, or *petaflops*. Achieving these incredible speeds is critical to future scientific, medical, and business discoveries. Many countries, among them the United States, China, France, and Japan, have made petascale computing a priority.[6]

In addition to a business's own computers and internal networks, the internet makes it effortless to connect quickly to almost anyplace in the world. As Thomas Friedman points out in his book *The World Is Flat*, "We are now connecting all of the knowledge centers on the planet together into a single global network, which . . . could usher in an amazing era of prosperity and innovation."[7]

Adapted from: OpenStax *Introduction to Business* (CC BY). Access for free at https://openstax.org/books/introduction-business/pages/13-introduction

The opportunities for collaboration on a global scale increase daily. A manager can share information with hundreds of thousands of people worldwide as easily as with a colleague on another floor of the same office building. The internet and the web have become indispensable business tools that facilitate communication within companies as well as with customers.

The rise of electronic trading hubs is just one example of how technology is facilitating the global economy. Electronic trading hubs are not reserved for large companies of developed economies, however. Alibaba is piloting an e-hub called eWTP in Malaysia that will provide access to small businesses. As Jack Ma, Alibaba co-founder, said at eWTP's launch, "There are a lot of free-trade zones for efficient trade facilitation, but only for big companies. There is no free-trade zone designed for small companies. I have been shouting everywhere, screaming, that every government should do it."[8]

Many companies entrust an executive called the chief information officer (CIO) with the responsibility of managing all information resources. The importance of this responsibility is immense. In addition to the massive expansion of information gathered by today's businesses, most of us are knowledge workers who develop or use knowledge. Knowledge workers contribute to and benefit from information they use to perform planning, acquiring, searching, analyzing, organizing, storing, programming, producing, distributing, marketing, or selling functions. We must know how to gather and use information from the many resources available to us.

Figure 19.3: Google's CIO, Ben Fried.

In today's high-tech world, CIOs must possess not only the technical smarts to implement global IT infrastructures, integrate communications systems with partners, and protect customer data from insidious hackers, but they must also have strong business acumen. Google's acclaimed tech chief Ben Fried manages the technology necessary to deliver more than 9 billion searches daily, with an eye towards greater business efficiency, growth, and profits.

Adapted from: OpenStax *Introduction to Business* (CC BY). Access for free at https://openstax.org/books/introduction-business/pages/13-introduction

Expanding around the Globe: E-Hubs Integrate Global Commerce

Thanks to the wonders of technological advancement, global electronic trading now goes far beyond the internet retailing and trading that we are all familiar with. Special websites known as trading hubs, or eMarketplaces, facilitate electronic commerce between businesses in specific industries such as automotive manufacturing, retailing, telecom provisioning, aerospace, financial products and services, and more. Virtually all Forex (Foreign Exchange) is done via trading hubs that provide an open market for trading of a variety of currencies. Because there are a large number of trades involving currencies, the price is discoverable and there is transparency in the market. By contrast, Bitcoin is mainly traded in smaller quantities, and there are often large discrepancies between prices for the cryptocurrency in different exchanges.

The trading hub functions as a means of integrating the electronic collaboration of business services. Each hub provides standard formats for the electronic trading of documents used in a particular industry, as well as an array of services to sustain e-commerce between businesses in that industry. Services include demand forecasting, inventory management, partner directories, and transaction settlement services. And the payoff is significant—lowered costs, decreased inventory levels, and shorter time to market—resulting in bigger profits and enhanced competitiveness. For example, large-scale manufacturing procurement can amount to billions of dollars. Changing to "just-in-time purchasing" on the e-hub can save a considerable percentage of these costs.

Electronic trading across a hub can range from the collaborative integration of individual business processes to auctions and exchanges of goods (electronic barter). Global content management is an essential factor in promoting electronic trading agreements on the hub. A globally consistent view of the "content" of the hub must be available to all. Each participating company handles its own content, and applications such as *content managers* keep a continuously updated master catalog of the inventories of all members of the hub. The *transaction manager* application automates trading arrangements between companies, allowing the hub to provide aggregation and settlement services.

Adapted from: OpenStax *Introduction to Business* (CC BY). Access for free at https://openstax.org/books/introduction-business/pages/13-introduction

> Ultimately, trading hubs for numerous industries could be linked together in a global e-commerce web—an inclusive "*hub of all hubs.*" One creative thinker puts it this way: "The traditional linear, one step at a time, supply chain is dead. It will be replaced by parallel, asynchronous, real-time marketplace decision-making. Take manufacturing capacity as an example. Enterprises can bid their excess production capacity on the world e-commerce hub. Offers to buy capacity trigger requests from the seller for parts bids to suppliers who in turn put out requests to other suppliers, and this whole process will all converge in a matter of minutes."[9][10][11]

Because most jobs today depend on information—obtaining, using, creating, managing, and sharing it—this chapter begins with the role of information in decision-making and goes on to discuss computer networks and management information systems. The management of information technology—planning and protection—follows. Finally, we'll look at the latest trends in information technology. Throughout the chapter, examples show how managers and their companies are using computers to make better decisions in a highly competitive world.

Data and Information Systems

Information systems and the computers that support them are so much a part of our lives that we almost take them for granted. These management information systems methods and equipment that provide information about all aspects of a firm's operations provide managers with the information they need to make decisions. They help managers properly categorize and identify ideas that result in substantial operational and cost benefits.

Businesses collect a great deal of data—raw, unorganized facts that can be moved and stored—in their daily operations. Only through well-designed IT systems and the power of computers can managers process these data into meaningful and useful *information* and use it for specific purposes, such as making business decisions. One such form of business information is the **database**, an electronic filing system that collects and organizes data and information. Using software called a **database management system (DBMS)**, you can quickly and easily enter, store, organize, select, and retrieve data in a database. These data are then turned into information to run the business and to perform business analysis.

Databases are at the core of business information systems. For example, a customer database containing name, address, payment method, products ordered, price, order history, and similar data provides information to many departments. Marketing can track new orders and determine what products are selling best; sales can identify high-volume customers or contact customers about new or related products; operations managers use order information to obtain inventory and schedule production of the ordered products; and finance uses sales data to prepare financial statements. Later in the chapter, we will see how companies use very large databases called data warehouses and data marts.

Adapted from: OpenStax *Introduction to Business* (CC BY). Access for free at https://openstax.org/books/introduction-business/pages/13-introduction

Companies are discovering that they can't operate well with a series of separate information systems geared to solving specific departmental problems. It takes a team effort to integrate the systems described and involves employees throughout the firm. Company-wide **enterprise resource planning (ERP)** systems that bring together human resources, operations, and technology are becoming an integral part of business strategy. So is managing the collective knowledge contained in an organization, using data warehouses and other technology tools. Technology experts are learning more about the way the business operates, and business managers are learning to use information systems technology effectively to create new opportunities and reach their goals.

In summary, businesses depend on information technology for everything from running daily operations to making strategic decisions. Companies must have management information systems that gather, analyze, and distribute information to the appropriate parties, including employees, suppliers, and customers. These systems are comprised of different types of computers that collect data and process it into usable information for decision-making. Managers tap into databases to access the information they need, whether for placing inventory orders, scheduling production, or preparing long-range forecasts. They can compare information about the company's current status to its goals and standards. Company-wide enterprise resource planning systems that bring together human resources, operations, and technology are becoming an integral part of business strategy.

Linking Up: Computer Networks

Today most businesses use networks to deliver information to employees, suppliers, and customers. A computer network is a group of two or more computer systems linked together by communications channels to share data and information. Today's networks often link thousands of users and can transmit audio and video as well as data.

Figure 19.4: Computer networks.

Networks include clients and servers. The **client** is the application that runs on a personal computer or workstation. It relies on a **server** that manages network resources or performs special tasks such as storing files, managing one or more printers, or processing database queries. Any user on the network can access the server's capabilities.

Adapted from: OpenStax *Introduction to Business* (CC BY). Access for free at https://openstax.org/books/introduction-business/pages/13-introduction

By making it easy and fast to share information, networks have created new ways to work and increase productivity. They provide more efficient use of resources, permitting communication and collaboration across distance and time. With file-sharing, all employees, regardless of location, have access to the same information. Shared databases also eliminate duplication of effort. Employees at different sites can "screen-share" computer files, working on data as if they were in the same room. Their computers are connected by phone or cable lines, they all see the same thing on their display, and anyone can make changes that are seen by the other participants. The employees can also use the networks for videoconferencing.

Networks make it possible for companies to run enterprise software, large programs with integrated modules that manage all of the corporation's internal operations. Enterprise resource planning systems run on networks. Typical subsystems include finance, human resources, engineering, sales and order distribution, and order management and procurement. These modules work independently and then automatically exchange information, creating a company-wide system that includes current delivery dates, inventory status, quality control, and other critical information. Let's now look at the basic types of networks companies use to transmit data—local area networks and wide area networks—and popular networking applications such as intranets and virtual private networks.

Connecting Near and Far with Networks

Two basic types of networks are distinguished by the area they cover. A local area network (LAN) lets people at one site exchange data and share the use of hardware and software from a variety of computer manufacturers. LANs offer companies a more cost-effective way to link computers than linking terminals to a mainframe computer. The most common uses of LANs at small businesses, for example, are office automation, accounting, and information management. LANs can help companies reduce staff, streamline operations, and cut processing costs. LANs can be set up with wired or wireless connections.

A wide area network (WAN) connects computers at different sites via telecommunications media such as phone lines, satellites, and microwaves. A modem connects the computer or a terminal to the telephone line and transmits data almost instantly, in less than a second. The internet is essentially a worldwide WAN. Communications companies, such as AT&T, Verizon, and Sprint, operate very large WANs. Companies also connect LANs at various locations into WANs. WANs make it possible for companies to work on critical projects around the clock by using teams in different time zones.

Several forms of WANs—intranets, virtual private networks (VPN), and extranets—use internet technology. Here we'll look at intranets, internal corporate networks that are widely available in the corporate world, and VPNs. Although wireless networks have been around for more than a decade, they are increasing in use because of falling costs, faster and more reliable technology, and improved standards. They are similar to their wired LAN and WAN cousins, except they use radio frequency signals to transmit data. You use a wireless WAN (WWAN) regularly when you use your cellular phone. WANs' coverage can span several countries. Telecommunications carriers operate using wireless WANs.

Adapted from: OpenStax *Introduction to Business* (CC BY). Access for free at https://openstax.org/books/introduction-business/pages/13-introduction

Wireless LANs (WLAN) that transmit data at one site offer an alternative to traditional wired systems. WLANs' reach is a radius of 500 feet indoors and 1,000 feet outdoors and can be extended with antennas, transmitters, and other devices. The wireless devices communicate with a wired access point into the wired network. WLANs are convenient for specialized applications where wires are in the way or when employees are in different locations in a building. Hotels, airports, restaurants, hospitals, retail establishments, universities, and warehouses are among the largest users of WLANs, also known as Wi-Fi. For example, the Veterans Administration Hospital in West Haven, Connecticut, recently added Wi-Fi access in all patient rooms to upgrade its existing WLAN to improve patient access, quality, and reliability. The new WLAN supports many different functions, from better on-site communication among doctors and nurses through both data transmission and voice-over-internet phone systems to data-centric applications such as its Meditech clinical information system and pharmacy management.[12]

Catching the Entrepreneurial Spirit: Documenting the Future

Potential customers of Captiva Software didn't share company cofounder and chief executive Reynolds Bish's belief that paper wasn't going away. They held to the idea that personal computers and the internet would make paper disappear, and they weren't going to invest in software to organize their documents. That almost caused Captiva to go under. "We really were afraid we weren't going to make it," said Jim Berglund, an early investor in Captiva and a former board member.

But Bish asked investors for another $4 million commitment—on a bet that paper was here to stay. Bish recalls a board member telling him, "Five years from now people are going to either think you're a genius or a complete idiot."

That conversation took place 20 years ago. Captiva Software was named one of the fastest-growing technology companies in San Diego in the early 2000s for its 172 percent increase in revenues. The company was then acquired by EMC Corp.—the sixth-largest software company in the world and top maker of corporate data-storage equipment, with projected annual revenues of more than $9 billion—for $275 million in cash, rewarding embattled early Captiva investors with 10 times their money back. (In 2016, Dell acquired EMC for more than $67 billion.)

Captiva began its journey to the big time in 1989 in Park City, Utah, as TextWare Corp., a small data-entry company. Cofounder Steven Burton's technical expertise, Bish's business background, and a credit card helped them get the business going. "It was pure bootstrapping," Bish said. "We did everything from going without a salary for a year or more to using up our credit cards."

Adapted from: OpenStax *Introduction to Business* (CC BY). Access for free at https://openstax.org/books/introduction-business/pages/13-introduction

Bish and Burton quickly saw the need for employees to enter data more directly and accurately. The software they developed still required clerks to type information from a paper document, but it could check for inaccuracies, matching zip codes to cities, for instance. In 1996, TextWare produced software that could "read" typewritten words on a scanned piece of paper, which significantly reduced the number of data-entry clerks needed. It found popularity with credit-card processors, insurance companies, shipping companies, and other corporations that handled thousands of forms every day.

TextWare acquired or merged with five firms, went public, changed its name twice, and in 1998 set up its headquarters in San Diego, California, after buying Wheb Systems, which is based there. In 2002, the company merged with publicly held ActionPoint, a San Jose, California, document-processing company, and changed its name to Captiva.

An estimated 80 percent of all information is still paper-based, according to market research firm Forrester Research. Captiva's flagship products, InputAccel and FormWare, process over 85 million pieces of paper worldwide every day, leaving no doubt that Bish's vision was on target. Paper is indeed here to stay.[13][14][15][16][17][18]

An Inside Job: Intranets

Like LANs, intranets are private corporate networks. Many companies use both types of internal networks. However, because they use internet technology to connect computers, intranets are WANs that link employees in many locations and with different types of computers. Essentially mini-internets that serve only the company's employees, intranets operate behind a *firewall* that prevents unauthorized access. Employees navigate using a standard web browser, which makes the intranet easy to use. They are also considerably less expensive to install and maintain than other network types and take advantage of the internet's interactive features such as chat rooms and team workspaces. Many software providers now offer off-the-shelf intranet packages so that companies of all sizes can benefit from the increased access to and distribution of information.

Companies now recognize the power of intranets to connect employers and employees in many ways, promoting teamwork and knowledge-sharing. Intranets have many applications, from human resource (HR) administration to logistics. For instance, a benefits administration intranet can become a favorite with employees. Instead of having to contact an HR representative to make any changes in personnel records or retirement plan contributions or to submit time sheets, staff members simply log on to the intranet and update the information themselves. Managers can also process staffing updates, performance reviews, and incentive payments without filing paperwork with human resources. Employees can regularly check an online job board for new positions. Shifting routine administrative tasks to the intranet can bring additional benefits such as reducing the size of the HR department by 30 percent and allowing HR staff members to turn their attention to more substantive projects.[19]

Enterprise Portals Open the Door to Productivity

Intranets that take a broader view serve as sophisticated knowledge management tools.

One such intranet is the enterprise portal, an internal website that provides proprietary corporate information to a defined user group. Portals can take one of three forms: business to employee (B2E), business to business (B2B), and business to consumer (B2C). Unlike a standard intranet, enterprise portals allow individuals or user groups to customize the portal home page to gather just the information they need for their particular job situations and deliver it through a single web page. Because of their complexity, enterprise portals are typically the result of a collaborative project that brings together designs developed and perfected through the effort of HR, corporate communications, and information technology departments.

More companies use portal technology to provide:

- A consistent, simple user interface across the company
- Integration of disparate systems and multiple sets of data and information
- A single source for accurate and timely information that integrates internal and external information
- A shorter time to perform tasks and processes
- Cost savings through the elimination of information intermediaries
- Improved communications within the company and with customers, suppliers, dealers, and distributors

No More Tangles: Wireless Technologies

Wireless technology has become commonplace today. We routinely use devices such as cellular phones, mobile devices, garage door openers, and television remote controls—without thinking of them as examples of wireless technology. Businesses use wireless technologies to improve communications with customers, suppliers, and employees.

Companies in the package delivery industry, such as UPS and FedEx, were among the first users of wireless technology. Delivery personnel use handheld computers to send immediate confirmation of package receipt. You may also have seen meter readers and repair personnel from utility and energy companies send data from remote locations back to central computers.

Adapted from: OpenStax *Introduction to Business* (CC BY). Access for free at https://openstax.org/books/introduction-business/pages/13-introduction

Bluetooth short-range wireless technology is a global standard that improves personal connectivity for users of mobile phones, portable computers, and stereo headsets, and Bluetooth wirelessly connects keyboards and mice to computers and headsets to phones and music players. A Bluetooth-enabled mobile phone, for example, provides safer hands-free phone use while driving. The technology is finding many applications in the auto industry as well. Bluetooth wireless technology is now standard in many vehicles today. Many car, technology, and cell phone companies—among them Amazon, Apple, Audi, BMW, DaimlerChrysler, Google, Honda, Saab, Toyota, and Volkswagen—already offer Bluetooth hands-free solutions. Other uses include simplifying the connection of portable digital music players to the car's audio system and transferring downloaded music to the system.[20]

Figure 19.5: The iPad Pro is an example of an ultramobile PC.

Although designing a true mobile replacement for the desktop PC has proved elusive for computer manufacturers, ultramobile PCs offer wireless functions many professionals want—web browsing, e-mail, Microsoft Office, and telephony. The Apple iPad Pro runs iOS 10, and with its 10.5-inch LCD touch screen and stylus, the mini-tablet provides the power of a desktop PC and freedom from pen and paper.

 An interactive H5P element has been excluded from this version of the text. You can view it online here: https://pressbooks.lib.vt.edu/fundamentalsofbusiness4e/?p=233#h5p-54

Private Lines: Virtual Private Networks

Many companies use virtual private networks to connect two or more private networks (such as LANs) over a public network, such as the internet. VPNs include strong security measures to allow only authorized users to access the network and its sensitive corporate information. Companies with widespread offices may find that a VPN is a more cost-effective option than creating a network using purchased networking equipment and leasing expensive private lines. This type of private network is more limited than a VPN, because it doesn't allow authorized users to connect to the corporate network when they are at home or traveling.

Figure 19.6: Virtual private networks (VPNs).

Adapted from: OpenStax *Introduction to Business* (CC BY). Access for free at https://openstax.org/books/introduction-business/pages/13-introduction

As figure 19.6 shows, the VPN uses existing internet infrastructure and equipment to connect remote users and offices almost anywhere in the world—without long-distance charges. In addition to saving on telecommunications costs, companies using VPNs don't have to buy or maintain special networking equipment and can outsource management of remote access equipment. VPNs are useful for salespeople and telecommuters, who can access the company's network as if they were on-site at the company's office. On the downside, the VPN's availability and performance, especially when it uses the internet, depends on factors largely outside of an organization's control.

VPNs are popular with many different types of organizations. Why? Security is one of the main reasons to always use a VPN to access the internet. Because all your data is encrypted once tunneled, if a hacker were trying to intercept your browsing activity, say, while you were entering your credit card number to make an online purchase, the encryption would stymie their efforts. That's why it's a particularly good idea to use VPNs in public settings such as coffee shops and airports.[21]

With the increase need for privacy and security, there are a number of different VPN service providers that have emerged in recent years offering various subscription plans. NordVPN is one example. NordVPN was launched in 2012 by childhood friends and within 10 years became known as the "world's leading VPN trusted by millions of people all over the globe".[22]

Software on Demand: Application Service Providers

As software developers release new types of application programs and updated versions of existing ones every year or two, companies have to analyze whether they can justify buying or upgrading to the new software—in terms of both cost and implementation time. **Application service providers (ASPs)** offer a different approach to this problem. Companies subscribe, usually on a monthly basis, to an ASP and use the applications much like you'd use telephone voice mail, the technology for which resides at the phone company. Other names for ASPs include on-demand software, hosted applications, and software-as-a-service. Figure 19.7 shows how the ASP interfaces with software and hardware vendors and developers, the IT department, and users.

The simplest ASP applications are automated—for example, a user might use one to build a simple e-commerce site. ASPs provide three major categories of applications to users:

- Enterprise applications, including customer relationship management (CRM), enterprise resource planning, e-commerce, and data warehousing
- Collaborative applications for internal communications, e-mail, groupware, document creation, and management messaging
- Applications for personal use—for example, games, entertainment software, and home-office applications

Figure 19.7: Structure of an ASP relationship.

Adapted from: OpenStax *Introduction to Business* (CC BY). Access for free at https://openstax.org/books/introduction-business/pages/13-introduction

According to recent surveys, more companies are currently using an ASP, and even moving their legacy systems to the cloud. Estimates suggest revenues from subscriptions to on-demand cloud services were about $180 billion in 2017. This sector is growing much more rapidly—three times faster—than traditional hardware and software.[23]

As this market grows, more companies are adding on-demand offerings to their traditional software packages. Amazon (Amazon Web Services), IBM, Microsoft, and Salesforce.com are among the leading cloud service providers.[24]

Until recently, many companies were reluctant to outsource critical enterprise applications to third-party providers. As ASPs improved their technologies and proved to be reliable and cost-effective, attitudes have changed. Companies, both large and small, seek cost advantages such as the convenience ASPs provide. The basic idea behind subscribing to an ASP is compelling. Users can access any of their applications and data from any computer, and IT can avoid purchasing, installing, supporting, and upgrading expensive software applications. ASPs buy and maintain the software on their servers and distribute it through high-speed networks. Subscribers rent the applications they want for a set period of time and price. The savings in licensing fees, infrastructure, time, and staff are significant.

Managed service providers (MSPs) represent the next generation of ASPs, offering greater customization and expanded capabilities that include business processes and complete management of the network servers. The global market for managed IT services reached $149.1 billion in 2016. This market is estimated to reach $256.5 billion in 2021, from $166.7 billion in 2017, at a compound annual growth rate of 11.5 percent for the period 2018 through 2021.[25]

In summary, today companies use networks of linked computers that share data and expensive hardware to improve operating efficiency. Types of networks include local area networks, wide area networks, and wireless local area networks. Intranets are private WANs that allow a company's employees to communicate quickly with one other and work on joint projects, regardless of their location. Companies are finding new uses for wireless technologies such as tablets, cell phones, and other mobile devices. Virtual private networks give companies a cost-effective secure connection between remote locations by using public networks such as the internet.

Management Information Systems

Whereas individuals use business productivity software such as word processing, spreadsheet, and graphics programs to accomplish a variety of tasks, the job of managing a company's information needs falls to **management information systems**: users, hardware, and software that support decision-making. Information systems collect and store the company's key data and produce the information managers need for analysis, control, and decision-making.

Adapted from: OpenStax *Introduction to Business* (CC BY). Access for free at https://openstax.org/books/introduction-business/pages/13-introduction

Factories use computer-based information systems to automate production processes and order and monitor inventory. Most companies use them to process customer orders and handle billing and vendor payments. Banks use a variety of information systems to process transactions such as deposits, ATM withdrawals, and loan payments. Most consumer transactions also involve information systems. When you check out at the supermarket, book a hotel room online, or download music over the internet, information systems record and track the transaction and transmit the data to the necessary places.

Companies typically have several types of information systems, starting with systems to process transactions. **Management support systems** are dynamic systems that allow users to analyze data to make forecasts, identify business trends, and model business strategies. Office automation systems improve the flow of communication throughout the organization. Each type of information system serves a particular level of decision-making: operational, tactical, and strategic. Figure 19.8 shows the relationship between transaction processing and management support systems as well as the management levels they serve. Let's take a more detailed look at how companies and managers use transaction processing and management support systems to manage information.

Transaction Processing Systems

Figure 19.8: Example of a company's integrated information system.

Adapted from: OpenStax *Introduction to Business* (CC BY). Access for free at https://openstax.org/books/introduction-business/pages/13-introduction

406 | Technology in Business

A firm's integrated information system starts with its transaction processing system (TPS). The TPS receives raw data from internal and external sources and prepares these data for storage in a database similar to a microcomputer database but vastly larger. In fact, all the company's key data are stored in a single huge database that becomes the company's central information resource. As noted earlier, the **database management system** tracks the data and allows users to query the database for the information they need.

The database can be updated in two ways: batch processing, where data are collected over some time period and processed together, and online, or real-time, processing, which processes data as they become available. Batch processing uses computer resources very efficiently and is well-suited to applications such as payroll processing that require periodic rather than continuous processing. Online processing keeps the company's data current. When you make an airline reservation, the information is entered into the airline's information system, and you quickly receive confirmation, typically through an e-mail. Online processing is more expensive than batch processing, so companies must weigh the cost versus the benefit. For example, a factory that operates around the clock may use real-time processing for inventory and other time-sensitive requirements but process accounting data in batches overnight.

 An interactive H5P element has been excluded from this version of the text. You can view it online here: https://pressbooks.lib.vt.edu/fundamentalsofbusiness4e/?p=233#h5p-55

Decisions, Decisions: Management Support Systems

Transaction processing systems automate routine and tedious back-office processes such as accounting, order processing, and financial reporting. They reduce clerical expenses and provide basic operational information quickly. **Management support systems (MSSs)** use the internal master database to perform high-level analyses that help managers make better decisions.

Information technologies such as data warehousing are part of more advanced MSSs. A data warehouse combines many databases across the whole company into one central database that supports management decision-making. With a data warehouse, managers can easily access and share data across the enterprise to get a broad overview rather than just isolated segments of information. Data warehouses include software to extract data from operational databases, maintain the data in the warehouse, and provide data to users. They can analyze data much faster than transaction-processing systems. Data warehouses may contain many data marts, special subsets of a data warehouse that each deal with a single area of data. Data marts are organized for quick analysis.

Adapted from: OpenStax *Introduction to Business* (CC BY). Access for free at https://openstax.org/books/introduction-business/pages/13-introduction

Companies use data warehouses to gather, secure, and analyze data for many purposes, including customer relationship management systems, fraud detection, product-line analysis, and corporate asset management. Retailers might wish to identify customer demographic characteristics and shopping patterns to improve direct-mailing responses. Banks can more easily spot credit-card fraud, as well as analyze customer usage patterns.

According to Forrester Research, about 60 percent of companies with $1 billion or more in revenues use data warehouses as a management tool. Union Pacific (UP), a $19 billion railroad, turned to data warehouse technology to streamline its business operations. By consolidating multiple separate systems, UP achieved a unified supply-chain system that also enhanced its customer service. "Before our data warehouse came into being we had stovepipe systems," says Roger Bresnahan, principal engineer. "None of them talked to each other. . . . We couldn't get a whole picture of the railroad."

UP's data warehouse system took many years and the involvement of 26 departments to create. The results were well worth the effort: UP can now make more accurate forecasts, identify the best traffic routes, and determine the most profitable market segments. The ability to predict seasonal patterns and manage fuel costs more closely has saved UP millions of dollars by optimizing locomotive and other asset utilization and through more efficient crew management. In just three years, Bresnahan reports, the data warehouse system had paid for itself.[26]

At the first level of an MSS is an *information-reporting system,* which uses summary data collected by the TPS to produce both regularly scheduled and special reports. The level of detail would depend on the user. A company's payroll personnel might get a weekly payroll report showing how each employee's paycheck was determined. Higher-level mangers might receive a payroll summary report that shows total labor cost and overtime by department and a comparison of current labor costs with those in the prior year. Exception reports show cases that fail to meet some standard. An accounts receivable exception report that lists all customers with overdue accounts would help collection personnel focus their work. Special reports are generated only when a manager requests them; for example, a report showing sales by region and type of customer can highlight reasons for a sales decline.

Adapted from: OpenStax *Introduction to Business* (CC BY). Access for free at https://openstax.org/books/introduction-business/pages/13-introduction

Decision Support Systems

A **decision support system (DSS)** helps managers make decisions using interactive computer models that describe real-world processes. The DSS also uses data from the internal database but looks for specific data that relate to the problems at hand. It is a tool for answering "what if" questions about what would happen if the manager made certain changes. In simple cases, a manager can create a spreadsheet and try changing some of the numbers. For instance, a manager could create a spreadsheet to show the amount of overtime required if the number of workers increases or decreases. With models, the manager enters into the computer the values that describe a particular situation, and the program computes the results. Marketing executives at a furniture company could run DSS models that use sales data and demographic assumptions to develop forecasts of the types of furniture that would appeal to the fastest-growing population groups.

Figure 19.9: There's push to add decision support systems to the clinical field.

Companies can use a predictive analytics program to improve their inventory management system and use big data to target customer segments for new products and line extensions.

Decision support systems help businesses by providing quantitative data and predictive models that aid problem-solving and decision-making. Now the health-care industry wants this technology in hospitals to improve the practice of medicine. Spearheading the effort for a clinical decision-support system is the American Medical Informatics Association, which believes a national DSS could help physicians with diagnosing and treating illnesses.

Executive Information Systems

Although similar to a DSS, an executive information system (EIS) is customized for an individual executive. These systems provide specific information for strategic decisions. For example, a CEO's EIS may include special spreadsheets that present financial data comparing the company to its principal competitors and graphs showing current economic and industry trends.

Adapted from: OpenStax *Introduction to Business* (CC BY). Access for free at https://openstax.org/books/introduction-business/pages/13-introduction

Expert Systems

An expert system gives managers advice similar to what they would get from a human consultant. Artificial intelligence enables computers to reason and learn to solve problems in much the same way humans do, using what-if reasoning. Although they are expensive and difficult to create, expert systems are finding their way into more companies as more applications are found. Lower-end expert systems can even run on mobile devices. Top-of-the-line systems help airlines appropriately deploy aircraft and crews, critical to the carriers' efficient operations. The cost of hiring enough people to do these ongoing analytical tasks would be prohibitively expensive. Expert systems have also been used to help explore for oil, schedule employee work shifts, and diagnose illnesses. Some expert systems take the place of human experts, whereas others assist them.

In summary, a management information system consists of a transaction processing system, management support systems, and an office automation system. The transaction processing system collects and organizes operational data on the firm's activities. Management support systems help managers make better decisions. They include an information-reporting system that provides information based on the data collected by the TPS to the managers who need it; decision support systems that use models to assist in answering "what if" types of questions; and expert systems that give managers advice similar to what they would get from a human consultant. Executive information systems are customized to the needs of top management.

Technology Management and Planning

With the help of computers, people have produced more data in the last 30 years than in the previous 5,000 years combined. Companies today make sizable investments in information technology to help them manage this overwhelming amount of data, convert the data into knowledge, and deliver it to the people who need it. In many cases, however, the companies do not reap the desired benefits from these expenditures. Among the typical complaints from senior executives are that the company is spending too much and not getting adequate performance and payoff from IT investments, these investments do not relate to business strategy, the firm seems to be buying the latest technology for technology's sake, and communications between IT specialists and IT users are poor.

Optimize IT!

Managing a company's enterprise-wide IT operations, especially when those often stretch across multiple locations, software applications, and systems, is no easy task. IT managers must deal not only with on-site systems; they must also oversee the networks and other technology, such as mobile devices that handle e-mail messaging, that connect staff working at locations ranging from the next town to another continent. At the same time, IT managers face time constraints and budget restrictions, making their jobs even more challenging.

Adapted from: OpenStax *Introduction to Business* (CC BY). Access for free at https://openstax.org/books/introduction-business/pages/13-introduction

Growing companies may find themselves with a decentralized IT structure that includes many separate systems and duplication of efforts. A company that wants to enter or expand into e-commerce needs systems flexible enough to adapt to this changing marketplace. Security for equipment and data is another critical area, which we will cover later in the chapter.

The goal is to develop an integrated, company-wide technology plan that balances business judgment, technology expertise, and technology investment. IT planning requires a coordinated effort among a firm's top executives, IT managers, and business-unit managers to develop a comprehensive plan. Such plans must take into account the company's strategic objectives and how the right technology will help managers reach those goals.

Technology management and planning go beyond buying new technology. Today companies are cutting IT budgets so that managers are being asked to do more with less. They are implementing projects that leverage their investment in the technology they already have, finding ways to maximize efficiency and optimize utilization.

An interactive H5P element has been excluded from this version of the text. You can view it online here:
https://pressbooks.lib.vt.edu/fundamentalsofbusiness4e/?p=233#h5p-56

Managing Knowledge Resources

As a result of the proliferation of information, we are also seeing a major shift from information management to a broader view that focuses on finding opportunities in and unlocking the value of intellectual rather than physical assets. Whereas *information management* involves collecting, processing, and condensing information, the more difficult task of knowledge management (KM) focuses on researching, gathering, organizing, and sharing an organization's collective knowledge to improve productivity, foster innovation, and gain competitive advantage. Some companies are even creating a new position, *chief knowledge officer*, to head up this effort.[27]

Companies use their IT systems to facilitate the physical sharing of knowledge. But better hardware and software are not the answer to KM. KM is not technology-based, but rather a business practice that uses technology. Technology alone does not constitute KM, nor is it the solution to KM. Rather, it facilitates KM. Executives with successful KM initiatives understand that KM is not a matter of buying a major software application that serves as a data depository and coordinates all of a company's intellectual capital. According to Melinda Bickerstaff, vice president of knowledge management at Bristol-Myers Squibb (BMS), any such "leading with technology" approach is a sure path to failure. "Knowledge management has to be perceived as a business problem solver, not as an abstract concept," Bickerstaff explains.

Adapted from: OpenStax *Introduction to Business* (CC BY). Access for free at https://openstax.org/books/introduction-business/pages/13-introduction

Effective KM calls for an interdisciplinary approach that coordinates all aspects of an organization's knowledge. It requires a major change in behavior as well as technology to leverage the power of information systems, especially the internet, and a company's human capital resources. The first step is creating an information culture through organizational structure and rewards that promotes a more flexible, collaborative way of working and communicating. Moving an organization toward KM is no easy task, but it is well worth the effort in terms of creating a more collaborative environment, reducing duplication of effort, and increasing shared knowledge. The benefits can be significant in terms of growth, time, and money.

At Bristol-Meyers Squibb, a major pharmaceutical company, Bickerstaff began the KM implementation by looking for specific information-related problems to solve so that the company would save time and/or money. For example, she learned that company scientists were spending about 18 percent of their time searching multiple databases to find patents and other information. Simply integrating the relevant databases gave researchers the ability to perform faster searches. A more complex project involved compiling the best practices of drug-development teams with the best FDA approval rates so that other groups could benefit. Rather than send forms that could be easily set aside, Bickenstaff arranged to conduct interviews and lessons-learned sessions. The information was then developed into interesting articles rather than dry corporate reports.[28]

Technology Planning

A good technology plan provides employees with the tools they need to perform their jobs at the highest levels of efficiency. The first step is a general needs assessment, followed by ranking of projects and the specific choices of hardware and software. Figure 19.10 poses some basic questions departmental managers and IT specialists should ask when planning technology purchases.

Questions for IT project planning

What are the company's overall objectives?

What problems does the company want to solve?

How can technology help meet those goals and solve the problems?

What are the company's IT priorities, both short- and long-term?

What type of technology infrastructure (centralized or decentralized) best serves the company's needs?

Which technologies meet the company's requirements?

Are additional hardware and software required? If so, will they integrate with the company's existing systems?

Does the system design and implementation include the people and process changes, in addition to the technological ones?

Do you have the in-house capabilities to develop and implement the proposed applications, or should you bring in an outside specialist?

Figure 19.10: Questions for IT project planning.

Adapted from: OpenStax *Introduction to Business* (CC BY). Access for free at https://openstax.org/books/introduction-business/pages/13-introduction

Once managers identify the projects that make business sense, they can choose the best products for the company's needs. The final step is to evaluate the potential benefits of the technology in terms of efficiency and effectiveness. For a successful project, you must evaluate and restructure business processes, choose technology, develop and implement the system, and manage the change processes to best serve your organizational needs. Installing a new IT system on top of inefficient business processes is a waste of time and money!

In summary, to get the most value from IT, companies must go beyond simply collecting and summarizing information. Technology planning involves evaluating the company's goals and objectives and using the right technology to reach them. IT managers must also evaluate the existing infrastructure to get the best return on the company's investment in IT assets. Knowledge management focuses on sharing an organization's collective knowledge to improve productivity and foster innovation. Some companies establish the position of chief knowledge officer to head up KM activities.

Protecting Computers and Information

Have you ever lost a term paper you worked on for weeks because your hard drive crashed or you deleted the wrong file? You were upset, angry, and frustrated. Multiply that paper and your feelings hundreds of times over, and you can understand why companies must protect computers, networks, and the information they store and transmit from a variety of potential threats. For example, security breaches of corporate information systems—from human hackers or electronic versions such as viruses and worms—are increasing at an alarming rate. The ever-increasing dependence on computers requires plans that cover human error, power outages, equipment failure, hacking, and terrorist attacks. To withstand natural disasters such as major fires, earthquakes, and floods, many companies install specialized fault-tolerant computer systems.

Disasters are not the only threat to data. A great deal of data, much of it confidential, can easily be tapped or destroyed by anyone who knows about computers. Keeping your networks secure from unauthorized access—from internal as well as external sources—requires formal security policies and enforcement procedures. The increasing popularity of mobile devices—laptops, tablets, and cell phones—and wireless networks requires new types of security provisions.

In response to mounting security concerns, companies have increased spending on technology to protect their IT infrastructure and data. Along with specialized hardware and software, companies need to develop specific security strategies that take a proactive approach to prevent security and technical problems before they start. However, a recent CIO article lamented the lack of basic security policies that companies only implement after a hack or data crisis.[29]

Adapted from: OpenStax *Introduction to Business* (CC BY). Access for free at https://openstax.org/books/introduction-business/pages/13-introduction

Data Security Issues

Unauthorized access into a company's computer systems can be expensive, and not just in monetary terms. Juniper Networks estimates that cybercrime will cost businesses more than $2 trillion in 2019, compared to just $450 million in 2001. The most costly categories of threats include worms, viruses, and Trojan horses (defined later in this section); computer theft; financial fraud; and unauthorized network access. The report also states that almost all U.S. businesses report at least one security issue, and almost 20 percent have experienced multiple security incidents.[30]

Computer crooks are becoming more sophisticated all the time, finding new ways to get into ultra-secure sites. "As companies and consumers continue to move towards a networked and information economy, more opportunity exists for cybercriminals to take advantage of vulnerabilities on networks and computers," says Chris Christiansen, program vice president at technology research firm IDC.[31]

Whereas early cybercrooks were typically amateur hackers working alone, the new ones are more professional and often work in gangs to commit large-scale internet crimes for large financial rewards. The internet, where criminals can hide behind anonymous screen names, has increased the stakes and expanded the realm of opportunities to commit identity theft and similar crimes. Catching such cybercriminals is difficult, and fewer than 5 percent are caught.[32]

Figure 19.11: Data security is under constant attack.

Data security is under constant attack. In 2017, cybercriminals penetrated Equifax, one of the largest credit bureaus in the nation, and stole the personal data of more than 145 million people. To date, it is considered one of the worst data breaches of all time because of the amount of sensitive data stolen, including consumers' Social Security numbers.

Firms are taking steps to prevent these costly computer crimes and problems, which fall into several major categories:

- *Unauthorized access and security breaches.* Whether from internal or external sources, unauthorized access and security breaches are a top concern of IT managers. These can create havoc with a company's systems and damage customer relationships. Unauthorized access also includes employees, who can copy confidential new-product information and provide it to competitors or use company systems for personal business that may interfere with systems operation. Networking links also make it easier for someone outside the organization to gain access to a company's computers.

  One of the latest forms of cybercrime involves secretly installing keylogging software via software downloads, e-mail attachments, or shared files. This software then copies and transmits a user's keystrokes—passwords, PINs, and other personal information—from selected sites, such as banking and credit card sites, to thieves.

Adapted from: OpenStax *Introduction to Business* (CC BY). Access for free at https://openstax.org/books/introduction-business/pages/13-introduction

- *Computer viruses, worms, and Trojan horses.* Computer viruses and related security problems such as worms and Trojan horses are among the top threats to business and personal computer security. A computer program that copies itself into other software and can spread to other computer systems, a computer virus can destroy the contents of a computer's hard drive or damage files. Another form is called a *worm* because it spreads itself automatically from computer to computer. Unlike a virus, a worm doesn't require e-mail to replicate and transmit itself into other systems. It can enter through valid access points.

  Trojan horses are programs that appear to be harmless and from legitimate sources but trick the user into installing them. When run, they damage the user's computer. For example, a Trojan horse may claim to get rid of viruses but instead infects the computer. Other forms of Trojan horses provide a "trapdoor" that allows undocumented access to a computer, unbeknownst to the user. Trojan horses do not, however, infect other files or self-replicate.[33]

  Viruses can hide for weeks, months, or even years before starting to damage information. A virus that "infects" one computer or network can be spread to another computer by sharing disks or by downloading infected files over the internet. To protect data from virus damage, virus protection software automatically monitors computers to detect and remove viruses. Program developers make regular updates available to guard against newly created viruses. In addition, experts are becoming more proficient at tracking down virus authors, who are subject to criminal charges.

- *Deliberate damage to equipment or information.* For example, an unhappy employee in the purchasing department could get into the company's computer system and delete information on past orders and future inventory needs. The sabotage could severely disrupt production and the accounts payable system. Willful acts to destroy or change the data in computers are hard to prevent. To lessen the damage, companies should back up critical information.

- *Spam.* Although you might think that *spam*, or unsolicited and unwanted e-mail, is just a nuisance, it also poses a security threat to companies. Viruses spread through e-mail attachments that can accompany spam e-mails. Spam is now clogging blogs, instant messages, and cell phone text messages as well as e-mail inboxes. Spam presents other threats to a corporation: lost productivity and expenses from dealing with spam, such as opening the messages and searching for legitimate messages that special spam filters keep out.

- *Software and media piracy.* The copying of copyrighted software programs, games, and movies by people who haven't paid for them is another form of unauthorized use. Piracy, defined as using software without a license, takes revenue away from the company that developed the program—usually at great cost. It includes making counterfeit CDs to sell as well as personal copying of software to share with friends.

Preventing Problems

Creating formal written information security policies to set standards and provide the basis for enforcement is the first step in a company's security strategy. Unfortunately, a recent survey of IT executives worldwide revealed that over two-thirds expect a cyberattack in the near future. Stephanie Ewing, a data security expert, states, "Having a documented, tested process brings order to chaotic situations and keeps everyone focused on solving the most pressing issues." Without information security strategies in place, companies spend too much time in a reactive mode—responding to crises—and don't focus enough on prevention.[34]

Security plans should have the support of top management, and then follow with procedures to implement the security policies. Because IT is a dynamic field with ongoing changes to equipment and processes, it's important to review security policies often. Some security policies can be handled automatically, by technical measures, whereas others involve administrative policies that rely on humans to perform them. Examples of administrative policies are "Users must change their passwords every 90 days" and "End users will update their virus signatures at least once a week."[35]

Percentage	Concern for protecting data
52	Aren't sure how to secure connected devices and apps
40	Don't immediately change default passwords
33	Don't think they can control how companies collect personal information
33	Parents admit they don't know the risks well enough to explain to children
37	Use credit-monitoring services

Figure 19.11: Five areas of concern regarding the protection of data.

Preventing costly problems can be as simple as regularly backing up applications and data. Companies should have systems in place that automatically back up the company's data every day and store copies of the backups off-site. In addition, employees should back up their own work regularly. Another good policy is to maintain a complete and current database of all IT hardware, software, and user details to make it easier to manage software licenses and updates and diagnose problems. In many cases, IT staff can use remote access technology to automatically monitor and fix problems, as well as update applications and services.

Companies should never overlook the human factor in the security equation. One of the most common ways that outsiders get into company systems is by posing as an employee, first getting the staffer's full name and username from an e-mail message and then calling the help desk to ask for a forgotten password. Crooks can also get passwords by viewing them on notes attached to a desk or computer monitor, using machines that employees leave logged on when they leave their desks, and leaving laptop computers with sensitive information unsecured in public places.

Adapted from: OpenStax *Introduction to Business* (CC BY). Access for free at https://openstax.org/books/introduction-business/pages/13-introduction

Portable devices, from handheld computers to tiny plug-and-play flash drives and other storage devices (including mobile phones), pose security risks as well. They are often used to store sensitive data such as passwords, bank details, and calendars. Mobile devices can spread viruses when users download virus-infected documents to their company computers.

Imagine the problems that could arise if an employee saw a calendar entry on a mobile device like "meeting re: layoffs," an outsider saw "meeting about merger with ABC Company," or an employee lost a flash drive containing files about marketing plans for a new product. Manufacturers are responding to IT managers' concerns about security by adding password protection and encryption to flash drives. Companies can also use flash drive monitoring software that prevents unauthorized access on PCs and laptops.

Companies have many ways to avoid an IT meltdown, as shown below:

- Develop a comprehensive plan and policies that include portable as well as fixed equipment.
- Protect the equipment itself with stringent physical security measures to the premises.
- Protect data using special *encryption* technology to encode confidential information so only the recipient can decipher it.
- Stop unwanted access from inside or outside with special authorization systems. These can be as simple as a password or as sophisticated as fingerprint or voice identification.
- Install *firewalls*, hardware or software designed to prevent unauthorized access to or from a private network.
- Monitor network activity with intrusion-detection systems that signal possible unauthorized access, and document suspicious events.
- Conduct periodic IT audits to catalog all attached storage devices as well as computers.
- Use technology that monitors ports for unauthorized attached devices and turn off those that are not approved for business use.
- Train employees to troubleshoot problems in advance, rather than just react to them.
- Hold frequent staff-training sessions to teach correct security procedures, such as logging out of networks when they go to lunch and changing passwords often.
- Make sure employees choose sensible passwords, at least six and ideally eight characters long, containing numbers, letters, and punctuation marks. Avoid dictionary words and personal information.
- Establish a database of useful information and FAQ (frequently asked questions) for employees so they can solve problems themselves.
- Develop a healthy communications atmosphere.

Adapted from: OpenStax *Introduction to Business* (CC BY). Access for free at https://openstax.org/books/introduction-business/pages/13-introduction

Keep IT Confidential: Privacy Concerns

The very existence of huge electronic file cabinets full of personal information presents a threat to our personal privacy. Until recently, our financial, medical, tax, and other records were stored in separate computer systems. Computer networks make it easy to pool these data into data warehouses. Companies also sell the information they collect about you from sources like warranty registration cards, credit-card records, registration at websites, personal data forms required to purchase online, and grocery store discount club cards. Telemarketers can combine data from different sources to create fairly detailed profiles of consumers.

The September 11, 2001, tragedy and other massive security breaches have raised additional privacy concerns. As a result, the government began looking for ways to improve domestic-intelligence collection and analyze terrorist threats within the United States. Sophisticated database applications that look for hidden patterns in a group of data, a process called data mining, increase the potential for tracking and predicting people's daily activities. Legislators and privacy activists worry that such programs as this and ones that eavesdrop electronically could lead to excessive government surveillance that encroaches on personal privacy. The stakes are much higher as well: errors in data mining by companies in business may result in a consumer being targeted with inappropriate advertising, whereas a governmental mistake in tracking suspected terrorists could do untold damage to an unjustly targeted person.

Increasingly, consumers are fighting to regain control of personal data and how that information is used. Privacy advocates are working to block sales of information collected by governments and corporations. For example, they want to prevent state governments from selling driver's license information and supermarkets from collecting and selling information gathered when shoppers use barcoded plastic discount cards. With information about their buying habits, advertisers can target consumers for specific marketing programs.

The challenge to companies is to find a balance between collecting the information they need while at the same time protecting individual consumer rights. Most registration and warranty forms that ask questions about income and interests have a box for consumers to check to prevent the company from selling their names. Many companies now state in their privacy policies that they will not abuse the information they collect. Regulators are taking action against companies that fail to respect consumer privacy.

In summary, because companies are more dependent on computers than ever before, they need to protect data and equipment from natural disasters and computer crime. Types of computer crime include unauthorized use and access, software piracy, malicious damage, and computer viruses. To protect IT assets, companies should prepare written security policies. They can use technology such as virus protection, firewalls, and employee training in proper security procedures. They must also take steps to protect customers' personal privacy rights.

Adapted from: OpenStax *Introduction to Business* (CC BY). Access for free at https://openstax.org/books/introduction-business/pages/13-introduction

Trends in Information Technology

Information technology is a continually evolving field. The fast pace and amount of change, coupled with IT's broad reach, make it especially challenging to isolate industry trends. From the time we write this chapter to the time you read it—as little as six months—new trends will appear, and those that seemed important may fade. However, some trends that are reshaping today's IT landscape are digital forensics, the shift to a distributed workforce, and the increasing use of grid computing.

Cyber Sleuthing: A New Style of Crime Busting

What helped investigators bring suit against Enron, Merck's Vioxx medication, and the BTK serial killer? Digital evidence taken from an individual's computer or corporate network—web pages, pictures, documents, and e-mails are part of a relatively new science called *digital forensics*. Digital-forensics software safeguards electronic evidence used in investigations by creating a duplicate of a hard drive that an investigator can search by keyword, file type, or access date. Digital forensics is also evolving into areas such as cloud computing and blockchain technology. For instance, it is estimated that as much as 3.9 million of the original 21 million bitcoins are "lost" on hard drives confined to landfills and flash drives located in the back of old office desks.[36]

But nowadays digital sleuthing is not limited to law enforcement. Companies such as Walmart, Target, and American Express have their own secret in-house digital forensics teams. And what if you're in New York and need to seize a hard drive in Hong Kong? No problem. Over 75 members of the Fortune 500 now use technology that allows them to search hard drives remotely over their corporate networks. Digital forensics makes it possible to track down those who steal corporate data and intellectual property. Broadcom, a semiconductor chip designer, used computer forensics to investigate and apprehend former employees who were attempting to steal trade secrets. In the process, Broadcom gathered incriminating e-mails, including deleted documents, that gave it solid evidence to use the 2013 Federal Computer Fraud and Abuse Act to stop the former employees from starting up a rival firm.[37][38]

However, there is a downside to having these advanced capabilities. If this kind of software falls into the wrong hands, sophisticated hackers could access corporate networks and individual computers as easily as taking candy from a baby—and the victims would not even know it was happening. In an age of corporate wrongdoing, sexual predators, and computer porn, your hard drive will tell investigators everything they need to know about your behavior and interests, good and bad. Cybersleuthing means we are all potential targets of digital forensics. As evidenced by the huge increase in identity theft, personal privacy—once an unassailable right—is no longer as sacred as it once was.

Adapted from: OpenStax *Introduction to Business* (CC BY). Access for free at https://openstax.org/books/introduction-business/pages/13-introduction

The Distributed Workforce

Insurance company Aetna shuttered 2.7 million square feet of office space, saving the company $78 million, while American Express estimates it saved between $10 to $15 million dollars per year by expanding its distributed workforce. Was this a sign that these company were in trouble? Far from it. Instead of maintaining expensive offices in multiple locations, they sent employees home to work and adopted a new model for employees: the distributed workforce. Employees have no permanent office space and work from home or on the road. The shift to virtual workers has been a huge success, and not only do companies save on their personnel and related costs, but they also have happier, more productive employees.

Aetna and American Express are not alone in recognizing the benefits of distributed workers, especially in companies that depend on knowledge workers. Work Design Collaborative LLC in Prescott, Arizona, estimates that about 12 percent of all workers in the United States fall into this category, and in urban areas the number could be as high as 15 percent. There are estimates that this trend could eventually reach 40 percent over the next decade, as long commutes, high gas costs, and better connecting tools and technologies make this an attractive option for many workers who like the flexibility of not working in an office.[39]

Already, employees use the internet to conduct video-conferenced meetings and collaborate on teams that span the globe. On the downside, working from home can also mean being available 24/7—although most workers consider the trade-off well worth it.

According to recent statistics, close to four million U.S. workers work from home at least half of the time. Remote workers continue to be recruited by companies of all sizes, including Amazon, Dell, Salesforce, and others.[40]

Intel has a successful virtual-work program that has been popular with working parents. "Technology allows working remotely to be completely invisible," says Laura Dionne, the company's director of supply-chain transformation. At Boeing, thousands of employees participate in the virtual-work program, and it has been a critical factor in attracting and retaining younger workers. Almost half of Sun Microsystems' employees are "location-independent," reducing real estate costs by $300 million. Additional benefits for Sun are higher productivity from these workers and the ability to hire the best talent. "Our people working these remote schedules are the happiest employees we have, and they have the lowest attrition rates," says Bill MacGowan, senior vice president for human resources at Sun. "Would I rather settle on someone mediocre in the Bay Area, or get the best person in the country who is willing to work remotely?"[41]

Adapted from: OpenStax *Introduction to Business* (CC BY). Access for free at https://openstax.org/books/introduction-business/pages/13-introduction

Grid and Cloud Computing Offer Powerful Solutions

How can smaller companies that occasionally need to perform difficult and large-scale computational tasks find a way to accomplish their projects? They can turn to *grid* or cloud computing, also called *utility computing* or *peer-to-peer computing*. Cloud and grid technology provides a way to divide the job into many smaller tasks and distribute them to a virtual supercomputer consisting of many small computers linked into a common network. Combining multiple desktop machines results in computing power that exceeds supercomputer speeds. A hardware and software infrastructure clusters and integrates computers and applications from multiple sources, harnessing unused power in existing PCs and networks. This structure distributes computational resources but maintains central control of the process. A central server acts as a team leader and traffic monitor. The controlling cluster server divides a task into subtasks, assigns the work to computers on the grid with surplus processing power, combines the results, and moves on to the next task until the job is finished. Figure 19.12 shows how typical grid and cloud setups work, and the differences between the two.

Figure 19.12: *How grid and cloud computing work.*

With utility computing, any company—large or small—can access the software and computer capacity on an as-needed basis. One of the big advantages of cloud computing is that companies can update their inventory in real time across their entire organization. For example, suppose you are an appliance retailer and have several outlets throughout the Midwest. If you have one model of a Whirlpool washing machine in your Des Moines, Iowa, store, and a salesperson in your Chicago location can sell that model in Chicago, the sale can be accomplished pretty easily. They can finalize the sale, create the shipping instructions, and update the inventory record automatically—and the Chicago consumer's needs will be met.[42]

Amazon, Google, IBM, Salesforce.com, Oracle, and Hewlett-Packard Enterprise are among the companies providing as-needed cloud and grid services. Although cloud and grid computing appears similar to outsourcing or on-demand software from ASPs, it has two key differences:

1. Pricing is set per-use, whereas outsourcing involves fixed-price contracts.
2. Cloud and grid computing goes beyond hosted software and includes computer and networking equipment as well as services.

Adapted from: OpenStax *Introduction to Business* (CC BY). Access for free at https://openstax.org/books/introduction-business/pages/13-introduction

The cloud and grids provide a very cost-effective way to provide computing power for complex projects in areas such as weather research and financial and biomedical modeling. Because the computing infrastructure already exists—they tap into computer capacity that is otherwise unused—the cost is quite low. The increased interest in cloud and grid technology will continue to contribute to high growth.

In summary, IT is a dynamic industry, and companies must stay current on the latest trends to identify ones that help them maintain their competitive edge, such as digital forensics, the distributed workforce, and grid computing. With digital forensics techniques, corporations, government agencies, attorneys, and lawmakers can obtain evidence from computers and corporate networks—web pages, pictures, documents, and e-mails. Many knowledge workers now work remotely rather than from an office. Companies adopting the distributed workforce model gain many benefits, such as cost savings, more satisfied and productive employees, and increased employee retention. Cloud computing harnesses the power of computers, online software, and data storage to create a virtual computing environment that is invisible to the user. A company can access the cloud on an as-needed basis instead of investing in its own supercomputer equipment. Outsourcing a portion of the company's computing needs provides additional flexibility and cost advantages. Companies can also set up internal grids.

An interactive H5P element has been excluded from this version of the text. You can view it online here: https://pressbooks.lib.vt.edu/fundamentalsofbusiness4e/?p=233#h5p-57

Adapted from: OpenStax *Introduction to Business* (CC BY). Access for free at https://openstax.org/books/introduction-business/pages/13-introduction

Key Takeaways

- Using software called a **database management system (DBMS)**, you can quickly and easily enter, store, organize, select, and retrieve data in a database. These data are then turned into information to run the business and to perform business analysis.
- **Databases** are an electronic filing system that collects and organizes data and information.
- **Enterprise resource planning (ERP) systems** unites all of a firm's major departments into a single software program. For instance, production can call up sales information and know immediately how many units must be produced to meet customer orders.
- The **client** is the application that runs on a personal computer or workstation.
- The **server** manages network resources or performs special tasks such as storing files, managing one or more printers, or processing database queries.
- An **application service provider (ASP)** is service company that buys and maintains software on its servers and distributes it through high-speed networks to subscribers for a set period and price.
- **Managed service providers (MSPs)** are next generation of ASPs, offering customization and expanded capabilities such as business processes and complete management of the network servers.
- **Management information systems (MISs)** are the methods and equipment that provide information about all aspects of a firm's operations.
- **Management support systems (MSSs)** are information systems that use the internal master database to perform high-level analyses that help managers make better decisions.
- A **decision support system (DSS)** is a management support system that helps managers make decisions using interactive computer models that describe real-world processes.

References

Parts of this chapter are adapted from Chapter 13 of Lawrence J. Gitman, Carl McDaniel, Amit Shah, Monique Reece, Linda Koffel, Bethann Talsma, James C. Hyatt. (2018). *Introduction to Business*. OpenStax. CC BY 4.0. Access for free at https://openstax.org/books/introduction-business/pages/1-introduction. OpenStax *Introduction to Business* may be accessed for free at: https://openstax.org/books/introduction-business/pages/1-introduction

Figures

Figure 19.3: Google's CIO, Ben Fried. Interop Events. 2012. CC BY-NC-ND 2.0. https://flic.kr/p/dgqb3J.

Figure 19.4: Computer networks. Christina Morillo. 2018. Pexels license. https://www.pexels.com/photo/engineer-holding-laptop-1181316/.

Figure 19.5: The iPad Pro is an example of an ultramobile PC. Roberto Nickson. 2019. Unsplash license. https://unsplash.com/photos/hLgYtX0rPgw.

Figure 19.6: Virtual private networks (VPNs). Kindred Grey. 2022. CC BY 4.0. Added command center by Soremba from Noun Project, server by aLf from Noun Project, and computer by Marco Livolsi from Noun Project (Noun Project license). https://archive.org/details/19.5_20220627.

Figure 19.7: Structure of an ASP relationship. Kindred Grey. 2022. CC BY 4.0. Added computer by Marco Livolsi from Noun Project (Noun Project license). https://archive.org/details/19.6_20220627.

Figure 19.8: Example of a company's integrated information system. Kindred Grey. 2022. CC BY 4.0. https://archive.org/details/19.7_20220627.

Figure 19.9: There's push to add decision support systems to the clinical field. National Cancer Institute. 2019. Unsplash license. https://unsplash.com/photos/NFvdKIhxYlU.

Figure 19.11: Data security is under constant attack. Tima Miroshnichenko. 2020. Pexels license. https://www.pexels.com/photo/a-computer-monitor-5380589/.

Figure 19.12: How grid and cloud computing work. Kindred Grey. 2022. CC BY 4.0. Added server by aLf from Noun Project, computer by Marco Livolsi from Noun Project, iPad by Mourad Mokrane from Noun Project, Laptop by Saeful Muslim from Noun Project, iPhone by Mr Robot from Noun Project, Earth by Cristiano Zoucas from Noun Project, and person by mim studio from Noun Project (Noun Project license). https://archive.org/details/19.11_202206.

Notes

1. Home. John Daly. (n.d.). Retrieved from: https://www.dalyinvestment.com/
2. "Innovative Technologies," TD Ameritrade Institutional, http://www.tdainstitutional.com, accessed February 21, 2018
3. Daly Investment Management website, https://www.dalyinvestment.com, accessed February 21, 2018
4. Daly Investment Management Facebook page, https://www.facebook.com/dalyinvestment, accessed February 21, 2018
5. Jason Compton, "Meet the Supercomputer Driving a Business Boom in the UK," Forbes, https://www.forbes.com, Junes 14, 2016.
6. Patrick Thibodeau, "U.S. To Have 200-Petaflop Supercomputer by Early 2018," Computer World, https://www.computerworld.com, June 21, 2016.
7. Thomas Friedman, The World Is Flat (New York: Farrar, Straus and Giroux, 2005) p. 8.
8. Bhavan Jaipragas, "Free Trade for Minnows: How Alibaba Gave Malaysia's e-Hub Hopes a Boost," This Week in Asia, http://www.scmp.com, November 20, 2017.
9. Asian Companies Count Losses—Hatch Ways to Cope with Weak Dollar," Reuters, https://www.reuters.com, January 24, 2018
10. Rob Verger, "This Is What Determines the Price of Bitcoin," Popular Science, https://www.popsci.com, January 22, 2018
11. Bhavan Jaipragas, "Alibaba's Electronic Trading Hub to Help Small and Medium-sized Enterprises Goes Live in Malaysia," This Week in Asia, http://www.scmp.com, November 3, 2017
12. Jason Newton and Jesse Gosselin, "VA Looks to Install WiFi after News 8 Story," WTNH News 8, http://wtnh.com, February 20, 2017.

13. "Why Captiva?" https://www.emc.com, accessed February 21, 2018
14. EMC corporate website, "About Us," https://dellemc.com, accessed February 21, 2018
15. "Lucera Uses Connectivity Routes of Chicago, New York, London and Tokyo as a Trading Hub in Trading Increases," BSO, https://www.bsonetwork.com, October 19, 2017
16. Ron Miller, "$67 Billion Dell–EMC Deal Closes Today," Tech Crunch, https://techcrunch.com, September 7, 2016
17. Brian Sherman, "Input Management and Opportunities for the Reseller Channel: An Interview with Wayne Ford, VP of Partner Alliances at Captiva," ECM Connection, http://www.ecmconnection.com, December 27, 2005
18. Kathryn Balint, "Captiva's Paper Chase Paying Off," San Diego Union-Tribune, December 9, 2005, pp. C1, C5.
19. Toby Ward, "Technology, the Intranet, and Employee Productivity," Prescient Digital Media, http://www.prescientdigital.com, accessed February 21, 2018.
20. John Quain, "Alexa, What Happened to My Car?" The New York Times, https://www.nytimes.com, January 25, 2018.
21. Michael Franco, "The Beginner's Guide to VPN's," Life Hacker, https://lifehacker.com, November 20, 2017.
22. NordVPN. (2022, August 3). About Us and our policies. Retrieved from: https://nordvpn.com/about-us
23. Chris Preimesberger, "Why Cloud Services Became the New Normal in 2017," eWeek, http://www.eweek.com, January 4, 2018.
24. Bob Evans, "How Cloud Heavyweights Microsoft, Amazon and IBM Will Transform Cloud Computing in 2018," Forbes, January 3, 2018, https://www.forbes.com.
25. "Global Managed IT Service Providers Market 2018-2021," PR Newswire, https://www.prnewswire.com, January 17, 2018.
26. Kathleen Hickey, "Data Warehouses Integrate Supply Chains," World Trade, February 1, 2006, p. 42.
27. Sami Barry, "The Strategic Role of a Chief Knowledge Officer," Helbling and Associates, Inc. Insights, https://www.helblingsearch.com, September 27, 2012.
28. Milon Gupta, "How Strategic Leaders Use Storytelling," Strategic Thinking, http://www.strategicthinking.eu, November 2, 2015.
29. Chris Low, "Information Security Policies Every Business Must Implement," CIO, https://www.cio.com, August 16, 2017.
30. Steve Morgan, "Cyber Crime Costs Projected to Reach $2 Trillion by 2019," Forbes, https://www.forbes.com, January 17, 2016.
31. Sean Michael Kerner, "IDC Analysts Identify IT Security Trends at RSA," eWeek, http://www.eweek.com, April 22, 2015.
32. Ibid.
33. Jack Cloherty and Pierre Thomas, "Trojan Horse Bug Lurking in Vital US Computers Since 2011," ABC News, http://abcnews.go.com, November 6, 2014.
34. "Effective Planning and Preparation Can Reduce Impact of 2018 Cyber Security Attacks, Data Breaches," Yahoo Finance, https://finance.yahoo.com, January 30, 2018.
35. Adapted from Tony Bradley, "Top 5 Concerns to Focus on for Privacy Day," Forbes, https://forbes.com, January 27, 2017.
36. Patrick Watson, "Why Bitcoin Has Inflation Risk," Equities.com, https://www.equities.com, January 13, 2018.
37. Kaveh Waddell, "CSI: Walmart," The Atlantic, https://www.theatlantic.com, April 3, 2017
38. Dave Smith, "Computer Fraud and Abuse Act 2013: New CFAA Draft Aims to Expand, Not Reform, the 'Worst Law in Technology'," International Business Times, http://www.ibtimes.com, March 28, 2013
39. "Remote Work is 'the New Normal,'" Fast Company, https://www.fastcompany.com, February 28, 2018.
40. Michael Guta, "3.9 Million Americans—including Freelancers—Now Work from Home at Least Half the Week," Small Business Trends, https://smallbiztrends.com, April 2, 2018.
41. Andrea Loubier, "Benefits of Telecommuting for the Future of Work," Forbes, https://www.forbes.com, July 20, 2017; Michelle Conlin, "The Easiest Commute of All," Business Week, December 12, 2005, p. 78.
42. Paul Trujillo, "5 Reasons Small Businesses Need the Cloud," B2C Community, https://www.business2community.com, January 30, 2018.

About the Author

About the Previous Author

Fundamentals of Business, 4th edition is adapted from a work produced and distributed under a Creative Commons license (CC BY-NC-SA 3.0) by a publisher who has requested that they and the original author not receive attribution.

We wish to extend our gratitude to the original author for portions of her book which were remixed and adapted to form portions of Chapters 1-15 and 17-18 of *Fundamentals of Business*. If the publisher and author are both willing to allow us to provide attribution to the author while retaining use of the Creative Commons license and continuing to provide free public access, we will gladly and publicly thank the original author here.

About Stephen Skripak

Stephen J. Skripak is (retired) Professor of Practice in Management at Pamplin College of Business, Virginia Tech (2005 – 2021) and former Associate Dean for Graduate Programs (2006-2014). He is a senior executive with 25 years of business leadership experience, including positions as General Manager and Chief Financial Officer with divisions of Fortune 500 companies. His background includes financial services, consumer packaged goods, apparel, and industrial companies, with emphasis in turnaround situations. He was the lead contributor and subject matter expert for the 2016 and 2018 editions of *Fundamentals of Business*, and reviewed the 2020 and 2022 versions of the book.

Lead Contributor

Ron Poff is Assistant Professor of Management Practice in the Management Department at Pamplin College of Business, Virginia Tech, where he teaches management courses. He began his career as an enlisted member of the US Navy Reserves before entering his primary career in supply chain operations then sales and marketing, where he served in executive roles with large corporations for over 25 years. As an entrepreneur, he then founded his own marketing agency. His education includes a B.S. in Business Management, M.S. Marketing, and a Graduate Certificate in eMarketing. He is the project lead, chief contributor, and coordinator of contributors for the third (2020) and fourth editions (2022) of *Fundamentals of Business*.

Contributors to the Fourth Edition

Howard Haines is Assistant Professor of Practice in the Department of Management at the Pamplin College of Business at Virginia Tech. His research includes understanding the successful skills and strategies of experienced/expert entrepreneurs and how they can be used in experiential education to teach novice entrepreneurs. He is the past Associate Director of the Apex Center for Entrepreneurs working with student founders and helping instructors across campus to bring entrepreneurship into their classrooms. He has also set up and taught entrepreneurship training and degree programs at various accelerators and universities. Prior to his time in academia, Howard worked in various leadership roles in startups, small-medium sized businesses, and in larger corporate entities like Amazon and American Express. He is a Ph.D. Candidate in Entrepreneurship and contributed all of the new material to Chapter 7: Entrepreneurship and Small Business Development in the fourth edition of *Fundamentals of Business*.

John Andy Travers is Adjunct Faculty in the Department of Management at the Pamplin College of Business at Virginia Tech and an Instructor in the Department of Management at Radford University. He holds an MBA from the University of Missouri – Columbia. His work in industry includes working as the General Manager for the Roanoke Valley Wine Company, at US Foods as a Division Director of Operations then as a Regional Director of Ethics and Compliance. He also worked as the Director of Operations for Orvis and worked closely with Orvis UK. He contributed new material for the fourth edition to Chapter 4: Ethics, Chapter 14: Marketing, and Chapter 16: Hospitality and Tourism Management.

Editorial Team

Kindred Grey is the OER and Graphic Design Specialist in the University Libraries at Virginia Tech. She received her B.S. in Statistics and Psychology from Virginia Tech in 2020 and has worked in University Libraries since then, assisting to publish open textbooks. Kindred's design abilities are demonstrated in the visual elements of this book: cover art, interior color palette selection, and creation of new and adapted figures. She prioritizes accessibility of textbooks without compromising design. She provided project coordination and editorial assistance, including tracking and updating the over two hundred figures and tables which were reviewed, revised, or replaced through the course of the project. Kindred's contributions have resulted in a text that is accessible to a wider range of readers and uses visual content to illustrate and more clearly convey conceptual information. She has worked on the third and fourth editions of *Fundamentals of Business*.

Anita Walz is Associate Professor, and Assistant Director of Open Education and Scholarly Communication Librarian in the University Libraries at Virginia Tech. She received her MS in Library and Information Science from the University of Illinois at Urbana-Champaign and has worked in university, government, school, and international libraries for over 20 years. She is the founder of the Open Education Initiative at Virginia Tech and the managing editor of several open textbooks adapted or created at Virginia Tech, many of which may be found here: https://vtechworks.lib.vt.edu/handle/10919/70959. She has provided overall planning, project coordination, day-to-day supervision, and oversight of the book since its inception in 2016.

Past Reviewers / Contributors

Anastasia (Katy) Cortes is Instructor of Management at Pamplin College of Business, Virginia Tech. She has over 25 years of management and business teaching experience at Virginia Tech and Hollins University. She is also a contributing author to OpenStax' *Management*, Denis Collins' *Business Ethics: Best Practices for Designing and Managing Ethical Organizations*, and the Testbank for *Fundamentals of Business*. She was critical to the review, content improvement, and layout of the first edition (2016) of *Fundamentals of Business*. Without her, the first edition of *Fundamentals of Business* (2016) and thus, subsequent editions would not exist.

Jonathan De Pena was a student reviewer for the 2016 edition.

Lisa R. Fournier, PhD is an Adjunct Instructor of Management at Pamplin College of Business. Lisa brings a blend of practical experience and academic research to the classroom. Her business journey began as an entrepreneur during her undergraduate at Western Carolina University. After selling her first business in imprinted sportswear, she worked in several emerging-growth companies as a strategic implementer throughout the 2000s. She has worked in a variety of industries, including healthcare informatics, criminal justice, beverage, auto, and others. She holds an MPM in project management (Western Carolina). In 2012, Lisa was awarded a Doctorate in Strategic Leadership from Regent University. She went on to start and operate a benefit corporation and entrepreneurial learning lab for four years in downtown Norfolk, VA. On divesting the assets to the local Norfolk community, Lisa brought her experience to Virginia Tech, where she teaches social entrepreneurship and business classes. Lisa's contributions to the 3rd edition (2020) of the book include review, substantive edits in several of the chapters, and contribution of original text.

Lauren Holt was a recent Virginia Tech graduate with degrees in Professional and Technical Writing and Biological Systems Engineering at the time of her contributions to the 2020 version of this book. Lauren's contributions to this textbook include Pressbooks editing, copyediting, and cover design.

Sarah Mease is the former Digital Publishing Assistant at Virginia Tech Publishing at the University Libraries at Virginia Tech and contributed to the 2020 edition of the book. Sarah provided review and feedback regarding proposed original figures for the book. Sarah holds a BA in English from Virginia Tech.

Nina Lindsay was a student reviewer for the 2016 edition.

Kathleen (Katie) Manning was a recent graduate of the Pamplin College of Business at Virginia Tech where she majored in Accounting and Information Systems at the time of her contribution to the book. She started her professional career in Fall 2020 at Deloitte in their Risk and Financial Advisory practice. Her contributions to this textbook include review from a student perspective, substantive additions regarding the chapter on Accounting, and assistance with editing and formatting.

Richard Parsons is Professor of Practice in Hospitality and Tourism Management at Pamplin College of Business, Virginia Tech. He is a senior executive in the hospitality industry with over 30 years at Marriott hotels in financial, brand and corporate sectors. He contributed to the 2016 edition of the book.

Sachi Soni was a student reviewer for the 2016 edition.

Michael Stamper is Data Visualization Designer and Digital Consultant for Arts at the University Libraries at Virginia Tech. Michael provided review and feedback regarding proposed original figures for the third edition (2020) of the book, including an emphasis on color contrast and accessibility. He holds a BA in Graphic Design and Art History, and a Masters in Fine Arts with an emphasis in Interactive, Graphic, Information Design and Data Visualization, both from Indiana University-Bloomington.

Gary Walton is Professor of Practice in Hospitality and Tourism Management at the Pamplin College of Business, Virginia Tech. He has thirty nine years in the hotel industry including twenty three years as the General Manager of the Hotel Roanoke and Conference Center. He contributed to the 2016 edition of the book.

Blake Warner was a second year student in the Pamplin College of Business at Virginia Tech during the time of his contribution to the text (2018). He is majoring in both Management and Finance. He is a part of many programs at Virginia Tech, including the Honors College Student Council and Pamplin Global Mentors. His contributions to this textbook include assistance with editing and formatting, as well as providing fresh ideas and insight on how to emphasize diversity throughout the text.

Version Notes

The book you are reading is the fourth edition of *Fundamentals of Business*. This book was adapted from an openly licensed textbook provided by the Saylor Foundation from a publisher who requested that they and the author not be listed. Below is a record of changes made in updating the book from the 3rd Edition to the 4th Edition.

Overall or Major Changes

- Updated data to the most recently available throughout the book;
- Updated graphics and photos;
- Added interactive, live-data graphs for key economic indicators in Chapter 3: Economics and Business;
- Reorganized and added significant additional content to Chapter 4: Ethics and Social Responsibility;
- Renamed and substantially expanded content in Chapter 7: Entrepreneurship and Small Business Development;
- Added additional content to chapters 8, 10, 12, 13, 14, and 17;
- Addition of completely new chapter — Chapter 19: Technology in Business;

Specific chapter-level changes

Chapters 1, 2, 3, 9, 11, 15, and 18

- Minor edits; as described above.

Chapter 4: Ethics and Social Responsibility

- Moved these sections forward in the chapter
    - Addressing Ethical Dilemmas
    - Making Ethical Decisions
    - Revisiting Johnson & Johnson
    - Refusing to Rationalize
- Expanded section on Ethical Tests to Help With Decision Making
- Added
    - Quote from Warren Buffett
    - "Issues of Honesty and Integrity" and graphic for the two-frogs story
    - Sections: Time and Pressure, Theft, and Lying and Deception
    - Section: Your Actions Matter–See Something, Say Something and new subsection on Legislative Action for Organizational Change
    - Section: Government Changes Helped Introduce New Business Stakeholders, including the Rise of Government Intervention in Business, The Rise of the Consumer, Intervention in Business by Academia and Mass Media
    - Reorganized: ethical frameworks in a section: Frameworks for Business Ethics, which covers CSR, ESG, and CSV.
    - Added Figure on Top 10 publicly traded companies fighting climate change in 2022
    - Included Prevention of Sexual Harassment, and Workforce Diversity under areas of corporate responsibility subsection titled "Employees"

Chapter 5: Business in a Global Environment

- Removed case study: Economic and International Impact of US Hospitality & Tourism

Chapter 6: Forms of Business Ownership

- Replaced end-of-chapter video

Chapter 7: Entrepreneurship and Small Business Development

- Renamed chapter "Entrepreneurship and Small Business Development"
    - What is entrepreneurship? What does Entrepreneurial mean?
    - Who is an entrepreneur?
    - When does entrepreneurship occur? When does it end?
    - Where does entrepreneurship occur?
    - Types of entrepreneurship
    - Entrepreneurial Ecosystem
    - How to do entrepreneurship?
    - Startup Financing
    - Beyond Founding
    - Added sections:
- Updated end-of-chapter Key Takeaways

Chapter 8: Management and Leadership

- Added section/subsection on
    - Managers and Information Technology
    - Project Management

Chapter 10: Operations Management

- Added subsection: Site Selection Example
- Replaced Chick-fil-A blog post with shorter description of Southwest Airlines orientation toward customer needs

Chapter 12: Managing Human Resources

- Added definitions and subsection on Diversity, Equity, Inclusion and Belonging (DEIB) in Action
- Added end-of-chapter video

Chapter 13: Union/Management Issues

- Added of two end-of-chapter video news interviews that provide are more current perspective of union activity

Chapter 14: Marketing: Providing Value to Customers

- Replaced dated social media examples featuring Starbucks with a chart listing Top Social Media Campaigns of 2021
- Added section: Advertisers Jump on Podcasts and Videos

Chapter 16: Hospitality and Tourism

- Updated global impact of tourism graphic to acknowledge pre-Covid-19 pandemic tourism with global tourism in 2020.
- Expanded section on Wineries, Cideries, Local Craft Beer, and Distilleries

Chapter 17: Accounting and Financial Information

- Added sections:
    - Careers in Financial Management
    - How do finance and the financial manager affect the firm's overall strategy?
- Added end-of-chapter video

Chapter 19: Technology in Business

- This chapter is completely new to the fourth edition. Parts of this chapter are adapted from Chapter 13 of Lawrence J. Gitman, et. al. (2018). Introduction to Business. OpenStax. CC BY 4.0. Access for free at https://openstax.org/books/introduction-business/pages/1-introduction.